CAMBRIDGE STUDIES IN RUSSIAN LITERATURE

Portraits of early Russian liberals

CAMBRIDGE STUDIES IN RUSSIAN LITERATURE

General editor HENRY GIFFORD

Portraits of early Russian liberals

A study of the thought of T. N. Granovsky, V. P. Botkin, P. V. Annenkov, A. V. Druzhinin and K. D. Kavelin

DEREK OFFORD

LECTURER IN THE DEPARTMENT OF RUSSIAN,
UNIVERSITY OF BRISTOL

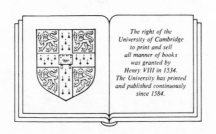

*The right of the
University of Cambridge
to print and sell
all manner of books
was granted by
Henry VIII in 1534.
The University has printed
and published continuously
since 1584.*

CAMBRIDGE UNIVERSITY PRESS

CAMBRIDGE

LONDON   NEW YORK   NEW ROCHELLE

MELBOURNE   SYDNEY

C.1

Published by the Press Syndicate of the University of Cambridge
The Pitt Building, Trumpington Street, Cambridge CB2 IRP
32 East 57th Street, New York, NY 10022, USA
10 Stamford Road, Oakleigh, Melbourne 3166, Australia

© Cambridge University Press 1985

First published 1985

Printed in Great Britain at the University Press, Cambridge

Library of Congress catalogue card number: 84-29211

British Library Cataloguing in Publication Data
Offord, D.
Portraits of early Russian liberals: a study of the thought of
T. N. Granovsky, V. P. Botkin, P. V. Annenkov, A. V.
Druzhinin and K. D. Kavelin. – (Cambridge studies in
Russian literature)
1. Liberalism – Soviet Union – History – 19th century
2. Soviet Union – Politics and government – 19th century
I. Title
320.5'1'0947   DK189 . 055   c . 1

ISBN 0 521 30550 0

For Dorinda

Contents

Foreword

'Despotism or socialism – there is no other choice', wrote Alexander Herzen early in the 1850s.[1] To the twentieth-century reader Herzen's words inevitably have a prophetic ring. The Russian autocracy, after all, took on an increasingly reactionary character from the middle of the 1860s. At the same period there began to develop vigorous revolutionary groups dedicated to the transformation of the old society and, from the late 1870s, to the destruction of the autocracy. Political middle ground was difficult to occupy, especially since Russia lacked a coherent bourgeoisie which might have had a vested interest in defending such ground against the supporters of the established order, on the one hand, and the vociferous champions of the masses, on the other. That is not to say that the majority of Herzen's contemporaries perceived their political options in such stark terms as Herzen himself. On the contrary, many of them, and in particular the thinkers who are the subjects of this study, did seek a middle course in the 1840s and 1850s. They desired a freer and more just society than that which they saw around them in mid-nineteenth-century Russia, but not a society in which social and moral distinctions would be more or less completely obliterated. And yet the choice of which Herzen spoke could not easily be avoided in a country lacking any tradition of free political discussion or any history of gradual reform. Thus in the 1840s Granovsky, Botkin, Annenkov, Druzhinin and Kavelin had all found themselves in opposition to the autocracy – although they were not rebellious by nature – by virtue of the fact that they contributed, in varying ways, to the great intellectual awakening of that decade and thereby implicitly challenged the official obscurantism. But in the 1850s, when the pace of economic, social and intellectual change quickened, all these thinkers declined to give unqualified support to the forces of opposition which they themselves had helped to unleash. And, when finally forced at the end of the 1850s to clarify their position on the political spectrum, those who remained (Granovsky was by now dead) had little alternative but to accept the *status quo*. Their desire to preserve what they loved best in the old order of things proved stronger than their enthusiasm for a brave new world in which so much – including, it must be said, their own status – would be irretrievably lost.

My use of the term 'liberal' to describe the thinkers who tried to hold to this middle course stands in need of some qualification. The term is not one which Granovsky, Botkin, Annenkov or Druzhinin customarily applied to themselves. In any case political terminology tended to be loosely used in the period with which I am chiefly concerned – that is, roughly the years 1838–61 – for the Russian political consciousness, as opposed to the literary and moral consciousness, was as yet poorly developed. Moreover, when they did use the term 'liberal' these thinkers did not necessarily use it in the sense intended in the present study. An entry in Kavelin's diary is illuminating in this connection. In August 1857 he recorded an interview he had had with the empress who had asked him why he had the reputation of 'the most desperate liberal, *qui veut le progrès quand même*'. Kavelin had replied that in his student days, in the early 1840s, and subsequently when he had been a professor at Moscow University, in the middle of that decade, he had been a 'great liberal' and that 'the most extreme theories' had entered his head. He had not, he told the empress, 'gone into political liberalism', but had been a 'sincere' fervent socialist . . .'. It had been correct to call him an extreme liberal in that 'all the liberals', Granovsky, Belinsky, Herzen and others, had been his friends.[2] Clearly the term 'liberal' as it is used here by Kavelin denotes nothing more precise than a person who deplores the spirit of the Russian régime, one of the idealistic and 'critically thinking' members of the burgeoning intelligentsia. The term certainly does not imply adherence to any specific political beliefs; indeed, Kavelin adroitly removes its political dimension.

A much more exact meaning is given to the term, however, in a series of articles written by Chernyshevsky in 1858 and 1859 on the subject of French political history.[3] Chernyshevsky understands by 'liberalism' a certain set of values, attitudes and predictable responses to social and political questions which, taken together, make up a distinctive political outlook. His classification is one which both Marxists and non-Marxists might now be able to accept in its broad outline (though they would disagree profoundly, of course, about the wisdom and value of the tenets Chernyshevsky describes). The fundamental characteristics of liberalism, as Chernyshevsky perceives it, provide a useful starting-point for a description of the outlook of the thinkers examined in the present study. The liberal desires gradual reform, from above. He values social and political stability. He hopes to solve problems by conciliation and compromise. He greatly fears sudden radical change and particularly socialist revolution. To these characteristics we may add others for which Chernyshevsky has even less sympathy and to which he devotes little attention, namely: toleration of opinions different from his own; emphasis on the dignity of the individual; and a belief in the power of the enlightened individual, a noble in the spiritual as well as the social sense, to exercise some influence on the development of his society. Together with these characteristics goes a tendency to uphold absolute values, immutable standards of truth, goodness and beauty. It is this broad set of characteristics that is implied when the term 'liberal' is used in the present work. Most or all of these characteristics are to be found in the thought of each of the individuals I have examined and they lay at the heart of these individuals' disagreements with the early Russian socialists.

A few words should be added on the form my study of these 'liberals' has taken. It seemed best to give portraits of the individuals rather than to provide a chronological survey of their combined *œuvre* during the 1840s and 1850s. For these thinkers never made a concerted attempt to put forward the liberal outlook, even in the 1850s when their views began to harden in response to the challenge from the more radical wing of the intelligentsia. Still less did they contemplate the formation of a political party intent on undertaking some joint practical activity. On the contrary, they were dilettanti who happened as a result of their common background and shared cultural interests and experience to respond in similar ways to the major historical events and intellectual and cultural developments of their day. Their individual paths crossed at many points and their careers followed a remarkably similar course. But in the final analysis they remain above all individuals, each of whom made a distinctive contribution to Russian intellectual life – Granovsky in historical scholarship, Botkin and Annenkov in travelogues and literary criticism (and, we should add, in conversation), Druzhinin in fiction and literary criticism, and Kavelin in juridical and socio-political writings. Because I have

chosen to examine these thinkers individually, however, I have had
to provide a substantial introductory chapter in which the major
currents and landmarks in Russian thought in the 1840s and 1850s
have been briefly surveyed. It is against the background sketched in
this introductory chapter that the intellectual biography of Granovsky, Botkin, Annenkov, Druzhinin and Kavelin must be seen.

By comparison with their radical contemporaries these thinkers
have received very little attention in twentieth-century scholarship.
Early in the Soviet period Belchikov made a brief study of the
criticism of Annenkov and Druzhinin, and there are passages on the
historical scholarship of Granovsky and Kavelin in Rubinshteyn's
survey of Russian historiography, published in 1941.[4] But it was not
until the post-Stalinist period that Soviet scholars began to examine
the mid-nineteenth-century Russian liberals in any detail. Tsagolov, in his book of 1956 on economic thought in Russia in the last
years of serfdom, includes a substantial chapter on the views of
Kavelin (who, as a leading contributor to the discussion of the
abolition of serfdom, has interested Soviet scholars more than the
other subjects of this study). Rozental laid important foundations
for the study of the emergent liberal faction in the intelligentsia of
the 1850s, and of Kavelin in particular, in her series of articles which
appeared in the late 1950s and early 1960s, and Kitayev, in a
monograph of 1972, made a more exhaustive study of the thought of
Kavelin, together with that of Chicherin and Katkov. Levin too has
a useful section on Kavelin in an unfinished work on Russian social
thought in the period of reforms which was published after his death
in 1974. Those thinkers whose main contribution was to aesthetic
and literary rather than to socio-economic debate have been most
fully examined by Yegorov, who in the mid 1960s published three
articles on Botkin and one on the literary criticism of Annenkov and
who has also incorporated useful passages on Druzhinin in his book,
published in 1982, on the 'struggle of aesthetic ideas' in the 1850s.
There are also, of course, brief surveys of Botkin, Annenkov, and
Druzhinin in the major histories of Russian literary criticism.[5] And
yet even if the outlook of the Russian liberals of the mid nineteenth
century has now come to be regarded by Soviet scholars as an
important intellectual and political phenomenon worthy of serious
study, it is still treated as having no intrinsic merit, as Kitayev makes
clear on the first page of his monograph.[6] To the Soviet scholar
liberals such as Kavelin are 'faithful defenders of the interests of a

gentry drawn into bourgeois reform',[7] irritating antagonists whom
Chernyshevsky and Dobrolyubov had to overcome in their struggle
to lay the foundations for socialism in Russia and whom later generations of Russian revolutionaries, particularly Marxists, have
scorned or spurned as more or less cynical class enemies. Lenin's
own vitriolic denunciations of liberalism, and of Kavelin in particular, have combined with the constraints of Marxist methodology
to make a less clearly predetermined appraisal of these thinkers
impossible in the Soviet Union. Even the views of Botkin, Annenkov and Druzhinin on imaginative literature are presented typically
not only as an obstacle in the path of the advocates of utilitarian
aesthetics (which they were) but also as a will-o'-the wisp which
major writers such as Turgenev and Tolstoy, who were briefly lured
by them, eventually resolved much more decisively than was in fact
the case not to pursue.

The major work published in the West on Russian liberalism is
Leontovich's book, which first appeared in German in 1957; but
Leontovich is interested primarily not in the liberal members of the
independent intelligentsia but in reforming bureaucrats, to whose
role in history he attributes great importance. There is also a lucid
account of the development of Russian liberalism from the 1860s by
George Fischer, but the thinkers examined in the present study do
not belong to the period in which Fischer is interested and are not
mentioned by him. Nor has any other work in English, as far as I am
aware, dealt at all comprehensively with more than one of the five
thinkers on whom I concentrate, although the names of most or all
of them are bound to occur in any account of mid-nineteenth-
century Russian thought or indeed in any biography of the major
imaginative writers of that period. Granovsky has perhaps fared
better than the rest (the monograph on his historical scholarship by
Priscilla Roosevelt is particularly searching and coherent), though
Kavelin's contribution to Russian liberalism in the second half of
the 1850s has also been helpfully surveyed by Daniel Field. Even
Andrzej Walicki, in his excellent history of Russian thought,
recently translated into English, has only five pages in all on the
roles of Granovsky, Botkin and Kavelin in the intellectual life of the
1840s and 1850s and makes but a few passing references to Annenkov and Druzhinin. Thus it is a large lacuna in our knowledge of
Russian intellectual life in the mid nineteenth century that the
present study is intended to fill, and the lacuna is an important one

for several reasons. For, in the first place, these liberals do indeed
exemplify, as Soviet scholars contend, a certain mode of thinking
and a particular political tendency, albeit one which was destined to
be eclipsed by the vigorous development of a socialist movement in
Russia. In the second place, they have a value in themselves as, in
Isaiah Berlin's words, 'morally sensitive, honest, and intellectually
responsible men' who lived in an age of 'acute polarisation of
opinion' (and whose dilemma has since their own time grown 'acute
and world-wide').[8] In the third place, they are leading representatives of that broad current in Russian thought which it is customary
to describe as 'Westernism' but which, being more amorphous than
Slavophilism, has been much less clearly defined. In the fourth
place, they were on the closest terms with major imaginative writers
such as Turgenev, Grigorovich, Nekrasov, Goncharov and Lev
Tolstoy during the very period in which Russian literature was
coming into full bloom and have therefore more than a passing
importance for the historian of classical Russian literature. An
acquaintance with their thought, moreover, helps us to place in
clearer perspective the now better known individuals and groups –
Belinsky, Herzen, the Slavophiles, Chernyshevsky and Dobrolyubov – whose views often found their clearest expression in endorse-
ments or, more frequently, criticisms of positions that Granovsky,
Botkin, Annenkov, Druzhinin or Kavelin at one time or another
adopted.

A word should be added about the readership at which the
present study is aimed. It is, of course, hoped that the specialist in
Russian thought will find something of interest here, but the work is
not intended for the specialist alone; it is designed also to throw
light on areas which to Western undergraduates studying Russian
history, literature and politics and to the general reader with an
interest in Russian culture remain comparatively obscure. I have
not therefore taken it for granted that the reader will be familiar
with certain works such as Herzen's *Letters from the Avenue
Marigny* and Chernyshevsky's 'Anthropological Principle in Philosophy' which will be known to most specialists in the field, and
consequently I beg the specialist's indulgence in those instances
where some account of such works has seemed necessary in order to
render entirely comprehensible the thought of the individuals on
whom I have concentrated.

Finally, it is a pleasure to acknowledge my debt to those people whose help and encouragement have enabled me at last to complete my study. Warmest thanks are due to Henry Gifford, for his interest in my project since its conception some five years ago, for his willingness to read my work despite other more pressing obligations, for his helpful suggestions and for sharing with me his great erudition. This is also the place fondly to record my gratitude to two of my teachers, the late Nikolay Andreyev and the late Leonard Schapiro; it was their interest in Russian thought and history that kindled my own and their scholarly example that in large measure accounts for whatever merits my study may have (though responsibility for its mistakes and failings is, of course, entirely my own). I should like to thank too Professor Anthony Cross, for confirming for me a detail in the biography of Kavelin, and Professor Hans Reiss, for providing me with information on Goethe and Rötscher; the staff of the libraries of the University of Bristol and of the School of Slavonic and East European Studies in London and the staff of the British Library, who have given me much help over the last four years while I have been carrying out the research for my study; the editorial board of *Oxford Slavonic Papers* for permission to reproduce, as Chapter 3 of the present work, an article printed in that journal in 1983; and Iain White for his painstaking work on my typescript. I am also most grateful to Mrs Anne Merriman for her meticulous typing of my final, still disorderly manuscript and to Mrs Barbara Case for her typing of the papers and articles on which three chapters of this book were originally based.[9] Lastly, but most of all, I thank my wife, whose encouragement and moral support while I have been completing my work have been invaluable and whose perception of the issues I have examined is far sharper than my own.

Note on dates, transliteration and use of Russian terms

Dates

Unless otherwise indicated, dates given in the text are in the Old Style; that is, according to the Julian calendar which was used in Russia until February 1918 and which in the nineteenth century was 12 days behind the Gregorian calendar used then, as now, in Western Europe. (New Style dates are indicated by the abbreviation NS.)

Transliteration

The method used in the text, notes and bibliography is that of the *Slavonic and East European Review*. The name Gertsen and the place name Kiyev, however, are rendered in the commonly accepted forms Herzen and Kiev respectively, and for the sake of simplicity no indication is given of soft signs in Russian names (hence Gogol instead of Gogol') when they are used in the text. In the notes and bibliography soft signs are everywhere transliterated.

Use of Russian terms

Titles of Russian journals are left in their transliterated Russian form, but a translation of the title is given when the journal is mentioned for the first time in the text. All other titles are translated in the text. Whenever a Russian term occurs in the text it is explained if its meaning is not already clear.

1

Russian intellectual life in the 1840s and 1850s

Nicolaevan Russia; the growth of Russian literature; Chaadayev's 'Philosophical Letter'

'"Despotism still exists in Russia: it is the essence of my government, but it accords with the genius of the nation"', Nicholas I told the French Marquis de Custine, who travelled extensively in Russia in 1839. Custine's own observations abundantly confirmed the emperor's judgement. He found a régime under which everyone and everything depended upon the favour of one man. Deprived of liberty, the Russians had developed a 'taste for servitude'; 'great and small' alike were 'drunk with slavery'. Everywhere the traveller could find 'compulsory manifestations of submission'; he was among a 'nation of mutes', sixty million automata awaiting the 'wand of another enchanter' before they could again enjoy life. Existence would become 'insupportably dull to the individual who should allow himself to reflect', for to converse was to conspire, to think was to revolt and thought was not merely a crime but also a misfortune. The Russians had pretensions to 'good manners' and Western education, to be sure, for they were an 'imitative people' with a 'general passion for novelties' and were 'incessantly occupied with the desire of mimicking other nations', which they did 'after the true manner of monkeys'. Nevertheless Russia remained 'more nearly allied to Asia than to Europe', a 'monstrous compound of the petty refinements of Byzantium, and the ferocity of the desert horde'. She was a nation of 'enrolled and drilled Tartars', 'a barbarism plastered over, and nothing more'.[1]

Custine's observations on the nature of the Russian régime must have been unexceptionable to its critics. Nicholas was by all accounts every inch a king, but he visualised the state, as one historian has put it, as a 'well drilled army unit, that is, a polity embodying the principles of hierarchical subordination, close delimitation of the duties of each member, and the unchallengeable authority of the anointed leader'.[2] His manifesto of July 1826 promised a gradual amelioration of national institutions by reform from above, but in practice his autocratic power was never checked and the bureaucracy by which the Empire was administered remained cumbersome, inefficient, arbitrary and corrupt. Indeed, the means of repression at the disposal of the emperor were significantly strengthened in Nicholas' reign. The voluminous laws of June 1826 gave wide powers to censors and although in 1828 a more liberal law was devised it was applied in a draconian spirit and stiffened by further provisions after the French 'revolution' of July 1830. A special gendarmerie – the notorious Third Section of the emperor's own Chancery – was set up in June 1826, placed under the control of Count Benkendorf and given responsibility for the detection and punishment of all citizens whose activities or ideas seemed harmful to the state. The gravity of the problem of serfdom – to which Radishchev had so strikingly drawn attention in his *Journey from St Petersburg to Moscow* as far back as 1790 – was appreciated, it is true. 'There is no doubt that serfdom, in its present form, is a flagrant evil', Nicholas admitted in 1842. But to attempt to remedy the problem now, Nicholas continued, would be an 'evil even more disastrous'.[3] Measures taken to mitigate the position of the serfs between 1833 and 1848 dealt only with peripheral aspects of the problem or specific abuses. Nor did Nicolaevan Russia have any coherent bourgeoisie which might have fought vigorously in its own interests for the abolition of serfdom and for political freedom. The 'tradespeople', as Custine observed, were 'too few in number to possess any influence in the state' and were besides 'almost all foreigners'[4]; a secular professional class, consisting of lawyers, doctors, academics, had barely begun to appear because the educational system was undeveloped; and the upper bureaucracy was drawn mainly from the ranks of the aristocracy and owed its allegiance to the Crown. The Russian social order of the 1840s therefore had a superficial appearance of immutability which was sustained by the theory of 'Official Nationality' (veneration of the 'truly Russian conservative principles of Orthodoxy, autocracy and nationality')[5] expounded by Count Uvarov, Minister of Education from 1833 to 1849. Benkendorf succinctly gave expression to the official complacency when he wrote: 'Russia's past is admirable; her present more than magnificent; as to her future, it is beyond the grasp of the most daring imagination.'[6]

And yet if Custine's impressions of the nature of the Russian régime were more or less accurate, nevertheless he failed altogether to perceive the beginnings of a cultural and intellectual life which would shortly rival that of his native France. (He rashly asserted, for example, that 'under such an order of things, real life is too serious an affair to allow of a grave and thoughtful literature'; art would 'never be a hardy plant' in Russia.)[7] In fact an intelligentsia was coming into being which, with its spirit of independence, was altogether at odds with officialdom. Two immense and, as we shall see, interrelated tasks, above all others, preoccupied that intelligentsia, in the 'marvellous decade' of its development, between 1838 and 1848, during which Custine had visited Russia: the creation of an original and humane literature, and the solution of the question as to Russia's historical relationship with Western Europe.

The rich literature which had begun to blossom in Russia in the 1820s and 1830s with the appearance of the poetry and prose of Pushkin and Lermontov and the stories of Gogol soon acquired an importance with which imaginative literature was not endowed in societies where independent educated opinion found freer expression. Literature did not explicitly put social problems, let alone offer solutions to them, but it did obliquely raise them in fictional form. It was demanded, as Mirsky has put it, that 'every time a novelist gave his work to the world, it should contain things worth meditating on and worth analysing from the point of view of the social issues of the day', and the demand was one which the novelists could never ignore.[8] (As this topical dimension to Russian literature developed, so writers quickly turned from poetry to prose, from subjective lyricism to examinations of reality which purported to be more or less objective, and, once prose had established itself, from the short sketch to the novel in which the fate of the individual could be examined against a larger and sometimes panoramic social backcloth.) Not only did literature stir thought and feelings, however, it even seemed to a beleaguered intelligentsia to sustain civilised life itself: it would shake minds out of what Polevoy called their *'banal vegetable inertness'*.[9] It had an 'organic' quality, a vitality quite out of keeping with the social reality of Nicolaevan Russia, which by contrast was described by the intelligentsia as dormant, stagnant or moribund. Imaginative literature was a solitary source of light in the 'kingdom of darkness'.[10]

The literature which thus began to flourish in the reign of Nicholas I was itself a product of the introduction into Russia of Western European culture and values. Peter the Great had prepared the ground for this westernisation of Russian culture by his far-reaching reforms and innovations at the beginning of the eighteenth century. But it was only after the Napoleonic wars, in which Russia had played an important role, that it became necessary for educated Russians to think deeply about the relationship of their nation to Western Europe. They had to ask themselves, in view of their country's new prominence in European affairs, whether Russia was simply a backward nation aping Western forms and dependent upon the West for any progress she might make; or, to put the question another way, whether Russia had an individual identity of her own which entitled her to play an international role commensurate with her political prestige among the European nations after 1815. Chaadayev, in the gloomy atmosphere that prevailed in Russia after the failure of the Decembrist revolt in 1825, gave the most pessimistic answers to these questions in his first *Philosophical Letter*, which was published in 1836. Writing from 'Necropolis', the 'city of the dead' – by which he meant Moscow – Chaadayev compared Russia to the West in the most unfavourable terms. The Catholic form of Christianity, together with the 'ideas of duty, justice, law, and order' had endowed Western European civilisation with a coherence and a continuity, an organic unity, altogether lacking in Russia, whose history was merely a series of unconnected jolts. The fate of the members of the educated minority in Russian society could be compared to that of the nation as a whole (the analogy between an individual and his people was a popular one at this period). They lived a groundless and aimless existence. In their homes they were 'like campers', in their families 'like strangers' and in their cities 'more nomadic than the herdsmen' who grazed their animals on the Russian steppes. They lived 'only in the most narrow kind of present without a past and without a future in the midst of a shallow calm'. In order to 'take up a position similar to that of other civilised people' they would have in a certain sense to 'repeat the whole education of mankind'.[11] They were in fact 'superfluous men', like Pushkin's Onegin and Lermontov's Pechorin, paralysed by introspective self-analysis, incapable of sound moral choices and living out their lives without useful purpose.

Slavophilism

Chaadayev's highly unflattering answer to the question as to Russia's relationship with Western Europe was soon to be challenged by the so-called Slavophiles, whose doctrines arguably constituted the steadiest intellectual landmark in Russia in the 1840s. That is not to say that the small number of thinkers – Khomyakov, I. Kireyevsky, P. Kireyevsky, K. Aksakov, I. Aksakov and Samarin – who were chiefly responsible for the formulation of the body of thought that came to be known as Slavophilism reached unanimous agreement on the main questions of interest to them, still less that they formed any political grouping. Many of the major essays in which their views were most clearly expressed, moreover, were not written until the 1850s, so that there is some justification for the view that even as late as 1844–5 Slavophilism was 'more a premonition that a doctrine'.[12] Nevertheless the views of the Slavophiles on the civilisation of Western Europe, on the one hand, and on Russian Orthodoxy and the Russian people and their institutions, on the other, did already in the mid 1840s have a greater coherence than those of their opponents.

It must be said that the Slavophiles were themselves steeped in Western learning and much influenced by notions derived from Western thinkers, such as the concept of *Volkstum*, or national distinctiveness, which had been advanced by Herder and introduced into Russia through the philosophy of Schelling.[13] Nevertheless Slavophilism is imbued with a deep hostility to Western European civilisation, which the Slavophiles tended to view – despite some acknowledgement of national variations – as a monolithic edifice built on the foundation of rationalism. An early but very characteristic statement of this view was contained in I. Kireyevsky's essay, 'In Reply to A. S. Khomyakov', published in 1839. Kireyevsky posits three elements which he believes lie at the root of Western civilisation: the Roman form of Christianity; the heritage of the Barbarians who destroyed the Roman Empire; and the classical heritage of pagan antiquity. This classical heritage, which was lacking in Russia, seemed to Kireyevsky to represent in essence the triumph of man's 'formal reason over everything else within him and outside him'. The Roman Church, when it became separated from the Eastern, Orthodox Church, had suffered a similar fate: 'rationalism' had triumphed over 'inner spiritual reason' in its teachings, which had as a consequence been corrupted. The Pope had become first the head of the Church in place of Christ and then, finally, an infallible secular ruler. The 'totality of faith' had come to rest on 'syllogistic scholasticism'. Even the emergence of the institution of knighthood – which Kireyevsky viewed most unfavourably; he described knights errant as brigands serving the Church by slaughtering the innocents in return for a promise of expiation – was attributable to the pernicious influence of a Church prepared to sell its purity for temporal advantage. This supposed ascendancy of formal reason over faith and tradition seemed to Kireyevsky to explain the 'entire present fate of Europe', its philosophy, its conception of 'industrialism as the mainspring of social life', its 'ideal of soulless calculation', the grasping ethos of the July monarchy in France, the veneration of 'external formal relations' and private property and the individual's sense of isolation (we should now say 'alienation'). All the best minds of Europe, Kireyevsky claimed, were currently complaining of the 'condition of moral apathy, of the lack of convictions, of the universal egoism' which he attributed to the ruinous influence of a Church that had lost the true spirit of Christ's teaching.[14]

The loss of firm spiritual foundations afflicted Russia too inasmuch as the Russian educated class had been a prey, since the reforms of Peter the Great, the 'destroyer' of what was Russian,[15] to the same maladies as the West. This theme was developed by Khomyakov in his essay on 'The Opinions of Foreigners about Russia', published in 1845 in *Moskvityanin (The Muscovite)*, which was the main organ for the expression of Slavophilism at this period. For one hundred and fifty years, Khomyakov complained, Russians had placidly accepted any new system of fashion, the fruits of the labours of German philosophers and French tailors, without ever questioning their truth or quality. Russians took it on trust, for example, that political economy – a discipline much despised by the Slavophiles, a 'science of wealth', as Kireyevsky once called it[16] – could have validity without making any reference to man's moral motivations; or, again, that jurisprudence was entitled to the status of a science even though it took no account of conceptions of moral law which alone could give human law some binding force. This tendency to Europeanise Russian culture inevitably bore certain 'fruits', notably a proud disdain for all that was native. Thus a profound rift developed between the spiritual and intellectual essences of the nation, between its autochthonous life and the alien culture which had been grafted on to it.[17]

The key to the resolution of this duality was to be found, the Slavophiles believed, in Christianity as it had been preserved in Russia, that was to say Orthodoxy. Unlike the Catholic Church, the Orthodox Church had not been compromised over the centuries – or so the Slavophiles contended – by association with secular power, nor had it given rise to a tradition of rationalistic philosophical speculation, or to a materialistic legal system sanctifying private property-ownership. It had therefore remained true, as its designation 'Orthodox' implied, to the pure Christian doctrines as they had been established at the early ecumenical councils between the fourth and seventh centuries. It also gave its members a sense of true brotherhood, of conciliarism (*sobornost'*) or community within the Christian fold, a concept to which Khomyakov in particular devoted much attention in his ecclesiological writings. These Orthodox principles – belief in the primacy of faith over reason, of spiritual over rational wisdom, emphasis on 'inner freedom' as opposed to submission to external authority and on Christian brotherhood rather than republican '*fraternité*' – the Slavophiles fondly believed would provide a firm basis for the future development of Russian society. Indeed, they even hoped, as Kireyevsky intimated in a celebrated 'Review of the Contemporary Condition of Literature' (1845), that their Orthodox Christianity would serve as a 'necessary supplement' to the culture of Western Europe and a source of renewal for a dying civilisation, the distinctive contribution to history of a tribe which had not hitherto had a universal significance.[18]

The moral principles embodied in Orthodoxy were preserved, the Slavophiles believed, among the Russian people, the mass of the peasantry who had been relatively untouched by Westernisation and were therefore unaffected by the formalism, rationalism and individualism that were supposed to pervade Catholic cultures. The Russian people kept alive a sense of real justice, 'not merely that dead justice which the legalist-formalist will justify, but the living justice to which human conscience conforms and to which it submits'. Khomyakov describes the function of the arbitrator (*posrednik*) in order to illustrate the point. The arbitrator carries no formal authority but by virtue of his impartiality and 'conciliatory benevolence' enjoys a moral authority to which the Russian will readily submit. Russian peasant society, therefore, was still bound together by 'bonds of true brotherhood, not conditional agreement'. The different attitudes of the people towards their late sixteenth- and early seventeenth-century rulers, Boris Godunov and Mikhail Romanov, again demonstrated their observance of 'purely moral principles' which were quite alien to the Western world. They had regarded Godunov as a man who had insinuated himself into power, having pushed aside his rivals, and the legality of his election as their ruler was merely external, apparent rather than real. Mikhail, on the other hand, they regarded as a man whom they had elected themselves and therefore gladly entrusted their fate to him. Their ability to make this distinction again showed their understanding of the difference between formal and true legality.[19]

Above all, the unspoiled, truly Christian character of the Russian people was expressed in the *obshchina*, or peasant commune. By their practice of periodically repartitioning the land available to them in accordance with the changing needs of the families in the village community, by their communal use of resources such as woodland, pastures and fishing grounds and by their discussion of their corporate affairs at an assembly at which all had a voice, the Russian peasants seemed to the Slavophiles to reveal a spirit of collectivism analogous to the brotherly ethos of the Orthodox Church and antithetical to the individualism regnant in Western society. The commune was therefore a 'moral choir', as K. Aksakov once described it, an active social expression of the concept of conciliarism.[20] It is worth noting that this view derived some support from the Prussian aristocrat, von Haxthausen, who travelled in Russia in 1843 and whom some of the Slavophiles met personally. Haxthausen described the commune as 'one of the most remarkable and interesting political institutions in existence'. Drawing attention to the peasants' practice of dividing the land equally among the commune's members, he suggested that the institution reflected the feeling of the Russian peasant that the land was a common heritage to be shared among all the members of the great 'national family'. He also anticipated that the commune would protect Russia both from the 'pauperism and proletarianism' of the modern West and from the 'doctrines of communism and socialism' to which bourgeois society was inevitably giving rise.[21]

It is useful, finally, to bear in mind the quite precise and understandable causes that may be postulated for the emergence of

Slavophilism. On one level it may be interpreted as a riposte to the scathing criticisms to which Russian culture had been subjected since the mid 1830s, notably by Chaadayev and Custine. (Khomyakov's 'article on foreigners' opinions of Russia begins with a complaint about the mixture of 'fear and contempt' in foreigners' accounts of their travels in Russia and bemoans their abuse of Russian hospitality.)[22] But on another level Slavophilism may legitimately be seen as the expression of a desire to cling to an economic and social order that was by the 1840s being threatened. The leading Slavophiles were all from wealthy families with large landed estates and their values were those of the pious nobleman gravitating towards an idyllic rural community of which he was the unchallenged paternalistic head. This order would not long survive the further decay of the gentry, the economic and social ascendancy of more plebeian elements and the further penetration into Russia of poisonous Western doctrines, based on rationalism and egoism, and of European capitalism, which the Slavophiles found repellent.

'Westernisers' and some Western influences on their thought

Understandable as Slavophilism may have been as an expression of wounded national pride, it was by the mid 1840s already taken quite literally by a large section of the intelligentsia as a provocative defence of outmoded values and of a social and political order that supposedly derived strength from them. As such, Slavophilism came to serve as a sort of landmark by which thinkers who were not Slavophiles and who aspired to a way of life more civilised than that of Nicolaevan Russia could plot their own intellectual position and from which they attempted to distance themselves. Thus it helped in a negative, as well as a positive, way to shape the intellectual life of the 1840s, by stimulating the discussion of values diametrically opposed to it. That is not to say that the main opponents of the Slavophiles – whom it is customary to designate 'Westernisers'[23] and who included Belinsky, Bakunin, Herzen, Granovsky, Botkin, Annenkov and Kavelin – loved Russia any less dearly than the Slavophiles themselves. We have only to recall Herzen's famous image of two-faced Janus or the two-headed eagle, which looked in different directions, East and West, but in whose breast there beat the same heart,[24] to underline the fact that a sense of patriotic commitment was not the exclusive property of the Slavophiles. But it is arguable that the Slavophiles' juxtaposition of a moribund West and a vital Russia, of rationalism and spiritual truth, of the rights of the individual and the supremacy of the collective, of juridical and moral law, and the adverse comparison of the former with the latter term in each pair, greatly helped the 'Westernisers' to clarify their own views of the Western values and institutions which were being decried.

It has to be said, however, that once a common antipathy to Slavophilism has been taken into acount the 'Westernisers' appear even less united as a group than their opponents. It is therefore perhaps best to consider them as the products of common Western intellectual influences rather than as the exponents of specific ideas to which all subscribed. And of all these influences the first and most important was the philosophy of Hegel, which all the 'Westernisers' imbibed in one form or another in the late 1830s (and which the Slavophiles saw as the last stone in the edifice of Western rationalism, the stone in fact that finally brought the whole edifice crashing down). Granovsky, Bakunin and Botkin all belonged, and Herzen was close, to the circle of the saintly Nikolay Stankevich, who played such an important role in the introduction of German philosophy, particularly that of Hegel, into Russia. Together they plunged 'headlong into the "German sea"', to use Turgenev's expression.[25] They discussed Hegel 'incessantly', Herzen recalled:

> there was not a paragraph in the three parts of the *Logic*, in the two of the *Aesthetic*, the *Encyclopaedia*, and so on, which had not been the subject of desperate disputes for several nights together. People who loved each other avoided each other for weeks at a time because they disagreed about the definition of 'all-embracing spirit', or had taken as a personal insult an opinion on 'the absolute personality and its existence in itself'. Every insignificant pamphlet published in Berlin or other provincial or district towns of German philosophy was ordered and read to tatters and smudges, and the leaves fell out in a few days, if only there was a mention of Hegel in it.[26]

Philosophy in general was an attractive subject for noble minds denied other pabulum, but Hegelianism had particular merits for the Russian intelligentsia. It was not only the latest but also among the most intellectually demanding, stimulating and comprehensive of systems. Moreover, Hegel's examination of the relationship between the finite and the infinite, the individual and the Absolute had an almost religious significance that was appealing to intellectuals who had lost faith in Christianity in its official, Orthodox form. Hegelianism encouraged them to seek the infinite in themselves and others and to look on love as a means of communing with the Absolute of which each individual was a partial expression. Furthermore, this belief that the individual, indeed every manifestation of everyday reality, was an aspect or moment in the universal and eternal process of the self-realisation of the Absolute gave enlightened individuals, however anonymous they might seem in tsarist society, some larger significance than they had hitherto discerned. Again, Hegel's view of philosophy as a means of overcoming or resolving antagonisms – division is the 'source of *the need of philosophy*', he once wrote[27] – offered comfort to 'superfluous men' suffering from a sense of spiritual fragmentation and disharmony. His dialectical method, which could be applied – and indeed was applied by his contemporaries and successors – to numerous areas of knowledge, was attractive too. For the notion that history, human societies and cultures moved inexorably through various stages of development, thesis and antithesis, towards a higher synthesis of the preceding forms was reassuring to intellectuals in a society which seemed static and far from perfectible. Not that the dialectical method could be fully understood by the logical understanding, what Hegel called *Verstand*, which is brought into play by the exact sciences; the method also required *Vernunft*, a form of reason capable of perceiving not rigid and static concepts but the concept of identity-in-difference, the passing of one thing into its opposite. And this perception, which Hegel required of his disciple, itself gave his system an esoteric and revelationary quality that was not displeasing. We might add that the general obscurity in which Hegel's system is shrouded may well have enhanced its appeal too; at any rate many of the Russian thinkers who fell strongly under Hegel's influence in their youth never properly extricated themselves from the linguistic thickets into which Hegel and his German disciples had led them.

In particular fields of knowledge as well as in the realm of general principles Hegel laid important foundations for Russian thinkers. His view of the state as an expression of the Spirit at a given stage of its development seemed to furnish grounds for an attitude of resignation on the part of the individual towards political orders like the Russian that were apparently immovable. If the unfolding of history was ineluctable, it was also legitimate. (The political quiescence encouraged by this view for a while seemed to some Russian thinkers to derive support from Hegel's axiom that the 'real is rational', which was taken to mean that existing régimes, by virtue of the very fact that they existed, were legitimate.) At the same time Hegel stressed the importance of 'world-historical individuals' (*die weltgeschichtlichen Individuen*), figures such as Alexander the Great, who might be seen as the instruments of the will of the developing Spirit and who were to exercise a fascination for several Russian thinkers even after the initial reverence of those thinkers for Hegel had diminished. Hegel also elaborated a view of art – as a vehicle for the perception of the Absolute, in the form of a beauty higher than that to be found in everyday reality – which remained influential in Russian aesthetics at least until the 1860s.[28]

Enthralling as Hegelianism was for the Westernisers and durable as some aspects of the system were to prove among them, however, it could not for long dominate the thinking of an intelligentsia instinctively critical of the tsarist régime and contemporary Russian society. The leading Westernisers therefore soon began to search for a philosophy less conservative than Hegelianism in its political implications (though even their rejection of Hegel often presented itself to them in Hegelian terms, as a sort of negation of his philosophy). Thus Bakunin repudiated his own reconciliation with reality by laying particular emphasis on the principle of antithesis in Hegel's triad and in his famous essay, 'The Reaction in Germany', published in Leipzig in 1842, celebrated negation for its own sake: the 'passion for destruction', Bakunin declared, 'is a creative passion'.[29] The Westernisers were assisted in their attempts to cast off the influence of Hegel by the so-called 'left-wing' or 'young' Hegelians, who in the late 1830s and early 1840s were seeking to return to philosophy the political dimension it had possessed in eighteenth-century France, and in particular by Feuerbach, whose major work, *The Essence of Christianity*, was first published in 1841. Following David Strauss, who in his work, *The Life of Jesus* (1835–6), had interpreted Christ's life and teachings in a historical perspective, Feuerbach set out to demonstrate that man's God was not a perfect being with an objective existence of His own but rather a subjective creation of man's consciousness, a '*mirrored image of man*' arising out of man's need to give some substance to his idealistic strivings. 'Man's being conscious of God', Feuerbach asserted, was 'man's being conscious of himself'. God was the 'manifested inward nature, the expressed self of man', religion the 'solemn unveiling of man's hidden treasures, the revelation of his most intimate thoughts', the 'open confession' of what he secretly loved. Religion had traditionally presented God and man as antitheses: God was the infinite, man the finite being; God was perfect, eternal, holy and omnipotent, man imperfect, temporal, sinful and impotent. Thus religion had alienated man from himself by opposing him to his own objectified latent nature. Feuerbach, on the other hand, by presenting God as inalienable from man's own consciousness, sought to restore unity to man's being and thereby to give man a new status. That which ranked first in religion, namely God, should in fact rank second, since it was 'merely the projected essence of Man'. And if it were the 'nature of Man' that was 'man's Highest Being', then 'man's love for Man' was bound in practice to become man's first and highest law. '*Homo homini Deus est*', Feuerbach concluded, Man's God was Man himself.[30]

Feuerbach had provided the basis for a new humanist view of a self-confident man responsible to no higher authority. At the same time he had destroyed – if his arguments were accepted – one of the bases of political quiescence. These implications of Feuerbach's work – which were to be re-emphasised by Chernyshevsky in the 1850s – were immediately perceived in the 1840s by the Russian Westernisers. Annenkov tells us that *The Essence of Christianity* was 'in everybody's hands' and suggests that nowhere did it make 'such a tremendous impression' as in the Westernisers' circle and 'nowhere did it so rapidly obliterate the vestiges of all preceding outlooks'. Herzen in particular was a 'fervent exponent of its propositions and conclusions' and with his usual acuity connected the 'revolution it revealed in the realm of metaphysical ideas with the political revolution heralded by the socialists'[31]. In his own essays of the early 1840s – particularly 'Buddhism in Science', which completed the cycle 'Dilettantism in Science', and the 'Letters on the Study of Nature'[32] – Herzen eloquently argued the case of man against great impersonal forces and rigid intellectual and, by inference, political systems. Thus the Westernisers' rejection of Hegelianism, facilitated by acquaintance with Feuerbach, was tantamount, as Walicki has observed, to a 'struggle for the rights of the individual and for the vindication of *active* participation in history'.[33] It signalled a shift from introspective contemplation to practical examination of reality.

As the new rebellious and pragmatic mood gained ground in
Russia in the early 1840s, so the hold of German thought on Russian
intellectual life, notwithstanding the popularity of Feuerbach's
work, was weakened. Attention turned again to France, a country
which suffered more than any other land, in the opinion of the
conservative aristocrat, Custine, from the contemporary disease of
a 'hatred of authority'[34] and in which republican sentiments were
again brewing in the early 1840s. Educated Russians now voracious-
ly read the *romans-feuilletons* of Eugène Sue, who had described
the wretched life of the lower classes in the modern city, and the
novels of George Sand, who herself had been much influenced by
the socialist teachings of Pierre Leroux. The work of contemporary
French historians on the revolution of 1789 was also in harmony
with the current mood in Russia. Thus even the moderate Turgenev
lavishly praised the tenth volume of Michelet's *The French Revolution*, a 'masterpiece' which came 'from the heart' and had 'blood
and warmth'.[35] The Russian intelligentsia became acquainted too at
this period with the socialist doctrines which were being disseminated in France. They studied the ideas of Leroux, a disciple of
Saint-Simon who had preached the need to organise society not for
the benefit of the nobility but in the interests of *'la classe la plus
nombreuse et la plus pauvre'*.[36] In the teachings of Fourier they
found plans for 'phalansteries', ideal communities in which man's
natural passions would be regulated and subordinated to the principle of social harmony. (Fourier had devoted followers in Russia,
notably the eccentric nobleman, Petrashevsky.) They could study
further utopian schemes in Cabet's *Voyage to Icaria* (1840) in which
the author envisaged an egalitarian society collectively operating
the means of production and a broad system of social services. And
in Louis Blanc's *Organisation of Labour* (1839) they could examine
the case for a democratic form of socialism under which all would
have the right to work and a guaranteed minimum wage and the
governing principle of which was expressed in the slogan 'From
each according to his capacities: to each according to his needs'.[37]

That these socialist teachings enjoyed great popularity among the
Westernisers there can be no doubt. Annenkov, returning to St
Petersburg from France in the autumn of 1843, found that the works
of Proudhon, Cabet, Fourier and Leroux were now being passionately debated in Russia and that all sorts of expectations were
being based on them.[38] It cannot be too strongly emphasised,

however, that these socialists were 'utopian', or 'critical-utopian', to use the term applied to them by Marx and Engels,[39] and that their significance for the Russian intelligentsia of the 1840s lay not so much in any practical proposals they made as in the moral concern they aroused to mitigate the social ills caused by a vigorous, expanding capitalist economy. They did not therefore give rise in Russia to any movement that was properly speaking political. Indeed, hardly any 'political conversations in the proper sense of the word' ever occurred at the meetings of circles in the Westernist intelligentsia at this period, Annenkov tells us:

the basic principles governing society were not touched upon at all. It was considered idle to debate them and people started talking about them only when in their application they reached the point of either comic or tragic absurdity. Up until such time they were things which everyone regarded as long since dead and buried.[40]

This evasion of political issues was not merely due to the fact that the censorship prevented explicit reference in the press to Russia's social problems and the abuses tolerated by the régime, but also to the fact that discussions still had the important, perhaps primary function of refining the intellect and character of the participants rather than providing practical solutions to concrete problems.[41] Russian thought in the 1840s tended still to dwell in the abstract aesthetic and moral spheres even after it had largely freed itself from Hegelianism and it was indeed for this reason that political divisions among the 'Westernisers' were slow to appear despite fundamental differences in outlook.

Belinsky

Like Bakunin, Belinsky for a while interpreted Hegelianism as a means for the vindication of reality. Coming to Hegel's philosophy after an acquaintance with Fichte, whose exaltation of the ego seemed to legitimise the Romantic revolt of individuals such as Schiller's 'fair-souled' heroes, Belinsky found in Hegel a certain solace. It was with a profound sense of relief, he told Stankevich in 1839, that he had encountered the Hegelian dictum 'Might is right and right is might';[42] the exhausting struggle with reality could be abandoned. Hegel's assertion that the real is rational Belinsky took to mean that the individual was bound, logically and morally, to

reconcile himself with historical and social reality. This reconciliation with reality – which was admittedly more unequivocally
stated in Belinsky's published articles than in his private correspondence – found expression in a celebrated review, published in
Otechestvennyye zapiski (*Notes of the Fatherland*) in 1839, of
F. Glinka's 'Sketches on the Battle of Borodino'. The state, Belinsky declared here, was the 'highest factor in social life'; only by
becoming a 'member of the state' did the individual cease to be a
'slave of nature'. Dumb animals lived without authority; but man,
even in his natural state, dwelt under 'rational forms of sovereignty
and subordination' and acknowledged power and the duty of filial
obedience. Man could not remember when he had first bowed down
to regal authority, because that authority was not established at any
particular time by any single enactment of man's but was an eternal
manifestation of God's will. This paean to absolutism Belinsky
bolstered with a quotation from the appeal by Shakespeare's
Richard II to the divine right of kings:

> Not all the water in the rough rude sea
> Can wash the balm off from an anointed king;
> The breath of worldly men cannot depose
> The deputy elected by the Lord.[43]

'Society', then, was the 'highest reality' for Belinsky in this phase,
and reality demanded full recognition and acceptance by the individual; otherwise it would crush the individual 'under the leaden
weight of its gigantic palm'.[44]

Belinsky's Hegelian conservatism went hand in hand with insistence on the value of an uncommitted art, for which he argued the
case in an essay of 1840 on the German literary historian, Menzel,
who had criticised Goethe for remaining aloof from contemporary
political matters. Belinsky takes to task such 'little great men' as
Menzel who did not see the state in Hegelian terms as a living
embodiment of an eternal idea and a rational organism developing
in accordance with 'immutable laws contained in its own essence'.
Not realising that the state had a will of its own which was higher
than that of any individual, Menzel and his like failed to appreciate
that great men such as Russia's Peter were only divine envoys who
perceived and carried out God's will, not their own. Thus they
argued as if the individual should measure the 'infinite kingdom of
the Spirit' by the petty yardstick of their own moral premises, as if

the individual himself could change the fortunes of his society. Belinsky then proceeds to condemn those who, in the belief that art might serve society, emulate the Romans and order their poets to assist the intending social reformer by extolling republican virtues. Art might indeed serve society if the artist followed his free inspir- ation and like a Shakespeare or a Goethe presented life in all its complexity. But if political or sectarian demands were made of art then elegant works of literature would quickly be supplanted by 'rhymed dissertations about abstract and rational subjects, by dry allegories . . . or finally by the crazed progeny of petty passions and partisan frenzy'. French literature (particularly the recent writings of Hugo, Dumas, Sue and George Sand, but also the works of sententious neo-classical dramatists and the blasphemous Voltaire) seemed to Belinsky to provide copious examples of these faults: it was 'furious' (*neistovaya* – an epithet shortly to be applied to Belinsky himself!) and reflected the existence of 'petty sects, insig- nificant systems' and 'ephemeral parties' and preoccupation with the 'questions of the day'.[45]

These views of Belinsky's on art, which are not often given much prominence, will in due course be seen to be strikingly similar to those advanced in the mid 1850s by Botkin, Annenkov and Dru- zhinin. Belinsky himself, however, soon repudiated his Hegelian conservatism – which was a source of great embarrassment to friends such as Granovsky and Herzen – and began to make impassioned criticisms of the reality he had tried so earnestly to vindicate. The shift is marked by two long articles on Lermontov published in *Otechestvennyye zapiski* in 1840 and 1841 respectively. In the first of these articles, on Lermontov's *Hero of our Time*, Belinsky dissociated himself from conservative critics by refusing to condemn Lermontov's Byronic hero. Pechorin had a 'strength of spirit and a power of will' which were out of the ordinary; even in his vices one could glimpse 'something great', like lightning among thunder clouds. He was fine, 'full of poetry'; his passions were 'storms' which cleansed the soul. There were indeed grounds, then, for seeing Pechorin as a 'hero of his time'.[46] And in his second article, on Lermontov's poetry, Belinsky makes a more explicit defence of the Romantic rebel in disharmony with his spiritually impoverished environment. Here he praises Lermontov for exal- ting negation. Lermontov, through his poetic ego, had expressed the spirit of the age: he had perfectly captured Russian society at a certain historical moment, in a period of yearning, of anguish and ambition. His poetry came from the depths of an 'outraged spirit'; it was the groan of a man for whom the 'lack of an inner life' was an evil a thousand times more terrible than physical death. And who among the poet's generation would not find in Lermontov the 'key' to his own despondency, spiritual apathy and inner emptiness?[47] Thus the powerless individual, submitting to fate and historical destiny, like the 'poor Yevgeniy' of Pushkin's *Bronze Horseman*, and the artist serenely recording and transmuting this reality into a sublime creation, were now replaced in Belinsky's scale of values by the social rebel at odds with an irrational environment and by the artist who strove to remould reality not *in* his art but *by means of* it.

Belinsky's rejection of Hegelianism did not take place unaided or all at once (his correspondence with Botkin bears witness to this fact). Nor did Belinsky dismiss Hegel as of no significance even after he had rounded most vehemently on him. He admitted even in 1843 that Hegel had transformed philosophy into a science and himself retained a dialectical conception of history, seeing progress as the negation of fixed, anachronistic social patterns.[48] But his renunciation of the concept of reconciliation with reality did have two fundamental consequences. Firstly, it enabled him to give free voice to his instinctive protest on behalf of the dissatisfied intellectual against the particular absolutism under which he lived. And, secondly, it permitted him to develop a new view of art and a conception of the artist as having a civic responsibility in his own society. Neither of these conceptions, any more than any others of Belinsky's, was sustained without struggle and inconsistencies, but they did dominate Belinsky's thought during the last seven years of his life.

It is understandable that Belinsky's protest on behalf of the oppressed individual, owing to its politically subversive implications, should have found more overt expression in the critic's correspondence than in published articles such as those on Lermontov. One of the most famous manifestations of this protest is the tirade contained in a letter of October 1840, to Botkin, in which Belinsky curses his 'foul desire for reconciliation with foul reality!':

Long live the great Schiller, mankind's noble advocate, the bright star of salvation, the emancipator of society from the bloody prejudices of tradition! Long live reason, and may ignorance vanish! as the great Pushkin exclaimed. The *human personality* is now higher for me than history, higher than society, higher than mankind. This is the idea and the thought of the age!

The philosophers of the French enlightenment and their revolutionary disciples, execrated during the period of reconciliation with reality, now emerge as the 'vanguard of humanity'.[49] A few months later, in another letter to Botkin, Belinsky again fulminates against Hegelianism and the tyranny it seemed to justify, this time in terms strikingly similar to those to be used by Ivan Karamazov in his own rejection of higher authority in Dostoyevsky's novel:

The fate of the subject, the individual, the personality, is more important than the fates of the whole world and the health of the Chinese emperor (that is to say Hegelian *Allgemeinheit* [universality]) ... I humbly thank you, Yegor Fyodorych [he means Hegel, whose names were Georg Wilhelm Friedrich], I bow down before your philosopher's cap; but with all due respect to your philosophical philistinism, I have the honour to inform you that if I succeeded in climbing to the highest rung on the ladder of development I would ask you when I got there to give me an account of all the victims of the conditions of life and history, all the victims of contingencies, superstition, the Inquisition, Philip II, and so on and so forth, otherwise I would throw myself head first off the highest rung.[50]

Belinsky's new revolutionary spirit naturally led him now to glorify the 'destroyers of the old', such as Voltaire and the French Jacobins and to turn to socialism almost as a religion. Socialism, he told Botkin in September 1841,

has become for me the idea of ideas, the being of being, the question of questions, the alpha and omega of faith and knowledge ... It (for me) has engulfed history, and religion and philosophy ...[51]

The second major consequence of Belinsky's rejection of Hegelian conservatism – his construction of a new, more subjectivist aesthetic opposed to the ideal of Olympian detachment on the part of the artist – was closely bound up with his desire to unleash the destructive inclinations of the disaffected intellectual. Art and literary criticism would be vehicles for revolt against the intolerable political and social order.

It should be stressed at the outset that Belinsky's rebellion by no means entailed rejection of all his earlier pronouncements on literature in general or Russian literature in particular. His insistence that art be firmly rooted in reality, for example, is not new (though he is to change his view as to what subject matter it is preferable for the artist to choose). He continues in the 1840s to develop the major themes of his first published essay, 'Literary Reveries' (1834), namely that a literature of Western European form was a denizen growth in Russia and could only acquire a distinctive national character as writers began to instil authentic native content into the foreign forms and to record the experience of their own people. He continues also to insist on the need to defend the integrity of art. (It will be of great importance to bear this point in mind when we come to examine the disputes between the radicals and liberals in the 1850s about the heritage of Belinsky and the character of Russian literature in his day.) No matter how 'profound, true, even holy' the idea of a work of art might be, he argued in 1844 in the fifth of his eleven essays on the significance of Pushkin in Russian literature, the work would remain trivial, false and lifeless if its author were not a poet by nature.[52] And in his vitriolic 'Reply to *Moskvityanin*' (1846) he reiterated that the artist needed unconditional freedom in choice of subject matter and insisted that art could only effectively serve certain ideas or tendencies if it remained 'first and foremost art'.[53]

Nevertheless 'pure art' did seem inadmissible to Belinsky in the 1840s. Indeed, such a concept, which was of 'purely German origin', could only have arisen among a 'contemplative, cogitative and dreamy' people; it could not possibly have appeared among a 'practical people'[54] (to which category the Russians might now claim to belong, by virtue of the spirit of the Westernisers' thought since the early 1840s). Art had the indispensable social role of promoting consciousness, which led to social well-being;[55] or, as Belinsky put the matter, with greater freedom, in his famous 'Letter to Gogol' (1847), it was part of the writer's task to awaken in the Russian people a sense of their 'human dignity lost for so many centuries amid dirt and muck'. Only literature, 'despite the Tartar censorship', showed signs of 'life' and 'movement' in Russia. It was for that reason that the writer's calling was held in such high esteem there and had 'long since eclipsed the tinsel of epaulettes and multi-coloured uniforms'.[56] Literature had therefore more than ever become the expression of social problems and content had come to prevail over form in importance. To seek to deny art the right of serving public interests, moreover, was to debase it rather than to elevate it, for it would be thus deprived of its most vital element, its idea, and turned instead into an 'object of sybaritic pleasure, the plaything of lazy idlers'.[57] The writer mindful of his social responsibility could not content himself with the mere objective reproduction of reality; he had to attempt to capture from the 'chaos of contradictory opinions and aspirations' that which was typical and general in his place and time. He had to peer beneath the surface and discern the 'secret spiritual motives' which underlay the actions of his characters and give a sense of 'something whole, complete, united and self-contained'.[58] He had to perceive, as Dobrolyubov and later Marxist critics were to insist, the most characteristic phenomena of a given epoch and organise their presentation in such a way as to reveal the underlying spiritual and social processes at work in it.[59]

Belinsky's literary criticism in the 1840s, then, was a vehicle, firstly, for his struggle on behalf of the restless intellectual and the downtrodden masses with tsarist absolutism and, secondly, for the promotion of a literature that would express the nation's social conscience. However, it also had yet another dimension, serving as a medium for Belinsky's criticism of Slavophilism and his advocacy of an opposing 'Westernism'. Admittedly Belinsky's assessment of Slavophilism was not altogether negative. The Slavophiles had posed a question of fundamental topical importance – the question of the relationship of Russia to the West – and had prompted others to think deeply about it. They were even right up to a point when they drew attention to the 'duality' of the Russian intellectual with his Western learning and *mores* and the consequent lack of moral vigour which prevented him from properly expressing his national character.[60] (This was after all precisely the problem which had haunted Chaadayev and bedevilled the 'superfluous man', whose introspective inertia – 'reflection', as it was termed – was familiar to the intellectuals of the 1840s themselves.) But at the same time the Slavophiles made the mistake of taking superficial phenomena, such as dress and customs, for expressions of deeper national character. They held the 'most strange opinion', Belinsky scoffed in one of his essays on *Eugene Onegin*, that a Russian man in a frockcoat and a Russian woman in a corset were no longer Russians and that the Russian spirit made itself felt only where there was a 'homespun coat, bast shoes, raw vodka and sour cabbage'.[61] They advanced certain 'hazy, mystical prejudices about the victory of the East over the West' and looked back nostalgically to the 'obtuse and stagnant patriarchal way of life' which obtained in pre-Petrine

Muscovy.[62] But in fact Russia belonged not to the 'East', by which Belinsky understood Asia, but to Europe, to which it was united by virtue of its geographical position, its Christian religion and its new civic life, the product of the Westernisation undertaken by Peter the Great, whom Belinsky revered. Belinsky demanded therefore not a return '*aux temps primitifs*', but a natural course forward, by means of 'enlightenment and civilisation'.[63] That is by no means to say that Russia would henceforth slavishly follow the West. For, in the first place, Belinsky argued in his 'Survey of Russian Literature for 1846', alien content would never supplant native content; rather it would grow into it with time, just as the food a man consumed was transformed into his flesh and blood and thus sustained him. And, in the second place, the age of transformation in Russia was now complete; Russia had extracted as much benefit from Peter's reforms as it could. The time had come for Russia to develop 'autochthonously, out of herself'. This development would not be assisted by attempts to bypass or leap over the age of reforms and return to pre-Petrine times; but nor would it be helped by indiscriminate and superficial borrowing from the West. Russians should cease taking European forms and externals for 'Europeanism' and admiring what was European simply because it was not Asiatic; rather they should love, respect and aspire to what was humane in Western civilisation and judge, on the basis of what they had already received, how much more they needed to take.[64]

Belinsky's views on the historical question of the relationship of Russia to the West are interlinked with his views on the question of literary history as to the degree of independence manifested by Russian literature. In the same way that European dress and, more importantly, European *mores*, did not prevent the educated Russian from being Russian, so European influences did not diminish the naturalness of Russian literature now that it had acquired a distinctive national content.[65] This idea is developed at greater length in Belinsky's last annual survey of Russian literature, for the year 1847, in which he clearly senses the coming of age of Russian literature. Whereas in 1834 he had boldly declared that Russia did not have a literature[66] – if by 'a literature' one meant a coherent body of works organically inter-related and expressing the spirit and preoccupations of a nation – by 1847 he did believe that such a literature was in existence. (Belinsky himself had presided over its formation and to a considerable extent moulded it by his judgements.) Russian literature had freed itself from foreign influences and in the process had increasingly come 'close to real life, to naturalness'; it had become a 'faithful mirror' of Russian reality. Pushkin had contributed greatly towards the development of this process (his *Eugene Onegin* Belinsky had described as an 'encyclopaedia of Russian life')[67]. But it was Gogol who had completed the process. All of his works were devoted 'exclusively to portrayal of the world of Russian life' which he had been able to depict with 'such amazing fidelity and truth' because he had shown 'complete freedom and independence' from all the 'rules and traditions' associated with particular schools. He had expressed 'originality and distinctive character' and had raised Russian literature from something foreign and 'rhetorical' to something national and natural.[68]

Gogol had inspired a whole school of writers – the so-called 'natural school' – which, Belinsky rightly said, now occupied the centre of the Russian literary stage. It is difficult to say precisely which writers belonged to the school since the term was broad and loosely used, but several men of letters who in their maturity were to acquire great prominence – Nekrasov, Turgenev, Saltykov-Shchedrin, and Dostoyevsky – as well as Herzen, the lexicographer Dal and other writers influential and popular in the 1840s though now more or less forgotten – Grigorovich, Sollogub, Butkov, Grebyonka and Panayev – belonged to it by virtue of some of their works at least. While it could not be claimed that these writers produced, in the 1840s, many works which were of great individual or lasting merit – and Belinsky did not conceal this fact – their emergence did seem to Belinsky to mark Russia's literary coming of age, for they heeded his plea that art base itself on 'real life' (that is to say, the life of the common people). Taking their lead from Gogol, as Belinsky had interpreted him (that is to say, as a faithful painter of Russian reality) these writers resolved to deal with the 'prose of life', with 'ordinary', everyday reality and introduced into their work strata of Russian society – the lower *chinovniki*,* the urban poor, the peasantry – which had not hitherto received much serious attention in imaginative literature in Russia. In practice the choice of such subject matter inevitably entailed concentration on the seamy side of Russian life and on the nation's social problems. Grigorovich's celebrated stories, *The Village* (1846) and *Anton the*

* Officials in the tsarist bureaucracy.

Unfortunate (1847), for example, give an unalleviated picture of the poverty and misery of a peasantry overburdened by taxation, cruelly exploited and subject to universal injustice. Treatment, as well as choice of subject matter, took a new departure. Conforming to the spirit of an age in which the natural sciences were making rapid progress and the rigour of their method being applied to more and more disciplines, including the humanities, the writers of the 'natural school' strove to reproduce society, its classes, customs, manners and language, in short the 'way of life' (*byt*), in meticulous detail and with scientific precision. They even borrowed from the natural sciences some of their favourite terminology, such as 'anatomy', and gave the title *The Physiology of Petersburg* (1845) to the immensely popular collection of sketches which constitutes in a sense their manifesto. Even their choice of genre reflected their concern to record what Nekrasov described as 'all the mysteries of our social life, all the mainsprings of the joyful and sad scenes of our domestic existence, all the sources of what happens on our streets':[69] for these writers consolidate the tendency to write in prose rather than poetry and excel at the sketch, a journalistic genre apparently more suitable for recording information than for sophisticated analysis of character.

Objective as they claimed their intentions were, however, the writers of the 'natural school' in practice barely concealed their sympathetic attitude to the poor or their hostility to the affluent upper classes. (They were accordingly chided for their choice of subject matter by critics of conservative persuasion, who were themselves in turn harangued by Belinsky for their unwillingness to have their sybaritic existence disturbed by distressing accounts of slums in which whole families huddled together, starving and shivering under a few tattered rags.)[70] The potentially subversive significance of their writings, moreover, was increased by their implicit assertion of the dignity and humanity of the common people. The legitimacy of the institution of serfdom, for example, was undermined by the fact that the landowners portrayed by Turgenev in his *Sportsman's Sketches*, which began to appear in 1847, were clearly morally inferior to the serfs over whom they had absolute legal jurisdiction. Belinsky, who was close to Turgenev at the period when the latter began his cycle of sketches, was quick to point the moral that could be deduced from the portrayal of the poor by the writers of the 'natural school' as the equals, in human terms, of members of the upper classes. The poor were deserving of sympathy rather than contempt for the vices which a harsh environment had bred in them. After all, Christ's 'loving and merciful glance' had not been offended by the sight of 'festering sores on a body barely covered by filthy rags'; he had permitted the first stone to be thrown at the fornicatress only by him whose conscience was clear.[71]

There is in Belinsky's heritage to the Russian intelligentsia one further element that is of the greatest importance, but which is less tangible than any of the views he advanced at one time or another on the relationship between the individual and the state, the relationship between Russia and the West or the role of art and criticism in Russian life. It is the magnetic power of his personality and the immense force of his moral example, to which memoirists unanimously bear witness. Of unprepossessing appearance and small stature, painfully shy and gauche in society, Belinsky lacked too the breadth of culture and knowledge of foreign languages which were customary in the circles he frequented. These disadvantages, however, were greatly outweighed by the ferocious moral commitment and sincerity which earned him the same appellation, 'furious' (*neistovyy*), that he himself had once applied to contemporary French literature and which at the same time inspired loathing and perhaps a certain dread in Russian officialdom. He was one of those rare individuals whose passionate, innate moral sense drives them to defend with fanatical conviction, uncompromisingly and at any cost, regardless of personal peril, whatever they believe to be truth and justice. One could not endure an 'outraged sense of truth and human dignity', he thundered in his letter to Gogol, after the publication of the *Selected Passages from a Correspondence with Friends*, in which the novelist had lamely defended the serf-owning order; 'one cannot keep silent when lies and immorality are preached as truth and virtue under the cloak of religion and the protection of the knout'.[72] It goes without saying that what Annenkov describes as Belinsky's fanatical ... quest for justice and truth'[73] coloured his literary judgements and gave rise to impassioned demands that his readers show a 'religious respect for the human dignity' of one's fellows, and live altruistically and serve some noble 'idea'.[74] But even more in his private life than in his writings Belinsky's 'sacred spark'[75] fired contemporaries and inspired those who knew him to pursue the truth in the service of

Russian letters irrespective of their temperaments and instinctive political preferences. Thus Herzen, Ogaryov, Nekrasov and Panayev, on the one hand, and Granovsky, Botkin, Annenkov, Kavelin and Turgenev, on the other, were unanimous in their acknowledgement of Belinsky's moral example, although the two groups were subsequently to disagree profoundly about the practical goals to which that example should properly encourage the intelligentsia to aspire.

Herzen's thought after his emigration in 1847

A more immediate source of disagreement among the 'Westernist' intelligentsia than the question of the nature of Belinsky's heritage was the development of Herzen's thought in the late 1840s. Having taken the decision to leave the stifling Russia of Nicholas I, Herzen almost at once became disenchanted with the West, in which he arrived early in 1847. This disenchantment is recorded in his *Letters from the Avenue Marigny*, the first three of which were published in *Sovremennik* (*The Contemporary*) in October that year. Before his arrival in Paris the French capital had been closely connected in Herzen's mind with 'all the best hopes of modern man'; he had entered the city 'with a trembling of the heart, with timidity, as once people had entered Jerusalem or Rome'. The Paris he found in 1847, however, was an epitome of 'moral corruption, of spiritual weariness, emptiness, pettiness'. It was no less moribund than Nicolaevan Russia, though moribund in a different way. If in Russia it was the government and its legion of functionaries which spread gloom throughout the land, in France it was the bourgeoisie which poisoned society with its exploitation and its values. The heir of a 'brilliant nobility and a coarse plebeianness', the bourgeois combined the worst failings of both and had none of the qualities of either. He was wealthy as an aristocrat but parsimonious as a shop-keeper. He exhibited a rowdy, ostentatious patriotism. He had devised a morality 'based on arithmetic, on the power of money, on love of order'. He was a despot in his family, but had a hypocritical partiality for sexual innuendo, flirting and a little debauchery 'on the quiet'. His *mores* were perfectly expressed in the vulgar vaudevilles which played every evening to packed houses. The best source for the study of this repugnant phenomenon was the worthless drama of Scribe, the 'courtier, flatterer, preacher, buffoon, teacher, jester and poet of the bourgeoisie'. The bourgeois would cry in the theatre touched by his own virtue as it was portrayed by Scribe, moved by the 'heroism of the office and the poetry of the shop-counter'. The bourgeoisie might have been momentarily acceptable, Herzen supposed, as a negation of the obsolete aristocracy, but did not have the capacity to behave with dignity in victory. The class lacked a 'great past' and had 'no future'. In a fourth 'Letter from the Avenue Marigny', published in *Sovremennik* in November 1847, Herzen continued this attack, accusing the bourgeoisie of turning the desire for profit into a 'passion, a religion', and describing it as history's *'lex talionis'*, retribution for the one-sidedness of the previous age when people had concentrated on political affairs and neglected economic questions.[76]

Revolted by the prevailing class in the France of Louis-Philippe, Herzen devoted much effort during the first years of his exile to the formulation of a brand of socialism according to which Russia, thanks to the special qualities of her unspoiled peasantry, was to play a leading role in Europe's social regeneration. Although he had recently been among those who had berated the Slavophiles for their belief in Russia's national exclusiveness and superiority, he himself now argued that 'Europe', such as it was, had completed its role. Admittedly Russia's own history to date was poor, but in the 'national character' and the 'national life' there lay the guarantee of future greatness. To the Slavs in general – an intelligent, strong race richly endowed with various qualities – Herzen attributed a remarkable capacity to 'adapt themselves to everything, languages, customs, arts and mechanical processes'. On the Russian peasant he lavished especial praise: what a marvellous people lived in the villages, Herzen had never seen their like elsewhere. In particular Herzen admired the supposed instinctive socialism which found expression in their commune. He now fully endorsed Haxthausen's opinion that each rural commune was a miniature republic which governed its own internal affairs. The commune gave to all without exception a place at the table; the land belonged to all, not to individuals; each person had a right to the use of as much land as any other; each member who held land had a right to a voice in the discussion of the commune's affairs; the officers of the commune were democratically elected at a general assembly. The commune had existed since time immemorial; it had saved the Russian people from 'Mongol barbarity' and 'German bureaucracy' and now it might help them to avoid the miseries of capitalist development. For since nothing in history was 'absolutely necessary', since there was 'no invariable predestination', it was possible that Russia might attain to socialism without passing through all the phases of Western European historical development: or at least she might pass through those phases only 'in the same way that the foetus passes through the inferior stages of zoological existence'. The nation's 'youth' might indeed be an advantage, as the Slavophiles had supposed.[77]

Russia after 1848 and the reinvigoration of intellectual life in the mid 1850s

The 'revolution' of 24 February 1848 in Paris and the uprisings it helped to precipitate in Prussia, Austria, Hungary and elsewhere, had the effect in Russia of inaugurating a period known as the 'dismal seven years' (*mrachnoye semiletiye*) which was oppressive even by comparison with what had gone before and which ended only with the death of Nicholas in 1855. Frightened by the spectre of revolution – and the worst official fears seemed to be confirmed by the discovery by the police of the Petrashevsky circle – the government took a series of draconian countermeasures. Censorship was placed under the supervision of a secret committee chaired by the extreme reactionary, Count Buturlin, and operated, in the words of the very moderate Annenkov, with a harshness that was 'almost savage'.[78] Uvarov was replaced as Minister of Education by Prince Shirinsky-Shikhmatov, whose obedience to the tsar was absolute: 'I have no thought, no will of my own', he once said, 'I am only a blind instrument of the will of the sovereign.'[79] Philosophy came to be regarded as a subversive subject; lectures on certain branches of it were discontinued in the universities and the teaching of logic was entrusted to theologians. The number of university students was reduced from 4,600 in 1848 to 3,600 in 1854[80] and the degree of government control over the universities was increased by the extension to the Minister of Education of the power personally to appoint or dismiss rectors and deans. Official corruption and self-advancement through embezzlement might have proliferated quite freely, as Annenkov claimed;[81] but it was not an atmosphere in which intellectual life could flourish and the period is notable both for the despondency of the intelligentsia and for the dearth of major contributions to thought and imaginative literature – a dearth by no means entirely explicable by the emigration of Herzen in 1847, and the deaths of Belinsky in 1848 and Gogol in 1852.

In the mid 1850s, however, this régime, which to many had the appearance of being timeless, came to an end. Military defeat in the Crimea at the hands of the British and French armies fighting at an immense distance from their native lands underlined the fundamental weakness of the régime and the pressing need for major change. At the same time the death of Nicholas and the accession to the throne of Alexander II, a man of relatively liberal temper, made it possible realistically to contemplate such change and to discuss it more freely. By far the most important practical manifestation of the new mood was the initiation of discussion of the abolition of serfdom and the preparation of appropriate legislation. The strategic and economic need to modernise Russia as well as the force of the moral arguments against serfdom were appreciated more clearly now, and in any case the increasing peasant unrest of the late 1850s gave the problem a new urgency. 'It is better to abolish serfdom from above than to wait until the serfs begin to liberate themselves from below', Alexander told an assembly of the Moscow nobility in March 1856.[82] The tsar himself initiated the preparations for the emancipation by setting up a secret committee to examine the problem, which met for the first time in January 1857. By spring 1859 'editorial commissions' were ready to collate the material submitted by the numerous provincial committees which had made reports during the previous year. And in October 1860, when these commissions had completed their work, the Chief Committee, under the chairmanship of the Grand Duke Constantine, prepared the final proposals which were incorporated in the emancipation edict of 19 February 1861.

In the new atmosphere which prevailed after 1855 intellectual life was suddenly reinvigorated. One manifestation of the new vitality was the blossoming of imaginative literature again after seven barren years. A remarkable crop of works appeared between 1855 and 1861, among them Turgenev's novels, *Rudin* (1856), *A Nest of Gentry* (1859), and *On the Eve* (1860), Tolstoy's *Sebastopol Stories* (1855–6), Pisemsky's *A Thousand Souls* (1858), Goncharov's *Oblomov* (1859), Ostrovsky's play, *The Thunderstorm* (1860), Dostoyevsky's *Notes from the House of the Dead* (1860), Nekrasov's narrative poem, *The Pedlars* (1861), and the sketches of numerous lesser writers, such as N. Uspensky and V. Sleptsov, who began to chronicle the poverty of the masses in a journalistic style. Publicism again began to flourish too: the journals *Sovremennik* and *Otechestvennyye zapiski* now achieved a circulation of approximately four thousand which was very large for the time; others, such as *Biblioteka dlya chteniya (Reading Library)*, were revived under new editorship and still others, such as *Russkaya beseda (Russian Conversation), Russkiy vestnik (The Russian Herald)* and *Ateney (The Athenaeum)*, sprang up in response to the increased public interest in topical cultural and social questions. Furthermore, as the attention of the educated public came at last to rest on concrete practical questions, so these journals took on a political character which had been lacking in the intellectual debate of the previous decade and which now helped to bring into sharper focus the views of those 'men of the 1840s' who remained prominent in intellectual life.

Three distinct currents of thought in Russian intellectual life in the immediate pre-reform years need to be considered here; we may label them Slavophile, liberal and radical. Slavophilism was undoubtedly reinvigorated in these years and its main tenets forcefully restated; indeed, it is to this period that some of the clearest statements of the doctrine actually belong. In 1855, for example, K. Aksakov wrote his 'Memorandum' for Alexander II 'On the Internal State of Russia' in which he argued that the Russian people had no desire for political rights. On two important occasions in their history, in the ninth and seventeenth centuries, Aksakov argued, the Russians had invited some outsider, in the first instance a Varanggian prince and in the second Mikhail Romanov, to rule over them and assume responsibililty for their political affairs. The Russian people were unassertive and tranquil, Aksakov contended (disregarding the evidence of the great peasant rebellions of Russian history); they wished only to preserve their 'internal communal life' and their customs and to lead the 'peaceful life of the spirit'. Russian governments showed wisdom in proportion as they understood this need of the masses to lead a life free of mundane political distraction.[83] In the following year, 1856, I. Kireyevsky published his article 'On the Need for and Possibility of New Principles for Philosophy', a further critique of the rational spirit thought to underlie Western civilisation. Faith, together with 'poetry' – by which Kireyevsky meant noble moral striving – had died in the Western world, where industry alone seemed important

now. Only the Orthodox religion could protect the believer from
the moral bankruptcy of which Western capitalism seemed to
Kireyevsky to be a product, for only Orthodoxy preserved a proper
distinction between the provinces of the reason and the spirit,
between human thought and divine revelation.[84] Finally Khomyakov, in his 'Epistle to the Serbs' (1860), reiterated the belief that
outside the Orthodox Church there was no clear conception or
sense of Christian brotherhood.[85]

The second main intellectual current of the mid 1850s, liberalism,
represented a development of the moderate Westernism of the
1840s. Since three of the leading representatives of this current –
Botkin, Annenkov and Kavelin – are subjects of the present study
only the most superficial examination of it need be made here. Its
exponents were for the most part enlightened bureaucrats or
academics; that is to say, individuals who had a vested interest in the
preservation of the existing structure in its general features, but who
for practical and moral reasons wished to bring greater justice and
efficiency to their society and its traditionally corrupt administration. (It is worth noting that the training and occupations of these
men also disposed them to take a more or less sober view of a given
subject and to seek conclusions based on serious rational argument.) In St Petersburg the main circle of liberals was that of
Kavelin and included N. A. Milyutin, who played an important role
in the work of the editorial commissions preparing the ground for
the abolition of serfdom and was in autumn 1858 appointed deputy-
minister of the interior. In Moscow, after the death of Granovsky,
the liberals gathered around A. V. Stankevich (younger brother of
the student of German philosophy) and included Botkin, the
brothers Ye. F. and A. F. Korsh, the eccentric doctor and translator
of Shakespeare, Ketcher (to whom Herzen devotes some memorable pages in *My Past and Thoughts*),[86] and Kudryavtsev, a classical
historian and professor at Moscow University (who died, however,
in 1856). In 1857, these men, all of whom had belonged to the
Westernist circles of the 1840s, were joined by a younger thinker,
the historian and jurist Chicherin.[87] The main forum for the expression of the views of these liberals was the journal *Russkiy vestnik*,
founded in 1856, which under the editorship of Katkov soon
achieved a popularity comparable with that of *Sovremennik*.[88] In
addition to the articles published in the legal press, however, the
liberals also produced a considerable literature of draft proposals

and articles on social and administrative questions, much of which circulated in manuscript form inside Russia or was published in anthologies printed by Herzen in London on his free press under the title *Voices from Russia*.

The writings of these liberals reveal a great reluctance to tamper with the principle of monarchic government in Russia and a belief that change could best be effected from above, within the existing political framework. Chicherin in particular emphasised the leading role played by the state in the historical development of nations: the state was the 'highest form of communal life, the highest manifestation of nationality in the social sphere'.[89] In an article on de Tocqueville's work, *The Old Régime and the Revolution*, he argued that the French historian had underestimated the historical role of absolutism and elsewhere he even went so far as to praise Louis XIV.[90] Admittedly his revival of the Hegelian enthusiasm for the strong state led to a breach with *Russkiy vestnik*, when Katkov refused to publish his article on de Tocqueville. Nevertheless this enthusiasm was quite consistent with the general tendency of the Russian liberals of this period to count upon the benevolence of the autocrat. Perhaps because of the air of expectancy after the death of Nicholas and because, too, of the manifest relative liberalism of the new tsar, they looked to Alexander II with optimism and affection. Ketcher may have gone further than most when he drank a toast to Alexander while kneeling in front of his portrait; but all expressed unqualified approval of and gratitude for Alexander's initiation of discussion of the problem of serfdom. At the same time, however, they were clearly frightened by the possibility that the government would lose control if reform were delayed too long or carried out too quickly and they were alarmed by the growing peasant unrest of the post-war years. Thus Chicherin, haunted by the prospect of great social upheaval, praised England as the country of 'judicious progress' which had protected itself from revolutionary storms by the passing of reform at opportune moments in its history.[91] And Babst, a professor of political economy, while criticising conservatives who defended the old order without acknowledging the need for change, alluded to a 'law of gradualness', which he supposed was the basic law of social development, and denied the inevitability of revolutions, which, he believed, were brought about by bad government[92].

Chernyshevsky

The liberals of the 1850s were concerned to a certain extent to continue the debate of the 1840s with the Slavophiles. A polemic of 1856–7 between *Russkiy vestnik* and *Russkaya beseda* reflected this concern. Chicherin was not untypical when he rejected such Slavophile concepts as 'basic Russian principles' and 'Orthodoxy' as devoid of real content.[93] Nevertheless liberals did share with Slavophiles an enthusiasm for gradual and moderate reform, as opposed to sudden and radical change, which prompted Katkov in 1857 to describe their respective journals as 'two sisters'[94] and which tended to mark them off at least as sharply from the third main grouping in the intellectual life of the period, the radicals, as from one another.

This fissure between liberal and radical thought in the mid and late 1850s can with justification be seen as the sign of a change that was taking place in the social composition of the intelligentsia. The advocates of moderate change, liberals and Slavophiles alike, were in the main older and relatively affluent men, many of them from the ranks of the landed gentry, while the radicals were for the most part *raznochintsy* (that is to say men of mixed, more plebeian social origin, from the *meshchanstvo** or lower clergy), who challenged the aesthetic, ethical, social and political beliefs of the 'men of the 1840s' and scoffed at their civility and restraint. Turgenev's Bazarov in *Fathers and Children* (1862) is the consummate literary portrait of the new type, but their most influential spokesman is Chernyshevsky; and, since it was precisely the desire to oppose Chernyshevsky's views that gave clarity to liberal opinion in the second half of the 1850s, we should pause to examine those views at some length.

It is important to emphasise that Chernyshevsky and his disciples derived their main inspiration from the rationalist, scientific tradition with which the 'men of the 1840s' had become familiar only after an infatuation with heady Hegelian concepts. The discoveries of the 1820s and 1830s in such fields as electricity, medicine and biology had stimulated interest in the natural sciences with their rigour and exactitude, their rejection of *a priori* hypotheses and their acceptance of only what could be empirically demonstrated. Scientific method began to be applied not merely to physics, chemistry, biology, astronomy and geology, but also to other areas

* Lower middle class.

which had not previously been considered amenable to such rigorous rational analysis, namely the study of man's behaviour, his society and his institutions. It is in the 1830s, after all, that the foundations are laid for the modern disciplines of psychology and sociology (the latter term itself was coined by Comte, one of the earliest advocates of the wider application of the new methodology), and for the 'scientific socialism' of Marx and Engels, which postulates inexorable laws of economic and social development. In Russia – where the study of mathematics and the natural sciences began to flourish in the 1850s and 1860s; Lobachevsky and Mendeleyev are outstanding early examples of this development – radical thinkers now began to place great faith in science both as a means of securing material improvements for society and as a discipline with the aid of which they would find infallibly correct answers to ethical, social and political problems. Scientific allusions abound in Chernyshevsky's writings, and, although their purpose appears on occasion to be to dazzle the reader with the author's erudition, there is no doubt that they are also intended to point up by analogy the accuracy of the conclusions Chernyshevsky draws. 'That part of philosophy which examines questions relating to man, just like the other part which examines questions relating to external nature', he boldly states, 'is based on the natural sciences.' The latter had developed to such an extent that they already provided material for the 'exact solution of moral problems'.[95]

It is also important to bear in mind both the breadth of the intellectual challenge to established beliefs which Chernyshevsky posed in his day and the way in which his assaults on separate bastions of the old outlook form part of a general campaign. Chronologically his first attack is on old aesthetic beliefs, and it is proper to begin a survey of this thought with an examination of this attack since it was in the realm of literature and literary criticism – the fields with which the intellectual life of the 1840s had been chiefly preoccupied – that the first battles of the mid 1850s were fought. In his dissertation, *The Aesthetic Relations of Art to Reality*, presented for a master's degree and published in book form in 1855, Chernyshevsky set out to demolish the idealist conception, derived from Hegelian aesthetics, that there coexisted a real world – the mundane, concrete actuality of everyday life, with all its joys and sorrows – and a superior, enduring world of perfect forms to which man aspired in his religion and philosophy and the beauty of which might be captured for posterity by the great artist. This traditional conception rested on an intuitive assumption, concerning the unverifiable existence of a higher reality, which Chernyshevsky, as a devotee of scientific method, could not accept. Moreover, the idealist aesthetic had deeply conservative implications repugnant to the socialist. For insistence on the comparative imperfection of everyday actuality and the exhortation to the artist to seek beauty in a transcendent reality encouraged an attitude of resignation towards earthly suffering and thus permitted the creation of an art devoid of any fierce sense of civic responsibility. In order to combat this indifferentism Chernyshevsky redefined the concept of beauty as that which reminds us most vividly of real life; the 'beautiful', he asserts, is 'life' itself. By this means he focuses the attention of the artist on reality with all its defects and topical social problems. He lowers the status of art too: its new function is merely to reproduce reality, to teach by serving as a '*Handbuch*', a handbook, for the reader; in short, to be of direct and palpable use to society.[96] This utilitarian view of art – to which the later doctrine of 'socialist realism' owes much – provoked heated objections from outside the radical camp. Dostoyevsky was to argue that, paradoxical as it might seem, only an artist unconstrained by demands for socially important content and political *parti pris* could produce works capable of deeply affecting the public and thereby benefiting society.[97] And the urbane Turgenev – for whom the beauty of the work of art was perhaps the only durable refuge for man in his tragic passage through life's misfortunes – was moved to uncharacteristically abusive denunciation of Chernyshevsky's dissertation, which he dismissed as 'a vile book', 'carrion', and even of Chernyshevsky himself, to whom he referred in his private correspondence as the 'one who smells of bugs'.[98]

Chernyshevsky's arguments for a utilitarian and politically committed art found expression in his 'Essays on the Gogol Period of Russian Literature' (1855–6), a series of nine voluminous articles containing extensive quotations from Belinsky's writings, which Chernyshevsky interpreted as social commentary.[99] After 1857, however (that is to say, from the time of the emergence of Dobrolyubov as a major critic to whom the literary section of *Sovremennik* could be entrusted), Chernyshevsky devotes relatively little attention to literary subjects and turns instead to philosophical, economic and political questions. The clearest statement of his philosophical views is contained in the essay on the 'Anthropological Principle in Philosophy' which was published in two instalments in *Sovremennik* in 1860. Chernyshevsky attempts in this essay to popularise the materialist and determinist views with which the Russian intelligentsia was becoming familiar through the work of German thinkers such as Vogt (notorious for his assertion that the brain secretes thought just as the liver secretes bile), Moleschott (who argued in his book, *The Circuit of Life* [1852], that mental processes should be seen purely as the product of physical stimuli) and Büchner (who explained consciousness as a physical state of the brain brought about by the movement of matter, and whose *magnum opus, Force and Matter* [1855], is commended by Turgenev's Bazarov as more worthwhile reading than Pushkin for the belated education of the *passé* older generation). The implications of the crude materialism preached by these thinkers were far-reaching. With their denial of the existence of spirit, they furthered the erosion of religious belief begun by Feuerbach (to whom Chernyshevsky alludes frequently and with approval). The weakening of religious belief served, in turn, to undermine absolute moral values, the concept of some immutable standard of good and evil and belief in a divine justice whose operation might compensate for the imperfections of earthly justice. Furthermore, by explaining character and thought as products of physiological and environmental factors over which man had little control, these thinkers paved the way for a view of man as unfree and therefore not responsible for his actions. (Indeed, Büchner himself drew important sociological conclusions from his materialism, explaining crime, as Robert Owen had done, as the product of bad social conditions.)

Following these writers Chernyshevsky, in his 'Anthropological Principle in Philosophy', denies the existence of a spiritual aspect in man. The 'observations of physiologists, zoologists and medical men have driven away all thought of dualism in man', who possesses his 'real nature' and no other. (Chernyshevsky is thus carrying out a simplification analogous to that which he has carried out in aesthetics: in both instances two conventional planes of reality are reduced to one.) Chernyshevsky then proceeds to assert that thought is the product not of intuition or innate impulse but of sensation and stimuli, and he makes the apparently shocking assertion that the thought processes occurring in Newton's brain when he was discovering the law of gravity are qualitatively similar, although of course far removed in scale, to those which occur in the brain of a hen seeking out grains of oats in a pile of dirt. The will Chernyshevsky belittles by describing 'wanting' as merely a phenomenon in a whole chain of cause and effect in which external factors play the main role. Character he treats as moulded by circumstances. Just as the fact that one man becomes a carpenter and another a blacksmith shows merely that under certain circumstances some men become carpenters and under other circumstances they become black-smiths, so 'in exactly the same way, under certain circumstances a man becomes good, under others he becomes bad'. Crimes, or 'bad actions' as Chernyshevsky calls them, are explained accordingly as the product of poverty; indeed, a man commits a 'bad action – that is, harms others – almost only when he is obliged to deprive them of things so as not to remain himself without the things he needs'.[100]

In the same essay Chernyshevsky puts forward a utilitarian ethic that was to have equally far-reaching importance for the radical intelligentsia. Whereas it was conventional to attribute to man altruistic as well as selfish impulses, Chernyshevsky again rejects dualism. Man's actions, he contends, are invariably governed by self-interest. At the same time man is a rational creature and is therefore amenable to the argument that his own best interest lies in the last analysis in co-operation with his fellows. According to Chernyshevsky's doctrine of 'rational egoism', man therefore must be taught to derive his selfish satisfaction from performing actions which are of benefit to others. As to the question of how we may judge which actions are good and which are evil, Chernyshevsky abandons absolute moral standards, the 'moral imperatives' of the Kantian idealist, and applies a relativistic criterion. An act is good or bad in relation to its consequences; it is good if it is useful, and the greatest good is that which is useful to the greatest number. Thus the 'interests of mankind as a whole stand higher than the interests of an individual nation; the common interests of a whole nation are higher than the interests of an individual class; the interests of a large class are higher than the interests of a small one'. This ethic, inasmuch as it subordinates the interests of the individual or the minority to those of the larger group, is consistent with a socialism in which individual liberties are unimportant by comparison with collective welfare. The ethic also seems to Chernyshevsky to allow of mathematical evaluations which had a pleasing exactitude: the gradation of interests was 'not open to doubt', for it represented 'merely the application to social problems of the geometrical axioms: "the whole is greater than the part", "the larger quantity is greater than the smaller quantity"'.[101]

Chernyshevsky's excursions into the realms of philosophy should be treated both as an attack on prevailing values – which was continued by even more iconoclastic successors such as Pisarev and Antonovich – and at the same time as an attempt to lay theoretical foundations for socialism. His vision of the socialist future is glimpsed in his novel, *What is to be done?* (1863), the heroine of which, Vera Pavlovna, runs an efficient co-operative of seamstresses and beholds in one of her dreams a communistic rural utopia housed in a building reminiscent of that monument to scientific progress, the Crystal Palace. During the late 1850s, however, Chernyshevsky is concerned not so much with the description of a future utopian epoch as with the examination of ways of inaugurating it. Like Herzen, he comes to fix his attention on the peasant commune. In numerous articles written even while the emancipation of the serfs was being considered by the government he tried to underline the practical advantages as well as the moral virtues of communal landholding, taking issue, for example, with those who saw the commune as an unproductive and inefficient agricultural unit. And in his most notable essay on the subject, under the characteristically opaque title 'A Critique of Philosophical Prejudices against Communal Landholding' (1858), he advanced the view – which was to provide an important foundation for the later Populist revolutionaries – that backward nations did not have to go through all the stages of development through which other nations had passed in order to reach the higher levels of development. In other words, Russia might arrive at a socialism based on the commune without passing through the protracted capitalist phase of development, with all its attendant social misery, which had developed in the West after the collapse of feudalism there.[102]

The 'Critique of Philosophical Prejudices against Communal Landholding' was directed partly against liberals who argued for gradual social change, and in a number of other articles, written during the same period as the articles on communal landholding but dealing ostensibly with the far removed subject of foreign political history, Chernyshevsky develops this attack against moderate opinion. Discussing Cavaignac, the French general who had ruthlessly suppressed the workers' uprising in Paris during the 'June days' of 1848, for example, he condemns the betrayal of the working class by 'moderate republicans' whose political ambitions the workers had helped to realise. The apparent joining of forces by these 'moderate republicans', representing the bourgeoisie, on the one hand, and the working class, on the other, had in any case been a sad *mésalliance*. If the republicans and workers had understood one another they could under no circumstances have begun to work together against the Orléanist government, because the antagonism between them was even greater than the causes of their dissatisfaction with the ministry of Guizot. The 'moderate republicans', morever, were ingenuous, indecisive and unpractical people:

behind the glitter and noise of their abstract formulae they saw and heard nothing, and each event was for them an unexpected thing to which they yielded without a struggle until, at last, they were completely ousted from the power of which they had been unable to make use.

For once Cavaignac had eliminated the threat from the working class, Louis-Napoleon took power himself and consolidated it with his *coup d'état* of 1851.[103]

An even clearer statement of Chernyshevsky's view of liberalism as ineffectual is contained in his article on the 'Struggle of Parties in France in the Reign of Louis XVIII and Charles X'. The subject of the restoration of the Bourbon monarchy in France after the Napoleonic wars, the conflict between moderate republicans and loyalist supporters of the monarchy, and the eventual overthrow of Charles X in the July days of 1830 provided Chernyshevsky with another opportunity to comment obliquely on political developments in Russia after the Crimean War. The article was written, Chernyshevsky explicitly declared, to explain the author's 'dislike' for liberalism as it was represented by Guizot, Thiers, de Tocqueville and others. 'Liberals' were not to be confused with 'democrats' or 'radicals', for their fundamental concerns were different. 'Democrats' sought as far as possible to break the domination of the upper classes over the lower classes in society. By what means the laws were changed and the new social order defended, these were matters of almost complete indifference to them. 'Liberals', on the other hand, would not allow the balance to be tipped in favour of the lower classes, because the latter, owing to their lack of education and their poverty, were indifferent to the matters that most concerned the liberals, namely the right of free speech and a constitutional structure. Again, the 'democrat' was irreconcilably hostile to the aristocracy, whilst the liberal almost always believed that it was only if it maintained a certain degree of 'aristocratism' that a society could attain to a liberal order. 'Liberals' usually harboured a 'mortal enmity' towards democrats since they believed that 'democratism' led to despotism and would be 'fatal to freedom'. The 'radical' – who for Chernyshevsky's polemical purposes is to be identified with the 'democrat' – believed that the main faults of a given society could be eliminated only by the 'complete rebuilding of its foundations, not by trivial improvements of its details'. A radical in China, for example, Chernyshevsky asserts – using the conventional 'Aesopian language' in order to allude to the state of affairs in Russia – would be an 'adherent of European civilisation'; in the East Indies he would oppose the caste system. Radicals invited censure from the liberals because they were prepared to bring about reform by means of material force – a transparent reference to revolution – and were prepared in order to achieve their end to sacrifice the freedom of speech and the constitutional forms which the liberal cherished.[104]

The liberals, then, desired political freedom, but political freedom introduced gradually, and extended little by little with as few upheavals as possible. Even freedom of speech would have to be kept within bounds to ensure that it did not become a vehicle for the demands of the masses. The franchise would have to be limited too. Liberalism might seem attractive, Chernyshevsky argued, for a person protected by good fortune from material hardship, for freedom was a 'very pleasant thing'. But freedom was always understood by liberals in a very narrow and purely formal sense, as an 'abstract right, permission on paper, the absence of legal prohibition'. The liberal could not understand that a legal right only had value when a person had the material means to make use of it. He himself was not forbidden, he wrote, to eat off a golden dinner service, but, since he did not have the funds to satisfy that 'elegant idea', he did not value this particular right and was willing to sell it for a rouble or less. By the same token the masses, who were in most countries ignorant and illiterate and lacked the funds to acquire education for themselves or their children, would hardly value the right of free speech. The liberals therefore lacked popular support and were doomed to impotence.[105]

In another celebrated article, on Turgot, the French physiocrat who had served Louis XV and Louis XVI in the 1770s, Chernyshevsky obliquely expresses his fear that the practical result of the ascendancy of liberalism in Russia would be the growth of a capitalist economy which would create even greater hardship than the system it replaced. Although progressive in his time as an opponent of feudalism who reduced aristocratic privilege, Turgot had also helped to clear the path for a *laissez-faire* economy based on the principle of self-interest, '*chacun pour soi*', the emergence of which Chernyshevsky already detected to his chagrin in the Russian countryside.[106] Turgot had understood that the labour of slaves was unproductive, but he had forgotten this consideration when he came to discuss the worker who was free in name but in fact a 'slave of poverty'. Thus having given man dignity by abolishing the *jurandes* or restrictive guilds and the use of forced labour for the construction of roads he had straightaway abandoned the poor to the 'whim of chance', leaving them to fend for themselves in a fiercely competitive system. Therefore freedom, Chernyshevsky was saying in answer to liberals whose endeavours might lead to the development of capitalism in Russia, might simply allow the strong to profit at the expense of the weak.[107]

Thus in his articles on French politics Chernyshevsky argued in the clearest terms possible in tsarist conditions that it was naïve to expect adequate social change to take place in Russia as a result of gradual reform from above. Liberals, whether they intended it or not, served the government rather than the masses; moreover, their own interests were diametrically opposed to those of the masses, although this appeared not to be the case while autocracy stifled all classes alike.

Russia after the emancipation of the serfs

The emancipation of the serfs did not succeed in satisfying the demands of the most important elements in Russian society. Conservative landowners rued the passing of their privilege. Sections of the liberal gentry clamoured for further reform which would bring them political rights. Socialists considered the provisions of the emancipation edict inadequate and argued that the material condition of the rural mass was not substantially altered, since the peasant, although he was now juridically free, bore a crippling financial burden in the form of the poll-tax (which was not abolished until 1885) and the dues payable for the land allotted to him. The peasants themselves remained dissatisfied because they did not immediately receive as their own unencumbered property the land which they had traditionally believed belonged to them. In many cases they refused to accept the provisions of the edict when they were explained to them and at the village of Bezdna, in Kazan province, misunderstanding resulted in the outbreak, in April 1861, of a serious riot which was put down by troops at the cost of 102 lives. Nor did the emancipation help to heal social divisions. In fact, it generated a new antagonism which the government, liberals and socialists all feared equally. For it facilitated the development of capitalism in Russia by creating a potential mobile labour force which drifted into economic dependence on the more well-to-do elements of the rural community or on the burgeoning class of urban industrialists and entrepreneurs.

The radical intelligentsia, which had acted with some caution while the reform was being prepared, soon began to make demands for more far-reaching change after the publication of the edict. In July 1861 a leaflet entitled 'The Great Russian' was scattered in St Petersburg and Moscow; its authors appealed to the 'educated classes' to relieve the incompetent government of its power. A second number of the leaflet, which was distributed in September, contained a demand for a 'good solution of the peasant question', and the liberation of Poland and a 'constitution', and in the same month a third number of the leaflet carried the prediction that popular rebellion would break out in 1863 if these demands were not met.[108] In a more militant proclamation, addressed 'To the Young Generation' by M. L. Mikhaylov and N. V. Shelgunov and printed on Herzen's press in London, the prospect of revolutionary violence was faced with equanimity and the young were urged to explain the evils of the tsarist order to the people and the troops.[109] A further and still more bellicose proclamation, entitled 'Young Russia', written in prison by a former Moscow University student, Zaichnevsky, was scattered in St Petersburg and Moscow in May 1862. Zaichnevsky criticised Herzen for expressing the naïve hope that socialism might be introduced by peaceful means in Russia, predicted a 'bloody and implacable' revolution which would demolish the 'foundations of contemporary society' and summoned the youth to take up their axes and 'beat the imperial party without pity'.[110] Meanwhile student disturbances had broken out in St Petersburg University in September 1861 in protest against the plans of the new Minister of Education, Putyatin – formerly an admiral – for a stricter régime in the institution. And in the spring of 1862 public tension was heightened by a series of fires which badly damaged certain quarters of St Petersburg. The cause of the fires was not reliably established, but conservatives fanned the widespread suspicion that radicals had been responsible for starting them. Taken together all these factors weakened any remaining enthusiasm on the part of the government for reform (although, it is true, provision was made in 1864 for the establishment of *zemstva** and further legislation, approved in the same year, recast the nation's antiquated judicial system). The return to repressive policies was marked by the arrest in 1862 of numerous persons, including Chernyshevsky, who were suspected of political offences, and by the brutal suppression of the Polish revolt in 1863.

The climate after 1861, then, was not one in which liberal counsels for moderation and gradual reform from above were any longer heeded. The greater freedom after 1855 had permitted rational discussion of the nation's problems, as the thinkers who are the subjects of this study had hoped it would. But it had also briefly facilitated the expression of extreme views of which the liberals themselves could not approve and which encouraged the government again to adopt the conservative stance that liberals had tried for two decades to persuade it to abandon. The emancipation of the serfs, of course, could be interpreted as to some extent the product of the enlightened and humanitarian attitudes which liberals had long advocated; but, ironical as it may seem, the great reform also marked the end of the period in which liberals were able to exercise some effective and distinctive influence in the nation's intellectual life. Suspected by conservatives of a subversive radicalism and berated by radicals for a caution that rendered their opposition ineffectual, they had after 1861 either to resign themselves to impotence or to compromise their former ideals by expressing a political allegiance that was to some extent incompatible with them.

* elective district councils (singular *zemstvo*).

2

Timofey Nikolayevich Granovsky (1813–1855)

Granovsky's status in the intelligentsia and the reasons for his neglect

In October 1855 Turgenev addressed to the editors of the journal *Sovremennik* an obituary notice, which was headed by an epigraph from Schiller, *'Auch die Todten sollen leben'* ('the dead must also live'), and began with an account of a funeral Turgenev had attended the day before:

Yesterday Granovsky's funeral took place. I am not going to describe to you how much his death affected me. His loss may be reckoned society's loss and will be received with bitter perplexity and grief in many hearts throughout Russia. His funeral was a moving and deeply significant occasion; it will remain an important event in the memory of everyone who took part in it. I shall never forget the long procession, the coffin gently rocking on the shoulders of the students, the bare heads and young faces ennobled by an expression of honest and sincere sorrow, nor how many people in spite of themselves tarried among the scattered graves of the cemetery even when everything was over and after the last handful of earth had fallen on the remains of the beloved teacher ... [1]

The occasion was not the pretext for an overtly political demonstration, as the funerals of prominent figures in the Russian intelligentsia were later to become. But in the dignified mourning described by Turgenev there was expressed a sense of loss which was both a more fitting tribute than public disorder to the man who was being buried and a more telling indication of his significance in the national life. A man had been lost who had not only established himself, during fifteen years as Professor of World History at the University of Moscow, as the most revered teacher of his generation but who had also been, in Herzen's words, one of 'the most luminous and remarkable personalities'[2] in the intellectual life of Russia in the 1840s, itself remembered as a 'marvellous decade'.[3]

However, by comparison with Belinsky and Herzen, with whom

contemporaries tended to rank him as an equal, Granovsky has received little attention from students of Russian thought.[4] There are perhaps three reasons for this comparative neglect. The first lies in the volume and nature of Granovsky's work itself. Granovsky published relatively little, and those monographs on universal history which we do have, ranging from his master's dissertation on medieval Pomeranian cities and his doctor's dissertation on the French Abbot Suger to essays on Alexander the Great and Tamburlaine, relate only obliquely to the Russian intellectual life of his time. His lectures to his students and his public lectures, for the most part, were not published, and, although substantial parts of his courses on ancient and medieval history have been reconstructed from the notes of students[5] (who must have been extremely diligent and nimble), such transcripts must obviously be treated with some caution. Most of his own manuscripts have been lost; in any case the mature lecturer tended to extemporise even on those rare occasions when he came to the lectern equipped with a lecture written out in its entirety, and it seems that the full force of his lectures was lost in the transcription.

The second probable reason for Granovsky's neglect lies in the nature of the intellectual life of his time. For, in spite of the dynamic growth of publicism, intellectual authority tended, in the 1840s at any rate, to derive as much from the stature of an individual in the circle of his intimates as from his public utterances. This stature, moreover, owed much in circles still imbued with notions of moral nobility to personal qualities with which Granovsky was richly endowed. 'One comes across few such loving, sincere, saintly and pure natures', wrote Belinsky in 1840; Granovsky had a 'pure, noble soul', an engaging innocence and a warmth that instantly conveyed itself to others.[6] To Herzen too Granovsky was an 'affectionate, serene, indulgent spirit', who possessed a 'wonderful power of love' and a nature 'so remote from the irritability of diffidence and from pretentiousness', 'so pure, so open' that he was extraordinarily easy to get on with.[7] Indeed, all sources describe him as a gentle, compassionate and conciliatory man who lived for others rather than for himself and gave generously of his time to those who came to him for help and advice. But these qualities are less manifest to subsequent generations than the persuasiveness of ideas committed to print and there is therefore some force in Panayev's warning that it is almost impossible to

explain the reputation of Granovsky to those who had not known
him.[8]

A third reason for the relative neglect of Granovsky, however,
undoubtedly lies in the complexion of his thought. For although he
died in 1855, just before the period in which many Russian writers
and thinkers felt obliged to make a choice between what might be
broadly termed liberalism and socialism, nevertheless in essence
Granovsky had already made his own choice, in favour of liberalism. His thought is therefore naturally less attractive to Soviet
scholars than that of his contemporaries Belinsky and Herzen,
whose more revolutionary leanings were in the second half of the
1840s already becoming a source of friction among the so-called
Westernisers. Admittedly Granovsky continues to be respected in
Soviet historiography as a scholar and, more importantly, as a
humanitarian intellectual who, because of his premature death,
never had the need or the opportunity to translate his views into
explicitly political terms. He cannot therefore be deemed to have
reneged on an earlier commitment to opposition to the Russian
autocracy or be tainted by association with the critics of those
radicals who began in the late 1850s to lay the theoretical foundations for a socialist revolutionary movement. But the fact remains
that his outlook is in many respects very close to that of Botkin,
Annenkov and Kavelin – with all of whom he had been on intimate
personal terms – who did in the second half of the 1850s become
leading representatives of a liberal tendency in Russian thought that
was scorned by Chernyshevsky and that has been despised ever
since by Russian socialists as half-hearted, ineffectual and hypocritical.

It is the purpose of this chapter to attempt to re-establish the fact,
which has thus become rather obscured, that Granovsky did indeed
play one of the most important roles in Russian intellectual life in
the 1840s and thereby to account for the high regard in which he was
held by his contemporaries. This purpose may best be served not by
giving a strictly chronological survey of his work but by dealing with
each of the three main aspects of his contribution to Russian
intellectual life – as historian, as a leading 'Westerniser' and as a
thinker occupying a liberal position on the political spectrum.
Admittedly Granovsky's thought did undergo certain changes or
was modified in the course of time, but not so much as to make this
thematic approach unsatisfactory in his case; indeed, the tenor of

his thought, like its tone, remained remarkably stable in a period when others, particularly Belinsky and Herzen, were prone to more or less abrupt changes of course.

Formative influences on the young historian

Granovsky was born on 9 March 1813 in the provincial town of Oryol, the eldest of five children, three sons and two daughters, of an official of the government salt board. Granovsky's grandfather, a self-made man who had set out in life with nothing, had eventually acquired an estate near Oryol which assured the family of a sub-stantial income. As a child Granovsky was frail but energetic and soon displayed a lively mind, quickly absorbing the teaching of the scriptures which his loving grandfather set him to study at a very early age. His education, however, followed the haphazard course so common in the 1820s: it was entrusted to a succession of foreign tutors who had remained in Russia after the Napoleonic wars. The advantage of this system was that it enabled Granovsky to develop an early fluency in French and to gain a good knowledge of English, but its defect was that it gave his reading no pattern. At the age of thirteen the boy was taken to Moscow where he attended a private boarding school in which he remained for two years, though with little profit. In the spring of 1831 he began service in a department of the Ministry of Foreign Affairs in St Petersburg, but after a very short time decided that he wished to study at university. He now prepared himself for entry with great determination and in difficult circumstances: his mother – to whom he had been very close and from whom he perhaps inherited his better qualities – had died in 1831 and his father virtually forgot about him, sending him money from Oryol only infrequently. Nevertheless Granovsky succeeded in gaining admission to the law faculty of St Petersburg University, which he entered in August 1832 and from which he graduated with distinction in 1835. He remained in St Petersburg and began to acquire some repute in literary circles, on the strength of which he was invited by Count Stroganov to prepare himself for a teaching post in Moscow University, of which Stroganov was the enlightened curator.

Preparation for the job of teaching history necessarily entailed a prolonged period of study abroad, and Granovsky was duly sent to Germany at official expense. He arrived in Berlin at the beginning of June 1836. He immediately set about improving his German and in the autumn began to attend the lectures of some of the many eminent scholars who were teaching in the Prussian capital at that time, the historian Ranke, the geographer Ritter, the historian of law Savigny and the philosopher of history, Gans. During his stay abroad Granovsky also travelled extensively, visiting Dresden, Prague (where he met Šafařík and other leading Czech men of letters) and Vienna, which made a most unfavourable impression on him (he found its people philistine, regimented and, by comparison with the inhabitants of Berlin, provincial). In Germany he felt quite at home. 'I love my country, I should like to be useful to it', he wrote to one of his sisters in April 1837, 'but the life I lead here suits me. When I build castles in Spain, it's always in some corner of Germany ... '[9] Not that his sky was cloudless: he had developed signs of serious chest illness even before he was twenty and ill health, aggravated by his tendency to work without sparing himself, continued to afflict him while he was abroad. Indeed, he was still not fully recovered when he returned to Russia in 1839, accomplishing the last part of the journey against doctor's orders, in a wild dash from Warsaw to Kiev.

What intellectual influences had Granovsky undergone when he returned to Russia in 1839 on the threshold of his academic career? As a student in St Petersburg he had already read the work of leading historians such as Guizot, Thiers, Thierry, Gibbon and Robertson. In Berlin he had been deeply affected too by Ranke, Ritter and Savigny, who together with other German scholars were bringing about a transformation in the study of history by their insistence on the need for meticulous research and painstaking observation, dispassionate consideration of the evidence and critical appraisal of sources. He was greatly impressed in particular by Ranke's lucid and 'practical view of things' as it was reflected in his lectures on the history of the French Revolution;[10] by Ritter's ideas on the interaction between man and his natural environment and on the creative role played by man in adapting natural conditions to his own needs; and by Savigny's view of law as a means of legitimising the existing order of things and by his view of the state as a natural product of the inner life of a people. Most important of all the German influences on Granovsky, however, was that of Hegel, whose philosophy Granovsky began seriously to study in the spring of 1837. 'Study German and start reading Hegel', he wrote to a friend at that time:

He will calm your soul. There are questions to which man cannot give a satisfactory answer. Hegel doesn't solve them either, but everything that is *at the present time* accessible to man's knowledge, and knowledge itself, is wonderfully explained in his work . . . [11]

A knowledge of Hegel would ensure that one did not take a one-sided or subjective view of things, for the German philosopher emphasised the rationality and harmony that one could perceive in the universe if one considered nature, art, religion, politics, indeed all knowledge, in all their fullness. Hegel explained the eternal and ephemeral significance of every phenomenon in the development of the Spirit and his method was therefore of great interest to the historian. And in any case Hegel's doctrines and dialectical method had such a great influence on so many branches of knowledge in the 1830s that they inevitably affected the work even of thinkers and scholars who had not actually studied them at first hand.[12]

Granovsky's acquaintance with German philosophy – which he imbibed together with Stankevich, to whom he was very close during his years in Berlin – probably helped to nourish his innate idealism and to increase the yearning for moral perfection which is so pronounced in his scholarship. He also undoubtedly derived from Hegel both his view of the history of mankind as the history of a spirit which developed and in the process came even nearer to perfection, and his interest in the supposed dialectical movement of history, the inevitable rise and fall of given societies. His study of Hegel did not, however, lead Granovsky to the extreme conservative political conclusions briefly defended by Belinsky. Indeed, Belinsky's reconciliation with reality Granovsky found repugnant. 'In fact, he's talking nonsense,' he wrote to Stankevich in autumn 1839 with Belinsky in mind. 'Philosophy' (which Granovsky, like many of his contemporaries, was equating here with Hegelianism) had done a lot of harm to Belinsky: it had prejudiced him against the French, about whom Belinsky did not allow one to speak unless one admitted that they were 'people without feeling, without depth, *poseurs*', and it had prompted some eccentric literary judgements, for example the proposition that Pushkin's *Boris Godunov* was equal in merit to anything written by Shakespeare.[13] Nor did Granovsky himself ever share the disrespect which Belinsky showed in his Hegelian phase for French culture. On the contrary, he accorded high praise to George Sand; '*C'est un des plus grands talents de l'Europe*', he wrote to one of his sisters in January 1840, there was 'so much simplicity, elegance and nobility' in her writing – sentiments he was to reiterate two years later.[14] Again, he retained throughout his life, irrespective of his attitude towards Hegel, a passionate love for the work of Schiller, who to Russians of the 1830s was the poet of rebellion and whom Belinsky accordingly denigrated in 1839. Granovsky's love of Schiller developed while he was in Germany: he would frequently see performances of Schiller's plays and after them would return home 'happier, better and more capable of work', he told his eldest sister in October 1836, shortly after his arrival in Berlin.[15] In January 1838 he was reading the correspondence of Schiller and Goethe with delight.[16] And in 1840 he described Schiller as 'more than a great poet', the 'heroic defender of all the great interests of humanity.'[17] Not suprisingly this 'respect for Schiller' was a major cause of Granovsky's discord with Belinsky in 1839: the judgement of Belinsky (and Katkov) that Schiller's *Wallenstein* was a 'pitiful, insignificant work, declamation without life' Granovsky found quite unacceptable.[18] Most importantly, this admiration for Schiller throws light on Granovsky the historian, who himself was to defend the 'great interests of humanity' against tyranny and injustice. It betrays the strong poetic streak which contemporaries found in Granovsky's nature and which is reflected in his enthusiasm for such works as the Icelandic *Edda* and the medieval Spanish epos[19] – on both of which he published essays – and in his liking for Emerson's view of history.[20]

There is, finally, one further influence on Granovsky that should be mentioned, namely Tacitus, the chronicler of Republican Rome. Granovsky had embarked on an advanced study of Latin early in his stay in Berlin, in 1837, and was soon able to read the Roman poets and historians in the original. He was to use Tacitus' work as an important historical source on the life of the ancient German tribes and he paid tribute to Tacitus' 'circumspection and conscientiousness' as an historian.[21] But it was evidently not so much Tacitus' historical scholarship that interested Granovsky as his excellence as a representative of the tendency – which Granovsky later suggested was typical of the classical historians – to treat history as an art form. 'I am working but little for history in general at the moment', Granovsky wrote to a friend in 1837, 'because I am reading and rereading Tacitus not as an historian but as an artist':[22]

What a soul this man had. After Shakespeare, nobody has given me such pleasure. I had wanted to make notes from him, study him as an historian, and I did nothing because I read him as a poet. There is more truly human, sad poetry in him than in all the Roman poets put together. He has little love, but then on the other hand what noble hatred, what fine contempt! You will agree with me when you read him. Of the modern historians no one will rival him ... [23]

Some of Tacitus' judgements, of course, particularly his contempt for the early Christians and the equanimity with which he viewed Nero's cruel persecution of them, were profoundly alien to the humanitarian Granovsky writing in another age. But undoubtedly the elegance of Tacitus' writing, the nobility of his character (which gave a certain serenity to his vision), his resolution to write *'sine ira et studio'*,[24] (without indignation or partisanship) – these qualities were most congenial to Granovsky, who had resolved at the outset of his career to dissociate himself, as an historian, from a 'one-sided, consequently fruitless, political tendency'.[25]

Granovsky as professor at Moscow University

In view of the strong influence exerted on Granovsky by German thinkers and scholars of the first half of the nineteenth century, we may loosely call him their disciple, though his admiration for Tacitus, Thierry, Emerson and many other historians who were not Germans makes it clear that he was always eclectic. However, it is not in comparison with those thinkers and scholars, nor even as an historian at all, that Granovsky should in the last analysis be judged. His work, for all its erudition and careful scholarship, retained something of the flavour of the cultivated pursuit of the dilettante; it contained no trace of what Panayev called the 'pedantry of inveterate scholars'.[26] But then, as Turgenev admitted in his eulogy, Granovsky had no pretension to the calling of historian in the strict sense of the word.[27] His significance lay not so much in the solidity or originality of his scholarship as in his ability to turn history, as others were turning imaginative literature and literary criticism, into a channel for the expression of independent thought and enlightened values. It was a role which the authorities of Nicolaevan Russia themselves unintentionally encouraged the historian to play, by their restriction of free debate or even the most harmless intellectual intercourse. (We learn from a letter Granovsky wrote to one of his sisters in April 1840, when he was completing his first session as a university teacher, that he had been obliged to refuse an invitation to dinner with his students on the grounds that the government did not approve of gatherings of that sort.)[28] And yet the official attempts to prescribe the content and tendency of history served only to lend the discipline – and at various times other disciplines too, such as classics and philosophy – a larger and more overtly political significance than it would otherwise have had. Granovsky, together with a number of colleagues in Moscow University, such as Redkin, Professor of Jurisprudence, and Kryukov, Professor of Ancient History, was fully conscious of this larger significance of his discipline. 'Our professors,' wrote Herzen,

brought with them their cherished dreams, their ardent faith in learning, and in men: they preserved all the fire of youth, and the lecturer's chair was for them a sacred lectern from which they were called to preach the truth. They took their stand in the lecture-room not as mere professional savants, but as missionaries of the religion of humanity.[29]

Their convictions were not to be submerged in their scholarship but given free rein in it. Thus Granovsky is not a historian as one of his own favourite German historians, Niebuhr, conceives him, a man whose path lies 'on the brink of the abyss of pedantry'.[30] On the contrary, he makes out of his narrow academic speciality what Annenkov called a 'flourishing oasis of science', a piece of territory where he could make pronouncements which had a bearing on the life, morality and ideas of his own time and hint at thoughts which could not yet be openly expressed.[31] He himself admitted that he had convictions and that he put them forward in his lectures; indeed, if he had not had them he would not have chosen to lecture.[32] Nor was he averse even to using his discipline for the purpose of conducting polemics: in general, he admitted to his friend, Ketcher, in 1843, though with a somewhat exuberant exaggeration, 'I want to polemicise, abuse and insult'.[33]

That Granovsky would shortly turn historical scholarship so effectively into a medium for the enlightenment of Russia could not easily have been predicted on the basis of his début in the lecture theatre in the autumn of 1839. His own description of the occasion survives in a letter to Stankevich:

I have to tell you that at my first lecture I disgraced myself in the most ignominious way. This is how it happened: the great hall, where congregation is held, was set aside for my début. This hall is terribly badly constructed: even Ivan Ivanovich Davydov's voice is lost in it, so what must become of mine? I arrived at the university very boldly, Golokhvastov arrived and off we set. In I come and see over 200 students sitting there . . . and a lot of other people as well. I got terribly scared, everything went dark before my eyes and I couldn't find the rostrum. Seriously. Golokhvastov was vainly making noble gestures with his right hand. The damned steps to the rostrum had got lost. I couldn't see them for the life of me. Finally Krylov took pity and gave me a shove up from behind, so that I jumped up into place with my eyes closed. The audience must have been smiling. The thought that if I opened my eyes I would see this smile made me read *blind*, that is to say I mumbled in a fast patter and virtually in a whisper what I could recall of my notes (which were just commonplaces), and after a quarter of an hour I bowed and left.[34]

This inauspicious beginning, however, was soon forgotten. Admittedly Granovsky's weak voice and imperfect pronunciation (he was known by the nickname of 'lisper' [*shepelyavyy*] among his friends) did not seem to equip him for stirring oratory; but he more than made up for these disadvantages by the quality of his language, which was always concise, simple and devoid of jargon, and by what a contemporary described as a 'fullness of thought and a fullness of love' which were apparent not only in his words but also in his noble appearance.[35] His popularity grew rapidly among his own students and in the winter of 1843–4 he established a wider reputation with a series of public lectures on the apparently remote subject of the Merovingian and Carolingian kings. It was this series of lectures which for the first time underlined the more than purely academic significance of Granovsky's historical scholarship. The lectures resembled not so much esoteric academic gatherings as something between social occasions and political rallies. Contemporaries considered them portentous indications of the existence of an independent public opinion in Russia. They attracted, Annenkov recalled, 'not only men of science, all the literary parties and all [Granovsky's] usual captive audience, the students of the university, but also the entire *educated* class of the city, from old men who had just left the card tables to young ladies who hadn't yet had a rest after their exploits on the dance floor', from government officials to distinguished men of letters.[36] The lectures were tumultuously applauded and the course ended with a wild and emotional scene which Herzen describes at length in his memoirs. 'When at the end, deeply moved, [Granovsky] thanked the audience', writes Herzen,

everyone leapt up in a kind of intoxication, ladies waved their handker-
chiefs, others rushed to the platform, pressed his hands and asked for his
portrait. I myself saw young people with flushed cheeks shouting through
their tears: 'Bravo! Bravo!' There was no possibility of getting out.
Granovsky stood as white as a sheet, with his arms folded and his head a
little bent; he wanted to say a few words more but could not. The applause,
the shouting, the fury of approbation doubled, the students ranged themselves on each side of the stairs and left the visitors to make a noise in the
lecture room. Granovsky made his way, exhausted, to the council room; a
few minutes later he was seen leaving it, and again there was endless
clapping; he turned, begging for mercy with a gesture and, ready to drop
with emotion, went into the office. There I flung myself on his neck and we
wept in silence.[37]

Granovsky's Westernism

What values, though, did Granovsky contrive to express in his
lectures and writings which could give rise to these extravagant
expressions of gratitude and enthusiasm? On the broadest level
there was in Granovsky's scholarship a warm, compassionate
humanism that posed an implicit challenge to a brutish and obscu-
rantist régime. Reviewers immediately noted this quality. 'What
roundedness in each lecture, what a broad view and what humanity!' wrote one of those present at the public lectures; 'this is a work
of art, a story full of love and energy'. A 'broad and much encom-
passing love' informed the lecturer's words, wrote another com-
mentator, 'love for what is arising, which he joyfully greets, and
love for what is dying, which he buries with tears'.[38] It was a quality
on which his devoted biographer, A. V. Stankevich, younger
brother of the Hegelian to whom Granovsky had been so close in his
youth, chose to dwell in the concluding passage of his work.[39]
Granovsky, then, belongs to that long and broad humanist tradition
in European culture which dates back as far as the Renaissance and
whose representatives take a warm and catholic interest in all man's
religious, artistic, scientific and political strivings.

On another level there is in Granovsky's work a vein of social
protest which could easily be detected by a public already adept at
the elucidation of allegory and which humanitarian men of his
generation were bound to welcome. Some of his passages on the

Middle Ages, for example, had a special pertinence for an educated class which believed their own country had in many respects not progressed beyond those times. Relations between lord and serf in Western Europe in the feudal period had much in common with relations between landowner and peasant in the Russia of the 1840s – a relationship which was beginning to attract the attention of imaginative writers but which the government, having refused to contemplate the abolition of serfdom, considered too sensitive an issue to be allowed open discussion. The rights of the lord over his serfs in Western Europe in the tenth and eleventh centuries, Granovsky proclaimed in his lectures, were not yet defined by law. The lord had the right of life and death over his serfs, took money and other taxes from them and could try and sentence them at will. His authority was the most severe and dismal despotism. From the unlimited power of one individual over a herd of people – and the 'slaves' of feudal times merited that description – there naturally developed a mocking and wilful attitude of lord to common man, a contempt for human dignity.[40] Never was the condition of the masses more burdensome and degrading, never did individuals or a social group as a whole achieve such unbridled freedom.[41] In Granovsky's doctoral dissertation too there are references, which have an equally transparent application to the Russia of his time, to the 'predatory' feudal lord or the lawless barons who considered social order incompatible with their personal rights and civilisation with oppression.[42] Elsewhere Granovsky condemns tyrannical institutions and underlines the harmful effects of their barbarousness. The Spanish Inquisition, for example, is held responsible for the decline of Spain's prosperity and the coarsening of her people, who were naturally noble and gifted.[43]

There was, however, yet another, equally important level of meaning in Granovsky's historical scholarship, beyond its broad humanism and its obvious implicit condemnation of the Russia of the 1840s with her irresponsible arbitrary government and her serf-owning lords bound by no law. For this scholarship reflected the broader concern of the intelligentsia in the age of Nicholas I to establish Russia's national identity and thence to plot her destiny (which in fact radical thinkers were rather prone to depict as no less glorious than, if different from, the destiny conceived by conservatives). To a large extent, of course, the search for an answer to the riddle of Russia's national destiny was carried out in imaginative literature, and indeed the blossoming of that literature was one indication of the growth of a distinctive consciousness. But the search could also be conducted in the field of history. Like other European peoples who were becoming conscious of their nationhood during the Romantic period, the Russians began in the 1820s, 1830s and 1840s to develop an interest in their historical past, which found expression in their enthusiasm for the historical novels of Zagoskin and Lazhechnikov, in the *Philosophical Letters* of Chaadayev and in the earnest if fanciful researches of the Slavophiles. And Granovsky, even though his field was universal and, in particular, medieval Western European history, used the discipline to make one of the most serious contributions to the debate which these researches generated.

It is worth emphasising at the outset that Granovsky was no more an advocate of indiscriminate aping of things foreign than other major so-called Westernisers, such as Belinsky and Herzen. He complains, for example, in a review of a book by a fellow historian, Kudryavtsev, of the latter's needless introduction into his work of linguistic borrowings from Western European languages, such as *shef*, *fortuna* and *traditsiya*.[44] Nor is he any less conscious than the Slavophiles of his Russianness or less determined than they to fulfil a patriotic duty. He looks on the connection with the native land as the basis of a people's morality, and agrees with a correspondent that 'real activity' is possible 'only on one's native soil'.[45] He possesses that same 'sense of duty' which compels all his contemporaries to attempt to serve their country in whatever sphere circumstances might permit[46] (and which it is tempting to trace to the more general notion of service which it was incumbent on the noble to give to his sovereign). He complains of the ignorance of Russia which he encounters in his travels abroad. (A young German woman had asked him during his stay in Berlin, for example, whether it was true that outside St Petersburg and Moscow Russian women still wore Tartar costume. 'Not exactly', Granovsky had replied, 'for our provincial ladies have as clothes the furs of wild animals which they kill themselves in the hunt.')[47] Finally, and in a different key, in a speech delivered to his students in 1845, shortly after his defence of his master's dissertation, Granovsky anticipates 'noble' and 'long' service of 'our great Russia', Russia which strides forward with contempt for the slanderous foreigners – he is no doubt referring to Custine, among others – who see in Russians 'only frivolous imitators of Western forms without any content of [their] own'.[48] He is therefore surely foremost among those West-ernisers of whom Herzen was thinking when he conceived his felicitous image of the double-headed eagle which looked in differ-ent directions, East and West, for its inspiration, but in which there beat the same Russian heart.

Nevertheless Granovsky was also scathingly critical of those people – and he had the Slavophiles in mind – who loved 'not the living Rus, but a decrepit phantom summoned by them from the tomb', people who profanely worshipped an idol created by their own fanciful imagination.[49] As early as 1839 he emphatically rejects the main Slavophile propositions, concerning the decay of the West, the wisdom of the writings of the fathers of the Greek Orthodox Church and the damage supposedly done by Peter the Great in tearing away the Russians from their own historical heritage. Kireyevsky was saying these things in prose and Khomyak-ov in verse. It was irritating that they were gaining a following among the students; indeed, 'Slavonic patriotism' was regnant in Moscow, Granovsky lamented. He intended, however, to rebel against it from the rostrum.[50] His master's dissertation too contains implicit criticism of the Slavophiles, in so far as they are equated in it with those historians who 'remould the past in accordance with personal whim or national vanity'. Granovsky examines the existing body of knowledge on the medieval Pomeranian townships of Jomsborg and Wollin. Medieval chroniclers and writers of the age of the Reformation had tended to confuse these two townships, the first of which was a Norman fortress on the Baltic and the second a Slavic settlement in the same region. Popular imagination and later historical scholarship had gone even further and had fused the two settlements into a myth of the magnificent city of Vineta, a northern Venice which had been engulfed by the sea in divine retribution for its pride in its wealth and the ruins of which were said to be sometimes visible beneath the waves off the Pomeranian shore. This glorious legendary city, however, existed only in the imagin-ation of misguided scholars, Granovsky contended; it had no more basis in historical fact, we are intended to infer, than the similarly romantic fantasies of the Slavophiles.[51]

It was in the history of the West rather than in a supposedly more glorious Russian national past that Granovsky thought the key to Russia's destiny should be sought, and in his writings and lectures

on Western Europe in the Middle Ages he outlined the heritage
which Russia seemed to lack. In the first place, of course, the West
had enjoyed a vigorous intellectual tradition. The medieval school-
men, for instance, for all their shortcomings, had exuded a healthy
confidence in the power of human reason; their conviction that the
truth could be taken by storm like a medieval castle might have been
naïve, but they had lent the European mind a noble curiosity and
developed in it considerable powers of logic.[52] In the second place,
the West had a democratic tradition which Russia lacked. Western
European peoples had long since promoted concepts of freedom
and constitutional forms of government. Spanish history, for
instance, offered examples as early as the fourteenth century which
greatly interested Granovsky. 'A wonderful people!' Granovsky
wrote of the Spaniards.

They understood constitutional forms at a time when people didn't have
any conception of them anywhere else. In 1305 the Spanish Cortes had laid
down that during their sessions the King's troops should leave the town:
otherwise votes would not be free. They had many such laws. Present-day
Europe is still fighting for what they had then.

And it was as a result of his interest in this subject that Granovsky
was in 1838 considering the formation and decline of free urban
communes in the Middle Ages as a possible theme for a master's
dissertation.[53] He also greatly admired the Quakers, whose social
and moral theories, he believed, were based on a deep respect for
human dignity, and he praised their democratic community, their
egalitarianism and their practice of settling matters by discussion
among elected representatives.[54]

   In the third place, the West had greatly benefited – so Granovsky
believed, unlike the Slavophiles – from aspects of classical civilisation which had been passed on to medieval Europe through the
Roman Empire, notably the institutions and experience of civilian
administration and Roman law.[55] One example of the wisdom of
Roman legislation – and an example of which Nicolaevan Russia,
with its inequality before the law, would do well to take note – was
the *lex frumentaria*, according to which the poorest citizens were
entitled to a monthly allowance of grain at a quarter of the going
rate.[56] Granovsky also noted that even in feudal times individuals
were to be found who had improved their own imperfect societies
by instilling in them certain principles inherited from the ancient
world. Louis IX of France, for example, by his own sense of law and

by the introduction into his courts of jurists imbued with the ideas of Roman legislation, had invested monarchic authority with the 'moral radiance of incorruptible justice' and had disposed the people to see the king as a dispassionate judge.[57]

It is worth pausing briefly at this point to emphasise the cardinal importance of Granovsky's admiration of the heritage of Roman law in Western Europe (even though that admiration is only succinctly expressed) and to underline the significance that the concept of legality had for the liberal political philosophy which we find in an embryonic form in Granovsky's historical scholarship. Owing to the lack of interest, within the Orthodox Church, in the pursuit of rational as opposed to spiritual wisdom, and as a result too of the relatively late beginning of the attempt substantially to secularise her culture, Russia lacked a strong and ancient tradition of jurisprudence just as she lacked a related history of philosophical and political speculation of the sort that had flourished in Western Europe since the Renaissance. Enlightened individuals such as Radishchev, who himself had a legal training, did from the time of Catherine II bemoan the absence in Russia of the concepts to which such a tradition might have given rise. Radishchev found no sense of natural justice or legality in the Russian administration either at national or local level or indeed on the estates of the gentry who, like Russian officials, are able throughout the *Journey from St Petersburg to Moscow* to commit acts of callousness and brutality with impunity. And yet even within the intelligentsia the supporters of Western legal concepts still had their powerful detractors in the 1840s and '50s. To the Slavophiles in particular Roman law and the Western system of formal, secular justice operating on the basis of statute as well as custom seemed a manifestation of pernicious rationalism, a corrupting influence on Christianity. For them the moral law laid down in Christianity in its Orthodox form was absolutely binding and for the purpose of regulating everyday conduct in the community it required the support of convention, not legislation and highly developed secular judicial agencies. Granovsky, then, in commending the concept of a temporal law to which all were subject, irrespective of their social standing, was again implicitly attacking both tsarist society and the opponents of his Westernism within the intelligentsia. The former was indefensible because its members' accountability for their conduct tended to vary in relation to their social status and because examples of arbitrariness were legion; and the latter were to be reproached for showing less interest in the physical protection of the individual citizen and the definition of his rights than in the preservation of his supposed moral and spiritual well-being. At the same time, however, Granovsky was raising a subject of particular importance to men of liberal outlook. For a sense of legality in society was a necessary adjunct to the liberty which liberals hoped the individual (or the enlightened individual, at least) would enjoy. Like the other Russian Westernisers of the 1840s Granovsky was concerned, as we shall see, to free the individual from the various forms of oppression which had stifled him. But once the iron grip of the autocratic state had been loosened, once the individual had broken away from Aksakov's 'moral choir' and marked himself off from the uniform community, he would need certain indefeasible rights and liberties and the protection of the law if he were to pursue his interests in safety and without hindrance.

It is characteristic, however, of the thought of the Westernisers of the 1840s, with their interest in ethical questions, that Granovsky should have attached great importance not only to the intellectual vitality and the democratic and legal traditions of Western Europe but also to its Christian ethos, which, he believed, had exercised an immense civilising influence. For one thing the Western Church, he contended, had directly helped to improve the condition of the serfs, by giving them shelter, accepting them into its ranks and conferring on those who lived on church lands greater rights than those enjoyed by serfs living on the lands of laymen. More importantly, the Church had indirectly mitigated the evil of serfdom by instilling moral ideals in the representatives of secular authority.[58] The moral education of the monarchy is the major theme of Granovsky's doctoral dissertation on the twelfth-century Abbot Suger, who in his capacity as representative of the Church and through his close personal relationship with Louis VI gave the secular powers a conception of their purpose and duty which they had hitherto lacked. From the time of Suger the monarchy had begun to restrain the centrifugal forces of feudal society, subordinating separate baronial interests to the general weal of the state, and to strengthen the moral bases on which society rested and which gave rise to a deep sense of law. Seen in this light the Church was not an instrument of oppression in the service of the state; rather the state was the agent of the Church in the defence of those who had been oppressed by feudalism in the course of its long ascendancy.[59]

There is one further respect in which religious or moral ideas seemed to Granovsky to have conferred on Western civilisation benefits which Russia had not enjoyed. They acted as a cohesive force, they lent societies a certain unity which was attractive to men of cosmopolitan and liberal temper, such as Granovsky, who hoped for the erosion of the more blatant divisions in Russian society and wished to avoid the conflicts to which such divisions might shortly give rise. Therefore Granovsky, like Chaadayev in his *Philosophical Letters*, admires those men who by their vision and will had created the conditions in which such unifying ideas could be disseminated. Above all he praises Charlemagne, to whom one of the most memorable lectures of his public series of 1843–4 was devoted. By stopping tribal migrations, by bringing separate peoples under a single administration and by giving them a common law and religion, Charlemagne had laid the foundations for a great civilisation which, in spite of all its subsequent schisms, had retained something common to all its disparate constituent parts.[60] Not that Granovsky considers Christian doctrine the only source of unifying ideas, or Western European monarchs the only men capable of promoting them: he also offers a favourable assessment of Alexander the Great's pre-Christian vision of universal empire, his attempt to merge victorious Greek and vanquished Persian into one nation and his creation of the possibility, through the foundation of the city of Alexandria, of a confluence of the ideas of East and West.[61]

It is in the light of Granovsky's emphasis on the unifying role of the great historical individual, inspired by some profound moral idea, that we should consider his admiration for Peter the Great, the ruler who more than any other had attempted to bring Russia into the mainstream of European civilisation. Whilst the Slavophiles viewed Peter with hatred as being chiefly responsible for the divorce of Russia from her sacred past, Granovsky looked on him as the only Russian ruler who had been capable of giving his country a sense of high national purpose. As early as 1839 Granovsky complains that Peter is not understood in Moscow circles, where he is not regarded with the gratitude due to him.[62] Much later, in 1854, he rebukes Herzen for casting aspersions on Peter. 'The longer we live', wrote Granovsky, 'the more the image of Peter towers before us.'[63] And in 1855 he describes his awe of a portrait of Peter,

painted just after the ruler's death, which he had seen during a visit
to Pogodin's house. He had almost sobbed contemplating this
'divinely beautiful face'. The 'tranquil beauty of the upper part' was
impossible to describe: only a 'great, infinitely noble and holy idea'
could have laid on its brow the 'stamp of such tranquillity'. But the
lips were tight with grief and anger, as if they were still trembling,
still involved in the cares and anxieties of life. What a man was
Peter, who had given Russia a 'right to a history' and who almost
single-handed had announced Russia's historical mission.[64] Like
Chaadayev, then, Granovsky looked on Peter as the great man who
had thrown down for Russia the 'cloak of civilisation'.[65] Like
Chaadayev too he seems not to have baulked at the ruthlessness
with which such rulers as Charlemagne, Alexander and Peter set
about translating their vision into reality, even though in the process
they crushed those hapless individuals, such as the 'poor Yevgeniy'
of Pushkin's *Bronze Horseman*, whose interests and dignity Granovsky was at the same time so anxious to protect.

The spirit of chivalry

There is another manifestation of Granovsky's reverence for
Western European civilisation, besides his interest in its law, its
liberties, its Christianity and its sense of moral unity, which
deserves particular attention, namely his enthusiastic appraisal of
the institution of knight-errantry. Like Roman law, the Western
Church and the figure of Peter the Great, this institution excited
animosity among the Slavophiles; I. Kireyevsky, for instance, on
more than one occasion devoted bitterly critical passages to it.
Granovsky, on the other hand, regarded the institution and its
representatives with something akin to awe. Partly inspired perhaps
by the novels of Walter Scott, which he first read at an early age and
for which he retained a lifelong fondness,[66] he returned repeatedly
to the subject with an almost juvenile relish, devoting articles full of
sympathy and enthusiasm, for example, to the Castilian hero
celebrated in the epic *El Cid* and to the late fifteenth- and early
sixteenth-century French knight, Pierre Terrail de Bayard, the
knight *'sans peur et sans reproche'*.[67] The institution of knighthood, Granovsky argues, reflected the ennobling influence of the
Catholic Church on Western European civilisation. Numerous
practices and qualities of the knighthood, he contends, emanated

from the Church – for example, fasting, prayer, chastity, renunciation of material concerns, abhorrence of avarice, the concept of service to a master or mistress, the defence of the weak, such as widows and orphans. Thus within feudal society, which was based on the oppression of the weak by the strong, there arose its very antithesis, an institution dedicated to the defence of the otherwise defenceless.[68]

On one level, of course, the knighthood was an expression of the spirit of the Middle Ages and, together with the Church which had moulded its character, the finest achievement of that time, the product of a quest for moral improvement.[69] But it is also tempting to interpret the institution, as it is presented by Granovsky, in a very loose sense, as a model for or moral example to men of another time who found themselves in a society not altogether dissimilar to the feudal order in which the institution of knighthood had originated. There was after all a distinctly chivalric quality in the Russian circles of the late 1830s and 1840s with their cult of the '*schöne Seele*' (the impeccable spirit), and with their admiration of Schiller. Indeed, the group of Westernisers of the 1840s, among whom Granovsky was one of the luminaries, was explicitly likened by Annenkov to a 'knightly brotherhood, a fighting order' with no written code but a unity that was clearly understood.[70] And Granovsky in particular appears to have been governed both in private and his public life by precisely such a chivalrous code. He was saddened to think, as he wrote, for example, to his fiancée in June 1841 shortly before their wedding, that so many marriages which had begun with true love on both sides became a source of unhappiness for both partners when love degenerated into a 'kind of indifference' and when the remnants of mutual affection were sustained only by habit. Such a marriage was not for him: 'I should prefer to lose you straightaway', he told his fiancée,

rather than come to this point of *Spiessbürgerthum* [philistinism] in marriage. It would be death for me if I had to replace the bonds which at present unite us by those of egoism and habit.

And he reassured himself with the thought that love could not be worn out except in a heart 'devoid of all other serious and noble interest'. If a man had a 'beautiful vocation', if he and the wife of his choice were 'moral beings' and intent on their moral improvement, then love would last as long as life itself.[71] His own marriage, to a woman ten years his junior, seems by all accounts to have lived up to these idealistic expectations and to have benefited from the same spirit of generosity and altruism which Granovsky brought to his teaching career and which earned him such affection and popularity among his students.

The same quixotic attitudes came to the fore in a curious episode which took place in Moscow University in 1848. Granovsky and some of his colleagues took exception to the conduct of one Professor Krylov who had publicly execrated his wife for her liaisons with his students. Krylov, in acting as his wife's 'executioner', seemed to be behaving in a manner unworthy of a university teacher, who, Granovsky felt, should set a moral as well as intellectual example to his students. Unfortunately Krylov stubbornly refused to vacate the post which he was held to have brought into disrepute, whereupon Granovsky and his colleagues tendered their resignations in the hope that their example might show future students that a professor could not be 'vicious with impunity'. As a matter of fact, even this stratagem failed in Granovsky's case; he was forbidden to take early retirement on the grounds that he would have to remain at his post for at least a further two years in order to redeem the cost of his stay as a student in Germany in the 1830s.[72] But the episode did clearly reveal a way of looking at the world which always affected the actions and coloured the thought of the 'men of the 1840s' and of which we need to be aware if we are fully to understand their lives and work. Nor was this quixotism without value, even though some of its manifestations were plainly absurd and its application in the Krylov affair of doubtful worthiness. For it indicated the existence of and encouraged a moral commitment, that love of some ideal outside oneself for which Turgenev, himself a member of Granovsky's generation and circle of friends, was later to praise Cervantes' tragi-comic hero in his famous essay, 'Hamlet and Don Quixote'.[73] It persisted beyond the 1840s, too, finding expression in Botkin's admiration for the Spanish *caballero* and even in Druzhinin's commendation of the English gentleman, and coming to the surface again in the avowedly chivalric idealism of the Populists of the Chaykovsky circle of the early 1870s.[74]

Granovsky's moderation: sources of friction with Belinsky, Herzen and Ogaryov

In the atmosphere of the Russia of the 1840s, where ideas and convictions were defended with passion, even ferocity, it was perhaps inevitable that Granovsky's relations with the Slavophiles, several of whom were his close personal friends, would sooner or later deteriorate as a result of his attacks on their views and his enthusiasm for aspects of Western culture. A reconciliation was attempted at the end of his course of public lectures in 1844 and a dinner arranged at which Westernisers and Slavophiles embraced and kissed one another; but the effusive expressions of friendship, as Herzen drily noted, did not prevent those who had been present from disagreeing more than ever only a week later.[75] Passions were inflamed by a lampoon written by Yazykov in which Granovsky was addressed as an '... eloquent bibliophile, The oracle of young ignoramuses, ... the frivolous companion Of depraved ideas and hopes.'[76] Granovsky's relations with P. Kireyevsky deteriorated to such a point that the two men almost came to a duel. K. Aksakov, sensing that differences were now too great to be overcome, called on Granovsky in the early hours one morning, woke him up, threw his arms round his neck and bid him a tearful farewell.[77] In 1847 Granovsky became embroiled in an ill-humoured polemic with Khomyakov on the abstruse historical question of the moral calibre of the Franks, whom Khomyakov had called a 'corrupt tribe' and whom, as a non-Slavonic race, he was eager to portray as truculent, mendacious and perfidious.[78] And as the years went by Granovsky spoke of the Slavophiles with increasing bitterness.[79]

However, it was not only the Slavophiles from whom Granovsky grew apart as a result of the clarification of his views on Russia and the West in the 1840s. For as they defined their own response to Slavophilism, so the Westernisers began to become aware of differences among themselves too. At first these differences seemed relatively superficial, but their seriousness increased as external circumstances began to change and eventually they proved to be fundamental.

There is no doubt but that temperamental differences, perhaps as ever, played some role in producing this split within the ranks of the Westernisers and in determining the stance of Granovsky in particular. Granovsky had by all accounts a peaceable and instinctively conciliatory nature. In Herzen's words, he 'often brought together in their sympathy with him whole circles that were at enmity among themselves, and friends on the brink of separation'.[80] Fine qualities he would recognise and acknowledge wherever he found them, regardless of partisan considerations. He was therefore quite able to respect the Kireyevsky brothers and even at a time when he disagreed profoundly with their views to say that he saw in them more 'holiness, straightforwardness and faith' than he had ever seen in anyone else.[81] Similarly, after his disagreements with Herzen in the mid 1840s he could still write to him, in 1847: 'I remain an incurable Romantic . . . I am an extremely personal man, that is to say I value my personal relationships, and my relationship with you has not been easy of late. Give me your hand, *carissime!*'.[82] This strength of personal attachment, what he himself called a 'sacred corner' of his heart, was something Granovsky could not give up.[83] It was perhaps the source of the defence of the dignity of the individual in Granovsky's writings; but it also precluded the extreme ideological commitments and animosities which revolutionary socialism was shortly to require. Granovsky belonged very clearly to the generation of the 'fathers' who in Turgenev's novel could not subordinate things which were sacred to them – love, friendship and art – to a new social and political outlook supposedly underpinned by science.

Granovsky's conciliatory temperament contrasted vividly with that of Belinsky, who was given to fanatical enthusiasms and tacked wildly between opposite intellectual havens. It was characteristic of him, for example, that he could write in 1839, at the time of Belinsky's reconciliation with reality: 'Our convictions are absolutely opposite, but that doesn't stop me from loving him for what is in him . . .'[84] All the same Granovsky did already criticise Belinsky for 'judging and laying down the law about everything in a dictatorial manner',[85] while in 1843 Belinsky tells Botkin that the one thing wrong with Granovsky is his 'moderation'.[86] (Interestingly Belinsky uses the word based on the French, *moderatsiya*, rather than *umerennost'*; it was as if the phenomenon of 'moderation' were itself of foreign origin and not to be confused with *umerennost'*, the virtue of non-commitment extolled by Griboyedov's bureaucrat, Molchalin, and later ridiculed by Saltykov-Shchedrin.)

This temperamental incompatibility naturally gave rise to differences of opinion between Granovsky and Belinsky. Their convictions – and in this both men agreed – were 'diametrically opposed' so that what was white for Granovsky was black for Belinsky and *vice versa*.[87] This difference found expression in an early, and as it turned out portentous, dispute of 1842 on the subject of the French Revolution. In a letter to Botkin – which the latter, according to the custom of the time, promptly read to Granovsky – Belinsky had expressed enthusiasm for Robespierre and the methods of Jacobin dictatorship. The millennium would be brought about on earth, Belinsky wrote, 'not by the honeyed and rapturous phrases of the perfect and fair-souled members of the Gironde, but by the terrorists – by the double-edged sword of the word and deed of the Robespierres and Saint-Justs'.[88] Granovsky replied that Robespierre was the 'shallow' and 'worthless' instrument of other people's will. Belinsky was no doubt attracted to him because Robespierre's revolutionary violence swept away so many members of that class, the aristocracy, which Belinsky detested. But how many petty personal impulses had lain behind Robespierre's actions? He was inferior to Saint-Just, a 'limited fanatic, but a noble and deeply convinced man', and his eloquence could not compare with that of the Girondins, not to mention Mirabeau. As a statesman, moreover, he was 'insignificant'. Admittedly Robespierre was a 'practical person' inasmuch as he was able to 'vulgarise' the larger questions of historical destiny which were at issue by interpreting them in the particular interest of himself and his party. But he lacked the vision of the Girondins, who understood that the purpose of the revolution was not merely to change external political forms but also to solve all the social problems and tensions which had been afflicting the world for so long. The Girondins had defined and drawn attention to all the questions which Europe was now pondering half a century later and they had declared that the revolution was not a 'French event' but a universal one. They had gone to their graves 'pure and holy' having fulfilled their mission on the theoretical level. Robespierre, on the other hand, had looked on the revolution as an exclusively political and an exclusively French event (although he said he believed the opposite to be the case). And it was he, finally, who had given the bourgeoisie a secure position from which it could be dislodged only by a new revolution.[89]

We may surmise that another early manifestation of Granovsky's moderation was his reluctance to follow his defence of the rights of women to its logical conclusion. He believed, his biographer A. V. Stankevich tells us, 'in the possibility of woman's high moral and intellectual development' and was always glad when he found women who were entitled to claim equality with men within the intelligentsia. (Granovsky's own wife, Herzen's wife and Panayeva had attained to this level of development; Yelagina, mother of the Kireyevsky brothers, played an important role in the intellectual life of the late 1830s and early 1840s as hostess of a famous salon, and Yelena Shtakenshneyder had a similar function in the late 1850s and early 1860s.) This approval of women's aspirations to intellectual equality with men, however, by no means implied a belief that women should enjoy full social equality, as the radicals of the late 1850s and 1860s were to demand. The notion that women should have made careers in business, trade or the law, for example, Granovsky appears to have found distasteful: 'I don't like women who know the laws', he is reported to have said on one occasion *à propos* of a woman who had successfully conducted some litigation. His attitude towards women, then, revealed the broad humanism that was characteristic of the Westernist intelligentsia in the 1840s and a certain gallantry that was typical of Granovsky in particular; nevertheless beneath this idealism there remained a strong respect for social convention, a view of woman as first and foremost wife, mother and, if domestic circumstances allowed, philanthropist in the local community.[90]

By the mid 1840s such differences between Granovsky and more radical contemporaries had begun to multiply and to take on a larger significance. One exchange, after which relations between the antagonists seem never to have been quite the same again, took place between Herzen and Granovsky in 1846 at Sokolovo, an idyllic spot just outside Moscow where in the summer of 1845 both men and their families had rented accommodation which in the following year once more became a meeting place for the leading Westernisers. Herzen's growing interest in the natural sciences and his reading of Feuerbach's *Essence of Christianity* led him towards a philosophical materialism incompatible with the preservation of religious faith. Science, Herzen claims to have observed at Sokolovo, obliged one to accept certain truths whether one liked them or not. Granovsky, however, refused to accept Herzen's 'dry, cold idea of the unity of soul and body' and clung instead to his cherished belief in the immortality of the soul.[91] This belief almost certainly provided Granovsky with some consolation after the loss of people very dear to him, particularly Stankevich and his own two sisters. But it is tempting also to surmise that Granovsky defended such a belief because he already sensed, as Dostoyevsky was to do in the 1860s, that without it man's life on earth would seem intolerably devoid of meaning. Man could not get by without some concepts or notions of 'some higher force, some law of being', he once wrote.[92] That is not to say that Granovsky found arguments to refute Herzen's new materialism; but he had powerful reasons of his own for refusing to accept it.[93]

Other sources of friction with members of the Westernisers' circle confirm Granovsky's moderation, his reluctance to follow the circle's more militant members to extreme conclusions. In January 1847, for example, he rebukes Ogaryov for intolerance, a subject vigorously debated by Botkin and Belinsky in the same year. He had a 'really profound hatred for any intolerance', Granovsky wrote, which did not respect views seriously arrived at by a thinking person. Intolerance was valuable and excusable, he felt, only in the youth who thought he had mastered the truth because he had read and taken to heart an intelligent and noble book, or in people with 'limited and crude' minds, such as the Protestant theologians of the seventeenth and even nineteenth centuries. The more limited a person was intellectually, the more easily he absorbed any little conviction which might enable him to sleep easily. Granovsky realised that his 'scepticism' might be seen as something 'unhealthy' or even a 'sign of weakness', but he was grateful to it for cultivating in him a 'true, humane tolerance'. It was a natural product of his study of history, for there was no science 'more inimical to any dogmatism'. (Whatever one might say about the natural sciences, they would never give one that 'moral strength' which history furnished.)[94]

At the same time Granovsky had to defend himself against renewed criticisms from Belinsky, who was embittered by what he saw as the failure of Granovsky and others to give sufficient support to *Sovremennik*. Indeed, Belinsky even accused Granovsky of trying to ruin *Sovremennik* by continuing to contribute to its main rival, *Otechestvennyye zapiski*. That Granovsky was prepared to write for two journals at the same time and that he was indeed pleased that there were two of similar orientation – such lack of partisanship was incomprehensible, almost offensive, to Bel-

insky.[95] Again, like Botkin, Granovsky disliked Herzen's *Letters
from the Avenue Marigny*, in which Herzen condemned the bourgeois order he found in Paris in 1847. The letters were 'very
intelligent in places', Granovsky commented, but there was 'too
much *frivolous* Russian superficiality' in them. They reminded
Granovsky of the way in which Frenchmen (he no doubt had
Custine in mind) wrote about Russia.[96] As for the proletariat,
whose suffering inspired the sympathy of Herzen for their cause,
Granovsky appears to have looked on this class dispassionately as
an inevitable by-product of the development of all 'historical societies' except the patriarchal states of the Orient.[97] He could
acknowledge the right of the proletariat, which was just making its
clamorous entry on the historical stage, to a higher standard of
living. He was also fully aware of the potential of the working class
as a historical force and was wont by 1849 to express his feeling that
the old world, faced with the emergence of this force, was doomed
to decay by quoting a quatrain of Goethe's:

> Komm her! Wir setzen uns zu Tisch,
> Wen möchte solche Narrheit rühren!
> Die Welt geht auseinander wie ein fauler Fisch,
> Wir wollen sie nicht balsamieren.[98]

On the other hand, Granovsky was doubtful, as the air of resignation which he shared with Goethe suggests, whether the triumph
of the proletariat would produce a wholly better society; indeed, he
feared it might mark the ruin of modern civilisation just as the
barbarian invasions had brought to an end the Roman era. In
particular, he suspected that conditions in a socialist society might
not allow the enlightened individual to flourish (and for Granovsky
the enlightened individual was not so much a member of an
aristocratic minority pursuing refined pleasure as a seeker after
elevated moral truths that were valuable to mankind as a whole).
Granovsky clearly perceived, then, that the reactionary forces in
Western society had themselves underlined the obsolescence of the
anciens régimes when they had resorted to violence to sustain those
régimes. But at the same time he believed that European civilisation was too closely connected with those obsolescent orders for
one to be able to predict with certainty what would become of it if
they collapsed or for one to relish the prospect of quick and easy
success for the new radicalism.[99] It is worth noting, finally, that this

ambivalent attitude of Granovsky's towards current events in Western Europe in the late 1840s was quite consistent with his interest as a historian in transitional epochs in the development of societies – a subject on which he read a paper at the home of Count Uvarov in 1849. He valued the youthful optimism of great historical movements as they first manifested themselves; but he also keenly sensed a tragic element in the decline of orders which had once been glorious.[100]

Granovsky's reluctance to embrace the new materialism or to condone intolerance towards the ideological enemy, his refusal wholeheartedly to welcome Herzen's attack on the Western European bourgeoisie – all of these reservations about the movement of Belinsky and Herzen towards a more uncompromising radical position were of a piece with Granovsky's larger objections to the socialist outlook. Western European socialism he saw as a phenomenon which could not be ignored by the historian or the thinking person; but with its utopian insights into the future this socialism was also a 'disease of the century'. It was harmful because it encouraged one to seek solutions to social problems outside the political arena; that is to say, outside the arena in which the liberal expected to be able to determine the course of historical development. As for the violence which would probably be necessary to usher in the socialist utopia – and which Herzen and Belinsky were able to contemplate with equanimity – Granovsky no more approved of it than of the abolition of those old values incompatible with the new socialist outlook.[101]

The role of the individual in history

It was consistent with the classic liberal position – of which distaste for extremism, intolerance and sweeping, violent change was one expression – that Granovsky should also seek, once the power of Hegel over him began to decline, to preserve confidence in the ability of the individual significantly to influence the course of historical events. In a book review published at the end of 1848 (that is to say, when his differences with Belinsky and Herzen had crystallised) Granovsky addressed himself to the thorny problem of the role of the individual in history. The modern science of the philosophy of history, he argued, had replaced the concept of chance in history with the concept of law or necessity. This determinism, or 'fatalism' as Granovsky preferred to call it,[102] had deprived the individual of much of his significance in history. Events were now seen not as the products of human will but as the inevitable outcome of the past. The individual was left only with the honour or shame of being the instrument of historical ideas ripe for fulfilment. This new view might have had more to commend it than the preceding one, prevalent in the eighteenth century, which had exalted chance; it was more rational and less capricious. But it was still 'dry', 'one-sided' and cruel. Determinism made it difficult to feel sympathy for the less fortunate generations and peoples in the historical process, by treating them only as a means for the attainment of certain historical objectives, instruments for the fulfilment of some overriding idea. It gave legitimacy to the notion that the ends justified the means. For what did it matter, once the deterministic view was accepted, if the means were of doubtful morality so long as they served ideas which were considered beneficial for mankind in the broadest perspective? In opposition to the deterministic view, therefore, Granovsky insisted that ideas were not like Indian deities which were dragged along on juggernauts in triumphal processions, crushing their worshippers as they progressed.[103] Admittedly man was not entirely free to make his own destiny, for his life was subject to the same laws as the life of nature. But these laws, Granovsky argued, did not operate in the same way in the different spheres. Natural processes are accomplished with greater uniformity and regularity than historical processes. Plants grow and bear fruit at certain seasons, but in history the fulfilment of a law, ultimately inevitable though it may be, could take anything from a few years to many thousands. Man might go irrepressibly towards a certain goal, but by which road he might progress and how long it would take him to attain his goal would depend on man himself. Thus the individual as Granovsky saw him was not so much an instrument as an 'independent champion or opponent of an historical law', the 'architect' as well as the 'material' of his history.[104] Indeed, if man were to be deprived of this freedom to mould his own destiny there would no longer be any value in the moral striving which Granovsky traced in history, or rather which he tended actually to equate with history itself. For determinism, as Dostoyevsky would soon argue with great force, relieved man of moral responsibility for his actions, turning him into what Granovsky called a 'blind, almost unconscious instrument of fatal predestination'.[105]

Granovsky's conception of the individual capable of affecting the course of history seems to be twofold. Firstly, there is the morally enlightened man of learning. The creation of such individuals and of a society which answered to their needs should be a major historical objective for a people. But the enlightened individuals would themselves promote that objective by enlightening an ever greater proportion of the masses. Indeed, the breaking down of the mass by the enlightenment of its individual members was a worthy and noble aim for the intellectual, a modern exploit (*podvig*). Nor could the masses be rescued from their plight without the intervention of the enlightened individual. For the masses did not possess, as some believed (Granovsky had the Slavophiles in mind), some 'general, infallible reason' which found expression in their traditions. On the contrary, like Nature or the Scandinavian God Thor, they were given to senseless cruelty or to a magnanimity that was equally senseless. Left to themselves, they stagnated under the weight of 'historical or natural contingencies'.[106] This view of the enlightened individual and his relationship with the masses was in fact another expression of Granovsky's disagreement of the late 1840s with Belinsky (who at the end of his life was declaring that the people were the 'soil which preserved the life-juices of any development')[107] and from Herzen (who, having arrived in the West promptly began to extol the Russian peasantry and their commune in terms reminiscent of those used by the Slavophiles). At the same time Granovsky may be seen, in the larger perspective, to be offering a definition of the distinctive moral, social and political role of an intelligentsia which was just coming into being as an independent force in Russian life and of which he himself was an outstanding early representative. It was a definition, moreover, which continued after his death to have a wide appeal even among sections of the intelligentsia basically unsympathetic to the liberal attitudes Granovsky represented. It foretokens, for example, the conception of the role of the intelligentsia offered by Lavrov and Mikhaylovsky, who at the end of the 1860s and in the early 1870s exhorted the 'critically thinking minority' to repay their debt to the masses by communicating to them the knowledge, in the form of socialism, which the intelligentsia had had the leisure to acquire at the people's expense.

The figure of the morally enlightened man of learning coexists in Granovsky's scholarship, however, with a second, Hegelian, incar-

nation of the individual capable of influencing historical development, namely the 'great man' chosen by Providence to implement
the beliefs and wishes of a given people at certain periods in their
history. Alexander the Great, Charlemagne and Peter the Great,
all of whom Granovsky revered, belong to this category. They have
something in common with the 'heroes' of Thomas Carlyle, whose
writings so fascinated Botkin and were translated by him in the
1850s. To say, as some contemporaries did, that such men were no
longer necessary was as absurd, Granovsky argues, as to suggest
that the human body could now do without one of its organs.[108] Not
that Granovsky's own statements on this subject are unexceptionable. Indeed, they inevitably sound rather hollow, coming as they
do at the beginning of his lecture on one such 'great man,' Tamburlaine, who left as his legacy to humanity the ruins of once great cities
marked by pyramids of human skulls.[109] Nor does Granovsky's
reverence for 'great men' appear to be consistent with his transparent compassion for the individual whose freedom or dignity may be
jeopardised by the ruthless authoritarianism of such men. But the
inconsistency does throw light on the character of the liberalism of
Granovsky and other 'men of the 1840s'. For it underlines the fact
that they should not be too closely equated with the British liberal
tradition, which developed in a society where absolute monarchy
had ceased to exist. They belong instead, as an American scholar
has recently pointed out, to that other 'classical' liberal tradition
which sprang up to the East of the Rhine and which, 'rather than
regarding the state as a potential threat to individual liberty,
emphasised its role as the chief guardian and promoter of freedom
for the individual'.[110] Within this tradition, conservative by comparison with that of Mill and Arnold, but liberal in its own context, the
enlightened monarch, no less than the civilised intellectual, had an
important role to play. Indeed, if revolutionary upheaval were to be
eschewed as a means of producing social change then it was perhaps
only the monarch who could begin to translate the ideals of the
intelligentsia into practice. Thus in a plan written in 1850 for a
textbook on universal history Granovsky offers a surprisingly indulgent interpretation of the Russian autocracy as an institution
capable by virtue of its impartial and selfless character of initiating
reform, and in October 1855, in a letter to Kavelin, even goes so far
as to say that Russia now needed not only Peter the Great but 'his
stick too'.[111]

Last years and legacy

Granovsky experienced particularly deeply the sense of gloom which afflicted the Russian intelligentsia in general during the 'dismal seven years' from 1848 to 1855. 'All around is emptiness', he wrote in 1849. 'May the present be cursed! Perhaps the future will be bright.'[112] He retained his post in Moscow University, but inevitably had to devote more of his time now to defending Russian scholarship from the blows being inflicted on it by the authorities than to making new contributions to it.[113] In 1847 he had sustained injuries which were to confine him to his bed for some weeks when he was thrown out of a rickety carriage on to the roadway. Now in the early 1850s he suffered repeatedly from ill health. At the same time his father died and the money saved by him was stolen, with the result that the fortune which should have been Granovsky's was lost and his father's estate was sold at a public auction. His financial affairs were made worse by his own weakness for gambling, which had first manifested itself in his adolescence but which became chronic now that he had lost some of his closest friends, such as Belinsky, Herzen and Ogaryov, and as the climate for men of letters became increasingly severe. Awareness of his own share of the responsibility for his indebtedness gnawed at his conscience and deepened the bouts of melancholy to which he had always been prone. Finally, in September 1855, just as the new age that followed the death of Nicholas I was dawning, he fell ill once more and on 4 October, after a sudden deterioration in his condition, he died, with his loyal wife at his bedside.

There is a passage in one of Granovsky's letters of 1848 in which, bemoaning the terrible depression which was again setting in, he goes so far as to suggest that Belinsky was fortunate to have died when he did, on the eve of the new dark age.[114] In a sense the judgement is one which might be applied to Granovsky himself. For his sudden and premature death in 1855, while it prevented him from contributing to the reanimated debate of the second half of the 1850s, also ensured for him the survival of a reputation untarnished by personal participation in acrimonious controversy. His 'enormous' influence on Moscow University and on the young generation, as Herzen recalled, 'outlived him; he left a long ray of light behind him'. Former students dedicated books to his memory, wrote 'warm, enthusiastic lines about him in their prefaces' and expressed a 'splendid youthful desire to relate their new work to the shade of that friend, to touch gently on his grave' as they began, to 'reckon their intellectual pedigree from him'.[115] Even for the radical younger generation of the late 1850s he remained what he had been for his own contemporaries, a revered figure who had honourably opposed the brutish régime by turning historical scholarship into a medium for the dissemination of humanitarian values. 'What could be a finer vocation?' asks Turgenev's idealistic student, Bersenev, in _On the Eve_, set in the mid 1850s, as he describes to Yelena his ambition to be a professor of history. 'Just think, to follow in the footsteps of Timofey Nikolayevich!'.[116] And it is in this spirit that Chernyshevsky and Dobrolyubov, the main tribunes of the younger generation, remember Granovsky. Both protest vigorously against the denigration of him in articles published in the journal _Russkaya beseda_ in 1856,[117] and Chernyshevsky, in a substantial review of the first edition of Granovsky's collected works, expresses profound respect for him as a 'servant ... of enlightenment'.[118] But it is very doubtful whether Granovsky would have been held in such esteem by the _raznochintsy_ if he had had the opportunity explicitly and publicly to put the liberal position which he had already privately delineated in his disagreements with Belinsky and Herzen. For Chernyshevsky and Dobrolyubov, in their publicism of the late 1850s and early 1860s, make increasingly strident attacks on this position, which by that time was being defended by Kavelin and Chicherin, both of them pupils of Granovsky's and advocates of gradual reform rather than revolutionary change.

Nor, finally, was the liberal of the 1840s subsequently to find any support among the conservative antagonists of the radicals. Dostoyevsky, writing from the standpoint of _pochvennichestvo_, 'native soil conservatism', gives a scathing portrait of the 'man of the 1840s' in the person of his Stepan Trofimovich Verkhovensky in _The Devils_. It is a portrait, moreover, for which Granovsky himself provided the main model, as we know from a surviving letter of Dostoyevsky's to his friend, Strakhov. Writing from Dresden early in 1870, at the time when the novel was being conceived, Dostoyevsky begs Strakhov to send him A. V. Stankevich's biography of Granovsky, which had been published in 1869. 'This book [Dostoyevsky uses the pejorative form _knizhonka_] is as necessary to me as air [to breathe] and as soon as possible', Dostoyevsky writes, 'as the most essential material for my work – material which I just can't do without. For Christ's sake don't forget it if it's at all possible to send it.'[119] Like Granovsky, the character Verkhovensky in Dostoyevsky's completed novel has been a distinguished lecturer and historical scholar, and has written a thesis on a medieval Northern European township and an article on knights errant; he has a chivalrous demeanour, a 'gentle and unresentful heart' and exquisite manners, a fondness for the West, a weakness for gambling and a proclivity to bouts of melancholy. But the idealism and eloquence which had made Granovsky so attractive to the generation of the 1840s are now presented by Dostoyevsky in a deeply offensive light. For Verkhovensky is a vain and egotistical lover of high-sounding phrases, an 'actor on the stage' who is unable to express himself without recourse to a foreign language and whose grand projects never come to fruition. He needs his listeners more than they need him, in order that he should have someone with whom to exchange platitudes over a bottle of champagne and to whom he may unburden himself of his 'remarkable thoughts'. And his main legacy is his nihilistic offspring,[120] for whose views, Dostoyevsky insists, the 'men of the 1840s' are directly responsible. 'If Belinsky, Granovsky and all that riff-raff were to have a look now', Dostoyevsky wrote to Strakhov in 1871 after the completion of his novel,

then they would have said: 'No, we never dreamt of that, no this is a deviation; let's wait a little while longer, and light will appear and progress will come to reign and mankind will be rebuilt on sound principles and will be happy!' They would never have agreed that having once stepped on to this path you will end up at nowhere other than the Commune and Félix Pyat.[121]

The fair-mindedness for which Granovsky himself was noted was not among Dostoyevsky's qualities. Granovsky may, through his scholarship and example, have helped inevitably, as Dostoyevsky suspected, to nurture a radicalism from which he personally would have recoiled; but it is perhaps unreasonable all the same to suggest retrospectively that he therefore treated serious ideas with irresponsible levity. He had in his own time spoken out honourably against an order that no longer had any moral legitimacy and he was not to know, before 1848 at any rate, that it was too late for his message to prevent, as he hoped it would, the growth of the social antagonisms which Dostoyevsky believes he exacerbated. Moreover, he must be credited with having helped, through his academic position and personal influence, to promote a certain moral awareness in the educated public. His utterances lacked the passionate force of Belinsky's, but they still compelled the intellectual to consider his duties, as a citizen, towards his society and, as a human being, towards his neighbour. And yet Dostoyevsky's judgement, splenetic or perverse as it may appear, does contain as ever a germ of truth and reveal a keen perception. For the dividing line between eloquence and empty rhetoric, *krasnorechiye* and *pustosloviye*, was indeed a thin one and Granovsky, like Turgenev's Rudin, that other embodiment of the most distinctive and typical attitudes of the educated man of the 1840s, was prone to cross it. Granovsky's beguiling lectures, like Rudin's perorations, inspired his audience and instilled in them noble ideals and thoughts of duty, sacrifice and selfless service of humanity. But we should not forget that they were delivered at a time when such sentiments could not be translated into social or political action, nor that they can be seen on close examination to reveal deep contradictions between a rational and an emotional view of human affairs, a scholarly and a poetic approach to history, a desire that women be emancipated and a hope that they might retain their conventional role, a religious scepticism and a stubborn adherence to belief, a love of liberty and an awe of supposedly enlightened despotism. To his contemporaries, then, Granovsky was an invaluable source of enlightenment, culture and inspiration, and by virtue of that fact alone he deserves attention and appreciation from any student of the age. But in the different historical conditions of a later period his outlook would indeed be seen to have a frailty which it was not difficult for both practical, utilitarian radicals and their pious, conservative antagonists to expose.

3

Vasiliy Petrovich Botkin (1811–1869)

Botkin's position in the Russian intelligentsia

One Sunday morning in the summer of 1858 Jane Carlyle, the wife of the Victorian essayist and historian, received an unusual visitor, and when he had gone she sat down to describe him to her absent husband.

Botkin (what a name!), your Russian translator, has called. He is quite a different type from Tourgueneff, though a tall man, this one too. I should say he must be a Cossack – not that I ever saw a Cossack or heard one described, instinct is all I have for it. He has flattened high-boned cheeks – a nose flattened towards the point – small, very black, deep-set eyes, with thin semi-circular eyebrows – a wide thin mouth – a complexion whity-grey, and the skin of his face looked thick enough to make a saddle of! He does not possess himself like Tourgueneff, but bends and gesticulates like a Frenchman.

He burst into the room with wild expressions of his 'admiration for Mr Carlyle'. I begged him to be seated, and he declared 'Mr Carlyle was the man for Russia'. I tried again and again to 'enchain' a rational conversation, but nothing could I get out of him but rhapsodies about you in the frightfullest English that I ever heard out of a human head! It is to be hoped that (as he told me) he reads English much better than he speaks it, else he must have produced an inconceivable translation of 'Hero-Worship'. . . . He was all in a perspiration when he went away, and so was I![1]

Clearly Mrs Carlyle found nothing in her bizarre visitor to suggest that he might have played a role of much importance in the intellectual life of his country. And indeed it must be said that Botkin's literary output was neither voluminous nor, for the most part, strikingly original. Much of his writing took the form of translations, articles based largely on foreign works or brief reviews of books and music. He wrote no fiction and the small amount of literary criticism which he produced is often diffuse and poorly argued.[2] At first sight, therefore, it seems hardly surprising that little attention has been devoted to Botkin by historians of Russian literature and thought. Only one Soviet scholar, Yegorov, has given a substantial and useful account of his life and work,[3] while Western scholars generally mention him only in passing as a friend of Belinsky, a 'Westernist', or, to use Isaiah Berlin's phrase, a 'philosophical tea-merchant'.[4]

However, one cannot lightly disregard a man who played a prominent role in the production of three major journals – *Moskovskiy nablyudatel'* (*The Moscow Observer*), *Otechestvennyye zapiski* and *Sovremennik* – and who at one time or another was the intimate of Stankevich, Bakunin, Belinsky, Herzen, Granovsky, Nekrasov, Turgenev, Fet, Tolstoy and many other leading men of letters. Granovsky, who grew close to Botkin at once when the two met in Moscow in 1839, found him warm, 'pure' and 'intelligent' though refreshingly free from any desire to exhibit his intelligence ostentatiously.[5] Turgenev greatly valued Botkin's literary judgements and it was partly at Botkin's suggestion that he made certain changes in his first novel, *Rudin*, prior to its publication in 1856. We know too from one of Turgenev's letters to the poet Sluchevsky that he considered Botkin the only person, apart from Dostoyevsky, to have entirely understood his character Bazarov in *Fathers and Children*.[6] As for Belinsky, his affection and respect for Botkin, for long periods during the last decade of his life, knew no bounds. It is not fanciful to suggest, therefore, that Botkin's importance in Russian intellectual life between about 1835 and 1860 was far greater than the relative oblivion into which he has been cast would seem to suggest. On the contrary, it is arguable that Botkin was one of those personalities who, although forgotten by subsequent generations, help to determine the dominant ideas and spirit of their age in as significant a degree as those few individuals whose work is for various reasons long remembered.

Not that Botkin's interest for the historian of ideas lies only in his influence on his contemporaries; for his own extremely complex intellectual development to a large extent mirrors the shifting preoccupations of the intelligentsia of his age and the eventual crisis within its ranks. It is by plotting this development, on the basis of memoirs and correspondence as well as Botkin's own published works, that I shall attempt to demonstrate Botkin's importance in the history of Russian thought. It will be necessary in the process to refer in particular to four major topics: firstly, the Russian enthusiasm for and subsequent rejection of Hegelian philosophy in the late

1830s and early 1840s (which I shall examine here primarily in terms of Botkin's relationship with Belinsky); secondly, the so-called 'Westernism' of the 1840s; thirdly, the mood of the Russian intelligentsia immediately before and after the European revolutionary disturbances of 1848; and, fourthly, the aesthetic and subsequent political controversy of the second half of the 1850s between the representatives of the so-called 'Pushkin' and 'Gogol' schools of Russian literature.

Before we turn to Botkin's intellectual biography, however, it is as well to emphasise that Botkin did not come from any of those milieus from which the Russian intelligentsia of the middle decades of the nineteenth century was mainly drawn. As the eldest son of a wealthy Moscow tea-merchant, he belonged to a social stratum despised equally by the predominantly aristocratic 'men of the 1840s' and the *raznochintsy* of the late 1850s and 1860s. Admittedly he himself, by virtue of his catholic cultural interests and largely by dint of his own efforts, managed to distance himself from this stratum and to gain access to the most cultivated circles of the intelligentsia of his day. He also brought enlightenment back to his own stratum, which was noted for its philistinism. Indeed, those of his eight brothers and five sisters who were themselves to mingle with the intelligentsia – his brother Mikhail was to become a painter and art historian, Dmitriy a notable art collector and Sergey an eminent specialist in the field of therapeutic medicine, while his sister Mariya married the poet Fet – owed much to Vasiliy Petrovich, who had himself directed their independent reading and cultivated their tastes. All the same he never completely deserted the class into which he had been born. He worked in the family business throughout the 1830s and 1840s and after his father's death in 1853 for a while played a leading role in the management of its affairs. Botkin, then, was a representative of the Russian entrepreneurial class as well as of the burgeoning intelligentsia and it will perhaps be as well to keep this fact in mind when in due course we consider his socio-political views.

It should be added, finally, that Botkin's personality, like his social status, had a duality which makes him somewhat enigmatic. There was in his nature a curious combination of the venomous and the angelic which contemporaries implied in their nickname for him, '*Kobra-Kapella*'.* He was known for an irascibility that would

* i.e. 'Cobra-Chapel'.

often cause him to erupt at the most trivial provocation; but at the same time he displayed a serenity and an evenness of character that were obviously attractive to volatile personalities such as Belinsky. Memoirists draw attention too to the disparity between his unquestionable aspirations to the ethereal and his irresistible attraction to carnal pleasure. No one among his generation of the intelligentsia, it seemed, was more suited than he to dwell in philosophical abstractions or to soar in the rarefied realm of beautiful art; and yet at the same time he would give himself up to debauchery that tended to shock his friends, sinking during one stay in France, so Annenkov tells us, into a 'whirl of Parisian love affairs and every other sort of adventure'.[7] It is tempting to suggest that it was a need to reconcile such conflicting spiritual and sensual requirements that finally produced the frankly hedonistic celebration of art which in the late 1850s betrayed Botkin's abandonment of earlier liberal principles.

Botkin's relationship with Belinsky

In order to appreciate the full extent of Botkin's contribution to Russian intellectual life in the first period of his activity, the late 1830s and early 1840s, it is necessary – as it was in the case of Granovsky – to bear in mind the nature of the circles frequented by men of letters at that time and to know something too of Botkin's intimacy with Belinsky.

Responsibility for fostering an independent culture in Russia rested with a handful of men, aristocrats in the main, whose small circles served as a refuge from the harsh reality of Nicolaevan Russia. Repelled by the political and social order of their country and by its official values, they dwelt in a rarefied atmosphere, giving themselves up to abstruse and idealistic philosophical discussion and finding consolation in epicureanism and a cult of noble friendship. In the convivial atmosphere in which these men frequently met, the 'most active, the most rapid exchange of ideas, news and knowledge' would combine with 'chatter, jest, supper and wine', wrote Herzen, fondly recalling this period of his life. Each member of the circle would communicate what he had read and discovered, out of discussion a general view would take shape and what had originated in the mind of one would become the general property of all.[8] Thus the dividing lines between the thought of various individuals were blurred and those who finally expounded their views most fully and articulately in published form were by no means the sole authors of them.

The atmosphere Herzen describes was one in which Botkin, despite his social origins, felt entirely at ease; indeed, he perhaps more than any other individual was instrumental in its creation. It was Botkin, Herzen recalled, who taught his contemporaries

not in gardens and porticos . . . but round the friendly dinner table, that a man may equally find 'pantheistic' enjoyment in contemplating the dance of the sea waves and of Spanish maidens, in listening to the songs of Schubert and scenting the aroma of a turkey stuffed with truffles.[9]

Above all Botkin possessed precisely the qualities valuable in a period in which Russians were sifting very copious foreign material in search of some precious indication as to their own destiny. He had the dilettante's catholic tastes and receptivity to new ideas; a facility in grasping the essence of what was new to him; sincere and spontaneous enjoyment of all the arts (few contemporaries could rival his knowledge of music and painting); the voracious appetite of the autodidact for new knowledge; and a love and experience of foreign travel and keen interest in the West. Most important of all, he had that command of foreign languages – he knew German and French well, had a fair knowledge of English, *pace* Mrs Carlyle, and taught himself Spanish and Italian – which was essential if Russians were to keep abreast of the latest philosophical and literary developments. Given the conditions of the time and the tastes and aptitudes of Botkin himself, therefore, it is not unreasonable to suggest that he exercised on his contemporaries an influence far more considerable than we should expect merely on the evidence of his published works.

No one was more appreciative of Botkin's qualities or more indebted to him than Belinsky, who was himself a *'central nature'*[10] – to use Turgenev's phrase – in the intellectual life of his time. Admittedly the ascetic Belinsky found Botkin's sensualism quite alien and in 1842 he told Botkin he was a 'monster' when he heard of the merchant's latest extravagances.

You old profligate [he wrote], you sinful old goat! It was with horror that I read your impious letter, with horror that I heard Kulchik's tales about your joint indecency, drunkenness, lust, gluttony and other seven deadly sins![11]

(Unfortunately Botkin's own letter, to which Belinsky was replying, does not survive!) But from the time of his introduction to Botkin towards the end of 1835, after the latter's return from his first journey abroad, Belinsky undoubtedly nourished an unusually intense affection for Botkin. 'From the first I loved you passionately', he wrote, 'I cannot love anyone more.'[12] In a letter of August 1837 to Bakunin he paints a glowing picture of his new friend, eulogising Botkin's infinite goodness, his clear, harmonious disposition, his receptivity to art and his renunciation of his own ego. Botkin was the 'first *holy* person' he had met, Belinsky wrote (with the exception, that was, of Bakunin's sisters, Belinsky added tactfully).[13] And by November 1837 Belinsky no longer loved Botkin as before; he was 'simply in love with him'.[14] Differences did arise, particularly in the spring of 1838, but by August all was well again and Belinsky assured Botkin that in his absence he had come to love him still more. Their mutual praise Belinsky now describes as a 'holy alliance, founded on a striving for truth'.[15] In the early months of 1839 Belinsky again feared that enmity had arisen between them and spoke of having been betrayed by Botkin, but by August they had settled their differences and Belinsky wondered why he had been so angry.[16]

One should make allowance, of course, for the predilection of the men of that time for exalted expressions of constant friendship and even, perhaps, for a characteristic Russian effusiveness. Belinsky's letters in general are in any case an extraordinary phenomenon, the extended outpourings of an ardent soul. Nevertheless Belinsky's correspondence with Botkin, which the celebrated literary historian Pypin described as 'one of the most curious and important facts' of Russia's modern literary history,[17] clearly has a special significance. Between 1838 and 1843 it is of a volume, comprehensiveness and intimacy unusual even by the standards of the correspondents themselves. No doubt the closeness of the two men may be partly explained in terms of the attraction of opposites: Botkin seemed to Belinsky to embody a psychological equilibrium so manifestly wanting in the critic's own nature. But intimacy came too of a special intellectual interdependence which persisted throughout this period in spite of the bewildering *volte-face* in both men's thinking. Botkin, like many of his contemporaries, was inspired by Belinsky's passionate enthusiasms; but Belinsky, the poorly educated *raznochinets*, for his part derived perhaps even greater benefit from Botkin's breadth of culture, artistic judgement and linguistic expertise.

Botkin, Belinsky and Hegelianism

One of Botkin's early services to Belinsky was in all probability to help to acquaint the critic with the tales of Hoffmann, who had been known to Russians since the 1820s but whose works were translated and eulogised with renewed vigour in the second half of the 1830s. A review written by Botkin in 1836 on the subject of Bessomykin's translation of Hoffmann's *Serapion Brothers* reveals him as an ardent devotee of the German writer who would be satisfied only with a translator who did the original full justice. Botkin himself made an abridged and by no means flawless translation of *Kreisleriana*, one of a whole series of Hoffmann's works appearing in 1838 in the journal *Moskovskiy nablyudatel'* for which Belinsky was currently the leading critic and the *de facto* editor.[18] Botkin is also reliably said to have written passages on Romanticism in Belinsky's articles.[19]

A more important function of Botkin's, however, was to serve as one of Belinsky's principal mentors in German philosophy, of which Botkin was for a period one of the most faithful apostles. He and his friends looked on Hegel, Botkin recalled a few years later, as the 'new Messiah' and bowed down to him 'like Buryats to their fetishes'.[20] On the frivolous level there is a celebrated anecdote which has Botkin together with others proposing toasts to all the Hegelian categories from 'Pure Existence' to the 'Idea'.[21] Again, Botkin's prolonged attachment to one of Bakunin's sisters, Aleksandra – an involvement which was almost *de rigueur* for the young intellectuals who visited the Bakunin estate at Premukhino – was fraught with all the earnest soul-searching and suffering which Hegelianism seemed to dictate. More importantly, for the 'edification' of his friends and the Russian public, as Botkin put it, he made numerous translations of articles in the Hegelian spirit.[22] In 1837, for example, he was translating a work by the German critic Marbach – himself a 'very mediocre man' in Granovsky's words, but an important populariser of the 'ideas of modern philosophy on the most serious questions'[23] – and was said by Belinsky to be 'in ecstasies over it'.[24] And in 1840, still in a mood of 'boundless idealism', to use Annenkov's words,[25] Botkin translated an article on Shakespeare by another German critic, Rötscher, who was the Russians' main source of Hegel's aesthetic doctrines at this period and with whom Botkin was particularly closely identified in the minds of his contemporaries.[26] Finally, in his own reviews of the late 1830s Botkin disseminates the view rooted in Hegelian aesthetics that the work of art is not a reflection of the ephemeral and the mundane but an attempt to illuminate a higher reality accessible only to the chosen few.[27]

It was probably on the basis of Botkin's researches and translations that Belinsky was able in 1838 to declare his admiration for Marbach,[28] and the title of his article of 1840, 'Menzel – a Critic of Goethe', in which he most clearly and unequivocally puts the case for pure art, seems to be derived from a chapter heading in Marbach's work on Goethe with which Botkin had acquainted him some two years before.[29] Belinsky himself enthusiastically expounds Rötscher's views on art in an essay of 1838 which he conceived as the theoretical introduction to a whole cycle.[30] Botkin, of course, was not the only source of these ideas for Belinsky; Stankevich and Bakunin were at least as important in this respect. Katkov, too, had had published in _Moskovskiy nablyudatel'_ in 1838 a translation of one of Rötscher's essays, which Belinsky deemed important.[31] But Hegelianism was a common obsession in years when Belinsky and Botkin were very close and in a letter to Botkin in 1840 Belinsky acknowledged, with German philosophy in mind; 'I could never teach you, but I am myself greatly indebted to you.'[32]

In the year 1840, however, Belinsky experienced his profound change of heart and turned his attention from abstruse speculation to the practical concerns of Russian reality. Thus in March he wrote to Botkin: 'To the devil with all the higher aspirations and objectives! We live in a terrible time, . . . we must suffer, in order that our grandchildren should live more easily.'[33] And in October he cursed the reconciliation with reality which had been induced in him by his literal interpretation of the Hegelian dictum 'the real is rational'.[34] He now criticised Botkin's continued allegiance to Hegelian philosophy and told Botkin that the Germans had muddled him and induced him to make misguided pronouncements about art.[35] He also took Botkin to task for grieving too much over the death of Stankevich at a time when Belinsky favoured facing up to unpleasantness, and for living 'in a world of heroism'.[36] These criticisms persisted into 1841. 'Your Rötscher is a pedant, a

German, a philistine', Belinsky now told Botkin, and the 'little Hegels' were 'pygmies'.[37]

And yet, far from cooling towards Botkin as his enthusiasm for Hegelianism in general and Rötscher in particular ebbed away, Belinsky appeared to grow even closer to him. 'I haven't loved anyone as I have loved you and I don't want to be closer to anyone else', he assures Botkin in Feburary 1840.[38] 'You are the only thing I have on earth, my only link with life; without you I am worse than an orphan, a corpse among the living.'[39] News of Botkin's intention to visit St Petersburg threw Belinsky into ecstasy; the very thought of it, he said, brought tears to his eyes. How much they would have to say to one another, how full of meaning each word would be, how lively and interesting every discussion. Belinsky did not much wish to talk to anybody but Botkin about all that was on his mind, particularly about art. When he and Botkin spoke about art they spoke also about life, and they understood one another.[40] There survive no fewer than nineteen letters written by Belinsky to Botkin in the course of 1840, three of which run to more than five thousand words, and it is mainly in these letters that Belinsky chronicles the profound spiritual and intellectual crisis endured by him in that year. It seems therefore that the wide-ranging dialogue with Botkin, now in the role of confidant rather than mentor, greatly helped Belinsky to clarify his own views in the period when they were most unstable.

Botkin, for his part, followed Belinsky in abandoning Hegelianism for a more critical approach to reality and a less esoteric view of art, though his conversion was slower and less categorical. He had never drawn the same reactionary political conclusions to which Hegel had led Belinsky, and Belinsky's notorious celebration of autocracy in his review of Glinka's 'Sketches on the Battle of Borodino' Botkin had merely found boring and unreadable.[41] Botkin may even have begun to waver in his allegiance to Hegelianism before Belinsky and he implanted some reservations about it in Belinsky's mind, for already in 1839 he was extolling Schiller, whose emphasis on the 'independent, free ego' gave rise to hostility to the existing order.[42] At any rate he asked himself in 1840 whether his ill-fated affair with Aleksandra Bakunina had not been intended to teach him the danger of 'fantastic conceptions of life' and to show him that 'poetry, truth and reality' consist in 'simplicity' and 'intelligibility', in acceptance rather than rejection of everyday reality.[43]

In November of the same year he lavished praise on the Flemish painter Teniers, who had been prepared to depict 'human nature in its mundane manifestations'.[44] And by 1842 he himself is drawing Belinsky's attention to the contemporary assault on the old institutions of marriage, religion and the state and predicting the rise of a new order on the ruins of the old. He is deeply impressed now by the poetry of Lermontov, a prophet of conflict and negation who exemplifies the contemporary revolt against authority, tradition and existing social conditions.[45] Not surprisingly Botkin's letter delighted Belinsky, who agreed with his friend's views on Lermontov 'down to the last iota' and also concurred with his opinion that the image of Pushkin's Tatyana in *Eugene Onegin* was sullied by her faithfulness to her husband[46] – an opinion shortly to find expression in Belinsky's own article on Tatyana. Botkin even sides with Belinsky in the critic's dispute of 1842 with Granovsky over the interpretation of the competing factions in the French Revolution, endorsing the view that Robespierre was '*la pythonisse et l'oracle de la Révolution* and a resolute opponent of the bourgeoisie'.[47]

As Botkin's views again merged with Belinsky's, so his value as mentor to the critic began to prevail once more: he was able to discuss with Belinsky new works on which their revolt was partly based and to bring others to Belinsky's attention. He followed closely the development of the German young Hegelian school of philosophy whose criticisms of their master Belinsky was grateful to receive.[48] Botkin underscores in a letter to Belinsky the significance of Feuerbach, who in his *Essence of Christianity* had interpreted the divinity as merely a projection of man's own consciousness.[49] And in the first of three articles which he published in 1843 on the subject of German literature he incorporates a virtual translation of part of Engels' pamphlet, *Schelling and Revelation*, in which Hegel's conclusions are described as 'often short-sighted' and the Young Hegelians are praised for applying Hegel's dialectic to examination of topical social issues.[50] Botkin now pleads too, in the spirit of the burgeoning 'natural school', for a literature that does not exclude the 'dark sides' of human life. In the second article he condemns the love poetry currently emanating from Germany, 'lyrical muck' as he calls it, which does not reflect the interests of the age. He rounds on Rötscher for his philistinism and his 'philosophical *Schulmeisterei*', preaching 'devoid of any rational, humane content'. And in the third article, which takes the form of a withering criticism of another

German author, Gutskow, he finally casts off the influence of the German philosophers, whose 'metaphysical constructions and abstract theoretical conclusions' had obscured the aspirations of modern society.[51] Botkin's development, needless to say, delighted Belinsky: 'I liked it more than all your previous articles,' he wrote about the last of the series on German literature,

perhaps because its content is closer to my heart ... You've given this putrid philistine frankfurter Gutskow a marvellous drubbing. And that's just how one would have wanted to fix that pork sausage Rötscher.[52]

Botkin's Westernism

In September 1843 there occurred in Botkin's life a bizarre, though rather characteristic episode which Herzen describes at length and with ironical wit in *My Past and Thoughts*: he married. His bride was a French seamstress, Armance Rouillard, with whom he had had a brief affair and with whom he had absolutely nothing in common. Preparations for the wedding, of which Botkin's father did not approve, were made with a secrecy in which Botkin and his fellow conspirators evidently took delight and were accompanied by much philosophical soul-searching. The ceremony itself was at last conducted with pomp in the Kazan Cathedral on Nevsky Prospect in St Petersburg. Romance did not survive the couple's voyage from Russia to France, however; disagreement seems to have arisen over George Sand's novel *Jacques* and Botkin to have concluded that his bride's sensibility was incompatible with his own. Relations deteriorated and the couple parted on arrival in France.[53]

Botkin was now to remain in the West for more than three years and this stay abroad marks an important phase in his intellectual development. His cooling towards German culture in general and a new affection for France are reinforced during this period. Like Annenkov, who at this time had some amicable correspondence with Marx, Botkin consorted with the most radical circles and, together with Bakunin and Grigoriy Tolstoy, informally represented Russia's anti-tsarist forces at an evening meeting in Paris in 1844 attended also by the French socialists, Louis Blanc and Pierre Leroux, and by Arnold Ruge and Marx on behalf of the German socialist camp.[54] Botkin's radicalism in this period is also attested by a surviving letter of 1845 to Ogaryov in which he condemns the '*bourgeois gentilshommes*' who use 'positive religion' as an instrument for the repression of the working class, characterises religion as a convenient means of explaining away all that was unacceptable in man's life and of encouraging quietism, and praises Feuerbach for his 'true understanding' of this subject.[55]

Botkin's contribution to Russian intellectual life during his stay abroad and the period immediately following it may most usefully be discussed in terms of 'Westernism', provided that we bear in mind the qualifications already made about this concept and treat it not so much as a coherent doctrine, nor even as a set of sharply defined ideas, but rather as a collection of shared attitudes which Botkin and others discussed and helped to disseminate. As was the case for many of his contemporaries, the most distinctive facet of Botkin's Westernism was opposition to Slavophilism and it was this opposition which helped to clarify his own attitudes. As early as 1842 Botkin includes in an article a jeering aside directed at the Slavophiles,[56] but his views are made clearer in letters to Annenkov in 1846–7. He did acknowledge that the Slavophiles had spoken one 'true word', *'narodnost''*. They had been the first to sense that the so-called 'Russian civilisation', with all its arrogance and presumptuousness, was in fact empty and derivative. But that was the extent of their achievement. Slavophilism had not produced a single 'sensible person', but only a 'gypsy' like Khomyakov, a 'noble somnambulist' like Aksakov or a 'monk' like Kireyevsky. The Slavophiles were all the 'most abstract theoreticians' who, when they came to make some positive pronouncement, preached narrow-mindedness and ignorance, defended a patriarchal social order, showed themselves unaware of the simplest economic principles, displayed intolerance and obscurantism and propagated the most egregious 'fantasies about the preservation of national prejudices'.[57] To Botkin, then, the argument about Slavophilism entailed at bottom a choice between 'ignorance' and 'civilisation'.[58] Westernism clearly stood for 'civilisation' which signified for Botkin – and he was typical in this – a respect for and rationalistic approach to knowledge; belief in the advantages of economic and industrial progress; greater social equality, at least on the moral and legal planes if not on the material one; intellectual and political tolerance; a belief in the necessity of the rule of law; and, of course, a respect – though not undiscriminating respect – for the Western countries in which these virtues found expression.

This moderate Westernism, and the civic spirit that went with it, found intermittent expression in Botkin's correspondence. In a letter to Annenkov, for example, Botkin defines it as the task of modern science to isolate the laws operating in the spheres of industry and politics in order that we may be able not only to criticise reality but also to explain it rationally. Thus, whereas the Slavophiles, as we have seen, dismissed political economy as a pernicious 'science of wealth', Botkin praised Adam Smith for discovering the discipline's basic laws.[59] Again, Botkin is pleased to note in 1846 that all social 'estates' – as it was customary for Russians at this time to call social classes – had for the first time participated jointly in the election of a town head in St Petersburg, thus taking a first step towards the erosion of social barriers.[60] As for Botkin's view of the function of literature in the mid 1840s, it continues to reflect his sense of civic purpose. The strength of Russian literature was conceived as lying in 'ideology' which had undergone a change since the days 'of long wandering in the German wastes' and now concentrated on the practical world. It was the 'French view' that was necessary for literature now; that was to say, a view 'resting on common sense and history, and keeping in mind the multitude, not the initiated and the chosen few'. Literary criticism had therefore to free itself from its Moloch, the false idol 'artistry' (*khudozhestvennost'*). In this respect Belinsky's articles on Onegin, particularly the one on Tatyana, were 'very good', though Botkin was not otherwise pleased with the state of Russian letters as he found them on his return in 1846.[61]

The most notable expression of Botkin's Westernism, however, was his major publication, the *Letters on Spain*. The *Letters* were the product of what Annenkov described as one of several '*hygienic* intermissions' in Botkin's Parisian debauches;[62] that was to say, a journey to Spain in the summer of 1845 in the course of which Botkin visited Burgos, Madrid, Aranjuez, Córdoba, Seville, Cádiz, Málaga and Granada (he also made a brief excursion to Morocco). Six of the *Letters* were published in *Sovremennik* between 1847 and 1849 and a seventh came out in 1851. In 1857 the whole series was published in a separate edition. The *Letters* were almost universally applauded,[63] although Botkin himself disingenuously asked Annenkov not to take them as coming from the heart and pleaded that they had been written in order to raise money badly needed by the author, to which end they had been prolonged unnecessarily.[64]

Botkin was not an imaginative or inventive writer, but he did have a sharp and impressionable mind and some descriptive talent. The *Letters* were endowed with a vividness and immediacy which reflected Botkin's enjoyment of the exotic side of Spain, its colour and vitality. His 'goatish nature', as Belinsky detected,[65] was thoroughly seduced by the Spanish 'worship of the body', by the 'naïve amiability' of the Andalusian women, who would wind themselves round their visitor 'like ivy', and by the sheer sensualism of their dance, while his higher nature was captivated by the deep religiosity expressed in the painting of Murillo, to which Botkin devotes a knowledgeable purple passage. The privations to be endured in Spain do not seem to have been very apparent to him until he briefly experienced the Anglo-Saxon comforts and sanitation of Gibraltar. Only from the gastronomic point of view was Spain found seriously wanting: for many a day Botkin was tormented by the repugnant and ubiquitous olive oil of the inns of La Mancha.[66]

The *Letters*, then, reflected Botkin's love of the alien culture he found in Spain and a deep sympathy for it; but they also contained indications that the Spanish historical destiny, national character and social order had a special pertinence for Russians of the 1840s. Works of travel literature in general, of course, may tell us as much about the sensibility of their authors as about the *mores* of the countries they describe. And, although Belinsky and Gogol both praised Botkin for writing about Spain with freshness and without preconceptions,[67] nevertheless it is worth stressing that Botkin was one of a long line of Russian travellers who went to the West fully cognisant of the debates agitating the Russian educated class and predisposed to perceive in foreign parts tendencies which might have a bearing on the enigmatic destiny of their own nation.

The points of similarity between Russia and Spain as it is perceived by Botkin are numerous and striking. Even the 'deserted fields' along the road between Burgos and Madrid remind him at the very outset of his journey of his native landscape. More importantly, Spain, like Russia, is an outpost of European civilisation: it has been isolated geographically, by its natural border, the Pyrenees, and historically, by the long period of subjugation to and struggle with an infidel invader. Botkin, it is true, shows a sympathy for the Moorish civilisation which is unusual for his time; but he also believes that the Moorish occupation had had the effect of preserving in Spain a civilisation which in some respects belonged as much to the Middle Ages as to modern times. Spain, like Russia again, was a country still largely unknown to Europe. It was also currently convulsed in the attempt to 'tear itself away from its past' and 'at the same time to preserve all its old, cherished traditions'; it was refashioning its constitution 'in a foreign manner' but retaining 'all its old ghastly administration'. Its intellectual life was largely concentrated in 'political newspapers, divided into irreconcilably quarrelling parties'. If it were to become a country of the first rank, then work, education, industry and diligence were needed, not words, exclamations, or comforting recollections of former glory. And for the moment the country's destiny was uncertain, a 'living riddle', as Botkin described it, using a word (*zagadka*) much beloved by his compatriots when they spoke about Russia's destiny. Like the Russia to which Gogol alludes as Chichikov's troyka speeds away at the end of Part I of *Dead Souls*, Botkin's Spain 'goes not knowing where its road will lead, without definite aim, without any plan and in complete ignorance of tomorrow'. Never before had Europe seen such a spectacle![68]

Whereas Botkin's comments on Spanish history and politics may, it seems, be applied *mutatis mutandis* to his native land, what he has to say about the character and *mores* of the Spanish people appears to have a more exemplary significance. Unlike the Russian masses, whom Botkin, for all his sympathy for them, was not prepared to idolise,[69] the Spanish common people expressed themselves with a common sense, lucidity and freedom which indicated perhaps what might be expected of a people not oppressed by serfdom. Again, the Spaniards as a whole and their upper class in particular exhibited a moral nobility, a sense of chivalry, a knightly temperament to which Botkin refers repeatedly. They were a people 'so noble, fine and full of dignity' and they displayed the virtues of the *caballero*, politeness, naturalness and hospitality. The bull-fight – which captivated Botkin and is the subject of a long description in his work – reflected the national ethos with its strict observance of a code of honour. Even the greatest matador is rebuked when he kills a bull with a stroke of the sword forbidden by the laws of tauromachy. Above all, the Spaniards displayed a sense of national unity and fraternity for which humanitarian men in Nicolaevan Russia necessarily yearned. Their dealings with one another were free and honourable irrespective of differences in social class. The Spanish noble was not proud, haughty, or condescending and did not consider it beneath his dignity to mingle with the crowd; nor was the common man envious of him or obsequious towards him. The peasant, the unskilled workman and the water-carrier would all speak to the grandee on an equal footing. Thus only wealth separated the various social 'estates'. Such supposed equality of personal status was clearly lacking in Russia, although Turgenev, by treating serfs as moral equals of their masters in his *Sportsman's Sketches*, published during the same years as the *Letters on Spain*, seems to postulate its feasibility there. But it is an ideal, we may infer, for which Russian society ought to strive, and not for moral reasons alone: for the existence of such equality in Spain made it unlikely that that country would undergo the revolutionary upheavals experienced by Germany, England and France, upheavals which Botkin doubtless meant his readers to consider a distinct possibility in Russia too.[70]

Botkin's moderation in the late 1840s and early 1850s

The *Letters on Spain*, while they contain the fullest expression of Botkin's progressive leanings in the 1840s, also mark the beginnings of that portentous rift in the ranks of the intelligentsia between, on the one hand, the men of liberal temper, like Botkin himself, who expressed these leanings with moderation, and, on the other hand, those such as Belinsky who were of more revolutionary disposition. There are several indications of this rift in Botkin's renewed correspondence with Belinsky in 1847. Admittedly the relationship between the two men was still warm after Botkin's return from Western Europe. Indeed, in November 1846 Botkin told Annenkov that his attachment to Belinsky was even stronger than it had been before.[71] And a year later Belinsky, responding to Botkin's suggestion that a 'black cat' had run between them, tried to dispel the impression of disharmony.[72] But points of difference were now too numerous and substantial for the former 'holy alliance' to be restored. One purely practical source of grievance was Botkin's willingness on his return to Russia to work for Krayevsky, whom Belinsky detested, on the journal *Otechestvennyye zapiski* as well as with Belinsky himself on *Sovremennik*.[73] (Granovsky, it will be recalled, was guilty of the same sin.) A more general question of principle concerned the degree of indulgence which should be shown towards those who expressed views with which one did not agree. Belinsky began in the last years of his life, as his hostility towards the established order became more and more uncompromising, to display an increasing intolerance which found expression in his repeated bitter denunciations of Gogol's *Selected Passages from a Correspondence with Friends*. Not that Botkin had expressed approval of Gogol's notorious defence of the serf-owning order; but he had reproached Belinsky for losing his temper over it. Tolerance of error, Belinsky replied, he could understand, but tolerance of baseness he would not tolerate. 'In general,' he harangued Botkin, 'you with your tolerance end up being intolerant by virtue of the fact that you exclude intolerance from the great and noble sources of human strength and dignity.' Belinsky, therefore, would remain proudly and firmly 'intolerant'. If he were to change he would from that moment consider that all that was humane and beautiful in him would have died.[74]

A second source of disagreement between Botkin and Belinsky was now their view of art. Whereas Belinsky in his later years became increasingly insistent that art should serve a civic purpose, Botkin began soon after his return to Russia to re-emphasise the virtues of artistry. Thus Belinsky defended certain passages in Grigorovich's story, *Anton the Unfortunate*, on the grounds that they provided valuable insights into the life of the Russian common people, whilst Botkin condemned them on the grounds that they were prolix.

You're a sybarite, Vasenka, [Belinsky wrote] you have a sweet tooth – just look, give you poetry and art and you'll savour it and smack your lips. But for me poetry and artistry are necessary only in sufficient degree to make the story true; that's to say so that it shouldn't lapse into allegory or resemble a dissertation.[75]

It is also significant in this connection that Botkin was shortly to praise Turgenev's *Sportsman's Sketches* on account of their artistry rather than their content. 'The Bailiff' and 'The Office' – two of the sketches which most clearly implied social criticism – gave Botkin as much pleasure, he told Annenkov, as the 'golden works of Cellini'.[76]

A third source of disagreement between Botkin and Belinsky concerned assessments of bourgeois civilisation and arose *à propos* of Herzen's *Letters from the Avenue Marigny*. Only Belinsky among the leading Russian intellectuals was prepared in 1847 to express more or less wholehearted enthusiasm for Herzen's criticism of the Western bourgeoisie. The 'sovereignty of capitalists' had covered France with 'eternal shame', he told Botkin in a long tirade based mainly on moral arguments and liberally laced with anti-Semitic sentiments. Woe to the state headed by the bourgeoisie, Belinsky concluded; it would be better to have a country governed by an 'idle, profligate riff-raff covered in rags', for they would be more likely than the bourgeoisie to display 'patriotism, a sense of national worth and a desire for the common welfare'.[77] Botkin, like Granovsky, however, did not share Belinsky's view. Admittedly one should not exaggerate Botkin's coolness towards Herzen's letters or his sympathy at this stage for the bourgeoisie which Herzen was indicting, for Botkin did confess to Annenkov that he had read the letters 'with the keenest pleasure' and assured Herzen that he was wrong to count him among the 'partisans of the bourgeoisie'; nothing repelled him so much as the 'spirit and morality of the bourgeoisie'.[78] But he did believe, as he confided to Annenkov, that Herzen had failed to ascertain clearly the significance of the bourgeoisie which he so despised. As a sceptic Botkin was unable, he said, to join either side of an argument when he saw that on each there were equal amounts of good sense and nonsense. The working class, as the oppressed class, had all his sympathy, but he could not help but add: 'God grant we may have a bourgeoisie!' At bottom this attitude was another expression of tolerance and moderation. Botkin was not prepared to imitate what he called the 'Slavic intolerance' shown by Herzen when he reprimanded Botkin for having the temerity not to agree with his opinion. And, as one who prided himself on fair-mindedness, Botkin felt compelled to defend the French bourgeoisie against the attacks of Russian outsiders who depicted it as some sort of 'rotten, revolting, pernicious monster which devours all that is beautiful and noble in mankind'. Such hyperboles were quite understandable when they came from a French worker living in a society where there was a conflict of interests; but Russia's 'intelligent Herzen' ought to have been able to take an independent view. Not that tolerance was easy to come by: indeed, only the English and French civilisations had yet acquired it.[79]

Botkin's disinclination to espouse the radical cause was greatly strengthened by the European uprisings of 1848 and by the new series of repressive measures taken in Russia as a result of them. In the atmosphere that prevailed during the 'dismal seven years' after

1848, Botkin was no longer bold enough to express the free-thinking sentiments to which he had formerly given voice. According to the memoirs of Panayeva he now became fearful of having conversations reported to the police by the servants and of being implicated by Dostoyevsky in the Petrashevsky affair; he would petulantly urge friends to destroy letters they had received from him; and on one occasion when there was a ring at the door late at night he rushed into the bedroom and hid under the bedclothes.[80] Panayeva, it is true, is not the most reliable witness, and her reminiscences of Botkin, whom she repeatedly portrays as pusillanimous and disloyal, are coloured by her sympathy for the more radical wing of the intelligentsia. But even Annenkov, an observer much more favourably disposed towards Botkin, tells us that some of the more 'nervous gentlemen', such as Botkin, 'all but went to pieces' in this period. Botkin moved from Moscow to St Petersburg, as the safer place to be, but still 'feared for every hour of his life'.[81]

One obvious consequence of this fear for his safety was Botkin's virtual withdrawal from publicism. Never a prolific writer, he now produced even less. Moreover, of the seven items which he is known to have published in the years 1850–4 inclusive, three were on the subject of music and represented to a large extent a flight from the harsh realities of the concrete world. The high purpose of music, he wrote, for example, was to tear us away from the prose of everyday life, albeit briefly. Cimarosa's opera, *The Secret Marriage*, now appealed to him because like an ancient fairy tale it reminded the care-worn adult of a joyful childhood.[82] Botkin's only article on Russian literature during this period, an essay published in 1850 on the poetry of Ogaryov, also reflects this mood. Ogaryov's poetry explored the state of the soul immersed in its inner world, and it was distinguished by its pensive charm.[83] Similar qualities Botkin found in the work of Turgenev, to whom he was particularly close at this time and whose stories at their best made on Botkin a 'truly poetic impression'.[84] And it is precisely the absence of a single 'drop of poetry' in Ostrovsky's play, *The Poor Bride*, that determines Botkin's lukewarm evaluation of it.[85]

Botkin's objections to radical thought in the second half of the 1850s

The reappraisal of values in the years following the death of Nicholas I, the accession to the throne of a tsar of more liberal temper, the traumatic experience of defeat in the Crimea and the ascendancy of a more plebeian class in the intelligentsia – these factors affected imaginative literature and literary criticism before any other area of thought. It was not so much that it now became possible once again to examine topical questions in literature and criticism; rather it suddenly became almost impossible *not* to take such questions into account. Previously the intelligentsia had been broadly united by its common love of art and by the similar social background of the majority of its members. But in the new conditions the rift of which we have seen the first indications in the late 1840s developed very rapidly in its ranks. Eventually this rift was to reveal irreconcilable political differences between the older and younger generations; but in the first instance it manifested itself on the ground on which the debates of the Russian intelligentsia had traditionally been conducted. That is to say, it concerned attitudes to imaginative literature and to types of artistic creation which seemed to be exemplified by the work of Pushkin and Gogol respectively. In this debate Botkin played an important role, although one which was at first characteristically complex and ambiguous.

On the one hand, there were several indications in 1855–6 that Botkin was not unsympathetic to the emergent radical camp, which exhorted writers, in the spirit of Belinsky's last injunctions, to put their talents to the use of society by examining important topical questions and by depicting Russian reality in the critical tone now supposed to have been characteristic of Gogol's writing. In the first place, Botkin was particularly close at this period to Nekrasov, editor of *Sovremennik* as Chernyshevsky rose to prominence on it and largely instrumental in turning the journal in a more radical direction. In the summer of 1855 Nekrasov stayed with Botkin, convalescing at his *dacha*.[86] In the second place, Botkin did defend the Gogolian tendency in Russian art, on the grounds that it was 'necessary for the benefit of society'; and he was correspondingly critical of frivolous art which had the purpose merely of amusing the public.[87] In the third place, he expressed approval of the work of Chernyshevsky. In April 1856 he told Panayev, for example, that the latest instalment of Chernyshevsky's 'Essays on the Gogol Period of Russian Literature' was 'very good' and in September said he had read a further article in the series 'with great sympathy': Chernyshevsky's articles were 'sensible' and attracted the attention of everyone who was at all interested in Russian literature.[88] He also defended Chernyshevsky's dissertation on the *Aesthetic Relations of Art to Reality*, in which Chernyshevsky had contended that the work of art was not a quest for transcendent beauty but a mere reproduction of reality. Whilst Turgenev abusively denounced Chernyshevsky's dissertation, Botkin suggested that the aesthetic concepts attacked by Chernyshevsky were indeed outmoded, dilapidated and good for nothing now that man's views on nature and reality were changing (although he did admit that Chernyshevsky's definition of art as a 'surrogate for reality' was 'preposterous'). In short, Chernyshevsky's dissertation, Botkin felt, contained a great deal that was 'intelligent and sensible'.[89]

On the other hand, despite Botkin's apparent toleration of Chernyshevsky's views in 1855–6, his bonds with those who would oppose Chernyshevsky's conception of art and his political attitudes were at the very same time being strengthened. Together with Druzhinin and Grigorovich, Botkin spent three weeks on Turgenev's estate at Spasskoye in the summer of 1855. The stay seems to have passed in an atmosphere of great harmony, marred only by Botkin's momentary rage at Grigorovich, who one day led the party through a tangled thicket and caused Botkin to get his feet wet.[90] Botkin now grows particularly close to Druzhinin, the most articulate spokesman of the so-called 'Pushkin school', who in an article of 1855 exalted Pushkin as the dispassionate artist whose serene, Olympian view of reality was the proper antidote to the satirical tendency associated with Gogol.[91] In 1856 Botkin and Druzhinin shared a *dacha* at Kuntsovo, and the following year travelled abroad together. Druzhinin's translation of *King Lear*, completed in 1856, was dedicated to Botkin. In September 1855 Botkin himself acknowledged in a letter to Druzhinin that 'political ideas' were the 'grave of art' and that 'philosophising' and a 'blind passion for theories and systems' were eroding 'poetic feeling'; indeed, they had killed the talent of Gogol.[92] Botkin also grows close and accords the highest praise to Tolstoy,[93] who had just appeared in literary circles in St Petersburg and who for a period fell strongly under the influence of Druzhinin. There are other indications too that Botkin's commitment to Chernyshevsky could have been of only the most superficial nature. In a letter of June 1856 he laments the recent 'terrible movement of Germany into the field of the natural sciences' – a development wholeheartedly welcomed by Chernyshevsky – and now bemoans the fact that lectures on philosophy in German universities are attended only by two or three people, the last of the Mohicans.[94] He attempts in the same year to persuade Nekrasov to replace Chernyshevsky on the editorial board of *Sovremennik* by Grigoryev,[95] shortly to be a leading exponent of the latterday Slavophile doctrine of *pochvennichestvo*. And he attends a dinner to commemorate the coronation of Alexander II and joyfully drinks a toast to the health of the new tsar.[96]

It is not surprising, in the light of these allegiances and sentiments, that Botkin began to endorse the values of the older generation when choices finally had to be expressed. In fact, his position was already clearly indicated by the interest he showed in 1855 in Thomas Carlyle, whom he described as one of the 'most remarkable contemporary writers of England'.[97] With a vigour and sense of purpose not characteristic of him Botkin accomplished a translation of Carlyle's lectures on Scandinavian mythology and on Dante and Shakespeare, which formed part of Carlyle's work, *Heroes, Hero-Worship and the Heroic in History*, and wrote a short foreword which was published with the first instalment of the translation in *Sovremennik* towards the end of 1855. (The other two instalments appeared early in 1856.)

Although Carlyle's lectures had been delivered in 1840 they contained a view of the world and a conception of art which had the clearest bearing on the crisis in Russian thought in the mid 1850s. Carlyle attempts to restore to the natural world the power and the mystery of which it was rapidly being deprived by the tendency of the age to describe it in scientific terms. He exalts the Scandinavian mythological view of the world, which with its awe for the great natural forces of sea, storm, sun, frost and fire, stood in sharp contrast to the contemporary conception of the universe as a machine. Carlyle accordingly reveres not the natural scientist, the critical or logical intellect, but the artist, the poet, the painter or man of genius whose function it is to 'discern the loveliness' of the world and glimpse the higher reality beyond the appearances of things. Is it not reckoned 'still a merit, proof of what we call a "poetic nature"', he asks, 'that we recognise how every object has a divine beauty in it; how every object still verily is "a window through which we may look into infinitude itself"'? The artist thus conceived cannot be judged as Chernyshevsky wished, in utilitarian terms. The poet such as Dante, who 'has once got into that primal element

of *Song* ... has worked in the *depths* of our existence' and
has perceived 'through long times the life-*roots* of all excellent
human things whatsoever' 'in a way that "utilities" will not succeed
well in calculating!'.

'We will not estimate the Sun by the quantity of gaslight it saves us', Carlyle
contends, and likewise 'Dante shall be invaluable, or of no value'.

Nor will such an artist exhibit 'narrow superstition, harsh asceti-
cism, intolerance, fanatical fierceness or perversion'. On the contrary, he will display the Olympian detachment advocated by
Druzhinin, what Carlyle calls a '*true* Catholicism', which makes his
work a 'kind of universal Psalm'. A people blessed with such a poet,
whose significance transcended national barriers, was rich indeed.
Italy, for example, politically dismembered though she currently
was, derived unity from the voice of Dante, who could 'speak forth
melodiously' what the nation's heart intended. On the other hand,
Russia, for all her strength, could not yet speak, for she had had 'no
voice of genius, to be heard of all men and times'; her 'cannons and
Cossacks' would all have 'rusted into non-entity', Carlyle declared
in an odd image, while Dante's voice remained audible.[98] These
concluding references to Russia Botkin chose to omit from his
translation, most probably because the offence they contained to
Russian national pride would have ensured a poor reception for
their author's work, but perhaps also because they no longer
seemed justifiable now that the reputation of Pushkin as the great
national poet had been firmly established by Belinsky. But they
must have strengthened Botkin's inclination to support Druzhinin's
view that Russian literature should be wrenched from its Gogolian
path on to a Pushkinian one, on which it could pursue eternal
artistic values rather than transient factional interests.

Interwoven with Carlyle's perception of the universe and the
artist's relation to it was a conception of history which had socio-
political implications no less meaningful for the Russian intelligentsia of the mid 1850s. For history, Carlyle asserted, was not the
product of any inexorable social forces or mass movements but 'at
bottom the History of the Great Men' who had worked in the world,
the heroes to whom his title refers. It was on loyalty to such
inspired teachers that society was based. 'All dignities of rank, on
which human association rests, are what we may call a *Hero*archy',
he wrote in a passage which inevitably provided comfort for men of

aristocratic temper and status whose hegemony in their society was threatened:

Society everywhere is some representation, not *in*supportably inaccurate, of a graduated worship of Heroes – reverence and obedience done to men really great and wise . . . They are all as bank-notes, these social dignitaries, all representing gold.

Carlyle was well aware that 'hero-worship' was unfashionable in the modern democratic age which denied the existence of great men or sought to account for them deterministically as products of their time. But faith that the great man would appear should be the cornerstone on which man might rebuild his society in 'these revolutionary ages', the 'one fixed point in modern revolutionary history' which otherwise would seem 'bottomless and shoreless'.[99] Such views clearly precluded unconditional respect for the masses or enthusiasm for the democratic sentiments with which Chernyshevsky was coming to be associated. Thus Botkin, through his translation of Carlyle, was obliquely aligning himself with the older wing of the intelligentsia, although he himself did not in fact share its aristocratic ancestry.

Any remaining doubts about Botkin's allegiance were shortly dispelled by his most important contribution to the debate between the 'Pushkin' and 'Gogol' schools, an article published in 1857 on the poetry of Fet. The article was partly inspired by Carlyle's work and, like his translation of *Heroes and Hero-Worship*, cost Botkin unusual effort.[100] It amounted to a defence of poetry as an end in itself in a prosaic age when economic, scientific and technological developments were tending to concentrate society's attention on matters that were apparently of more practical significance. The practical nature of the age, Botkin argued, by no means obviated the need for art. For man had an innate desire to express his thoughts and feelings in images. Poetic feeling resided in the nature of almost every man, though of course in varying degree. It was man's sixth and highest sense. But not only would the 'human spirit' therefore never be willing to live on the material plane alone; human society was in fact moved only by the 'moral ideas' which found expression in art. These ideas affected man's inner spiritual being, conditioned his view of life and hence left their mark on his everyday activity. Thus art in the final analysis had an incomparably greater practical effect than those thousands of phenomena which it was customary to call 'practical'. Moreover, paradoxical as it might seem, it was only 'art for art's sake', or 'free artistic creation' as Botkin preferred to call it, that could fulfil this function. Whereas false and empty works had no practical significance, since they exercised no influence on the human spirit, the true poet who did not set out to edify or to improve his reader could indeed have a beneficial effect on society through his spontaneous treatment of universally valid subject matter. Fet, finally, is praised as a true poetic talent who in a materialistic age has preserved originality, independence, lyricism, sincerity and a serene vision.[101]

The essay on Fet was quickly followed by a minor article on a theme calculated to enrage the advocates of utilitarian art and criticism: the use of the rose in classical antiquity. One knew that out of the beauty of nature, admired by the 'idle imagination' of poets, no useful artifice could be fashioned, he wrote facetiously, and proceeded to devote several thousand words to the subject.[102] But, like Druzhinin, Botkin seemed to sense already that the battle with the younger generation was being lost. Thus in 1857 he again went abroad and living in Rome became increasingly absorbed in a subject remote from topical issues, medieval Christian art. He even expressed a gloomy presentiment of senility, although in truth he was only 47.[103] His alignment with the fathers against the children was now conclusively demonstrated by the more overt expression of that political liberalism which had been implicit in his moderate Westernism of the 1840s and which was a corollary of his more recent pleas for a free objective art. On the basis of a stay in England in 1859 he now gives a sympathetic appraisal of the British bourgeoisie. He is attracted by the comfort of English life, and by the order, stability and solidity of English society. He enjoys the atmosphere of political freedom and the lively debates in the House of Commons. And in various ways he places his emphasis on the virtues of the ruling classes rather than the plight of the masses. He draws attention, as he had in his *Letters on Spain*, to the equality of the various social strata before the law rather than to their manifest material inequality. Like Druzhinin in the same period, he extols too the qualities of the 'gentleman' (which are not altogether dissimilar from those of the Spanish *caballero*). And he marvels at the effectiveness of an appeal published in *The Times* for relief for the paupers of London. Thus, avoiding the emphasis of his socialist compatriots who wrote with dismay of the misery of the masses under capitalism, Botkin chooses to describe in a favourable light the comforts enjoyed by the bourgeoisie and to express admiration for their apparent social concern.[104]

Botkin's conservatism in his final years

As the younger generation became more vociferous and icono-clastic on the morrow of the reforms of the early 1860s, so Botkin shed all vestiges of sympathy with them, and began to speak of them with contempt, comparing them unfavourably to his own contem-poraries. In the revolutionary party he saw concentrated all that was 'vile, splenetic and loathsome' in Russia. Chernyshevsky, Mikhayl-ov and their like were on the side of 'sedition and unrest, falsehood, thoughtlessness and barbarism'.[105] The humanitarian liberalism, to which Turgenev remained faithful to the end, now deserted Botkin and he became unashamedly reactionary. He approved of Katkov's views as they found expression in *Moskovskiye vedomosti (The Moscow Gazette)*; he was not sorry to see Dostoyevsky's journal, *Vremya (Time)*, banned by the censor-ship and he even rejoiced at the closure in 1866 of *Sovremennik*, with whose destiny he himself had once been so closely linked.[106] He favoured the ruthless suppression of the Polish uprising of 1863 in the name of Russian national self-interest, endorsed the expres-sion of patriotic feeling at the English club in Moscow when it entertained Katkov and spoke frankly in a letter to Fet of his hatred of the Poles.[107] The gendarme now seemed to him to provide the only hope for Russia's salvation.[108] His final years he lived out in bitterness, seeking futile pursuits in order to while away the time and surrounding himself with luxuries which his failing health would no longer permit him to enjoy. Former friends, even those who did not entirely share the values of the younger generation, turned away from him in disgust. Herzen, whom Botkin chanced to meet in the street in Switzerland, would not speak to him.[109] Turgenev was repelled now by Botkin's egoism' 'Oh . . . in every man', he wrote to Annenkov, 'there sits a beast which only love can tame.'[110] He also began to view Botkin's ever increasing epicureanism with distaste: when Botkin died, Turgenev remarked, he should be laid to rest in his coffin with a truffle in his mouth.[111]

Thus Botkin ended his days in alienation and isolation from many of those to whom he had formerly been close. Like Turgenev's

Pavel Kirsanov he seemed more at home abroad than in Russia, where he was now superfluous. In Berlin, he told Turgenev in 1866, he was like a fish in water: *Fidelio* was being performed and he could attend lectures on Byron's poetry and the philosophy of Schopenhauer.[112] In Russia the worth of the values he had once defended had by now been obscured by the arguments of both government and radical intelligentsia against the moderate liberal position. But that was not to say that Botkin's contribution to the intellectual life of his time had been unimportant, as Annenkov reminded the younger generation in an obituary to his friend in 1869. One should never forget, Annenkov wrote, 'through what jungles and thickets these honest servants of knowledge' had had to 'beat a track' for themselves and their successors.[113] And in the quest of these 'servants of knowledge' for enlightenment and civilised values – a quest which had given rise to a literature of the greatest wealth and vigour – Botkin had for a quarter of a century played a central role.

4

Pavel Vasilyevich Annenkov
(1813–1887)

Annenkov's contribution to Russian intellectual life

Annenkov's original contribution to Russian letters, like Botkin's, was small, and yet he too played a role in the intellectual life of the 1840s and 1850s that can scarcely be ignored. He is now generally remembered first and foremost as a memoirist and biographer whose account of the intellectual life of the period 1838–48, under the title *The Marvellous Decade*,[1] and whose writings on the life of N. V. Stankevich, Gogol and Turgenev remain invaluable sources for the student of mid-nineteenth-century Russian culture. (And it is indeed in these fields that Annenkov's creative talents found their freest expression.) But he was also the author of much literary criticism which, though frankly poor in quality and marred by a convoluted literary style, clearly reflected the intellectual currents of the time and indicated the hardening of opposition among the older members of the intelligentsia to the utilitarian view of art encouraged by Chernyshevsky. He wrote a much acclaimed biography of Pushkin which precipitated the controversy of the mid 1850s over the respective merits of Pushkin and Gogol. Furthermore, Annenkov was a gregarious man who by virtue of the breadth of his circle of acquaintances – he met, among other people, Heine and Herwegh, George Sand, Pierre Leroux, Proudhon and the young Marx and Engels – served as an important source of information for his contemporaries on the latest ideas circulating in Western Europe in the 1840s. Most important of all, perhaps, Annenkov was a traveller of great stamina and inexhaustible curiosity whose published 'letters' from Western Europe helped, like Botkin's *Letters on Spain*, to broaden the cultural horizons of the Russian reading public.

Annenkov was, of course, a dilettante, one of those intellectual 'tourists', Lavrov once scathingly suggested, for whom art and politics were but an 'ephemeral adornment' with which they might

briefly enrich their own lives.[2] His failure to apply himself seriously
to any particular subject was reflected in the superficiality of many
of his writings and even, on a mundane level, in his notorious
inefficiency as a proof-reader of his own works. But the 1840s were
years in which the restless amateur, whatever his shortcomings,
brought much that was valuable to an intelligentsia rapidly imbibing
a Western European culture of which it had hitherto had only a
rather scanty knowledge, and Annenkov's importance as a source
of enlightenment to his contemporaries therefore amply compensated for his mediocrity as a writer and thinker. His own temperament, moreover, must have suited him for this role and coloured his
convictions, as indeed Granovsky's nature had helped to determine
his own function. For Annenkov was amiable, pleasure-loving and
popular. 'Our good fellow' (*nash dobryy*) was the nickname by
which friends frequently referred to him in their letters. Grigoriy
Tolstoy, an eccentric Russian nobleman close to radical circles in
Paris in the 1840s, gave Annenkov a letter of recommendation to
Karl Marx in which he said that Annenkov was a person whom
Marx was bound to like: one only had to see him in order to grow
fond of him.[3] Turgenev wrote in a similar vein to Pauline Viardot in
1847: Annenkov was *'un charmant garçon aussi fin d'esprit qu'il est
gros de corps'*.[4] (Annenkov's corpulence and his love of food and
wine were a frequent source of amusement to his friends.) Granovsky, in a letter of 1854 to his wife, endorsed the general view of
Annenkov as a 'marvellous person'.[5] Not surprisingly, then,
Annenkov's opinions, like Granovsky's and Botkin's, were heard
with respect and enjoyment. At the same time he exercised a
conciliatory influence on his friends, showing in his personal dealings with others the toleration fundamental to the liberal outlook.
No sooner had Annenkov returned from abroad in 1848, Nekrasov
wrote in a letter to Turgenev, than he brought 'everyone together
and back to life again'.[6]

Annenkov belonged to precisely that generation which also
produced Belinsky, Herzen, Granovsky, Botkin, Kavelin and Turgenev and to the social background from which the majority of that
generation's more liberal members were drawn. He was born in
June 1813 (or, according to some sources, 1812) into a family of
middle-ranking gentry who had traditionally served the state and
who owned landed property in the then remote Volga province of
Simbirsk. Two of his brothers were to achieve high rank in the

tsarist hierarchy. Fyodor, who was eight years Pavel's senior, rose to the position of governor of Nizhniy Novgorod, and Ivan, a year older than Pavel, had a distinguished military career in the Life Guards' Cavalry Regiment, of which he himself wrote a history.[7] Pavel himself was educated in the St Petersburg Mining College and progressed as far as the courses on mining engineering, but did not complete them. (He could hardly have been suited to these studies.) He briefly attended lectures in the history faculty of St Petersburg University, but did not formally register as a student there and took no degree. He made a desultory attempt in 1833 to serve, at the rank of Collegiate Secretary, in the civil service in the Ministry of Finance, but he was evidently no more dedicated to this activity than to his academic pursuits. It was already the artistic world that interested him most of all. He frequented the literary circles of St Petersburg and in particular that which gathered around Gogol (whom Annenkov met for the first time at a literary *soirée* in about 1832) and which included former school-fellows of the writer from the Nezhin *lycée*.[8] These circles, however, were not preoccupied in the 1830s with the intense philosophical speculation and study of Hegelianism which absorbed Stankevich, Granovsky, Herzen, Botkin, Bakunin, Belinsky and others whose first intellectual home was Moscow. It is perhaps for this reason that Belinsky, who met Annenkov shortly after his own arrival in St Petersburg from Moscow, at first found him rather alien, although he did like him from the beginning.[9] At any rate Annenkov, as a resident of St Petersburg, had no important contact with the future Westernisers before his first journey abroad in 1840, and it is with that journey that his intellectual biography should properly begin.

'Letters from Abroad'

It is a little remarked but surely important fact that the magnificent development of Russian thought and literature in the 1840s, 1850s and 1860s went hand in hand not only with intense scrutiny of the works of Western European writers but also with the acquisition of much first-hand experience of life in the countries to which those writers belonged. Neither Pushkin nor Lermontov had ever crossed the frontiers of the Russian Empire, but the major Russian writers of the succeeding generations, such as Gogol, Turgenev, Tolstoy and Dostoyevsky, all travelled extensively in Europe, albeit with varying degrees of satisfaction. For the Russian educated class, the 1840s and 1850s were decades of great journeyings through foreign lands as well as intellectual and spiritual odysseys through European letters. These journeyings came to be regarded as an indispensable part of the education of a cultivated Russian, the final stage in a man's intellectual and moral upbringing. They gave breadth to his horizons and reinforced the civilised values with which his reading had acquainted him but which were wanting in his Russian environment. Moreover, extensive travel encouraged the toleration characteristic of the liberal intellectual who in the late 1850s was to find it difficult to accept the radicalism to which familiarity with Western doctrines (but not with Western societies) eventually led the *raznochintsy*. For an understanding of alien ways of life, familiarity with foreign customs and traditions manifestly respected by most people in the places in which they had sprung up – these insights were bound to dampen enthusiasm for revolutionary change according to some preconceived pattern with a supposedly universal validity. Again, awareness of the extent of human achievement in general and of the precious heritage of Western man in particular bred a fear of social cataclysms which might sweep away more than the ills it was hoped they would cure. Besides, political considerations were hardly ever uppermost in the minds of the Russian travellers of the 1840s and 1850s. Such considerations seemed unimportant amid the welter of impressions that were to be enjoyed for their own sake, such as the beauty of the constantly changing landscape, the rich and varied architecture, the delights of foreign cuisines and the simple luxury of a good dinner and a comfortable bed with clean sheets after a long day's journey in the Mediterranean summer. It is perhaps significant in this connection that enthusiasm for foreign travels of the sort made by Botkin and Annenkov diminished in the 1860s. Of course, the *raznochintsy* lacked the wealth and leisure at the disposal of the 'men of the 1840s'; nor could their impressions be so fresh once Western Europe had been so thoroughly traversed in all directions by their compatriots. But it is also tempting to suggest that the *raznochintsy*, with their firm political convictions and their comparatively rigid view of the world lacked the older men's intellectual curiosity, their thirst for fresh experience and their simple capacity for pleasure (or at any rate the sense of freedom from moral guilt which enabled the 'fathers' to indulge that capacity). Many *raznochintsy* did visit the West, but generally

speaking it was for some practical purpose, such as evasion of the
tsarist police, and they showed relatively little inclination to explore
the territory beyond the site they had chosen for their self-imposed
exile.

Annenkov's first stay in the West, which lasted from October
1840 to November 1843, furnished material for his series of thirteen
Letters from Abroad which were addressed to Belinsky and
published in *Otechestvennyye zapiski* in 1841, 1842 and 1843.[10] The
letters are impressionistic and are informed by no guiding ideas or
themes which might enable one to ascribe to Annenkov at this stage
any distinct political philosophy or even any very clearly defined set
of values. Nor did they have the *brio* which in many places was to
enliven Botkin's more celebrated *Letters on Spain*, let alone the
brilliance of Herzen's later essays in the same genre. But, as one of
the earliest attempts made in the age of Nicholas to acquaint the
Russian reading public with Western society and its heritage, the
letters do reflect more clearly and artlessly than other travelogues of
the decade the sense of delight and awe which understandably
overcame the Russian traveller when for the first time he left
Russia's sombre landscapes, provincial philistinism and physical
discomforts for the relative luxuriance, refinement and affluence of
the West. Thus, arriving together with Katkov[11] in Hamburg after
disembarking at Travemünde, Annenkov is immediately impressed
by the imposing Gothic architecture and the constant bustle of a
thriving commercial city with a stock exchange to which thousands
flocked every day and where, it seemed, all the newspapers of
Europe were available. The enthralled tourist attended a recital by
Liszt and with due reverence visited the scene of some of Hoffmann's drinking bouts. In Saxony he admired the rich soil and
splendid views. He spent 'two delightful weeks' in Dresden, where
he viewed paintings by Raphael, Murillo, Correggio and Titian and
where he marvelled at copies of exquisite statues from Italian
palaces and villas. And in Prague he found a legend at every step.
Hitherto, he remarked, he had only understood 'conditionally' all
that one might consider pleasing, but now, with first-hand knowledge, he understood it differently.[12]

The fifth, sixth and seventh letters of Annenkov's series 'from
abroad' are devoted to his first extensive wanderings in Italy, in the
course of which he visited, among other places, Venice, Ferrara,
Bologna, Ancona, Rome, Naples, Sicily, Pisa, Florence, Modena,

Parma, Piacenza, Milan and Genoa. (It was during this first visit to
Italy, incidentally, that Annenkov stayed in Rome with Gogol, who
was at that time writing the first part of *Dead Souls*, and acted as
amanuensis for the first six chapters of the novel.) These letters are
particularly worthy of note, and not merely because their comparative lengthiness and freedom suggest that Annenkov was increasing
in confidence as a descriptive writer as his travels and his record of
them progressed. More importantly, these letters reflect that deep
affection for Italy that was to be felt from this period on by many
members of the Russian intelligentsia. Such an attachment is not
altogether easy to explain, though no doubt it is partly due to the
beauty of the country and its light and radiance and to the Russian
perception of the character of the Italian people as carefree and
expansive and therefore in some measure similar to that of the
Russian as he liked to see himself. For Annenkov, however, Italy
had an additional attraction which was later to assume considerable
importance for men of liberal persuasion who feared the impover-
ishment of their lives and culture by the encroachment of political
concerns on them. Italy, and Rome in particular, had a timeless
quality, an apparent remoteness from the outside world, that made
it a haven of tranquillity not only for the weary traveller but also for
the refugee from the political bustle of the age. The place was a
monument to art and to the eternal value of artistic beauty.
Anyone entering Rome, Annenkov wrote,

detaches himself from the present, forgets newspapers, Europe, discoveries, and gives himself up to recollections of history and art: there is no
[subject of] conversation other than a statue, a painting, some new find in
this land already full of the masterpieces of the ancients.[13]

It is an idea to which Annenkov returns in the following, sixth
letter, written perhaps under the impression of the inspiration
Gogol was currently finding in the city. 'Imagine,' he asks his
readers,

that there is on earth a capital to which one must come in order to enter
into oneself and live in a sort of noble and fertile solitude in the midst of
antiquity and works of art, many of which are frontiers of creation which
people will not now cross. The voice of Europe comes here muffled and
barely audible; but this is not a Chinese separation from universal life,
rather something solemn and lofty like an out-of-town house in which some
great man has worked. Sometimes it seemed to me that Europe was
deliberately keeping this wonderful city, surrounded by dead fields with

the remains of aqueducts, tombs and theatres, as a villa to which to send her sons to calm down after turmoil, anxieties, factions and any disquiet.[14]

One would always be affected by the moral grandeur of such a city, a grandeur which found expression in the proud and independent character and inborn aesthetic taste of the people who now lived around Rome. And as soon as Annenkov departed from Italy and arrived in Geneva, 'on the soil of political, historical and philo-sophical questions and every sort of disquiet', he appreciated the ample pleasures of Italian life all the more.[15]

France, the country most closely associated in the minds of Russians of the 1840s with modernity and political concerns, made a comparatively unfavourable impression on Annenkov. As yet he showed no strong sympathy either for the socialist movement, which was gaining momentum there, or for the bour-geoisie which was prospering under the régime of Guizot (about whom Annenkov did not as yet have a great deal to say).[16] Several aspects of life, however, did strike Annenkov forcibly; for example, the omnipresence of women, who even worked in shops and restaurants, and the great freedom of the debate which was conducted in journals representing all sections of society and all political interests. But, if such freedom was enviable to a Russian in the age of Nicholas, nevertheless Annenkov regretted the price paid for the consequent intrusion of politics into every-day life: it drove away 'artistry' and 'pure inspiration'. He also disapproved of the popular 'almanacs' or 'physiologies', as they were known, whose authors were shortly to be emulated in Russia by the writers of the 'natural school'. These 'little books' gleamed in the booksellers' windows, often open at their 'most torrid pages', and their philippics against the prevailing order of things thus infected the passer-by whether he liked it or not. Eugène Sue, one of the most successful exponents of the genre, Annenkov as yet detested.[17]

On leaving France Annenkov travelled again in Germany, pro-ceeding down the Rhine from Cologne to Ems, Wiesbaden, Heidel-berg, Stuttgart, Ulm, Augsburg and Munich. (He went on to visit the Austrian Tyrol and Lake Constance too, before returning to Russia in the autumn of 1843.) For the traveller recently struck by the French preoccupation with contemporary reality, Germany, with its antithetical tendency to elevate everyday matters to the level of a weighty 'scholarly, historical or philosophical theme', offered a not altogether pleasant contrast. The French obsession with current affairs might have obscured the worth of those eternal values which Annenkov had cherished in Italy but, treated in the German manner, modernity lost its vivid colours, contemporary history became 'uninteresting' and 'abstract', and opinions took precedence over individuals, characters and passions.[18] This appreciation of the value of the middle ground, Annenkov's desire to counterbalance apparently antithetical tendencies, already went hand in hand with other attitudes which also foretokened the moderate position Annenkov was subsequently to occupy and which found expression in random observations in the closing letters of his cycle. Clearly he did not entirely approve, for example, of the 'spirit of criticism', which was so highly developed in the West. Again, he regretted the apparent intellectual chaos introduced into the modern world by the uncompromising struggle for the assertion of one's principles and proposed to seek solace and stability by supplementing the diet of modern polemical reading with draughts of timeless art:

After the pure crystal romance of Uhland, which resembles painting on glass, I read the vigorous imprecation of Anastasius Grün who represents the other side of the coin, a complement, as it were, to the old chivalric tendency of the Swabian poet. When the imagination tires I go over to Rückert and in the splendour of his verse and oriental images I forget all that is one-sided or harrowing in modernity . . .[19]

Finally, he has reservations about the modern tendency to view art as a means of securing aesthetic glory for a nation in the industrial age. It is a tendency that has given rise to an 'incessant, bewitching chain of pictures, drawings, figurines, candelabras, chandeliers, clocks, bronzes, diadems and so forth', but one which the great tramontane artists of the Renaissance would surely have deplored.[20]

Annenkov's views on politics and art, then, are not sharply defined in the early 1840s, and yet in his instinctive responses to what he saw and read during his first stay in Western Europe we may already discern the contours of the moderate position he was later to adopt. He loves peace and shuns turmoil. He reveres the artistic achievements of classical antiquity and the Renaissance, achievements which embody lasting values. And he fears the vulgarisation of art and life itself by politics.

Annenkov and Marx

As one who respected things European, on which he could furnish first-hand information, Annenkov naturally began to move in the Westernist circle of the intelligentsia when he returned to Russia in 1843. Belinsky he had already met towards the end of 1839 (though he was evidently not nearly so close to the critic at this period as Botkin: by the middle of 1840 the two had still not met on more than about ten occasions).[21] He had also called once on Botkin in the summer of 1840.[22] The other important members of the Muscovite Westernist circle, on the other hand, were known to Annenkov only by their reputations before his return to Russia and it was not until 1843 that he met Herzen and Granovsky.

Annenkov was an observant witness of the main developments which were taking place in Russian intellectual life at this time. He noted the impact of Granovsky's famous public lectures in the winter of 1843–4 and the increasing antagonism between his Westernist friends and the Slavophiles. He was also present at Sokolovo in the summer of 1845 when the first signs of discord began to be felt within the Westernist camp itself. Even inside Russia, though, Annenkov tended to lead an itinerant existence, dividing his time between Moscow, St Petersburg and his estate in Simbirsk province. He seems, moreover, to have made little contribution personally to the debates which were taking place in the mid 1840s. It is therefore reasonable to pay relatively little attention to this short phase of his life and to turn instead to his second stay in the West, for which he again left Russia at the beginning of 1846. He was to remain abroad for over two and a half years more, though now he travelled less and spent long periods in Paris, where he rented an apartment in the Rue Caumartin.

It was quite understandable that Annenkov should in the mid 1840s gravitate towards Paris, the European city most closely associated with new political ideas and movements. For the leading members of the Westernist intelligentsia, to whom Annenkov had grown close during his stay in Russia, had themselves by now taken on a much more radical complexion than they had had when Annenkov first went abroad in 1840. True to the spirit of this section of the intelligentsia, Annenkov tended during this his second stay in the West to cultivate acquaintances in radical circles, and these included not merely Slav *émigrés* such as Bakunin and, from early

1847, Herzen, but also Western socialists such as Marx. Annenkov, however, never wholly committed himself to any intellectual system or unreservedly accepted a particular point of view, and even during this period his radicalism proved to be cautious and equivocal. Scepticism already, or perhaps one should say still, informed all his major statements of opinion. It coloured his celebrated, though brief, correspondence with Karl Marx in 1846–7; his *Parisian Letters* of 1847–8; and his contributions (or at least what we can reconstruct of them) to the debate of those years on the role and value of the bourgeoisie in Western European history.

Annenkov called on Marx (and Engels) in Brussels soon after leaving Russia in 1846, in all probability in March,[23] and was well received. In his memoirs he has left a fine portrait of the young socialist's imposing bearing, although the portrait is darkened by Annenkov's perhaps retrospective imputation to Marx of the imperiousness and authoritarianism of a 'democratic dictator'.[24] Annenkov also gives a valuable account of a meeting at which Marx ferociously criticised the tailor Weitling for inciting the German workers, among whom Weitling had a considerable following, to take revolutionary action before conditions were ripe and before he himself was able to present to them a rigorous scientific doctrine explaining their predicament and defining their objectives.[25] Annenkov's relations with Marx remained warm after his departure from Brussels and he wrote the German socialist several letters (six are extant) after his arrival in Paris. Of these the most interesting concern Annenkov's reactions to Proudhon's book, *System of Economic Contradictions, or Philosophy of Poverty*. As a matter of fact, Annenkov had already written most favourably of Proudhon's book in his first *Parisian Letter*, where he praised Proudhon's independence among the various socialist factions and commended him for demonstrating that society's only salvation lay in the search for the '*law* according to which wealth develops correctly and by itself'.[26] In a private letter written later in the same month (November 1846), however, Annenkov diffidently sought Marx's opinion on Proudhon's book. Proudhon's ideas on God, providence and the duality of spirit and matter seemed very confused, Annenkov confessed, but the sections in his book which dealt with economic matters were 'unusually strong'. No book had ever shown so clearly, Annenkov declared (taking up a point also made in his first *Parisian Letter*), that civilisation could not renounce its achievements and that all that had been gained through the division of labour, the introduction of machinery and the development of competition had been won for ever. All the same, Proudhon's book evidently left Annenkov in some confusion, for he admitted that it had increased his doubts rather than dispelled them.[27]

Proudhon's book appeared at a time when Marx and Engels were still in the process of formulating the historical materialism which was shortly to find popular expression in *The Communist Manifesto* and which was to underpin their 'scientific socialism'. Having settled in Brussels after his expulsion from Paris by the French government early in 1845, Marx, in collaboration with Engels, had rapidly written *The German Ideology*, the two thinkers' first protracted statement of historical materialism, but no publisher had been found for that work. Thus it was not until the appearance, in 1847, of Marx's response to Proudhon's book, facetiously entitled *The Poverty of Philosophy*, that this fundamental aspect of Marxist doctrine was first publicly set out. And, since Marx's reply of December 1847 to Annenkov's rather perplexed letter represented the first reaction of the German socialist to Proudhon's book and contained a very precise outline of the work which was shortly to appear as *The Poverty of Philosophy*, this reply has assumed some importance in the broad history of socialist ideas as well as in the narrower record of the intellectual searchings of the Russian intelligentsia.

Writing with a sureness of which Annenkov, for all his desire to see opposing points of view, must have been envious, Marx dismissed Proudhon's book, which he had belatedly received and only quickly read, as 'bad, very bad'. Proudhon put forward a 'laughable philosophy' because he did not understand the complex structure of modern society in all its ramifications. Proudhon detected in history a series of social evolutions, a form of progress which he attributed, after the fashion of Hegel, to the operation of some universal reason. The solution of contemporary questions therefore lay not in a social movement but in 'dialectical rotations' taking place in Proudhon's own mind. History, in Proudhon's opinion, was made by scholars capable of stealing God's 'innermost thoughts'. Marx then proceeded to explain what he perceived to be the true nature of economic development. Certain stages in the development of a people's productive forces gave rise to certain forms of exchange and consumption and even to a particular social structure, a particular organisation of the family and social classes, and to a political structure which gave expression to that civil society. It was therefore a people's method of production and system of economic relations that determined their social and political existence. Moreover, the economic forms within the framework of which a people carried on its production, consumption, and exchange were '*transient and historical*'. As new productive forces were acquired so people changed their method of production and all the economic and other relations associated with the old method. It was therefore a mistake to see economic categories, as Proudhon, in common with other 'bourgeois' economists, saw them, that is to say as 'eternal laws'; rather they were historical laws valid only for a particular phase in the development of man's productive forces.[28]

Annenkov, replying to Marx's letter in January 1847, began with gushing praise for Marx's assessment of Proudhon's book. Marx's view, by virtue of its 'correctness, clarity and, most importantly, its attempt to remain within the framework of the real', had had a 'bracing' effect on Annenkov. One was constantly in danger of being dazzled by the 'false glitter of the abstract idea', for one so often gave in to the 'temptation to accept the supposedly magnificent constructions of the intellect wholly engrossed in itself as the last word of science and philosophy!' A friendly voice which opportunely brought one back to economic and historical facts carried so much more weight than systems of 'pure categories and logical contradictions' grounded not in real life, history and science but in the imagination.[29] Now there is no doubt that Annenkov had sound and genuine reasons for endorsing Marx's critique of Proudhon's book in this way. The Westernisers themselves, after all, had struggled to discard Hegelian notions, that 'junk' which Marx disparaged in Proudhon's book. Marx's determination to deal with the concrete, the practical, as opposed to the abstract and the theoretical, was also in keeping with the spirit of the Westernisers of the mid 1840s. Nevertheless it is not difficult to detect behind Annenkov's fulsome words a mind which was not ready to accept systematic and uncompromising explanations of complex phenomena. For the platitudes of the first part of the letter gave way to observations and further questions which betrayed Annenkov's reservations about Marx's interpretation. Annenkov was still inclined to think, for example, that what he called the 'critical part' of Proudhon's book deserved serious attention: Proudhon had made a valuable attack, for instance, on Louis Blanc's ideas. Again, the isolation in which Proudhon's views had placed him seemed to Annenkov to have a certain splendour. More importantly, Annenkov voiced the anxiety of the liberal worried by the possibility that socialism would achieve equality by tending to reduce the high standards attained by the minority rather than by raising the low standard at which the majority currently existed. He was disturbed by the thought that communism presupposed renunciation of some of the 'advantages of civilisation' and some of the 'prerogatives of the individual' which had been won with such difficulty. And did not communism, Annenkov asked Marx, presuppose a high standard of universal morality which it would be very difficult to attain? If that were the case communism would still be 'fine', but it would no longer be a 'necessary product of human development'; an attempt would have to be made to implant it, and the attempt would have only the same chances of success as any other experiment, any other instance of the forcible introduction of some innovation in society.[30]

These misgivings about socialism in its revolutionary and authoritarian form ensured that Annenkov's instinctive sympathy for the more cautious and peaceful anarchist Proudhon would not be eroded by Marx's rational arguments, however eloquent and persuasive they might seem. Indeed, Annenkov would in all probability have supported Proudhon's own exhortation to Marx, contained in a letter of 1846:

Let us give the world the example of a learned and far-sighted tolerance, but let us not, because we are at the head of a movement, make ourselves the leaders of a new intolerance, let us not pose as the apostles of a new religion, even if it be the religion of logic, the religion of reason.[31]

At any rate Annenkov's correspondence with Marx was soon to lapse after their exchange of letters on Proudhon in the winter of 1846–7. Marx's last extant letter to Annenkov, written in December 1847 from London, where Marx had gone in order to attend the second congress of the Communist League and to attempt to establish connections with the Chartists, contained not a polemical treatise but a short request for the sum of 100–200 francs which might, he hoped, ease his family's desperate financial plight.[32]

Annenkov's 'Parisian Letters' and his relations with Belinsky in 1847–8

Annenkov's *Parisian Letters*, which relate to the period November 1846 to January 1848, convey the same impression as his letters to Marx, namely that of a man deeply interested in the issues and currents of his day but determined to avoid firm commitment to any particular idea or faction. Like the earlier *Letters from Abroad*, the *Parisian Letters* were a loose collection of description, comment and anecdote on miscellaneous facets of foreign, in this instance Parisian, life from the current economic debates to collections of art and the quality of French metalwork. Although they are plainly more mature than the *Letters from Abroad*, the *Parisian Letters* still lack the perspicacity, exuberance and sheer artistry of Herzen's *Letters from the Avenue Marigny* (though it is possible that Herzen's choice of this genre owed something to the success of Annenkov's exploitation of it). Nor did Annenkov's letters reflect such strong personal sympathies as Herzen's with their admiration for the common people and their contempt for the bourgeoisie. With even-handedness, though, there went an intellectual shapelessness. The letters contained abundant raw material, but it was not clear how the reader was intended to construe it. The fault was perceived by Gogol, who told Annenkov that the letters showed much keen observation and accuracy, but the 'accuracy of a daguerreotype'. The author himself, Gogol felt, was like 'wax' which had not taken shape, 'albeit wax of the highest quality, transparent and pure'. It was not apparent to Gogol why the letters had been written and he gently rebuked Annenkov for failing to pose himself any 'serious question'.[33]

Annenkov's political position, in so far as one can infer it from the *Parisian Letters*, is closer to that of Granovsky and Botkin than to that of Belinsky and Herzen. Unlike the latter, he is prepared to underline the positive aspects of a society not nurtured under despotism of the sort to which Russians were accustomed. He valued the French ability to make dispassionate assessments and to carry out 'praiseworthy scrutiny of contradictory opinions', and he noted (wrongly, as it turned out) the stability of the existing order. Most striking of all, Annenkov was unenthusiastic about the various schools of socialist thought currently represented in France. In his very first letter he derided Pierre Leroux, who had 'changed the theory of the distribution of wealth in society' by insisting that the share of each should be determined not in accordance with his 'talent' but in accordance with his needs. This proposition Annenkov considered eccentric. It remained, he remarked facetiously, only to 'distribute social wealth according to temperaments, according to a partiality for brunettes or blondes . . . ' At the end of the same letter he also mocks Cabet's proposal that he and Considérant should hire a large hall and hold a public debate about the respective merits of their utopias – 'phantasmagorias', Annenkov calls them – in order to determine where it would be 'sweeter to drink and eat, in Icaria or the phalansteries', and to decide which thinker therefore had bestowed the greater benefit on mankind.[34]

Annenkov's attitude towards the French Revolution of 1789 is also unsympathetic. He treats it as a terrifying lesson, not a source of inspiration. His description of a current play on the subject, for example, is couched in terms of fear. Two or three times the audience had heard the well-known song (Annenkov is alluding to the 'Marseillaise') 'from which France had suffered so much'. On one occasion the 'fearful committee' appeared (Annenkov presumably has in mind the Committee of Public Safety). And once even the 'terrible assembly itself', that is to say the Convention, was shown, with Danton declaiming while Saint-Just presided. Anyone who valued the 'successes of European civilisation', Annenkov believed, would note with satisfaction the extent to which certain sounds had become muted and to which certain names had lost their potency. The public now seemed more easily moved by martial valour and by the thirst for glory than by revolutionary passions. This apparent change among the French public and the tendency to see the French Revolution as a thing of the past Annenkov considered an 'unbelievable success'.[35] That was not to say that he approved flippant denigration of leading figures of the French Revolution or of those who currently voiced social concern. He was offended, for example, by a play in which the beautiful image of Charlotte Corday had been distorted and by a parody of Pyat's play, *The Ragpicker of Paris*. But he could not muster the socialist's enthusiasm for the Revolution or his profound compassion for the masses. He was consequently unsympathetic when, on his return to Paris after a short absence in the summer of 1847, he found the populace in surly mood. The July festivities, the firework displays, the public concert in the Tuileries and the dazzling illuminations in the Champs-Elysées were all 'very sumptuous and rich', and yet the people seemed distracted. Admittedly current political scandals might preoccupy a few minds, but they were not sufficient grounds, in Annenkov's opinion, for 'remaining gloomy at such an entertaining spectacle'. Whenever would the people rejoice if not now?[36]

It was quite in keeping with the spirit of the time, however, that the indifference or even antipathy to socialism which was reflected in the *Parisian Letters* should not have prevented Annenkov from remaining on good terms with Bakunin, Herzen and Belinsky, who had by now adopted more uncompromising radical positions than any other leading members of the Russian intelligentsia. Indeed, Annenkov grew closer to Belinsky in 1847, the last year of Belinsky's life, than ever before. Disturbed by the increasingly ominous news from St Petersburg about Belinsky's health, Annenkov contributed 400 francs towards the cost of sending the critic on a journey to the West in order that he might visit a spa, consult doctors and also see at first hand the nations whose literatures and historical fortunes he had followed so closely. (Belinsky had never before been to the West.) Belinsky was greatly touched by Annenkov's generosity and even more by his friend's decision to postpone a journey he had proposed to make to Greece and Turkey and to travel instead to Silesia to meet Belinsky after his departure from Russia.[37] Annenkov duly arrived in Salzbrunn, where the waters were reputed to assist the curing of pulmonary complaints, in June 1847 (NS). It was here, in Annenkov's presence, that Belinsky composed his famous 'Letter to Gogol' in which, in response to some lines addressed to Belinsky at the end of a letter Gogol had sent to Annenkov, Belinsky furiously rebuked the novelist for betraying the writer's vocation. The restless Turgenev, who had also come to Salzbrunn to meet Belinsky, soon became bored by the inactivity forced on the company of the small provincial town and abandoned his friends on a flimsy pretext for Berlin and London. It was left to Annenkov alone, therefore, to accompany Belinsky to Dresden, Leipzig, Weimar, Eisenach, Frankfurt and Mainz, thence by boat up the Rhine to Cologne, on to Brussels and finally to Paris, where Belinsky remained until September, when he returned to Russia, without Annenkov, via Berlin.[38]

Evidently the modes of travel chosen by Annenkov were not always to Belinsky's liking. The ride to Frankfurt in a stage-coach shared with German travellers who smoked cigars and insisted on

keeping the windows closed he found particularly unpleasant. Nor
could life have been easy for the ascetic Belinsky with such a
bibulous companion. Annenkov was constituted in such a way,
Belinsky complained in a letter to his wife, as to require a régime
diametrically opposed to the one that suited Belinsky himself.
Annenkov had at first drunk a half bottle of wine with his dinner
each evening, but then found that it was better for his health to
drink a whole one. Annenkov could only be healthy in a noisy city
where one could not go to bed before two in the morning.[39] In spite
of these differences, however, Annenkov must have been of the
greatest value to Belinsky as he made his way, ailing and vulner-
able, through foreign lands for the first time. Annenkov was for
Belinsky a much travelled and worldly-wise guide, a well informed
tutor in the latest developments in European letters and politics,
and, no doubt, an amiable companion with whom Belinsky could
freely discuss all the questions that currently interested him.

Unfortunately Annenkov, who devoted the last three chapters of
The Marvellous Decade to Belinsky's visit to Western Europe, is not
only as digressive as ever on this subject but also concentrates on
Belinsky's moral and literary views (of which he offers his own
questionable interpretation) and tells us nothing of the content of
the social and political conversations which the two men must have
had.[40] We may assume from Belinksy's subsequent letters to
Annenkov, however, that these conversations touched upon such
topics as constitutional government, the position of the Russian
peasantry and the role of the bourgeoisie in European history, and
we may even infer Annenkov's views on the latter subject, at least,
with some certainty. Belinsky is no doubt taking up a matter they
had already discussed, for example, when in September, after his
return to Russia, he reports to Annenkov how the Prussian king had
contemptuously dismissed the *Stände*, the German Estates or
parliament, when the more radical members of the body began to
pose a threat to his authority. Annenkov himself had been sceptical
about the value of the Prussian system of 'parliamentary chatter',
though he had been curious, as he set out from Paris *en route* for
Silesia, to 'listen to the Germans holding forth'.[41] Belinsky seems to
be confirming that nothing could come of such an experiment, for
the people needed potatoes, not a constitution, which was desired
only by the educated town dwellers.[42] Again, Annenkov is the
recipient of a long letter written in December 1847, in which

Belinsky, with great accuracy, reports the deliberations currently taking place in the Russian government on the possibility of abolishing serfdom, which Nicholas himself was said to have described to members of the gentry as a brake on the development of trade and industry.[43] Finally, in his last letter to Annenkov, dictated on 15 February 1848, Belinsky returned to the subject of the bourgeoisie, which they had evidently discussed, together with Bakunin, Herzen and others, in Paris. Belinsky now considerably revised the opinions he had put forward only two months earlier in a letter to Botkin,[44] with the result that he came to occupy a position close to Annenkov's own. Reacting against Bakunin's and the Slavophiles' glorifications of the masses, Belinsky claimed to have cast off his 'mystical belief in the people'. The people had never liberated themselves. Everything had always been achieved by individuals. Belinsky regretted that in arguments with Annenkov on the subject of the bourgeoisie he had called Annenkov a 'conservative'; he was now ready to concede that Annenkov was an 'intelligent person' and that he, Belinsky, was an 'ass squared'. It seemed to Belinsky that the 'whole future of France' lay in the hands of the bourgeoisie, that 'all progress' depended on the bourgeoisie alone and that the masses would merely play an 'auxiliary role' from time to time. And, whereas Bakunin hoped that Russia would be spared the emergence of a bourgeoisie – indeed Bakunin, like Herzen, took an unreservedly negative view of this class – Belinsky, on the other hand, now stated that it was 'clearly apparent' that an 'internal process of civil development' would not begin in Russia until the Russian gentry was turned into a bourgeoisie.[45]

Annenkov's tolerant, indeed respectful, attitude towards the bourgeoisie combined with his firm belief in the value of so much that modern Western civilisation had achieved, from its material comforts to its intellectual freedom, to preclude any enthusiasm on his part for the revolutionary disturbances of 1848. He must have been filled with alarm by the prospect of the wave of revolutionary eruptions which Bakunin exultantly predicted in a letter of April 1848, a wave that would 'wash off the face of the earth the ruins of the old world' and leave the 'good, garrulous *Bürger* in a bad way, a very bad way'.[46] Certainly the account of the revolutionary events of February which Annenkov gave to Gogol on his return to Russia later in the year distressed the novelist.[47] Indeed, Annenkov's attitude towards these events was sufficiently critical for Herzen to warn Granovsky and other Moscow friends in a letter (which Annenkov brought back to Russia with him!) not to give too much credence to Annenkov's version of them. Annenkov had taken up what seemed to Herzen a strange position of undiscriminating 'fairness' which prevented him from perceiving any 'large truth'. He had been carried away by the spirit of the early days of the revolution and even in the late summer of 1848 remained under their influence. Annenkov believed a republic had already come into being, whereas Herzen thought the revolution was still in its early stages. And he continued to defend Lamartine, the effective head of the provisional government formed after the fall of the monarchy in February, whereas Herzen detested the man because he was 'milk pudding' trying to make himself out to be 'hot punch'.[48]

Annenkov's aversion to revolutionary upheaval was not to find clear expression in print until the late 1850s, by which time the discussion of such matters had taken on a more immediate significance for Russians themselves. But it already ensured that Annenkov's views after his return to Russia in 1848 would be very moderate and that in the disputes of the 1850s he would naturally side with members of his own generation, such as Botkin, who had already expressed their own misgivings about socialism and the commitments which adherence to its doctrines dictated.

Annenkov's creative writing and his views in the 1850s as expressed in his correspondence with Turgenev

It is not surprising that Annenkov, the intimate friend of writers such as Gogol and Turgenev and the dilettante living in an age when *belles-lettres* enjoyed the greatest popularity and prestige in Russia, should have tried his hand at creative writing. His first attempt at fiction, a short story entitled *Kiryusha*, published in *Sovremennik* in 1847, dealt with the well-worn subject of the world-weary man who has a sense of superiority over others but who lacks the capacity for genuine and spontaneous feeling, regrets the waste of his passing youth and inspires in a young woman a pure and innocent love which he cannot reciprocate. The story is flawed, however, by its implausible dialogue, its unconvincing characterisation and its surfeit of authorial analysis.[49] Belinsky thought the story was 'very presentable' and tried to persuade Annenkov to write another,[50] but *Kiryusha* was plainly deficient by the standards of the short prose works written at the time by Turgenev, Druzhinin and a host of other authors. Nor were Annenkov's subsequent attempts at creative writing, the novellas *The Artist* and *She will perish* (both published in *Sovremennik* in 1848), any more successful.[51] Even the well disposed Belinsky was hard pressed to find encouraging words about the novella *She will perish*: Annenkov was 'not a poet but an ordinary story-teller', he admitted, though he did add as a consolatory afterthought that Annenkov was 'unusual' among ordinary story-tellers.[52]

A more successful medium than fiction was the descriptive sketch of Russian life at which Annenkov tried his hand in the years 1849–51. Nine such sketches, under the title *Letters from the Provinces*, were published in *Sovremennik*.[53] The idea of recording his impressions of Russian provincial life in a form similar to that used in his two cycles of letters from Western Europe may have been suggested to Annenkov by Gogol, who in his letter of 1847, in which he had given his opinion of the *Parisian Letters*, speculated: 'What if, instead of giving a daguerreotype of Paris, which is better known to a Russian than anything else, you started to write notes about Russian towns, beginning with Simbirsk ... '[54] Like Turgenev's *Sportsman's Sketches*, the bulk of which belong to the same period, Annenkov's *Letters from the Provinces* assisted the Russian nobleman in his rediscovery of the countryside of his own Russian heartland, where he experienced a sense of spiritual ease and felt a breath of freedom lacking in St Petersburg.[55] The sympathetic portrayal of types and customs to be found among the Russian common people was also bound to have a certain appeal in a period when interest in the masses was growing but when compassion for them could not be overtly expressed. Nekrasov, editor of *Sovremennik*, advised Annenkov to concentrate on this aspect of his subject and claimed that the letters, although neglected by literary critics, had been greeted enthusiastically by the journal's readership and had given rise to lively debate and correspondence.[56]

It is for his general participation in the literary and political discussions of the 1850s rather than for these mediocre attempts at creative writing, however, that Annenkov deserves our attention here. The very breadth of the circle of his acquaintances – he was close to Tolstoy, Goncharov, Ostrovsky, Saltykov-Shchedrin, Fet

and Nekrasov as well as Botkin, Druzhinin and Turgenev, and he
came to know Chernyshevsky quite well – assured him of a position
of some importance in the intelligentsia. But he was also one of the
leading exponents, together with Botkin, Druzhinin and Kavelin,
of the liberal outlook that began to form in the mid 1850s in
response to the challenge addressed to the older generation by the
raznochintsy. This response found expression in Annenkov's
literary criticism and, more effectively, in his work as editor and
memoirist. It can also be traced in his voluminous correspondence
with Turgenev, the bulk of which survives and has been published,
and to which it is particularly fruitful to turn in the first instance.

After Annenkov's return from the West in 1848 his relationship
with Turgenev became, and thereafter always remained, very close.
To Annenkov, as we shall see, Turgenev represented an exemplary
artist as well as a friend, while to the novelist '*Annenkovius venera-
bilis*' was a jovial companion, a highly esteemed judge of art and a
valuable critic of Turgenev's own works. Thus in 1853 Turgenev
asked S. Aksakov not to judge Annenkov by his *Letters from the
Provinces*, for Annenkov had 'not a lot of talent', but to believe that
Annenkov was an 'extremely intelligent person, with fine and sure
taste'.[57] Turgenev repeated this praise in a letter to Annenkov
himself, comparing his friend to Merck, an eighteenth-century
German literary critic in whom Turgenev showed considerable
interest at this time. Merck Turgenev described as a man endowed
with an 'unusually sure critical vision', a person who had the gift of
detachment and was able to make disinterested judgements. 'You
have several of Merck's features', Turgenev told Annenkov, 'at
least I know no one in whom I would have greater faith at the
present time.'[58] Three years later he reaffirmed that only in Botkin
and Annenkov did he now find critical powers.[59] And, although he
was sensitive to criticism of his own works, Turgenev repeatedly
sought Annenkov's opinion of them before submitting them for
publication (indeed, it became 'a sort of superstitious habit' with
him to do so) and he set great store by Annenkov's judgements and
heeded his advice, which was always very much to the point and
'valuable'.[60] Thus early in 1853 Turgenev was anxious to hear
Annenkov's personal opinion of the first five chapters of his first
attempt at a novel, *Two Generations*, and did not wish to proceed
without Annenkov's advice.[61] In the same year Annenkov made a
portentous criticism of Turgenev's story, *The Inn*, comparing Tur-

genev's character Akim with the eponymous hero of Harriet Beecher Stowe's *Uncle Tom's Cabin* (which had appeared in book form in 1852 and was translated into Russian in the following year). Both Akim and Uncle Tom seemed to Annenkov to be polemical rather than primarily artistic creations, and he was repelled by the political implications of the two works, which were directed against the institutions of serfdom and slavery respectively.[62] Turgenev took the advice to heart and, having read *Uncle Tom's Cabin* himself, resolved not to attempt more works like *The Inn*.[63] And it is perhaps worth noting that when he did next succumb to the temptation to make a more or less political statement in his art – in the novel *Smoke*, published in 1867 – the work lacked the artistic quality characteristic of Turgenev's fiction and marked the beginning of the decline of his powers as a novelist.

The correspondence between Annenkov and Turgenev, whose opinions on art (and politics) were remarkably similar, reflected very clearly the increasing impatience of the two men with any didactic, polemical or political tendencies in art. Thus early in 1853 Annenkov had an unexpected difference of opinion with Katenin, a now aged dramatist of Pushkin's generation who had condemned Pushkin's 'little tragedy', *Mozart and Salieri*, on the grounds that Pushkin had gratuitously imputed to his fictional Salieri a crime, the poisoning of Mozart, of which the historical personage had not in fact been guilty. Annenkov's reply, to the effect that Pushkin had in his Salieri wished to create an artistic type embodying envy, had struck Katenin as a shameful condonation of Pushkin's calumny. But to Annenkov – and Turgenev agreed with him – art had a 'code of morals' all of its own, separate from society's code.[64] In the same year both Annenkov and Turgenev rued the presence of 'tendency' in Ostrovsky's play, *Don't Sit in Another's Sleigh*, and criticised Nekrasov for what Annenkov called the 'almost anti-poetic' content of some of his poetry which had just been published in *Sovremennik*.[65]

As the predilection for 'tendency' and topical content in literature was reinforced in the mid 1850s by Chernyshevsky's dissertation and criticism, so the resolve of Annenkov and Turgenev to support an art free of ulterior considerations grew even stronger. 'Obviously you won't fool an old campaigner with noise, gold, melodramas and so forth', Annenkov wrote to Turgenev towards the end of 1856, when the gulf between liberals and radicals was widening, 'and for old campaigners like you and me poetry is as necessary as a digestive tablet'![66] It was precisely because of their desire to preserve 'poetry', in the broadest sense of the word, that both Annenkov and Turgenev set such great store in the mid 1850s by the developing talent of Tolstoy.[67] And for the same reason Annenkov ecstatically welcomed Turgenev's highly lyrical and poetic novella, *Asya*, with which he was familiar in advance of its publication in 1858. Annenkov was deeply moved, he told Turgenev, by the reappearance in literature of 'human characters', by talk of the 'soul', nature and poetry. Turgenev's novella would sweep through the current '*bestial* literature' like a 'peal of church bells'. Of course, the beasts would probably not cross themselves. Moreover, *Asya* was so subtly composed that ears 'accustomed to the massive roar of jackals and hyenas' might never understand its message. Its poetry was of no value to Chernyshevsky, Dobrolyubov and their ilk, for such people considered poetry an 'invention of the Germans which one couldn't even buy eggs with' and which was consequently of less value than a 'one-rouble bank note'. All the same, *Asya* emitted an 'electric atmosphere' by which even the 'coarsest dispositions' were bound to be enthralled.[68]

Annenkov's reservations about the views of the younger generation on art were of a piece with objections, which he also voiced in his correspondence with Turgenev, to their utilitarian morality. Annenkov frequently visited Chernyshevsky in 1857 and became better acquainted with him. He even had a certain admiration for him, as he admitted to Turgenev: Chernyshevsky sustained *Sovremennik* almost single-handed and with steadfast purpose. But he could not accept Chernyshevsky's tendency to subordinate truth itself – another absolute value, like beauty in art – to his immediate political purpose. 'Truth, literary, economic, historical and so forth, has no significance for him', Annenkov complained.

His main objective is to come to the aid of need [*sic*], to respond to want, to support aspiration, nothing else matters for him. The dexterity with which he skirts the truth is amazing and is equalled only by the modesty with which he confesses his guilt before it with his thin little voice. This thin little voice is a terrible scoundrel. The next day he begins the same thing all over again without the slightest sign of improvement. His articles agitate you when you read them. They are not so much a sea but a Bethesda's pool which this new angel flies down to each month to stir up the water. The young rush there very readily![69]

By the end of the 1850s the 'new angel', with his relativistic view of art and truth, had gained the upper hand over the older champions of absolute values, and in a letter written to Turgenev in July 1859 Annenkov provided a sort of postscript to the conflict that had been taking place. He drew Turgenev's attention to a book written by David Strauss (already well known in Russia for his book, *The Life of Jesus*) on Ulrich von Hutten (1488–1523), the Franconian humanist, writer and knight. Annenkov had just read Strauss' book and recommended it to Turgenev because, although it dealt with the period of the Reformation, it also happened to be the best book Annenkov knew on 'contemporary Russia'. 'It is astonishing,' Annenkov wrote to Turgenev,

how this German has understood the personality of Belinsky and of the majority of our figures, their relations among themselves and their attitudes to contemporary social questions and, finally, what an amazing, lively picture he has presented of the struggle of our awakened forces, their decline in the period of the first clash, and their resurgence, pointing out even what will become of them in the near future.

Perhaps the Russians of Annenkov's time were small in stature beside Strauss' figures, but the characters were 'one and the same' and so was the background against which they were set. So much was Annenkov under the influence of Strauss' book that he begged Turgenev, who was in France at the time, to acquire for him a good portrait of Hutten, that 'Vissarion Grigoryevich [i.e. Belinsky] among knights'.[70]

Strauss' biography of Hutten, read in the light of these comments, gives a fascinating insight into Annenkov's perception – which in retrospect appears extremely fair and accurate – of the schism which had taken place in the Russian intelligentsia between the mid 1840s and the late 1850s. It is easy to appreciate why Annenkov should have associated Hutten, as he was portrayed by Strauss, with Russia's 'furious Vissarion'. 'There was something of the knight errant in Ulrich von Hutten', as Strauss had put it. Like Belinsky, he expressed a withering contempt for the old order of things. He was a man 'called to free self-development, and the liberation of others from bondage'. He was given to ferocious outbursts on behalf of the weak against the powerful and privileged. Thus he incited the Swabians to put an end to the 'tyranny' of a 'bloodthirsty minister', to deliver others 'from terror' and themselves 'from ignominy', and he pronounced vehemently against the

Roman Church when it no longer seemed morally worthy of its
pre-eminence in the Christian world. His invective was fearless: he
held neither his life nor his property so dear as to refrain for their
sakes from an honourable enterprise. 'Indignation', Strauss tells us,
was the 'nurse of Hutten's genius'. The 'fire which could not find
vent through the sword illumined his writings' and gave them a
'martial, heroic tone' which accounts for their 'imperishable
charm'. His mode of thinking was rhetorical rather than logical,
and, like Belinsky again, he tended to abandon himself to his
feelings. Even Strauss' description of Hutten's appearance must
have reminded Annenkov of his late compatriot, for there was
'something austere and even wild' in the pale face of this 'slim,
insignificant-looking man'.[71]

   The humanist enlightenment in which Hutten had participated
could credibly be compared to the flowering of Russian culture in
the 1840s, although its scale, of course, was very different, as
Annenkov had admitted. The humanist scholars had 'helped to
raise men's minds out of the mists of the departing Middle Ages into
a purer air'. They had fought 'ignorance and scholasticism by
opening up the new sources of culture in thorough knowledge of the
ancient languages'. Had not the Russian 'men of the 1840s' likewise
helped to break down the obscurantism of semi-feudal society by
spreading knowledge and acquainting their contemporaries with
the civilisation of the West? And had they not, like the humanists,
helped men to form 'style and taste' and enabled men's minds to
attain a 'wider scope' and a 'finer mould'? It is probable that
Annenkov even saw Granovsky as in some measure comparable to
Erasmus, the 'living representative of all that the Western nations
had gained by the survival of the study of the ancients' and perhaps
the 'most highly cultivated man of his time'. Erasmus, moreover,
had resisted the transformation of serene scholarship into zealous
reformatory pamphleteering. He had 'considered that the friends of
the revival of learning should go to work persuasively rather than
polemically'. He remained a humanist, while Hutten in his later
years – and again the comparison with Belinsky was irresistible –
became 'more and more of a Reformer' and found 'blemishes' in the
humanist outlook. He came to regard Erasmus as one who was
'denying the principles which had previously actuated him', while
Erasmus looked on Hutten as one 'who had forsaken the cause for
which they had laboured together'.[72]

It is difficult to say whether Luther, the main representative of the movement to which Hutten ultimately gave his allegiance, was associated in Annenkov's mind with Chernyshevsky. But certainly the German pastor, as Strauss presented him, exhibited the same immoderation, intolerance and single-minded determination to pursue a factional interest that the Russian liberals of the 1850s detected in the *popovich*.* Luther's writings had a 'vehemence, bluntness and passion' bound to lead to 'disturbance and schism' and attempts by Erasmus to restrain him made him only more reckless. One imagines Annenkov ruefully sharing Erasmus' sentiments as they are described by Strauss:

What was the use of insulting those whom your object was to cure? What was the use of extravagances which were sure to give offence? He thought that the wisdom, urbanity, which we find in the sermons of Christ and Paul, were entirely wanting in Luther's preaching ... [73]

And yet Hutten and Luther, like Belinsky and Chernyshevsky after them, were representatives of 'historical forces' which outstripped the humanists and the 'men of the 1840s' and left the precursors of the new movements at a disadvantage. For humanism was 'large-minded, but faint-hearted'. Lutheranism was 'more narrow-minded' but its 'concentrated force, which swerved neither to the right hand nor the left, was necessary to success'. Humanism could be compared to the 'broad mirror-like Rhine at Bingen; it must become narrower and more rapid before it can make a way through the mountains to the sea'.[74] Thus Annenkov, by emphasising the bearing of Strauss' book on the Russian intellectual life of his own day, seems with remarkable honesty and resignation to have appreciated the disadvantage at which the liberal 'fathers' found themselves as their conflict with the *raznochintsy* developed.

Annenkov's literary criticism

Before considering those writings of Annenkov's in which his concern about the crisis of liberal values found implicit expression, we should pause to examine briefly the literary criticism which he produced in the 1850s. In volume his critical output during this

---

* i.e. 'son of a priest'; *popovich* is a colloquial, jocular word derived from the word *'pop'* (priest) and *'ovich'*, a patronymic suffix, and was commonly applied to Chernyshevsky, Dobrolyubov and other radical publicists of the 1850s and '60s who emanated from the lower clergy.

decade was quite considerable, but his criticism does not merit such serious or detailed attention as that of Druzhinin, who made the clearest statement of the aesthetic principles of the liberals and most skilfully applied those principles. For Annenkov never convincingly exhibited in print the critical prowess and insight which Turgenev and many others respected in his conversations and in the random literary judgements to be found in his letters. No doubt this shortcoming is due partly to Annenkov's dilettantism which prevented him from sustaining a coherent and interesting argument. But it is also due in large measure to the inelegance and, at times, obscurity of his prose. Statements as abominable as the following, for example, are by no means exceptional in his criticism:

We have intentionally imparted to our interrogative phrase a proviso which fastens the subject of our discourse to contemporaneity, to the present minute and to a certain definite order of phenomena . . . [75]

Even the well-disposed Turgenev admitted that Annenkov's critical ability was clouded by hopelessly muddled expression of his ideas, and Nekrasov and Druzhinin, in an epigram written in 1856, mocked him for posing 'insoluble riddles'.[76]

In his critical articles of the early and mid 1850s (but not in his articles of the late 1850s) Annenkov confines himself for the most part to an examination of the artistic properties of the works he reviews and tends studiously to avoid discussion of the social questions which are raised, explicitly or implicitly, by a writer's work. In this respect he is a typical representative of the liberal (and conservative) schools of criticism whose 'aesthetic' approach Dobrolyubov parodies at the beginning of his famous review of Turgenev's novel, *On the Eve*.[77] The salient features of this 'aesthetic' approach are set out by Annenkov in a poorly argued article, 'Old and New Criticism', which was published in *Russkiy vestnik* in 1856. 'Artistry', Annenkov contended here, was the 'vital question' for modern Russian literature; beside it all other questions, such as the demand for a certain interpretation of reality, assumed secondary importance. The criticism of the 1840s – Annenkov had Belinsky's work in mind – had given too much weight to qualities other than artistic ones. It had admittedly given rise to a 'secondary world of art' filled with burning conviction; but it had also made possible the proliferation of tendentious works which would in due course overshadow much-prized masterpieces. In any case, art was better able to answer to society's needs if it was free of all constraint. Whenever certain services were demanded of it – for example, 'among peoples in their infancy' – then it stubbornly resisted them. It would remain dumb in such circumstances, no matter how 'brilliant' the themes it was called upon to develop. Like Druzhinin, Annenkov felt that Pushkin in particular had suffered from the new attempts to reduce the importance of artistry as an end in itself. And yet reading Pushkin, Annenkov argued, did bring practical benefits. For those who wished to 'think *nobly* and to feel *nobly*' Pushkin was still an unrivalled teacher. Through his work the Russian reading public had become acquainted not merely with metrical refinement but also with refined ideas and an understanding of and respect for the 'finest spiritual feelings'. The further development of the Pushkinian artistic tradition would therefore prove to be of far more practical use to modern Russian society than attempts to emulate Gogol, who in his later years had misguidedly yielded to pressure to inject an unproductive '*edifying* element' into his art.[78]

The principles Annenkov upheld in his essay on the 'old and new criticism' were quite consistently applied by him in his reviews. Already in 1848, *à propos* of the new 'realism' of the writers of the 'natural school', he was warning that free artistic creation would give way to purely mechanical fabrication if authors constantly portrayed the same topical characters: it would become possible to 'knock together a story in the same way that a carriage is constructed from ready parts'.[79] Again, writing in 1853 on works which dealt with the life of the common people, he pleaded for moderation in the treatment of contemporary reality. There was, he claimed, an 'immutable aesthetic law' which permitted the introduction of antitheses or contrasts into a work of art only on condition that they were not irreconcilably inimical to one another. Antitheses could only be the 'property of art' if the possibility existed that they might be reconciled. The stark juxtaposition of good and evil, black and white, refinement and coarseness, belonged to the realm of scientific observation rather than to art, as the experienced writer, with his sense of measure and 'harmonious relations', readily appreciated.[80] In a further article, in which he reviewed S. Aksakov's *Family Chronicle*, Annenkov returned to the idea that pure art, on which no constraints are placed, may heal ills at the same time as bringing them to light and contends that Russian literature would henceforth play an important role in the shaping of society only in proportion as writers succeeded in adhering to the canons of free creation.[81] And in an article of 1859, on Pisemsky's novel, *A Thousand Souls*, Annenkov again pointedly chooses to make 'purely aesthetic remarks' even though the novel, dealing as it did with Russian officialdom, had considerable topical significance.[82]

Among Annenkov's critical articles there is one, however, a review of Turgenev's *Asya* under the innocuous title 'The Literary Type of the Weak Man', which deserves closer attention here than the rest, for in it Annenkov strays further than usual into socio-political territory and argues the case, in effect, for the sceptical liberal intellectual. On one level this article represented a response to Chernyshevsky, who in a famous review of *Asya*, entitled 'The Russian at the *rendez-vous*', had presented the weakness of the hero of Turgenev's novella as a form of moral bankruptcy to which a serf-owning gentry was inevitably prone.[83] Annenkov did not deny that the 'weak' type, of which Turgenev's hero was an example, was inactive, sceptical and egoistic. But he did believe, unlike Chernyshevsky, that this type was 'the only moral type' in contemporary Russian life. For, in the first place, the 'weak' character could at least recognise his faults and laugh bitterly at himself. And, in the second place, this type, whatever his faults, was superior to those around him, for there resided in him 'education, humanity and ... an understanding of national character'. There was much for the weak man to do, too. This 'small detachment of people' should examine the faults which prevented them from being as active as they might be. They should come down 'into the civil and social life of the crowd, making new channels and paths in it', and they should recognise the importance of their 'calling'. All these demands on the 'weak' type were 'very modest', but then it was not sensible in Annenkov's opinion to set people extraordinary tasks which presupposed vast abilities. The tasks confronting contemporary Russian society seemed to be such as could only be solved by 'honest, constant, persistent work together'. The efforts of the 'extraordinary, exceptional, huge individuals so highly prized by Western Europe' were not what was needed here. True, there was a 'particular type of valour' without which one could not even conceive of the existence of the state. The ability to accept misfortune stoically, to endure poverty and persecution and to preserve one's moral dignity amid universal decay – this quality was 'heroism' in its own way, but a 'secondary, domestic' form of heroism which stood in the same relation to heroism as it was conceived in the West as 'petty bourgeois [*meshchanskaya*] drama' stood to 'tragedy'. Annenkov was quite willing, then, to accept that no 'majestic oaks', as he put it, would grow on Russian territory provided that the surrounding vegetation flourished and bore fruit. The 'only exploit' at the present time would be 'honest labour based on moral convictions', and the 'only valour' the moral education of one's fellows and the inculcation in them of a sense of 'duty'. The instrument of this progress, the 'antidote' to the lover of the 'high-flown phrase', the '*historical* material' from which contemporary life would be created, was the 'weak' type whom Turgenev had depicted and whom Chernyshevsky had derided.[84]

In literary terms Annenkov's praise of the 'weak type' may be taken as a defence of the 'superfluous man' (with whom Russian writers had been so much preoccupied since the 1820s and whom Turgenev repeatedly portrays in his novels and novellas) in preference to the 'positive hero', the more purposeful man of action of whom Turgenev's Bulgarian patriot Insarov, in *On the Eve*, is an early example and whose emergence Dobrolyubov welcomes in his review of that novel. Literary types, though, were taken, of course, to represent the Russian educated man of certain periods in what seemed his most characteristic incarnations, and behind them there lay various conceptions of what that educated man ought to aspire to be. As for the 'weak type', he is on one level an embodiment of the introspective intellectual of the 1840s, and Annenkov, in drawing attention to his merits, is reasserting his claim to a fair judgement by posterity. Whatever the faults of this character – and Turgenev himself had revealed these faults in his first completed novel, *Rudin*, the most topical passages of which had been written in St Petersburg under the guidance of Annenkov, Druzhinin and other friends – nevertheless he had exhibited a warm humanity and a sincere idealism that Annenkov doubtless considered particularly valuable and worthy of preservation in an age of iconoclasm. Beyond the literary and social or historical dimensions of fictional characters, however, there lay a further, political, dimension which was becoming more readily apparent in the new conditions of the late 1850s. The 'superfluous man', the 'weak type', the ineffectual Oblomov, had come by now to be identified with the liberal intellectual, a humane member of the enlightened minority but not one of tsarism's militant opponents, and Annenkov, in defending this type, is making a thinly veiled defence of the Russian liberal's cautious gradualism as against the impatient revolutionary quest of the *raznochinets*. Like Botkin and Kavelin, he was much troubled by the prospect of social upheaval. (He himself had witnessed such upheaval in Paris.) Therefore while bolder or more destructive spirits encouraged heroic and valorous 'exploit', what Populists of the 1870s were to call *'podvig'*, Annenkov greatly preferred 'small deeds' of the sort to which sections of the intelligentsia would turn in the 1880s, after the failure of attempts to stir the masses by propaganda and to wring concessions from the government by means of terrorism, and his literary criticism made this preference clear enough.

Annenkov's edition of Pushkin and his works on Stankevich and Gogol

Annenkov's literary criticism was voluminous and earnest, but his position in the literary and socio-political debates of the 1850s was more successfully, though obliquely, established in his work as editor, compiler and memoirist.

His outstanding achievement in this decade, and perhaps the achievement for which he most of all deserves to be remembered, was his edition of Pushkin's works, which precipitated the important debate over the respective merits of Pushkin and Gogol. The impulse for the edition may have come originally from Belinsky who, at the end of the last of his eleven monumental essays on the significance of Pushkin in Russian literature, noted that even ten years after the death of the poet no tolerable collection of his works had been published.[85] For several years in the early 1850s Annenkov laboured with uncharacteristic dedication at the task Belinsky had invited his contemporaries to undertake. Finally, in 1855, the first, biographical, volume of his edition appeared, followed by five volumes containing the poet's works and a seventh, supplementary volume which was published in 1857.[86] The meticulous and scrupulous biography, over four hundred pages long, was unanimously acclaimed. 'The biography of Pushkin makes the most gratifying impression' Turgenev told Tolstoy's sister and her husband, 'and everywhere one hears the most flattering judgements of Annenkov's labour.'[87] Katkov found the work 'truly estimable'.[88]

Nekrasov, whose views were already radical by comparison with Annenkov's, publicly stated that the biography was a 'major book', the outstanding literary phenomenon of 1855.[89] And even Chernyshevsky praised Annenkov for this and other contributions he had made to the intellectual life of the mid 1850s.[90] As a mark of their esteem leading men of letters, including Turgenev, Botkin, Druzhinin, Nekrasov and Panayev, held a dinner in Annenkov's honour on 17 February 1855 and presented him with a copy of the first volume of his edition which they had inscribed with a dedication to the author of the 'exemplary biography of Pushkin and the conscientious editor' of the poet's works.[91] The only serious reservation voiced about Annenkov's edition concerned the considerable number of misprints which Annenkov, perhaps losing patience as his work neared completion, had failed to detect in the proofs.[92]

Shortly after the appearance of the biography of Pushkin, Annenkov also completed a biography of Stankevich, which was published together with Stankevich's correspondence in 1857.[93] This work betrayed Annenkov's growing antipathy to Chernyshevsky's outlook in a number of respects. For one thing, Annenkov's insistence that Stankevich's overriding preoccupation was with aesthetic considerations could be construed as a riposte to Chernyshevsky's current repudiation of the Hegelian conception of art and beauty. This emphasis in Stankevich's thought, moreover, seemed to Annenkov to endow even Stankevich's lapses of artistic judgement with a 'much greater portion of truth and instructiveness' than certain other 'verdicts' – of a utilitarian nature, we are meant to infer – which were 'entirely unexceptionable' because they were 'entirely superficial'.[94] A more overt criticism of the radical outlook was implicit in Annenkov's assertion that Stankevich was a 'servant of the truth in pure, abstract thought', and 'in the example of his life', and that he could never serve that truth 'in the wild marketplace of modernity'.[95] Annenkov must have believed too that he himself had set about his task with an integrity and impartiality of which Stankevich would have approved and which sharply distinguished his biography from the highly tendentious appraisal of Stankevich's contemporary, Belinsky, in Chernyshevsky's recently completed series of 'Essays on the Gogol Period of Russian Literature'. Again, Annenkov's biography may plausibly be seen as an indictment of the Chernyshevskian ethical doctrine of rational egoism, for Stankevich is remembered by those who were close to him as perhaps the outstanding exponent of the view that selfish impulses should be suppressed and the ego given up to fulfilment of a noble duty. (It was Stankevich, after all, who had served as the model for Pokorsky, the fair-souled student so fondly remembered by his fellows in *Rudin*.) Stankevich had had the capacity 'to think not at all about himself and, without the slightest sign of bragging or pride, and without willing it, to carry everyone else along behind him into the realm of the ideal'.[96]

Seen from the vantage-point of the post-Nicolaevan period, Stankevich still seemed just as clearly as in his own lifetime the purest embodiment of the quixotic dreams of his generation, the incarnation of all the 'best moral traits, the most noble aspirations and hopes' of his contemporaries. And yet Annenkov's re-examination of him from that new vantage-point was bound also to serve as a sobering reminder to the 'men of the 40s' that the cherished time of their youth, with which Stankevich was so closely associated, was indeed long past. The members of Stankevich's generation, Annenkov wrote in the warm concluding passage of his biography, had 'raised all the questions currently engaging literature and science' and had laboured over them as best they could, and now they were beginning to retreat a little from the centre of the stage, giving way to others.[97] It is tempting even to suggest that the very fact that the surviving 'men of the 40s' felt a need in the late 1850s to record the spiritual history of their generation was itself indicative of a presentiment among them that their influence was declining. This presentiment certainly colours Turgenev's correspondence of the period in which the author complains – rather absurdly for a man of about 40 – of his approaching senility. But it is nowhere more clearly expressed than in a letter which Annenkov wrote to Druzhinin from Simbirsk, in September 1856:

We have died, Aleksandr Vasilyevich [Druzhinin], only there hasn't been a funeral. We lie in our tail-coats, Aleks. Vasilyevich, on cambric pillows, only there's no sacristan at the head of the bed. This is the absolute truth, and it came into my head when I read the list of themes you sent. Remember, the trip to Lombardy, acquaintance with Gogol, provincial letters, everything that is past and has had its day and is gathering dust ... for God's sake look for young people to dilute the spirit of decay with which our trough-mates, long since deceased, will inevitably affect you. Memoirs, commentaries, discussions of former theories and accounts of past life – all this has a whiff of the earth [i.e. the graveyard] about it and after all this the windows must be opened.[98]

In spite of the gloomy thoughts induced by recollections of the past, Annenkov could not resist taking up one of the subjects suggested by Druzhinin, namely the time he had spent with Gogol in Rome, and he promised to work it up for Druzhinin when he went to Moscow at the end of the month.[99] He kept his word, and his memoirs, under the title 'N. V. Gogol in Rome in the Summer of 1841', duly appeared in 1857, in two instalments, in *Biblioteka dlya chteniya*, the journal which Druzhinin now edited. The work was received almost as enthusiastically as the biography of Pushkin, and not merely because Annenkov was considerably more skilled as a memoirist than as a literary critic, but also, perhaps, because in it he remained for the most part aloof from the polemic – in which he was at the same time personally involved – about the respective merits of Pushkin and Gogol.[100] And yet even in those memoirs the identity of their author as a moderate 'man of the 1840s' could be perceived, especially in those passages in which Annenkov once again described his first journey through Italy. He claimed to have found among the Italian people that same chivalrous spirit that Botkin had detected among the Spaniards. The Italian nature, Annenkov reaffirmed, might attain to 'all kinds of beauty and nobility'. There was an 'innate Italian kind-heartedness' and a capacity for spontaneous feeling that was irrepressible among 'fresh peoples'. Even among the very poor he had become acquainted, Annenkov claimed, with individuals who bore themselves 'like heroes', 'marvellous characters' who, although humble butchers or tailors by trade, thought 'like knights'.[101] Cheered by these observations Annenkov retouched his idyllic picture of a people living a timeless existence untroubled by the tensions with which other societies were currently afflicted. In the little towns of the Apennines, for example, it seemed as if the departure of 'noisy, medieval life' had left a vacuum which was rarely filled by the 'gusts' of the modern world. Annenkov relished this lethargic way of life of a people who did not strive frenziedly to keep in step with their age, like the rest of Europe, but who instead quietly let time pass. He derived an 'inexpressible pleasure' from those 'happy valleys' which intersect the Apennines, leaving one only with the memory of their beautiful orchards. And he mentioned approvingly a book by a German criminologist, Mittermaier, who had put forward the thesis that the humane and gentle relations which, he supposed, existed between Italian landowners and their tenant farmers and between the farmers and their workers prevented the 'ulcer of class enmity' that afflicted other Western European countries from developing in Italy.[102] Not surprisingly Turgenev and Druzhinin both singled out these passages for particular praise. It was wonderful, Turgenev wrote, how Annenkov's description of his journey from Venice to Rome breathed 'Italy, spring, youth, the happiness of health and lack of cares'.[103] If only the Russian government, these men must have felt, could reduce the social inequalities and tensions in their own country then perhaps Russia too might avoid bloody domestic conflict and enjoy the tranquillity they thought they detected in the European country for which they had the deepest affection.

Fear of socialism and retreat

Annenkov's fear of the 'gusts' of the modern world found explicit expression in his memoirs on the revolutionary events he had witnessed in France in 1848. The first two instalments of these memoirs, entitled 'February and March in Paris, 1848', were published in *Biblioteka dlya chteniya* in 1859,[104] that is to say at the time when the moderate members of the older generation were beginning to sense, as Annenkov's enthusiasm for Strauss' book on Hutten implied, that their struggle with the younger radicals was being lost. Although Annenkov later admitted in the final instalment of these memoirs that the excesses of the French Revolution of 1789 were not repeated in 1848,[105] he still saw the events of 1848 as instructive for countries which had not undergone such upheavals. What dismays him most of all, it seems, is the unedifying spectacle of the unrestrained mob sullying beautiful objects associated with the régime that has collapsed. He describes the crowds cavorting in the Tuileries, the smashed busts of the King, the torn canvases of valuable paintings, the broken chandeliers. Magnificent carpets were ruined. Workers and their children adopted extravagant poses in imitation of princes and marquises, lolled on beds and in armchairs, flung royal possessions out of windows and flicked with grubby fingers through personal albums. The masses were in 'a sort of moral intoxication'. They had abandoned themselves to exultation in a place to which they had not previously had access. As for the republican clubs, Annenkov speaks of these with scorn. No sooner did they set about discussing matters publicly than 'fearful and impassioned nonsense came out'. The meetings made do with regurgitation of articles from journals, 'absurd imitation' of the clubs of 1793 and sometimes with 'brawling', which broke out once even in the club run by that 'evil genius of the city', the 'Paganini of conspiracies', Auguste Blanqui. The socialist leaders were blindly followed by the people, who seemed ready to take up arms on any pretext in the name of abstract concepts such as equality and fraternity.[106]

Fear of socialist revolution, however, did not dampen Annenkov's enthusiasm for reform in Russia in the late 1850s; in fact it made him all the more anxious that changes should be brought about in good time, before existing problems became too acute to solve without recourse to violence. Together with Turgenev and others he mooted the idea of a society to promote literacy among the lower classes and pondered the use of Sunday schools for the same purpose.[107] More importantly, he welcomed the plans being made for the abolition of serfdom. The news that committees of nobles were being set up to discuss the emancipation, for example, gave him great pleasure. The day was approaching, he wrote to Turgenev, when they would be able to say to themselves: 'I am now an entirely honourable man.' Of course, many people still bitterly opposed the emancipation; but even the opponents understood that the past was slipping away, never to return.[108] As the preparation of the reform proceeded, so Annenkov's admiration for the tsar who had initiated and guided the discussion increased. The 'tsar stands like a rock around which both clear and turbid waves are broken', he wrote, again to Turgenev, in November 1860; it had turned out that the tsar knew the 'whole history of the problem through and through' and that 'no cheating' at all was possible.[109] And on the day the edict was published Annenkov's loyalty to the sovereign exceeded all previous bounds. His pleasure was marred only by what seemed to him the ingratitude of the common people, who appeared to consider the emancipation no more than the long overdue confirmation of a natural right.[110]

As a matter of fact, it was not long before Annenkov began to perceive as clearly as the radicals the shortcomings of the emancipation, which he had at first welcomed as a 'banner of salvation' that would be gratefully seized by all and which he had interpreted as Russia's peaceful revolution.[111] Writing to Druzhinin in July 1861, he described the despondency of the peasants on his own lands in Simbirsk, to which he had just returned. The peasants were angered by the fact that the land they had been granted was not to be the unencumbered property they thought they deserved as a reward for all the sacrifices made and the blood shed for the fatherland by their forebears. Nothing remained for Annenkov but 'slavishly to follow the letter of the statute', though as liberally as possible, and to leave that 'agitated, far from becalmed and secretly embittered region'. He very much regretted that all his attempts to ingratiate himself with his peasants had come to nought, but he could not help respecting people who realised, albeit dimly, that the emancipation edict constituted not 'peace, but war, struggle and conflict'.[112]

This surprisingly frank admission of the failure of the emancipation edict, however, did not signal a decision by Annenkov to adopt a more radical position. On the contrary, it presaged further attempts to distance himself from those current tendencies in Russian intellectual life which for one reason or another he found uncongenial. It was perhaps indicative of a new willingness to withdraw from the fray that at the beginning of 1861 he announced some personal news which astonished all his friends: he intended to marry. Of course, it was laughable to talk about 'bliss and ecstasy' at his time of life, he confessed to Turgenev; but there was a warm affection, the object of which was, in Turgenev's words, a 'not very beautiful but kind and intelligent' woman of 28, Glafira Aleksandrovna Rakovich.[113] The ceremony duly took place, in February 1861, in the grand setting of St Isaac's Cathedral in St Petersburg, and was attended by the requisite number of generals and finely dressed ladies. And yet even two days after his wedding Annenkov continued, perhaps not entirely in jest, to speak of his marriage as a 'necessary, but extremely indecent and fairly absurd act'.[114]

Annenkov's essential conservatism and his alienation from the radical stream in Russian thought, moreover, soon became clearer. There was, for example, a chauvinistic streak in the 'Letter from Kiev' which he allowed Katkov to print in *Russkiy vestnik* in 1862.[115] His relations with Herzen and Ogaryov were strained by the support of the two *émigrés* for the Polish uprising of 1863.[116] And he wrote a sympathetic review of Pisemsky's novel, *The Stormy Sea* (1863), in which the 'nihilists' had been held up to ridicule, giving vent to his own impatience with radical protest.[117] The economic and political questions which now preoccupied the intelligentsia held little interest for him. It is not surprising, therefore, that from the late 1860s until his death in Dresden in 1887 he spent most of his time abroad with his family (his wife bore him a son and a daughter) returning to Russia only infrequently to put his financial affairs in order. He kept in touch with Russian friends, it is true, corresponding with Turgenev, in particular, and assisting the editors of *Vestnik Yevropy* (*The Herald of Europe*), a journal of liberal orientation set up in St Petersburg in 1866 and managed by Stasyulevich. But it is difficult to resist the comparison of Annenkov with Turgenev's Pavel Kirsanov, that typical representative of the 'men of the 1840s', whom we also find living out his days in Dresden in the epilogue of *Fathers and Children*. Like Kirsanov, Annenkov no longer had any firm purpose in Russia. The stage on which he had once occupied an honourable, if not a central, position had been taken over by younger men for whose values and manner he did not care. He had regrets, to be sure, but being of a pacific nature he was not inclined to prolong the contest: better by far to live with one's memories in the congenial surroundings in which Annenkov had first fully appreciated life's pleasures in the now distant days of 1841.

5

Aleksandr Vasilyevich Druzhinin
(1824–1864)

Judgements of Druzhinin by Soviet scholars and by his contemporaries

Aleksandr Vasilyevich Druzhinin, a younger man than Granovsky, Botkin and Annenkov (he was born in 1824), did not belong to that generation which came to maturity in the bleak years following the abortive Decembrist uprising and which passionately embraced and then rejected German philosophy in the late 1830s and early 1840s. (Indeed, he made no impact on Russian intellectual life until the publication of his novella, *Polinka Saks*, in 1847.) Rather he was the product of the intellectual ferment that Granovsky, Botkin and Annenkov had themselves helped to create. Furthermore, the nature of his contribution to Russian intellectual life in the middle of the nineteenth century was qualitatively different from that of the slightly older men. Whereas Granovsky exerted his influence mainly through the medium of historical scholarship, and Botkin and Annenkov, as dilettanti with broad cultural interests, made few outstanding contributions in any particular field, Druzhinin excelled as a literary critic. It was in this role that he broadly represented the liberal 'men of the 1840s' when in the mid 1850s they came to defend the integrity of art against Chernyshevsky and Dobrolyubov, who were beginning to make utilitarian demands of it. Since literary criticism, moreover, was the arena in which the contest between the liberals and the younger radicals was first fought, Druzhinin briefly achieved great prominence, though towards the end of the decade, when the radicals began to prevail, he faded quickly into the background.

It is true to say that Druzhinin has fared even worse at the hands of students of Russian intellectual history than Granovsky, Botkin or Annenkov, whose closeness to Belinsky has perhaps assured them of at least a small measure of indulgence from Soviet scholars. As the most unequivocal opponent of Chernyshevsky's aesthetic and of the ethical assumptions and political ambitions on which it rested, Druzhinin has understandably been variously dismissed by Soviet commentators as a critic whose ideas were inconsistent and unclear or whose 'epicurean' attitude towards art tended to impede the social movement against tsarist tyranny.[1] In political terms Druzhinin is classified by exponents of this line of thought as a 'liberal' or even a representative of the 'nobles' reaction in literature'.[2] It is occasionally suggested in his defence that his final indifferentism represents a retreat from his position in the 1840s, when he was supposedly sympathetic to the radical cause.[3] But generally speaking the attitude of Soviet commentators towards him is unreservedly hostile. Chukovsky, author of the longest Soviet essay on him, presents him as an untypical figure in the intellectual life of his period, and accuses him of spreading 'false legends' about Pushkin's alleged lack of social concern.[4] Yegorov, in a more recent article, describes him as 'two-faced in his attitude to the "external" world and to his friends', talks pejoratively of a 'notorious trinity' of Botkin, Annenkov and Druzhinin, and argues that, although these critics had much in common, Druzhinin should indeed be regarded as the most infamous of the three.[5]

The place accorded to Druzhinin by Soviet scholars, however, is not commensurate with his real importance in the intellectual life of the mid nineteenth century. A highly cultured man, well versed in painting and music as well as in all the major European literatures, Druzhinin was a many-sided and considerable talent: a writer of fiction in the spirit of the 'natural school'; literary editor of the journal *Sovremennik* between 1848 and 1855 and subsequently editor of the journal *Biblioteka dlya chteniya*, positions in which he showed great diligence and competence;[6] a translator, whose Russian versions of four of Shakespeare's plays have been highly praised by judges hostile to his aesthetic view as well as by contemporaries more favourably disposed towards him;[7] chief founder of a society to help needy writers;[8] an erudite historian of English literature, whose articles did much to acquaint the Russian public with the life and work of writers such as Sheridan, Charlotte Brontë, Thackeray and Crabbe;[9] and a biographer, notably of the Russian painter Fedotov.[10] He seems to have stood at the very centre of that group of writers and lovers of literature – Turgenev, Grigorovich, Ostrovsky, Botkin, Annenkov, Nekrasov – whose invaluable service it was to keep alive a tradition of independent thought and art during the 'seven dismal years' with which the reign of Nicholas I ended. There is much evidence to suggest, moreover, that, as a literary critic who more consistently than anyone else opposed the view that imaginative literature should be put to social and political use, Druzhinin achieved much greater influence in the literary circles of the mid 1850s than one might infer from the relative obscurity into which he was cast soon after his death in 1864 and in which he has remained ever since. One memoirist, for example, gives the name the 'Druzhinin circle' to the group which comprised the most eminent men of letters in the mid 1850s.[11] Nekrasov, writing at the end of 1856, confirmed that the 'literary movement' had 'grouped itself around Druzhinin'.[12] One of Turgenev's correspondents informed the novelist in the same year: 'Druzhinin is now a star of the first magnitude; everything revolves around him.'[13] And Tolstoy told Botkin that in Moscow, as well as St Petersburg, Druzhinin's style of literary criticism was very popular, particularly among the Aksakovs.[14]

Some insight into the eminence of Druzhinin in the mid 1850s is provided by the fact that the journal of which he took editorial control in 1856, *Biblioteka*, was in the first instance seen as a serious competitor to *Sovremennik*, to which Nekrasov and Chernyshevsky were currently giving an increasingly radical, utilitarian character. Turgenev, in January 1857, predicted a brilliant future for *Biblioteka* and hoped that *Sovremennik* would not be entirely crushed by it, although, he told Druzhinin, he was afraid it might be.[15] Panayev, Nekrasov's collaborator on *Sovremennik*, disputed Turgenev's view that *Sovremennik* would falter and that *Biblioteka* would kill it off, but he did admit that the editorial board of *Sovremennik* was not so widely read and well informed as that of *Biblioteka* and that it was stretched to the limit by such competition. And, if *Sovremennik* did collapse, Panayev added in a vindictive afterthought, it would be Turgenev's fault for helping Druzhinin.[16]

The attitudes towards Druzhinin of Turgenev and Tolstoy, arguably the two greatest writers to emerge from the St Petersburg literary circles of the mid 1850s, although variable, tend to support the impression of a writer and personality of unusual authority. Turgenev, it is true, was initially cool towards Druzhinin. 'I can't read Druzhinin's things', he wrote to Nekrasov in 1852; and again, at the end of 1853, in a letter to Annenkov, he disparages Druzhinin's fiction, which he found unbearably strained and false.[17] Even at this period, however, he highly praised Druzhinin's work on Fedotov,[18] and personal acquaintance with Druzhinin himself seems to have disposed Turgenev more favourably. Thus he asks Nekrasov, in a letter of autumn 1854, to shake Druzhinin's hand on his behalf: 'I came to like him from the time of our last trip to his place.'[19] The friendship was firmly cemented by the idyllic three weeks Turgenev and Druzhinin spent together, with Botkin and Grigorovich, on Turgenev's estate at Spasskoye in May and June 1855. 'Do you know that Druzhinin is an excellent fellow?' he now asked Nekrasov, and for some weeks after his friends' departure he talked ecstatically of their stay.[20] Familiarity with Druzhinin's literary criticism, as opposed to his fiction, also helped to change Turgenev's impression of Druzhinin. He was extravagant in his praise of Druzhinin's assessment, which appeared in 1855, of the importance of Pushkin in Russian literature: he had read Druzhinin's essay, Turgenev said, with great enjoyment; it was 'noble, warm, sensible and true', a masterly appreciation of Pushkin which could not have been bettered.[21] Druzhinin was a 'Russian *reviewer* in the most excellent sense of the word'.[22] For several years Druzhinin remained one of the chosen few to whom Turgenev was prepared to entrust his works for comment and discussion before they were submitted for publication and was present at first readings of *Rudin, A Nest of Gentry* and *First Love*.[23]

There was a period in the mid 1850s when Tolstoy too, between soldiering in the Caucasus and Crimea and travelling in Western Europe, fell under the influence of Druzhinin to such an extent that one of Turgenev's correspondents could write: 'Tolstoy simply almost idolises him. The reverence in which he holds Druzhinin as a critic is comic in the extreme.'[24] Like Turgenev, Tolstoy submitted his work to Druzhinin for a preliminary literary judgement. On sending him *Youth* he warned Druzhinin that the story was for his eyes alone and vowed that he would publish it only if he had Druzhinin's approval to do so.[25] Druzhinin appears even to have accomplished the rare feat of persuading Tolstoy to stop denigrating Shakespeare and to drink a toast to the dramatist.[26] Towards the end of 1856 Tolstoy began to cool towards Druzhinin, but he remained under his influence for some time still, and in later life never revealed the full extent of the attraction that Druzhinin's views had at one time held for him.

In the case of neither Turgenev nor Tolstoy was the influence of

Druzhinin permanent, but its temporary strength does invite attention. Moreover, the ambivalence of the attitudes of these writers to
Druzhinin is itself of great interest. For, in the first place, it is
indicative, in Turgenev's case at least, of the writer's own unease at
the growing conflict in the intelligentsia and of his difficulty in
aligning himself unequivocally with either faction. And, in the
second place, it may also reflect a certain difficulty on the part of
Turgenev and Tolstoy in judging Druzhinin the man as well as
Druzhinin the writer. For Druzhinin did not move quite so easily
and naturally in the intelligentsia as Granovsky, Botkin, Annenkov and Kavelin. Like most of the liberal 'men of the 1840s', it is
true, he was of noble origin. His parents were well-to-do members
of the gentry and he continued after his father's death to enjoy the
use of the family estate at Marinskoye, in the district of Gdov, in St
Petersburg province, to which he would periodically withdraw. He
was educated at home until he was sixteen, then studied at the
Corps of Pages, a military school in St Petersburg, and served
briefly as a Guards officer. His background, therefore, was quite
typical of the educated Russian in the 1840s. He also undoubtedly
enjoyed widespread respect, and not merely from those who were
like-minded. And yet one senses that he always remained at a slight
distance from even his closest collaborators, who, for their part, did
not on the whole address to him the warm and effusive expressions
of affection which were customary among friends in a beleaguered
intelligentsia. 'You belong to that category of people whom one
likes but little at first sight', Turgenev told him in 1855 with a
frankness which among other peoples would have been offensive,
'but to whom one becomes more attached the more one gets to
know them.'[27] Perhaps this slight remoteness of Druzhinin's was
due partly to an apparently alien streak in his temperament. Certainly Druzhinin cultivated virtues – the keeping of regular hours,
diligence, efficiency, neatness, reliability and a general belief in the
importance of being punctilious – which themselves seemed to the
expansive Russian intelligentsia to have a rather foreign quality.
More importantly, he was set somewhat apart by a phlegmatic
coolness which contemporaries associated with that people, the
English, with whom Druzhinin seemed to have the most affinity. He
was present at the carousals of the literary circles of the period, to be
sure, but he participated in them without quite the normal spon-
taneity. There was something strained or forced about his hedo-

nism; even in his conviviality, Grigorovich observed, one detected a certain melancholy.[28]

The novella 'Polinka Saks'

Druzhinin's literary output in the period between 1847 and the death of Nicholas I was prodigious. It included a large number of novellas and stories as well as substantial *feuilletons* which were published in *Sovremennik*. The significance of this *œuvre* was ephemeral and, since the bulk of it throws little light on either the intellectual life of the 1840s or the controversies of the 1850s, it does not for the most part merit detailed examination here. There is one constituent of it, however, which we should pause to consider, namely Druzhinin's first literary success, the novella *Polinka Saks*, which was published in *Sovremennik* in 1847, for not only did this novella have a great impact in its time but it also provides a key – though at first sight a rather misleading one – to the assessment of Druzhinin's later work.

Polinka Saks is an epistolary novella which traces the triangular relationship of Konstantin Saks, a thirty-two-year-old official with a promising career ahead of him, Polinka, his young bride, who has married at her father's wish rather than out of love, and Galitsky, a dashing social lion who is himself in love with Polinka. In the first letter the hero Saks tells his friend Zaleshin about his beloved Polya: he has been trying to educate her and instil good taste in her, and he hopes soon to be able to go out with her 'hand in hand to face life' with all its good and bad features. The second letter, written by Polinka to her friend Annette, gives us a further insight into the character of Saks and the nature of the relationship of the married couple. Polinka begins by saying that she had feared Annette was angry with her for not marrying her brother. In fact, it was Polinka's father who had wanted her to marry Saks, whom Annette has described as 'old and ugly'. Saks is a little bald, Polinka admits, but he is as noble a person as one could meet. He is rich and numbers painters and musicians among his friends. Polinka asks Annette, however, to excuse her for defending Saks: she realises that few people like him and most consider him eccentric, for he spends a great deal of money and yet seems unconcerned about his income. Her father suspects that he has unnecessarily lowered the *obrok* (quit-rent) paid by the peasants on his estate.[29] Polinka senses that

Saks is a jealous man and has asked Saks what he would do if she were to fall in love with one of his friends: he would kiss her and leave, he has replied, and would not regard the other man as guilty. Polinka cried like a child at such apparent coldness on her husband's part. She is herself trying to change Saks, she tells Annette at the end of her letter, in order to make him more like other people. In the third letter Zaleshin, writing to Saks, describes a recent visit he has had from a Prince Galitsky (in whom the reader without great difficulty perceives a potential rival to Saks for Polinka). Galitsky has the attributes of the superfluous man in one of his more destructive incarnations: he is 'proud as the devil' and has enjoyed a brilliant success in society. He was born an empty person and has studied little and poorly. He is a man of no convictions. In the fourth letter, from Annette to Polinka, we learn that Galitsky is in fact Annette's brother, whom Annette was hoping – as we have been told by Polinka – that Polinka would marry. Annette implores Polinka not to let Saks know of her brother's passion, for she fears Saks' anger, the more so since Saks, Annette alleges, once killed a young Russian in a duel fought in defence of a Parisian actress whom the man had tried to hiss and jeer off the stage. All the same Annette begs Polinka to let her brother see her, even though she would fear for his safety were Saks to find out about his love for Polinka.

These four letters constitute a prologue which introduces the characters and launches the plot. In chapter two Saks tells Polinka that he has to go to the provinces to investigate a case of theft by one Pisarenko (who, as it happens, had formerly handled the affairs of Galitsky's father). Polinka pleads with Saks not to leave her but he tells her that duty demands that he go and asks her to be more mature. As he is about to leave, Galitsky arrives – we learn in chapter three – on the pretext of delivering letters, though in truth he wants an opportunity to see Polinka. Chapter four consists of two letters from Galitsky. In one, addressed to Pisarenko, he bemoans the fact that men of principle like Saks fuss about honesty and asks Pisarenko to detain Saks in the country for as long as possible. In the other he describes to his sister Annette the considerable progress he is making in his relations with Polinka. The return of Saks, he predicts, will resolve the situation one way or the other. Saks loves Polinka, he is sure, but so does he, Galitsky. In chapter five Polinka writes to Annette explaining her dilemma: Saks has done her no wrong and is a good man; nevertheless she enjoys Galitsky's caresses. Saks, meanwhile, writes to Polinka, saying that he has heard about the appearance of Galitsky and gently asking her to be on her guard. He also reports that Pisarenko is dragging out the investigation (as Galitsky, the reader knows, has instructed him to do). Pisarenko, however, soon gives up his attempt to frustrate Saks' investigation and he even hands over to Saks the incriminating letter he has received from Galitsky. Saks immediately returns to St Petersburg and in his next letter, to Zaleshin, is in a vengeful mood. Zaleshin has advised him to be rational rather than to act as passion dictates, but Saks is after all a human being in love; it is easier to build theories in fiction than in real life. Polinka, meanwhile, blames herself for what has happened and waits anxiously for the anger of her husband to erupt. Her mother fails to reply to one of her letters, leading her to asume that she has been disowned by her family. Finally, as we learn from Galitsky's next letter to Annette, Saks has summoned Galitsky to an encounter at a specific time and place. Galitsky anticipates a duel or some trick which will wash away the stain to Saks' honour. To his astonishment, however, Saks entrusts Polinka to him and tells them to go abroad and marry. He orders Galitsky to make Polinka happy; or else, Saks warns, Galitsky will be lost.

In the final chapter Polinka is haunted by Saks' demand that Galitsky make her happy and by his warning that he will be watching over their relationship. We learn too that she is ill. She begins to become aware that she loves Saks and asks God's blessing for this person who 'even in separation gives life, resurrects, finishes the education that has been begun'. Saks visits her. She is too mature now to love Galitsky, for she has grown up as a result of Saks' self-sacrifice. She expects that after death – she is now very sick – Saks will look into her heart and find that her education has been completed, that she did value him and that she repaid him for his great sacrifice with all that a woman had to give, her boundless and ardent love. Saks will see from a letter she writes – which is to be sent to him when she dies – that she has thus become a woman through his noble influence. Saks meanwhile stops following the couple as Polinka seems to recover in the spring, and goes to stay with Zaleshin in the Crimea. There he receives Polinka's last letter, sent after she has died.[30]

This scarcely credible story was received in its time with an enthusiasm which it is difficult now to understand. Belinsky, in a letter to Annenkov, described Druzhinin's novella as a 'marvel' and made a further flattering reference to it in his 'Survey of Russian Literature for 1847'. There was much in it that was immature or exaggerated, he admitted, and the character of Saks was 'a little too ideal'; but the work contained 'so much truth, so much spiritual warmth and true, conscious understanding of reality', 'so much originality' (Belinsky uses the word *samobytnost'* here) that it had immediately attracted attention. The character of the heroine, Belinsky believed, had been particularly skilfully drawn: evidently the author knew Russian womanhood very well.[31] Turgenev was also greatly impressed by the novella.[32] The actress Aleksandra Shubert, encouraged by Dostoyevsky to take serious roles rather than the nonsensical ones in vogue in the theatre in the late 1850s, even tried to persuade Druzhinin to adapt *Polinka Saks* for the stage, though without success.[33] The narrator of Dostoyevsky's novel, *A Raw Youth*, describes the novella as a work which, together with Grigorovich's *Anton the Unfortunate*, had an 'unbounded civilising influence' on the generation that was growing up in the 1840s.[34] And Tolstoy, when in later life he compiled a list of works of literature which had made a great impression on him, ranked *Polinka Saks* alongside Pushkin's *Eugene Onegin*, Lermontov's *A Hero of Our Time*, Gogol's *Dead Souls*, Grigorovich's *Anton the Unfortunate* and Turgenev's *Sportsman's Sketches*: it had had an 'enormous influence' on him in his youth. Even as late as 1906 he outlined the contents of Druzhinin's story to his family circle and called the work beautiful.[35]

The main reason for the success of Druzhinin's novella, which appears sentimental and mannered to the modern reader, lies in the fact that it reflected very clearly the sensibility of a large section of the Russian intelligentsia in the mid 1840s. This was after all a period in which George Sand enjoyed considerable popularity in Russia, and the conception of *Polinka Saks* owes much to the work of the French writer (which Saks in fact reads to Polinka for her edification) and in particular to her novel *Jacques* (1834). The eponymous hero of *Jacques* – which, like *Polinka Saks*, is epistolary in form – is an experienced man of thirty-five who marries Fernande, a callow girl of seventeen. He believes that he has at last found happiness, but soon realises that Fernande's feeling for him is really veneration rather than love. Unable to live up to Jacques' ideals, Fernande falls in love with another man, Octave, and the world-weary Jacques stages an accident, flinging himself into an Alpine crevasse in order that the couple should be free to express their love for one another. Both George Sand and Druzhinin, then, examine in their respective works an eternal triangle consisting of a mature hero who behaves in the most selfless way in order to bring happiness to his young bride and her lover. Both authors show a couple who are incompatible and are critical of a society whose conventions have brought about the predicament. Both emphasise the power of romantic love, a passion which is a law unto itself and which threatens to break the traditional social bonds. Druzhinin, it is true, appears less concerned than George Sand to prosecute what an English reviewer of the French writer described as a 'perpetual war against the nuptial vow'.[36] His work also contains implicit criticisms relating exclusively to his own society; one can infer, for example, that Saks' humanitarian impulses, as illustrated by his lowering of *obrok* on his estate and by his determination to bring Pisarenko to justice, are frowned upon in Nicolaevan Russia as eccentric and slightly subversive. But in both *Jacques* and *Polinka Saks* the prevailing mood is libertarian and both authors place a high value on acts of self-sacrifice which demonstrate the superior morality of their hero.

It would be wrong, however, to see *Polinka Saks* merely as the product of an alien literary tradition. Druzhinin's novella enjoyed popularity in the late 1840s not merely because it was reminiscent of the work of George Sand but also because it answered to the needs of an intelligentsia which had of its own accord resolved to secure the liberation of the individual from the despotic control of awesome abstractions, be they philosophical systems such as Hegelianism, social conventions such as arranged marriages or authoritarian political régimes such as Russian autocracy. *Polinka Saks* belonged to the new body of humanitarian literature which Belinsky was attempting to promote in that very essay in which he reviewed Druzhinin's work. Indeed, the novella met precisely the specifications laid down by Belinsky himself for this new literature in which the idea of human dignity would be upheld.

One item in particular in Belinsky's criticism appears to have a special bearing on *Polinka Saks*, namely his tirade on Pushkin's narrative poem, *The Gypsies*. (It is perhaps not coincidental that this tirade, which forms part of the seventh of Belinsky's eleven essays on Pushkin, was published in 1844, the year in which Druzhinin wrote *Polinka Saks*.) Belinsky uses Pushkin's poem as the basis for a sermon on the need for his readers to cultivate in themselves a spirit of true Christian love and self-sacrifice. In Aleko, Belinsky argues, Pushkin had created a character ruined by egoism who was unable in practice to attain the nobility or the moral standards to which he pretended to aspire when he indicted the civilisation he had left behind. For Aleko's heart was poisoned by the jealousy which erupted in vengefulness when the gypsy girl he had seduced took another lover. The morally developed man, Belinsky contends, would not experience any sense of personal injury on discovering that the woman he loved had cooled towards him, for he would realise that it was the fancy of her heart rather than any deficiencies of his own that were to blame. He would not think of sacrificing the woman's happiness for his own sake by compelling her to stay with him. If love was gone it was impossible for a couple to live together; in marriage, which was a contractual obligation, a union might continue under false pretences, but if a relationship did not rest on true love then a morally developed person could not tolerate its continuation. As for talk of vengeance, that was old-fashioned now; daggers, poisons and pistols were the sordid theatrical effects of a 'morbid madness, animal egoism and wild ignorance'. All the morally developed person could do, when he realised that his love was no longer reciprocated, was act 'with all the self-renunciation of a loving soul, with all the warmth of a heart which has comprehended the sacred mystery of suffering': he would give his blessing to the object of his love and conceal his own grief as best he could.[37]

Thus Belinsky, writing *à propos* of Pushkin's vengeful hero Aleko, appealed to the educated Russian to strive to become a 'human being' by practising the noble morality he preached, by cultivating a 'religious respect, for the human dignity of one's fellows.[38] It is tempting in retrospect to see his tirade as a sort of manifesto for the Russian novel as it was to develop in the hands of Turgenev, Dostoyevsky, Tolstoy and Chernyshevsky, all of whom were greatly preoccupied with the theme of one's moral responsibility towards one's neighbour. But the tirade may also be seen in a narrower perspective, as an exhortation to the writers of the 'natural school' to give expression to the humanitarian values of the Westernist section of the intelligentsia. Druzhinin, in heeding this exhortation, not only established his literary reputation, but also produced one of the main works of imaginative literature in the Westernist spirit.

There is one further point that needs to be made concerning *Polinka Saks*, for it has a bearing on the development of Druzhinin's thought in the mid 1850s. For all its latent political significance as a piece of humanistic literature extolling self-sacrifice in the interests of the happiness of others, the novella was probably conceived first and foremost as a contribution to the *literary* and *ethical* movement of the 1840s, not as a plea for *social* change. It may be compared in this respect to Turgenev's *Sportsman's Sketches*, which began to appear in the same year. Like *Polinka Saks*, Turgenev's *Sketches* could be made to yield a socio-political meaning; but they also represented a literary experiment along lines laid down by George Sand in her pastoral novels and could equally be judged in terms of pure art. Indeed, the first sketch, 'Khor and Kalinych', was apparently conceived as a contrast between differing types of human character, represented by Goethe and Schiller respectively, and its topical significance was sufficiently veiled for Botkin to be able to describe it as an 'idyll'.[39] It would be misleading, therefore, to associate Turgenev's *Sketches* too closely with Belinsky's thought in the last years of his life. Similarly, we should beware of attributing to Druzhinin at the time of writing *Polinka Saks* any clearly defined political animosity to tsarism on which he later reneged. His work was undoubtedly written in the spirit of the age to which it belonged; but faithfulness to that spirit did not necessarily require the same political commitment which was implicit in Belinsky's writings of the 1840s and which was of course always explicit in Herzen's writings after his emigration.

On the eve of controversy with the radicals

In order to understand Druzhinin's role in the literary community after the publication of *Polinka Saks*, in the late 1840s and the first half of the 1850s, we need to bear in mind the fact that Belinsky's heritage had a dual nature. Insistence on the civic role of the artist was, of course, one of the precepts Belinsky had bequeathed, but it was not the only one. What impressed itself perhaps even more forcefully on his contemporaries was his demand that they love sincere and truthful literature as passionately as he and that they regard the cultivation of Russian literature in particular as a sacred cause, a patriotic duty.

It was, admittedly, Belinsky's view of art as an instrument of social criticism that appealed most of all to radical thinkers and writers such as Chernyshevsky, Dobrolyubov and Nekrasov. But other disciples of Belinsky's, such as Botkin, Annenkov, Turgenev and Goncharov – dilettanti rather than aspiring social reformers – were more attracted by Belinsky's passionate love of literature and his patriotic interest in its vitality, and they seemed in the first instance to be no less legitimate successors to the great critic than the radicals. Druzhinin was a typical representative of the latter group and a prominent participant in their literary festivities and carousals. Indeed, of all the men who had surrounded Belinsky it was Druzhinin who seemed in the 'dismal seven years' that followed the critic's death to be his natural heir. In his contribution to *Sovremennik* under the title 'Letters from a Subscriber from Another Town', which enjoyed great popularity in the early 1850s, he commented, as Belinsky had done, on the latest works of literature and on the state of Russian journalism. And at the end of the first letter of this series he took one of the current journals to task in terms which suggest a conscious attempt to emulate Belinsky. A journal should not be cold and indifferent to questions which preoccupy lovers of Russian literature, he wrote; a journal should have 'life, fire and conviction', for literature would perish if it lost its passion.[40]

As a matter of fact, Druzhinin's publicism began at an early stage to differ from Belinsky's in important respects. Already in this fourth 'letter' he suggests that he is reluctant to enter into polemics and regrets that the 'spirit of intolerance and exaggeration' has still not been entirely banished from Russian letters.[41] Moreover, he tends to dilute his serious criticism with content that is trivial, anecdotal or inconsequential. His review of Oliver Goldsmith's *Vicar of Wakefield*, written in 1850, for example, consists largely of biographical material and a plot summary.[42] Again, his immensely long essay on Johnson and Boswell, published in 1851–2, is light and inconsequential and lacks a serious central argument. Other works which he reviews, such as a novel by the comte de Tressan and Ann Radcliffe's *The Romance of the Forest*, are similarly devoid of any obvious relevance to the Russia of the time.[43] Much of his energy, finally, was devoted to frivolous *feuilletons* published under the title

'The Sentimental Journey of Ivan Chernoknizhnikov round the St Petersburg *dachas*'.[44]

Nevertheless, it was not immediately obvious after the death of Belinsky, in spite of the lack of polemical incisiveness in literary criticism, that serious divisions would open up between Druzhinin, Botkin and Annenkov, on the one hand, and Chernyshevsky, Nekrasov, Panayev and their supporters, who were to lay emphasis on the socio-political aspect of Belinsky's criticism, on the other. Even in 1855–6 writers shortly to go in very different directions still corresponded and collaborated with intimacy and goodwill. Nekrasov, wondering what to include in *Sovremennik* at the beginning of 1855, says Druzhinin's contribution is the 'most brilliant of all'; in August of the same year he writes a warm letter to Druzhinin in the hope of retaining his services for *Sovremennik* on a permanent basis; and in November he quotes Druzhinin to show that even in his lightest pieces Druzhinin is able to 'drop an intelligent idea, a warm word'. He advises everyone to read Druzhinin's articles on Pushkin; they showed 'what Russian criticism ought to be!'. He tells Druzhinin that he wishes they had been published in *Sovremennik*: Chernyshevsky's articles on Pushkin would have looked dull by comparison. And in 1855 Nekrasov seeks and obtains for *Sovremennik* Druzhinin's long articles on Crabbe.[45] Relations between *Sovremennik* and *Biblioteka* are good at first: Druzhinin prints some of Nekrasov's verse in the first number of *Biblioteka* which he edits and at the end of 1856 the two journals are subscribing jointly to foreign publications.[46] Druzhinin's personal relations with Panayev remain cordial.[47] Nor does Chernyshevsky immediately criticise Druzhinin: in October 1856 he writes a cautious note on the appearance of *Biblioteka*, admitting its right to differ and full of respect for Druzhinin. Even later in the year he is still conciliatory.[48] Moreover, Botkin, who is to be identified with Druzhinin's school rather than that of Nekrasov, Panayev and Chernyshevsky, was, as we have seen, still close to Nekrasov in the summer of 1855, when the two shared a *dacha*; and his article on Fet, in many respects a programmatic article for those who opposed the new direction of *Sovremennik*, was all the same published in that journal.[49] In short, differences of opinion did not always seem very important, provided that all continued to display their great love of Russian literature. Turgenev foresaw disagreement with Druzhinin in 1856, but dismissed it as 'nothing;' in the most important matters, he wrote, 'our intentions and tastes coincide'. What did it matter, he wrote again a little later, if they did disagree; for 'Truth . . . has more than one aspect.'[50]

All the same, the men of letters were being forced by the new historical conditions to contemplate choices they had not previously had to make and to form allegiances according to new criteria. The increasing acrimony of the remarks of some of the individuals who on a superficial level remained co-operative and conciliatory graphically illustrates this fact. Thus Druzhinin speaks of the 'smell of old carrion' which emanates from the writings of Chernyshevsky, to whom it became customary in the second half of the 1850s to refer as 'the one who smells of bugs'.[51] Nekrasov accuses Druzhinin of lying in an article on Gogol and refers to his way of thinking as 'sh . . . with cream', the 'stench' from which would alienate all that was 'alive' in the young generation from *Biblioteka*.[52] Panayev applies the epithets 'rotten' and 'superficial' to Druzhinin as a critic.[53] Chernyshevsky defies Turgenev to find in Druzhinin's work a 'single idea' which is neither banal nor plagiarised; even Grigoryev seems better to Chernyshevsky than Druzhinin: he may be mad but at least he is a human being, not a 'cesspit'.[54] The disintegration of the literary community was betokened too by the fact that Turgenev and Tolstoy, in spite of their hostile reactions to Chernyshevsky's dissertation and their respect for Druzhinin, remained faithful to *Sovremennik*, while Druzhinin criticised its position in the pages of *Biblioteka*. Writing to Turgenev at the beginning of 1857, Druzhinin clearly anticipated this imminent disintegration:

Thoughts and hearts are at one, and yet our work is never to blend into one comforting whole, forces are fragmented, interests run counter to one another. This situation is one of the strangest in the world and who can say how it will end? We are all scattered like twigs . . . [55]

'Pure' and 'didactic' art; the 'Gogol school' of Russian literature

Although Botkin and Annenkov made important contributions to the debate of the mid 1850s about the function of imaginative literature, it was Druzhinin who emerged as the chief spokesman for the older generation. Over the period 1855–8 he and Chernyshevsky responded to one another's views in numerous articles – many of them on major works of Russian literature – in the attempt to establish their respective interpretations of Russian literature and criticism and to prescribe the proper course for their subsequent development. Battle was first joined in reviews of the first volume of Annenkov's new edition of Pushkin's works, which appeared in 1855. The suggestion made by Chernyshevsky *à propos* of this edition that Pushkin's work was no longer of primary significance in the new literary age, whose main representative was Gogol, was challenged by Druzhinin in two essays which constituted a defence of the poet, in part ecstatic and itself poetic, against the 'too exclusive adherents of Gogol'.[56] Chernyshevsky, in his long series of articles under the title 'Essays on the Gogol Period of Russian Literature', published in *Sovremennik* between December 1855 and December 1856, again insisted on the pre-eminence of Gogol, whom he now described as the 'greatest of the Russian writers in significance'; indeed, never had there been a writer 'so important for his people as Gogol [had been] for Russia'. Chernyshevsky also devoted a large part of his series to analysis of the literary criticism of Belinsky, inserting massive quotations from Belinsky's articles and interpreting them as an insistent call for social utility and civic responsibility in art.[57] Druzhinin's articles, under the title 'Criticism of the Gogol Period of Russian Literature and our Attitude towards it', which appeared at the end of 1856, represent both a counter-argument to Chernyshevsky's series, as suggested by the title itself, and a programmatic declaration for *Biblioteka*, of which Druzhinin had just become the *de jure* as well as the *de facto* editor.[58] A series of articles by Druzhinin on Crabbe may also be taken as belonging to the polemic, for Druzhinin suggests that the English poet dealt in a superior way with subject matter similar to that presented by writers of the 'natural school' and encourages Russian writers to emulate him.[59] Finally, having debated the respective merits of Pushkin and Gogol and having offered different interpretations of the work and legacy of Belinsky, Chernyshevsky and Druzhinin proceed to apply the views on art which they have outlined to current authors such as Tolstoy, Saltykov-Shchedrin, Pisemsky and Ogaryov. To follow the arguments in this polemic chronologically would be tortuous and repetitive; but it is not difficult to describe in their totality the aesthetic credos and critical methods which emerge clearly and insistently from it.

In Druzhinin's view there were in the final analysis only two types of imaginative writer, the 'artistic' and the 'didactic'. The 'artistic' writer, whose 'slogan' was 'pure art for art's sake', believed that the interests of a given moment were 'transitory'; he served what was unchanging in human life, namely the ideas of 'eternal beauty, good and truth'. His art had no worldly moral, nor would any conclusions directly beneficial to his contemporaries be drawn from it; rather it was its own reward and object. He portrayed people as he saw them, without preaching as to how their deficiencies should be remedied (or, at least, if he did teach, he did so unwittingly). He lived in an elevated world and came down to earth as the Olympian Gods once had, firmly believing that it was on Olympus that he really resided. His voice would continue to be heard by posterity. Moreover, paradoxical as it might seem in view of the fact that he did not set out to teach, the Olympian artist such as Homer, Shakespeare or Goethe actually served as a mentor to mankind. People came to him in search of spiritual nourishment and went away with a lighter spirit. His work, created in a moment of inspiration for the sake of pleasure alone, in fact became a source of edification, the basis of our 'knowledge, of our good intentions, of our great deeds!'.[60]

The fate of the 'didactic' writer was at first sight far more brilliant and enviable than that of the artistic writer. Having cast himself into the waves of 'turbid modernity' he seemed to have more numerous sources of inspiration than the servant of 'pure art'. He used his gift in the interests of his fellows at a given historical moment, promoting political, moral or scientific goals of great importance, going among his contemporaries not as a dispassionate visitor from Olympus but as an earthly labourer for the public weal. He might indeed accomplish much that was useful for his society. And yet all such didactic writers, in their eagerness to influence the course of current events, inevitably impaired the artistic quality of their work. Furthermore, the fame of such writers, who were to be found among the youth of every country, would be short-lived by comparison with that of the artists they denigrated; their voices would quickly be 'swallowed up in the abyss of complete oblivion'. Who, Druzhinin asks, now remembered Goethe's detractors such as Menzel?[61]

Didactism had recently come to prevail – though only briefly – in Germany, with the emergence of such poets as Heine, Börne, Herwegh and Freiligrath, who had joined forces with representatives of the new philosophical systems and political movements (Druzhinin has in mind the 'Young Hegelians' and the early socialists). It had also taken root in France, partly under German influence but also as a result of the development of an indigenous socialist movement, in the 1830s and 1840s. George Sand had been intoxicated by the new social and aesthetic theories; Eugène Sue had seen the commercial advantages of injecting a didactic element into his writing; and young economists and historians had pursued their own disciplines in a similar spirit. At the same time the didactic tendency had established itself in Russia thanks to the enthusiasm of many Russian writers and critics – and Druzhinin himself, it should be noted, was among their number – for the German and French sources Druzhinin mentions. These Russian writers had come to regard 'realism, sentimentality of the new style and a didactic tendency in the basic idea' as the most important qualities in a work of art. So long as a work was instructive for the contemporary reader, treated a 'topical idea and did not offend against the rules of grammar, it was considered satisfactory and noteworthy'. And, as this utilitarian view of art gained ground, so a partisan spirit and the intolerance inseparable from it began to flare up in Russian literature.[62]

It was above all with the name of Gogol that the 'didactic' tendency had come to be associated in Russia. As a matter of fact, Druzhinin emphasises, Gogol's work was rich in eternal truths and independent of the views of any particular generation. Gogol did not show in his work only the 'aspirations, defects and weaknesses' of his own society at a specific moment, nor was he a 'poet of negation'. Indeed, in some of his works – for example, *A May Night, Old-World Landowners, Viy* and *Taras Bulba* – he revealed a tenderness which was all too easily forgotten, Druzhinin suggested, when one read the more sombre works for which he had come by the mid 1850s to be chiefly renowned. Nevertheless it was undeniable that many of Gogol's works, such as *Dead Souls, The Overcoat, Notes of a Madman* and *Nevsky Prospect*, did lend themselves to the didactic interpretation. Gogol had brought direct benefit to his society 'by teaching modern man, revealing the defects of modern society, ridiculing vice and interceding for the weak'. Thus, in spite of Gogol's timeless value as a perspicacious observer of mankind in general, it had still been possible to draw from his works copious lessons of contemporary and local significance. And the exigencies of the period in which he was writing had led critics (Druzhinin had Belinsky in mind) and readers to concentrate their attention on the negative, apparently satirical, dimension of his work.[63]

Didacticism and the critic's encouragement of it in Russian literature seemed to Druzhinin to have numerous adverse effects, which are repeatedly mentioned in his writings. Firstly, didacticism blunted the critical taste of the reading public and was even counter-productive inasmuch as it made readers indifferent to real social ills when, through constant repetition, their description became hack-neyed.[64] Secondly, the demand that Russian writers reveal the bad side of life had given to Russian literature for a whole decade a 'sour, sad, dreary and monotonously scowling' quality; or, to put the matter another way, the demand that writers point a moral, in order to facilitate the cure of social ills, had lent literature a 'hospital smell' of which it could not easily rid itself.[65] Thirdly, didacticism detracted from the realism of a writer's creation, for in 'eulogies and protests' there would never be 'real life'.[66] Lack of realism was evident, for example, in works purporting to describe the evils of serfdom, whose authors, in their anxiety to denigrate certain social types, quite overlooked real problems such as the misery produced by early rural capitalism.[67] Authors would create characters in an artificial way, writing according to a specific recipe: a writer would have in his head a 'satirico-sentimental apothecary's shop out of which would come certain ingredients, in a certain quantity, for the creation of given individuals in novellas and novels'.[68] And, fourthly, the demands of didacticism, paradoxical as the suggestion might seem, in fact tended to impose on writers an additional form of censorship: for not only did writers now fear reprimands from above if they portrayed a bad landowner, they were also in danger of reproach 'from below', to the effect that they were impeding the cause of progress, if they portrayed a good one.[69]

Druzhinin on Pushkin and 'poetry'

Whatever the 'ardent admirers' of Gogol might say, Russian litera-ture could not, in Druzhinin's opinion, live any longer on *Dead Souls* alone. It had been 'worn out and weakened by its satirical tendency'.[70] It was therefore necessary to counteract those who did so much damage by their attempts to teach society. If men of letters of the older generation did not resist the Russian youths who were currently aspiring to become Russian Börnes and Herweghs, Druzhinin told Botkin in August 1855, then those youths would not only commit many follies, they would also harm literature and invite official persecution of Druzhinin and his fellow writers and critics and force them to give up the 'little corner in the sun' which they had acquired for themselves at such high cost.[71]

The best means of counteracting the didactic tendency to which 'immoderate imitation of Gogol' had led was to re-establish Pushkin (who in the eyes of the 'arrogant' youths was merely an 'imbecile')[72] as the dominant influence on Russian letters.[73] Druzhinin's admiration, or rather adoration, of Pushkin knew no bounds. 'I tell you in all honesty', he once wrote to Annenkov, 'that any person who has the temerity to think ill of Pushkin I am prepared to beat with my own hands – with a stick, a bottle, a stone or some other offensive weapon.' Pushkin could on one level be treated as a 'truly practical person, wise in his worldly opinions, a truly modern figure standing firmly on the soil of his environment and precisely through this gaining such fame and weight in his country'.[74] But he was also to be worshipped as a 'moral benefactor and educator'. His life – that is to say his spiritual life as it was revealed in his poetry – served as an excellent lesson for succeeding generations: any Russian should be able to draw from it 'rules about how one should live, love, correct the mistakes of one's life, labour, love one's labour and one's country'.[75] Like other true artists, Pushkin did not fulfil this great moral vocation by design; he did not attempt to persuade his readers to adopt partisan points of view on specific topical issues. His influence came instead from his ability to awaken in Russians an appreciation of the 'poetry' of which literature had been deprived by the adherents of the 'didactic' school, the followers of Gogol.

There is a purple passage in Druzhinin's second essay on Pushkin in which he attempts to capture for his readers the elusive beauty which he himself perceives in Pushkin's work. The passage deserves to be quoted at length, since not only is it Druzhinin's most eloquent celebration of Pushkin's talent, but it also provides the key to Druzhinin's own artistic credo. 'Our eyes clear' when we read Pushkin's work, Druzhinin writes,

we breathe more freely: we are borne from one world into another, from artificial illumination into the simple light of day, which is better than any bright illumination, although illumination, at the proper time, also has its attractions. Before us stands the same way of life, the same people – but how calm, tranquil and joyful it all looks! Where previously we saw along the roadside only drab fields and all sorts of other rotten things, now we feast our eyes upon rural scenes of Russian antiquity, on dry and many-coloured valleys, with all our heart we hail the first days of spring or a poetic night by the river – the night on which Tatyana visited Yevgeniy's deserted house. The road itself, on which we recently thought, as we travelled along it, only of jolts and the drunken Selifan, takes on a different aspect and our journey seems not so fatiguing as before. The unknown plains have something fantastic about them; the moon illuminates the passing darkness like an invisible man, little sparks and imaginary leagues rush up before the coachman's eyes, and before the poet's eyes the spirits of the road, howling mournfully, begin their poetic flight. Winter has come; winter is the season of frostbitten noses and of the misfortunes of Akakiy Akakiyevich, but for our singer and those who venerate him winter brings with it the previous radiant scenes, the very thought of which makes our heart pound. The peasant triumphantly tears over the new path on his wooden sledge; the heavy red-footed goose steps carefully on the bright ice, preparing to swim, slips, and to its utter astonishment falls over. The storm clouds the sky in gloom, weeping like a child, howling like a beast and stirring up the thatch on the old shack; but even the wild howl of the swirling winter storm bears an intoxicating poetry. Happy is he who can seek out this poetry, who celebrates winter and autumn in his verse, and on a frosty late October's day sits by the fireside calling together in his imagination the dear friends of his heart, the faithful companions of his schooldays, and repaying their friendship with sweet songs, remembering not the evil in life but exalting the good alone![76]

Clearly the 'poetry' to which Druzhinin pays homage in this passage – implicitly, by his *mélange* of allusions to Pushkin's works, as well as explicitly – is to be understood not as a literary form, but rather as an attribute of 'pure art'. For 'poetry' is to be found, Druzhinin tells us elsewhere, in Botkin's *Letters on Spain*, Ostrovsky's plays, Turgenev's novellas and even in places in Saltykov-Shchedrin's satirical *Provincial Sketches* and the prose of the supposed satirist Gogol as well as in the verse of Fet and Maykov. Indeed, Pushkin's *prose* – which Druzhinin values far more highly than Belinsky, who had considered it relatively insignificant[77] – is no poorer in poetry than his verse.[78] Unfortunately Druzhinin's definitions of 'poetry' are vague, no doubt partly because the concept itself was nebulous. In one place he describes it, for example, as the 'sun of our inner world which apparently does no good deeds and gives no one a brass farthing, but all the same animates the whole universe with its light'.[79] But he does seem to associate poetry in its broadest sense with certain qualities to which he devotes much attention in his literary criticism and to which he refers in his essays on Pushkin in particular. The first of these qualities is Olympian detachment. The true artist, Druzhinin emphasises repeatedly, is independent. He upholds the 'theory of impartial and free creation' as it is understood by poets of the highest order, such as Schiller, Goethe, Crabbe, Wordsworth and Coleridge.[80] In Russian literature Pushkin above all others had displayed this virtue of detachment: 'Pushkin stood above all schools, above all counsels', he looked on all around him with 'toleration' and 'indulgence'.[81] Deriving from this detachment was a second quality of poetry with which Pushkin's work was also richly endowed, namely the rare ability to see both sides of a question, to present reality in all its complexity. For the detached vision was an all-embracing one. The Pushkinian artist took '*comprehensiveness*' as his 'slogan'.[82] He could therefore restore to art the 'lofty side' of life which the advocates of the 'didactic' tendency had tried to exclude from it.[83] Ostrovsky was a case in point: he was to be congratulated for having realised that the 'positive and bright side of simple Russian life' might be embodied in art as a part of the whole, 'as a fresh and necessary note in the general harmony'.[84] The true artist's view of the totality of human experience, moreover, would be neither idyllic nor full of 'stupid spleen', but would be informed by a third quality of 'poetry' as Druzhinin understands it, namely a serenity that came of love of the life studied deeply and faithfully described. The 'true poet', he wrote in one of his essays on Crabbe, would look with calmness on scenes in which 'pseudo-poets' found only objects for their sarcasm; he would find pleasure and joy where such poets saw only 'anguish' and the 'dirt of life'.[85] He was imperturbable and conciliatory where others were irascible and divisive. Thus, like Pushkin as Druzhinin characterises him, the 'true poet' would bring warmth and radiance to his world; communion with him would lighten the spirits of his fellow men.

Druzhinin was initially confident that the movement which he himself was leading against the further development of 'didacticism' in Russian literature would be successful. He was heartened by the appearance of numerous works, such as Goncharov's *Oblomov*, Turgenev's *A Nest of Gentry* and Ostrovsky's play, *The Ward*, in which artistry was plainly not sacrificed to 'didactic' requirements and which seemed to demonstrate the emancipation of Russian literature from the tutelage of 'didactic' criticism. The emergence of Pisemsky, with whom he co-operated on the editorial board of *Biblioteka*, was a source of particular joy to him. With his balanced view of rural life, Pisemsky had dealt a fatal blow to the works of writers like Grigorovich, who knew the masses they supposedly described about as well as a 'clerk of the provisions department' knew the life of farmers in Spain.[86] Above all Druzhinin is gladdened by the flowering of the talent of Turgenev and Tolstoy in this period. Turgenev's writings were a 'whole poetic encyclopaedia of the last twenty years'.[87] And Tolstoy's early stories in general and his *Sebastopol Stories* in particular already enabled one to predict that the whole world, 'with its bright and its dark sides', would be revealed to this writer, whom no one would be able to divert from an independent path.[88] Druzhinin therefore felt able to declare, by 1858, that the atmosphere had suddenly freshened and been cleansed of the stinking vapours that had accumulated.[89]

Druzhinin as a literary critic

Druzhinin's attitudes to the imaginative literature of his day are inseparable from his conception of the role of the critic.

Although in deference to the censors Druzhinin rarely mentioned Belinsky by name in his articles of the mid 1850s, instead referring vaguely to the 'criticism of the Gogol period of Russian literature', it is nevertheless obvious that he sees Belinsky's figure towering over the literature of the 1840s and 1850s. He does not regard Belinsky's legacy, however, as entirely beneficial. On the one hand, it is true, he does accord very considerable praise to Belinsky for his services to Russian literature. He acclaims Belinsky's love of enlightenment, his 'boundless sympathy for all that was sacred, beautiful and just in life and poetry' and his ability to act in his time as the voice of all who aspired towards truth. Belinsky had ecstatically greeted any new talent or useful labour. He had made a cold public accept and love the nation's art. He had evaluated the work of the great Russian writers and had been the first to realise the true significance of Pushkin and Gogol. He had separated the ephemeral from what was of lasting worth, given order to the confused history of Russian literature and shown the logic of that literature's development. In short, his work was of such great importance that the editors of any journal had to know and study it thoroughly and to define their attitude towards it.[90]

And yet, on the other hand, all things, Druzhinin felt, had their shortcomings, Belinsky's work included. Its faults derived mainly from the conditions in which Belinsky had worked. He had had no sound opposition. His articles had been met with complete approval, or with silence, or with unworthy abuse. As a result he had begun to lose the tolerance and the self-discipline so necessary for an understanding of the truth. He had become hasty and even arrogant in his judgements. He would rush to put into print ideas too recently and improperly assimilated. Some of his views, which he expressed expecting no objections to them, were infantile. He rarely weighed his arguments and grasped the pro and contra of an issue. He believed too naïvely that all that was new and young contained the seed of great transformations. In some of his harsher judgements he was unfair to authors of the second rank, such as Marlinsky, for a critic should be a 'teacher', not the 'unbridled opponent' of a writer. He was too hostile to those who were at least sincere in their love of Russian literature, too intolerant an exponent of the dictum 'If you are not with me, you are against me'. And, of course, Belinsky had been responsible for the introduction into Russian literature of that didactic tendency which Druzhinin considered it the main purpose of his own criticism to counteract. Thus, whatever the merits of Belinsky's work, Druzhinin would not submit to what he called 'critical fetishism'. He had never built 'literary idols' for himself, and now, in the new age, ten years after Belinsky's death, all his instincts rebelled when he encountered 'servile, pale, dry, talentless copies of the old original'. Having remained independent when Belinsky's star had been at its zenith, he was not going to sacrifice that independence now that it had declined.[91]

Now it is undeniable that as a critic Druzhinin did have some qualities in common with Belinsky. Not least, of course, he had a deep and sincere love of literature; like Belinsky he commended the faithfulness of literature to reality, as he perceived it at least; and in some respects his evaluation of Pushkin resembled that of Belinsky. But, just as he tried to turn Russian literature off the course on which Belinsky was thought to have placed it in his final years, so in many respects Druzhinin also diverted literary criticism from the channels into which Belinsky had directed it. There are in his works none of the large topical ideas of a significance transcending the purely literary which we find repeatedly in the writings of Belinsky, with their thinly veiled tracts on the plight of the educated man in the 1830s and 1840s, egoism and altruism, the stagnation of Nicolae-van Russia. In short, Druzhinin's criticism lacks the social, moral and political dimensions of Belinsky's publicism.

Let us take firstly the lack of the social dimension. Analysis of the society reflected in a work of art is rare in Druzhinin's writing. He is interested primarily in the formal artistic appreciation of a work, rather than in its social or historical context. In his review of the plays of Ostrovsky, for example, he sets out to explain their dramatic success, proceeding to look at their '*structure, characters and language*'.[92] And it is significant that in some instances where Druzhinin does make broader reference to social types – for example, when he is talking of the 'superfluous man' as described in Turgenev's work, or of the character paralysed by that lethargy which Dobrolyubov designated *oblomovshchina* – then he tends to minimise the peculiarity of those social types to Russia.

Secondly, let us consider Druzhinin's dilution of the moral content of literary criticism. Belinsky's reviews, in the 1840s at any rate, had glowed with a passion (*strast'*) that came of a strong sense of moral rightness or wrongness and a fierce commitment to what Belinsky perceived as truth and justice. Druzhinin, on the other hand, admires in the literary critic, no less than in the creative writer, a detachment or dispassionateness (*bespristrastiye*) which – like the toleration already advocated in Belinsky's lifetime by Granovsky and Botkin – was quite incompatible with such impassioned pleading. Repeatedly he commends this detachment and promises to remain impartial in his judgements. He will look, he says, 'without anger and prejudice' into charges made by *Sovremennik* against Ostrovsky.[93] Again, he claims his conclusion concerning Turgenev's work is 'impartial'.[94] Clearly he hopes to preside over the development of a new school of Russian writers, whose main characteristic will be that toleration and ability to resolve antagonisms which he admires in Pushkin but which he considers Belinsky and the writers of the 1840s to have lost. He seems to intend that *Biblioteka* should set the example for this new school, for he invites contributions to the journal from representatives of different points of view and promises to proceed in a measured way according to the dictum aptly taken from Goethe, '*ohne Hast, ohne Rast*' (without haste, without rest).[95] This determination not to engage the moral sensibility of the critic or reader, however, was not calculated to appeal even to some of the more moderate elements in the Russian intelligentsia of the second half of the 1850s. Turgenev, for example, criticised Druzhinin's article on Belinsky on the grounds that it was 'intelligent and impartial', but 'cold'. He repeated the criticism to Tolstoy, whom he tried to discourage from becoming too infatuated with Druzhinin: when *he* was young, Turgenev told Tolstoy in a paternal tone, 'only enthusiastic natures' had had an effect on him. Again, *Biblioteka* under Druzhinin's editorship would be 'efficient, respectable and useful', wrote Turgenev, but it would be too 'cold' and 'passionless' (*besstrastna*) and there would be little that was 'Russian' in it.[96] And there is indeed something very alien to the Russian intelligentsia in Druzhinin's exaltation of the literature and life of the 'practical' English people, of the virtues to be found, as he once put it, 'in cold and positive England'.[97] Passion and partiality, then, departed from literary criticism in the hands of Druzhinin, and with them went warmth, 'Russianness' and moral conviction.

Thirdly, let us consider Druzhinin's removal – or, rather, transformation – of the political quality that was inherent in Belinsky's impassioned moral outbursts (for with its exaltation of truth and its quest for the good Belinsky's work was necessarily subversive in the conditions of Nicolaevan Russia). It is interesting in this connection that contemporaries, even the more moderate among them, unanimously describe Druzhinin not as a liberal, as he is known to us in Soviet historiography, but as a *conservative*. 'He stood out among us all by his extreme conservatism', wrote Grigorovich in his memoirs.[98] Admittedly, Grigorovich may not always be the most reliable witness, but others support his view in this instance. Panayev mentions Druzhinin's 'rotten conservatism';[99] Herzen, talking of *Biblioteka* as it is characterised by Druzhinin's outlook, also mentions with indignation its 'conservative' character.[100] And Turgenev addresses Druzhinin in his correspondence as 'dearest of conservatives' and in an obituary to his friend, speaking of Druzhinin's love of England, suggests that in English conditions he would doubtless have found himself in the ranks of the Tories.[101] On what evidence, though, did these writers base their classification of Druzhinin as a 'conservative'? Not on Druzhinin's statements of a more or less political nature, for he spoke of the legitimacy of protest against the oppressive régime of Nicholas I, approved of the reformatory intentions of the post-Nicolaevan government and clearly favoured the abolition of serfdom. As late as 1859 he wrote, for example, with reference to the literature and criticism of the 1840s:

One can see a protest against everything that is now changing and being rebuilt *through the good aspirations* of our government: against the serf-owning order, which is now repenting in Russia [*sic*]: against embezzlement, bribery and corruption, with which the government is waging a noble struggle, against obscurantism . . . [102]

In Druzhinin's aesthetic credo, on the other hand, Panayev, Herzen and Turgenev did find good grounds for their classification of Druzhinin as 'conservative'. For this credo tended to undermine the case of the social reformer in several important ways.

In the first place, the credo's dispassionate quality seemed to render it politically innocuous and consequently in some small measure to diminish the pressure on a government traditionally reluctant to reform. What Druzhinin did not understand, Nekrasov complained, was that the only honourable course of action a man could take in the circumstances was indeed to indict and to protest.[103] Objectivity could all too easily be interpreted as indifference to the plight of the masses. In the second place, Druzhinin's suggestion that the true poet *loved* reality seemed as reactionary in its implications as the Hegelian formula, briefly adopted by Belinsky, that the 'real is rational'. That despotic, semi-feudal Russia might be described in serene terms was itself offensive to many; but to love the society in which one lived whatever its imperfections – as Druzhinin explicitly urged the poet to do[104] – that would have represented a political betrayal to those who could not accept tsarism and its institutions. In the third place, in the cult of the detached artist there seemed implicit an élitism as clear as that which Belinsky, early in the last phase of his career, had attacked in Pushkin's poem 'The Mob'.[105] The crowd, Druzhinin asserted, should raise itself up to the level of the poet, the poet should not descend to the level of the crowd; and by 'crowd' Druzhinin meant educated society, not the 'coarse' mass, the '*vile multitude*', which was too untutored to influence the poet at all.[106] And, in the fourth place, Druzhinin's view of art is broadly speaking that Hegelian view in which Chernyshevsky, in his dissertation on the 'aesthetic relations of art to reality', had tried to reveal reactionary implications. The world of poetry, Druzhinin wrote in one of his articles on Turgenev was a world 'governed by its own laws which have absolutely nothing in common with the laws of the simple, prosaic world'; it was an 'elevated world' clearly superior to everyday reality.[107] Naturally this aesthetic seemed to the political radical to divert attention from existing earthly misery to a supposed celestial serenity and to encourage precisely that tragic view of life and stoical resignation to unhappiness which we strongly sense in Turgenev's fiction.

Finally, 'conservatism' was also implicit in Druzhinin's work as a translator of Shakespeare, no less than in Botkin's work as a translator of Carlyle. Apparently determined to exclude overtly political views from literary criticism, Druzhinin chose to insinuate them instead through works which he could describe as 'pure art'. His translation of *King Lear* – and especially, Turgenev felt, the tenderness with which Druzhinin, in his introduction to the play, had described the character of Kent, the 'faithful servant, the ideal of the true loyal subject'[108] – seemed already to imply a sympathy for the threatened order in 1856. More telling, however, was Druzhinin's translation of *Coriolanus*, which came out in 1858 – that is to say the year in which the production of 'accusatory works', in Druzhinin's opinion, reached a peak.[109] Shakespeare's play concerns the limitation of the power of the nobility by the masses, who, in the new age, in Shakespeare's words, 'must have their voices'. Towards these masses Coriolanus, the great warrior and selfless patriot, shows 'soaring insolence'. He finds them fickle. 'He that trusts to you', he tells their representatives,

> Where he should find you lions, finds you hares;
> Where foxes, geese; you are no surer, no,
> Than is the coal of fire upon the ice
> Or hailstone in the sun.

He deplores their aspiration to 'curb the will of the nobility' and fears that the advance of democracy would weaken the state and jeopardise the peace:

> Where gentry, title, wisdom,
> Cannot conclude but by the yea and no
> Of general ignorance – it must omit
> Real necessities, and give way the while
> To unstable slightness.[110]

Both in Rome and in the camp of the enemy of the Romans, to which Coriolanus deserts, the voice of the nobility counsels reason and moderation against the crude impulsiveness of the mob, though their pleas are to no avail. Clearly Shakespeare's tribunes of the Roman people, with their blind disrespect for the general who had once saved them, are equated in Druzhinin's mind with the Russian *raznochintsy* who make strident demands on behalf of a benighted mass and express a plebeian scorn for the unpractical artist, noble in spirit as well as social rank. Druzhinin himself reveals an obvious sympathy for Coriolanus when in his essay on the 'criticism of the Gogol period' he describes him as 'one of those stern heroes' about whom Thomas Carlyle had recently lectured. And in the same article he seems to underline his belief that Shakespeare's play had a contemporary relevance for his own society: *Coriolanus* could be interpreted, he suggested, as a 'whole course of political wisdom'; it was a 'valuable tablet [*skrizhal'*] for rulers, economists, friends of mankind, thinkers and statesmen' who cared for their native land.[111] It was no doubt with precisely these considerations in mind that Turgenev congratulated Druzhinin on his choice of play to translate and that Botkin described *Coriolanus*, in a letter to Druzhinin, as having the 'greatest topicality'.[112]

Druzhinin's last years and his loss of influence

In the last years of his life, the early 1860s, Druzhinin seems to draw away from current and local realities. As reform is implemented and debate enlivened in Russia, he returns to the genre of the light *feuilleton* in which he had excelled in the early 1850s and in the field of criticism he writes almost exclusively about English literature. In his eagerness to assert the importance of art divorced from topical issues he seems sometimes to lapse in his judgement: he praises G. A. Lawrence's novel, *Guy Livingstone*, a crude and frivolous melodrama, because its spirit is 'completely opposite ... to the analytical, half-sad, half-satirical spirit of the main figures in modern art'.[113] But in any case this final phase of Druzhinin's literary career was neither long nor productive. From the late 1850s he was afflicted with failing health and a decreasing capacity for work, and in January 1864, not yet forty years of age, he died of consumption, which the harsh St Petersburg climate had helped to bring to an early crisis.

As a matter of fact, even as Druzhinin flourished as a critic the public began to cool towards the point of view he represented. Druzhinin is now 'harmless', wrote Chernyshevsky towards the end of 1856, 'because no one listens to him and no one reads him'.[114] His 'rotten tendency produces sympathy in no one except N. I. Grech and F. Bulgarin', Panayev affirmed in the following year, for it was a time when 'pure art, *"l'art pour l'art"* ', had 'no effect on the Russian public'.[115] And by 1860 Druzhinin had evidently ceased altogether to exercise any significant influence on Russian intellectual life. The journal *Biblioteka* which he had edited was now taken and read very little, if we are to believe Saltykov-Shchedrin: it was losing ground to *Sovremennik*, which satisfied the taste of the public for topical material and polemic. Even Tolstoy, whose epicurean side had been strongly drawn towards Druzhinin, could not accept his former mentor's views when the more sober moral side of his nature began to prevail: there was nothing to prevent lovers of the classics, of whom he was one, from 'seriously reading poems and novellas and seriously discussing them', he wrote to Fet in 1860, but 'something else' was needed now, and he, Tolstoy, favoured pedagogical work among the peasantry.[116] Meanwhile the poets, if they did not adopt a civic stance, were 'hooted into silence'[117] or, like Fet – whom Druzhinin so much admired and whose fate he rightly regarded as portentous[118] – they retired into seclusion and lamented the passing of the golden age of Russian poetry.

Thus Druzhinin's criticism and the art he valued went out of demand in a utilitarian age when Russia was undergoing its belated transition from virtual feudalism to rudimentary capitalism and when the great social and political change long awaited by the independent intelligentsia seemed at last to be imminent. Nor was it only in the field of aesthetics that the apostles of 'pure art', of whom Druzhinin was the leading representative, lost important territory, for their plea for an art that was detached, even-handed and tolerant overlapped with the more general intellectual and, in the final analysis, political position based on the same liberal values. And that political position – which, as we shall shortly see, was most clearly delineated in the second half of the 1850s by Kavelin – would not long be held once the literary battles had been lost.

There is finally a melancholy postscript to Druzhinin's biography which eloquently evokes the mood of emptiness and futility that men of liberal persuasion must have experienced by 1864 as a result of this defeat of the values they cherished. Shortly after Druzhinin's death a funeral feast was held in his honour at the Hôtel de France in St Petersburg. Botkin, Annenkov, Turgenev, Goncharov, Grigorovich and the diarist Nikitenko were present, but Nekrasov, who had made a hasty departure from Druzhinin's funeral a fortnight earlier, was conspicuously absent from this company, with which he was by now in a state of implacable hostility. There seems to have been no real grief, or sense of loss, or even the elation that might have come of a burning desire to emulate the deceased. The mourners dined and drank liberally, but the occasion was flat and ended with the eminent men of letters talking about women and exchanging, in Nikitenko's words, 'various revolting scandalous stories'. Turgenev, writing to Pauline Viardot the following day, complained of a hangover.[119]

6
Konstantin Dmitriyevich Kavelin
(1818–1885)

Kavelin's life, character and work

Konstantin Dmitriyevich Kavelin was born in 1818 into a family which owned landed property and serfs in the province of Ryazan. His father was Russian but his mother was Scottish, the orphaned daughter of one John Baillie, who had worked as an architect at the court of the Emperor Paul. His early education was haphazard, like Granovsky's: he was taught at home by a succession of more or less inadequate tutors, among them the young Belinsky, who for a short time in 1835 was employed to prepare Kavelin for examinations in Russian literature. (The critic was a source of inspiration to his impressionable adolescent pupil, but hardly competent as a teacher.) From 1835 to 1839 Kavelin studied in the law faculty of Moscow University and for a further three years remained in the city, living with his parents and continuing his studies privately. Here he began to mix with prominent members of the Westernist intelligentsia, such as Granovsky (who had a great influence on him) and the university professors, Redkin and Kryukov. He also met Chaadayev. At the same time he frequented Yelagina's salon, at which he came into contact with leading Slavophiles. In 1842 he moved to St Petersburg in order to serve in the Ministry of Justice. Here in the northern capital he resumed his acquaintance with Belinsky and grew close to Botkin, Turgenev, Nekrasov, Panayev and other prominent men of letters. It was his ambition, however, to pursue an academic career, and in 1844 an opening presented itself: he was offered the post of assistant in the Department of the History of Russian Legislation in the University of Moscow following his successful defence of a master's dissertation on seventeenth- and eighteenth-century Russian legal procedure, and was shortly promoted to the rank of professor. Not that Kavelin's career in Moscow University was to last for long, for he was one of those who in 1848 tendered their resignations in protest at Professor Krylov's treatment of his wife (who, as it happened, was the elder sister of Kavelin's own wife, *née* Korsh, whom Kavelin had married in 1845). Kavelin's resignation, unlike Granovksy's (see p. 64 above), was accepted and he moved once again to St Petersburg, where he seems to have endured the harsh intellectual climate after 1848 with more resilience than most. 'Only Kostya [i.e. Konstantin]', wrote Ogaryov to Herzen in 1849, offered the consoling sight of someone who preserved his youthfulness and who, working tirelessly, did not yield to the general depression.[1] Between 1848 and 1857 he worked in various capacities in the civil service, first in the Ministry of the Interior, then, from 1850 to 1853, as head of the education section of the headquarters of the military educational institutions and finally, from 1853 to 1857, as head of a department in the office of the Committee of Ministers. He also joined the Imperial Russian Geographical Society (whose members cautiously helped to prepare the ground for the emancipation of the serfs by collecting ethnographical and statistical material on the life of the peasantry) and accepted the position of secretary of the Imperial Free Economic Society, whose members fulfilled a similar function by disseminating the principles of 'rational agriculture'. His interest in the practical questions relating to the abolition of serfdom intensified in 1853, when on the death of his mother he inherited an estate and serfs in Samara province. And in the same period of his life he resumed his academic career, taking a chair in the Law Faculty of the University of St Petersburg in 1857 and remaining in it until 1861.[2]

Kavelin was in many respects – and not only by virtue of his social background and the circle of his friends – a typical representative of the 'men of the 1840s'. He had the same conciliatory nature as Granovsky and Botkin (a fact to which the breadth of the circle of his acquaintances throughout the 1840s and 1850s bears witness). He also had the passionate moral commitment to ideas and the wide-ranging intellectual curiosity which are so marked in Granovsky and Belinsky. Not that these qualities were the exclusive property of the older generation, of course; nor should we consider the patriotic fervour with which Kavelin's thought is imbued (and which obliterates any sense of partial spiritual allegiance to his mother's native Scotland) altogether alien to the younger generation of the intelligentsia. But Kavelin possessed too that warmth of heart and contagious enthusiasm so characteristic of the 'men of the

1840s' but less apparent among the younger radicals. Friendship, for example, he tended like Turgenev's 'fathers' to regard as a sacred personal bond rather than a form of collaboration based on intellectual affinity. He was not a skilled raconteur – his stories lacked colour, Turgenev felt[3] – but in debate he would captivate his audience as he held forth with vibrant voice and sparkling eyes. His ingenuous quixotism, it is true, gave him an eccentric or child-like quality in the eyes of some contemporaries. To Nikitenko, for example, he seemed a 'sweet, capable but unbalanced youth', an indisputably gifted person wanting, however, in judgement and profundity. His tilting at windmills might even be construed, Nikitenko thought, as a species of vanity.[4] And yet, on the other hand, quixotism, for all its shortcomings, was a valuable quality, for it ensured the preservation of a youthful vigour. Kavelin had two gifts, wrote one of Druzhinin's correspondents, which rarely go together: '*jeunesse de cœur et jeunesse de visage*'.[5] And in displaying that *jeunesse de cœur* throughout the 1850s Kavelin helped to sustain the spirit of the thought of the previous decade even as the value of its content was increasingly called into question.

Although Kavelin first makes an impact on Russian intellectual life later than Granovsky, Botkin and Annenkov, with the publication in 1847 of his *magnum opus* on the 'juridical way of life of ancient Russia', nevertheless his intellectual development follows a similar pattern to that of the other thinkers examined in this study. It is therefore as well to divide his career into the same broad phases as theirs: an early implicit opposition to Nicolaevan autocracy expressed through an enlightened 'Westernism'; indications in the late 1840s of differences of opinion with Belinsky which betokened the adoption of a moderate position when opinion began to polarise in the second half of the 1850s; lively participation in the debates of the post-Nicolaevan period and a growing aversion to iconoclasm and radical social change; and, finally, alienation from radical thinkers as their demands became more militant after the emancipation of the serfs in February 1861. We should at the same time, however, bear in mind the fact that Kavelin's contribution to the intellectual life of the 1840s and 1850s was also in some measure different both in quantity and quality from that of all the other subjects of this study. Unlike Granovsky, Botkin and Annenkov, at least, he was a prolific writer (though certainly not an elegant or a lucid one). Moreover, he did not write on the subject of imaginative literature, which preoccupied so many of his contemporaries, particularly Botkin, Annenkov and Druzhinin, in the 1850s. In fact, he was a poor judge of art (although he did love Beethoven); in literature he would seek first and foremost the dominant idea; sometimes he would altogether miss the point of a work, as Belinsky complained,[6] and he was inappreciative of an author's artistry. On the other hand, he was considered an authority on the subject of Russian legal history and the founder of the étatist school of historians. He was also a tireless advocate of reform, author of a major project for the emancipation of the serfs and of important essays on the question of the relationship of social classes in Russia. An examination of his thought, therefore, provides a further necessary dimension to our picture of the outlook of the liberal 'men of the 1840s', a dimension that is more explicitly social and political.

'A Brief Survey of the Juridical Way of Life of Ancient Russia' (1847)

By far the most important early work Kavelin wrote, and the one which established him at the age of 28 as a leading figure in the intellectual life of the nation, was the long essay published in *Sovremennik* at the beginning of 1847 under the title 'A Brief Survey of the Juridical Way of Life of Ancient Russia'. Kavelin applies himself in this essay to the task of finding the answer to a riddle which, he claims, no one has as yet been able to solve. What, he asks, is the nature of the principle which has governed the development of Russian history from its beginnings in the ninth century – when, according to the chronicles, Varangian princes had been invited to rule over the native Slav tribes – to the eighteenth century, when Peter the Great had embarked on that immense programme of westernisation with whose effects Russians were still in Kavelin's time trying to come to terms? A key to the riddle was to be found, he suggests, in the Christian religion, which had been officially introduced into Russia in 988. Christianity had revealed and nurtured in man an inner spiritual world of which primitive mankind had been only dimly aware; indeed, it had set this inner world 'infinitely higher than the external, material world'. With the release of man's spiritual energies, his personality (or we may also say 'individuality' – the Russian *lichnost'* is ambiguous) acquired a new importance, a 'great, holy significance'. In antiquity *'man as a man'* had no value, but with the advent of Christianity *'man and the human personality'* acquired a worth that was infinite and unconditional. Man became the 'living vessel of the spiritual world', the representative, potential, if not actual, of God on earth. He was no longer the 'slave of nature and circumstances' but their master. Most importantly, for Kavelin's purposes, the promotion of the Christian principle of man's unconditional worth and individuality inevitably had social consequences: man's 'moral and individual development' became the 'slogans of all modern history'.[7]

The Germanic tribes, having mixed with the Roman elements in the lands they had conquered and having accepted Christianity, founded states of a new historical type, which were imbued with the 'individual principle'. The Russian tribes, on the other hand, had taken quite a different historical course (although they were eventually to approach the same destination). Among the Russians the principle of personality or individuality had not existed in the early stages of their history. Their social organisation had been 'exclusively patrimonial', being based on the principle of kinship and blood relationships alone. The ancient Russians lived as one family in settlements under the rule of an elder; they recognised no political power or legal authority, devised no laws, set up no administration and owned no personal property. Even in the nineteenth century vestiges of the Russian's primeval view of his relationship with his community survived, Kavelin contended, in the terminology which the peasant customarily used when referring to other people, even to people with whom he had no family tie: the landowner he would address as 'father', his seniors as 'uncle' or 'aunt', 'grandfather' or 'grandmother', his juniors as 'children' and his equals as 'brother' or 'sister'. Nor was the development of the patrimonial way of life in ancient Russia affected by contact with other peoples, as may have been the case among the other Slavs. For no foreign tribes had settled among the Russians with the exception of the Varangians; and, whereas the Varangians had in other places left their imprint on the way of life of the peoples they subjugated, in Russia they themselves were quickly subordinated to the influence of the indigenous population. Nevertheless Russian social organisation did begin by itself to evolve from a patrimonial form towards one in which the individual was liberated from the bonds of kinship. Or, to put it another way, the principle of personality or individuality, which was characteristic of modern European societies, advanced in Russia at the expense of the patrimonial principle. Indeed, the distinct periods into which Russia's history could be divided coincided with the phases of this development.[8]

The patrimonial principle had begun to decay even in Kievan times. It had been the intention of Yaroslav, who ruled as Grand Prince of Kiev from 1019 to 1054, to use this principle to strengthen the political unity of Kievan Russia. All princes would belong to one clan, and each would have his allotted position in the hierarchy; at the head, as Grand Prince, would stand the eldest, that is to say the prince nearest by birth to the founder of the clan. On Yaroslav's death, however, his heirs had disputed his heritage and the interests of the individual families had taken precedence over the interests of the princely clan as a whole. Monomakh and his son Mstislav had briefly revived Yaroslav's system, but the fierce rivalries which followed Monomakh's death in 1125 marked the beginning of the irreversible decline of the patrimonial principle and the concomitant destruction of Russia's political unity. Out of the internecine strife of the twelfth and thirteenth centuries, however, there emerged a new type of prince – of which Andrey Bogolyubsky was an outstanding early representative – who denied his kith and kin a share of his domain and assumed unlimited authority. Paradoxical as it may seem, the Tartars had actually assisted the development of this type; for, since they valued the prince who was the best servant and who most promptly paid his tribute, seniority in the clan or family came to have less importance as a qualification for political power than certain practical personal merits. Thus it was the 'gifted, intelligent, bright Muscovite princes' who were best equipped to take advantage of the opportunities afforded by Tartar rule for self-aggrandisement. And, as their power increased, so these princes sacrificed the interests of the family to those of a state which was becoming indivisible. Admittedly this process was slow, but it was all the same an 'act of thought, of consciousness'. The individual had entered the historical arena. The emergence of the Muscovite state therefore marked at one and the same time a departure from a way of life based excusively on blood relationships and the beginning of the era in which the personality would operate independently in juridical and civil affairs.[9]

The Muscovite period of Russian history was the 'dawn of the new' and the 'twilight of the old'. It was marked off from the preceding and following epochs by the reigns of Ivan the Terrible (that is Ivan IV) and Peter the Great respectively. These two rulers, the 'two greatest figures in Russian history', had much in common. Both acknowledged the 'idea of the state' and were the 'most noble and worthy representatives' of this idea (though Ivan, as Kavelin somewhat ingenuously put it, acknowledged the idea 'as a poet', while Peter acknowledged it as a man who was above all 'practical'). No one before or after Ivan, except Peter, had acted so 'energetically' against the 'nobles' and regional rulers who oppressed the people. He ousted the boyars from all the main branches of administration and seats of power and entrusted positions of authority to his own appointees of common origin, who owed their ascendancy to him and were ready to serve the state. The formation of the *oprichnina* in 1565 should also be seen, Kavelin contended, as a manifestation of Ivan's intention to establish a service gentry in place of a hereditary nobility and to replace the patrimonial or blood principle by the principle of 'personal worth' in the government of the land. (It was quite wrong, Kavelin maintained, to suppose that Ivan intended by the creation of the *oprichnina* to separate himself from the Russian common people, whom he loved and wished to free from oppression by the boyars.) Thus Ivan the Terrible, as Kavelin eccentrically interpreted him, was a misunderstood genius who had failed only because Russia was not yet ready for the changes he tried to bring about. Forced to struggle with the 'half-patriarchal, senseless environment' in which he was destined to live, Ivan had eventually lost faith in his ability to carry out his 'grand designs' and it was under the burden of disappointment that he finally became a 'bigot, a tyrant and a coward'. His 'executions and atrocities', however, should not blind one to his greatness. In fact, it was because he was so great that he fell so far.[10]

Only Peter had understood Ivan; he was his 'great successor'. Endowed with a 'terrible will and amazing practical sense' and living in more propitious conditions over a century later, Peter was able to complete Ivan's work and set Russia on a new course. The individual personality, however, could not suddenly become independent, for it was quite undeveloped. It had to acquire content from the outside; the individual had to begin to 'think and act under foreign influence'. Such was the nature and significance of the age of intensive reforms initiated by Peter and only recently completed. In Peter the personality had renounced 'immediate, natural, exclusively national determinations'. (Kavelin means by this opaque assertion to say that with westernisation there began to appear individuals with a civic consciousness that was not entirely determined by their environment and indistinguishable from that of their fellows.) All Peter's private life and all his life as a statesman had constituted the 'first phase of the realisation of the principle of personality in Russian history'. Critics of Peter – and Kavelin was addressing the Slavophiles – argued that Peter's reforms had had detrimental consequences. They had served, Peter's critics alleged, to split Russian history into two quite distinct halves, to make Russians 'characterless, pitiable, ill-defined or undeveloped creatures' and to make a virtue out of repudiation of what was native in Russian culture. Kavelin conceded that such arguments did have an historical importance inasmuch as they revealed the attitudes of one part of Russian society as it had emerged after the reforms. But there was no truth in them. An 'impassable gulf' between old and new existed only in the imagination of the Slavophiles. The two Russias, pre-Petrine and post-Petrine, were not unconnected. On the contrary, there was an inner link between them, as Kavelin claimed to have shown by drawing attention to a supposed guiding principle in Russian history. 'We became Europeans', he declared, 'while remaining Russians as before.'[11]

Kavelin's long essay at once earned him the reputation of a 'magnificent historian' (the phrase belongs to Herzen).[12] And it did indeed have a considerable impact on Russian historical scholarship, for it contained the most popular early statement of the so-called clan theory, according to which ancient Russian social organisation was based on kinship. (In its broad outline this view was also advanced – with greater erudition and more meticulous scholarship – by the historian Solovyov in his master's dissertation of 1845, his doctoral dissertation of 1847 and the first volume, published in 1851, of his monumental *History of Russia*.) Moreover, Kavelin's essay contained the germ of the view of the Russian state which was to be propounded by the étatist school of historians, whose most notable representative was Kavelin's pupil Chicherin. The étatist historians were to echo the belief, implicit in Kavelin's veneration of Ivan the Terrible and Peter the Great, that the state was the source of progress, civilisation and, paradoxical as it might seem, individual liberty in Russia. (Clearly this glorification of the state owed much to Hegel, as did Kavelin's search for a

guiding principle in historical development, and even to Granovsky, in whom we have found a reverence for the 'great men' of
history.)[13]

The establishment of Kavelin's reputation as an historian,
however, was probably due more to the fact that his views were
congenial to the 'Westernist' circles of the intelligentsia of the late
1840s than to any intrinsic merits or original theses in his scholarship. For his essay was taken by Westernisers and Slavophiles alike
as the definitive statement of the Westernist conception of Russian
historical development. Botkin, it is true, thought the essay would
have been 'incomparably better' if it had not been written from the
'German-philosophical point of view',[14] but Belinsky received it
most enthusiastically. He was familiar in advance with the contents
of the essay and felt confident that the point of view taken by
Kavelin would ensure that the essay would be 'devilishly good',
'something highly unusual'. Having read it he declared that it was an
epoch-making work in Russian historical studies, and in his last
annual survey of Russian literature he reiterated his praise.[15] The
Slavophiles, on the other hand, were dismayed by the essay;
indeed, it was in answer to it (and to Belinsky's survey of Russian
literature for 1846, which was also published in the first number of
Sovremennik in 1847)[16] that Samarin wrote his own article 'On the
Historical and Literary Views of *Sovremennik*',[17] which Botkin, in
turn, described as a 'sort of Slavonic manifesto'.[18]

The relationship of Kavelin's essay to the current debate between
Westernisers and Slavophiles is clearly perceptible. Kavelin begins
by stating emphatically that the Russians are a European people
and that their history is to be considered together with that of the
Western peoples. Russian history – like Western European history
– represented a 'gradual *change* of forms, not their *repetition*'; it was
different, by virtue of this capacity to develop, from that of the East,
where from the beginning to the present time 'almost one and the
same thing' came into being over and over again.[19] Most importantly, Kavelin approved of the principle of personality or individuality which he maintained was governing the development he
detected in Russian history. The Slavophiles did not welcome this
principle. They did not wish to see the family and the analogous
commune weakened by individualism, because they would not
concede that if a man lived in the bosom of the family he lost
'resilience' and 'energy' and was lulled into torpor; on the contrary,

they believed that man was enriched by submerging his individuality in the larger brotherhood. Kavelin, on the other hand, contended that personality, conscious of its 'eternal, unconditional quality', was a prerequisite for any spiritual development among a people and that without it no people would play a significant role in the modern world. The gradual promotion of the principle of personality or individuality in Russian life, at the expense of the family principle beloved by the Slavophiles, was therefore to be regarded as both natural and desirable.[20] That was not to say that Kavelin's celebration of the principle of individuality consorted any better than Belinsky's or Granovsky's with veneration of rulers such as Peter in whose hands the state assumed its most authoritarian form. But it was consistent, despite the étatist conception of Russian history in which it was couched, with the Westernisers' crusade against a crude nationalism which engulfed the enlightened individual and stifled his noblest moral and civic impulses.

It is instructive, finally, to compare the conception of the role of the state in promoting individuality which is advanced here by Kavelin – a Westerniser who in the late 1850s was to become a typical representative of the emergent Russian liberalism – with that formulated by classical Western European liberal theorists. The task of identifying notions shared by a majority of those many thinkers of different periods and nationalities who are generally described as liberal is, of course, fraught with difficulty; but it would not be a great distortion of the truth to say that a principal concern of most Western European liberals has been the limitation of the extent to which the state may legitimately interfere in the affairs of its citizens. Humboldt, who discussed the cultivated individual's quest for personal fulfilment in his work on *The Limits of State Action*, held that the state should 'abstain from all solicitude for the positive welfare of citizens' and should not proceed one step further than is necessary to ensure their security from each other and from foreign enemies; for no other purpose should it limit their freedom.[21] This tendency to look on government as a purely protective agency became particularly pronounced in Victorian England, where it eventually gave rise to that extreme opposition to state intervention in the affairs of the individual which led Herbert Spencer to inveigh against public provision of even the most basic social amenities. John Stuart Mill, in his own famous inquiry into the 'nature and limits of the power which can be legitimately exercised by society over the individual', contends that while authority may historically have been necessary in order to protect the 'weaker members of the community from being preyed upon by innumerable vultures', it was nevertheless 'indispensable to be in a perpetual attitude of defence' against the 'beak and claws' of the 'king of the vultures' himself, since he would be 'no less bent upon preying on the flock than any of the minor harpies'. For Mill, following Humboldt, the assertion of individuality was 'one of the principal ingredients of human happiness, and quite the chief ingredient of individual and social progress'. And in the promotion of this individuality, which enhanced the value of the individual both to himself and to others, the state was entitled to exercise its power over a member of the community against his will only in order 'to prevent harm to others'.[22] Clearly no Russian liberal of the mid nineteenth century, least of all Kavelin, belonged to this libertarian Western tradition; rather it was in anarchism, which was to gain a large Russian following, that such opposition to the state was chiefly to find expression. Russian liberals might plausibly have argued, however, that the majority of their compatriots still dwelt in an age 'anterior to the time' when, in Mill's words, mankind had 'become capable of being improved by free and equal discussion' and that liberty, 'as a principle', therefore had no application in their country. Until such time there was nothing for them, as Mill gloomily predicted, 'but implicit obedience to an Akbar or a Charlemagne', if they were so fortunate as to find one.[23] Given Russia's backwardness and the political impotence of its small educated public, then, it is perhaps understandable that the emergence there of what has been described as the 'feeling, sensuous, thinking, creative individual released from bonds and liberated for self-realisation'[24] should have been associated with the ascendancy of precisely the sort of authoritarian ruler – Ivan the Terrible and Peter the Great in Kavelin's scheme, Charlemagne, Alexander the Great and Peter the Great in Granovsky's – whose iron grip on his subjects it was a principal concern of Western liberals to loosen. Thus while Western liberals enjoyed political rights and liberties and sought yet further restrictions on the authority of the state, Russian liberals – as Kavelin's subsequent career was eloquently to attest – emphasised the active, creative potentiality of the state as well as its passive, protective function and sought not so much to limit the power of their autocrat as to persuade him to use his power for the promotion of ends which they deemed worthy.

Kavelin's relationships within the intelligentsia in the late 1840s and 1850s

Kavelin's writings of the late 1840s and early 1850s represented for the most part an amplification of the basic views put forward in 'A Brief Survey of the Juridical Way of Life of Ancient Russia'. These writings reflect a continuing antipathy to Slavophilism, of which the most notable expression is his 'Reply to *Moskvityanin*', a lengthy rebuttal of the objections made by Samarin to his major essay. Taking up the Slavophile contention that Russians were ready for self-renunciation and self-sacrifice, Kavelin argues here for a greater realism. People had to be seen as they were, 'self-seeking and evil', not as the Slavophiles wished them to be, and society had to be fashioned accordingly. Until man was regenerated the best social order, in Kavelin's view, would not be the communal one envisaged by the Slavophiles but one in which the individual had the greatest scope for the expression of his personality which was consistent with the preservation of social stability.[25] Again, in a very long book review, published in 1848, he disputes the Slavophile notion that Western borrowing served to dilute Russian national distinctiveness. Just as a living organism assimilated the most varied food and drink and transformed them into its own flesh and blood, so a whole people, Kavelin argued, regarded everything from a particular point of view determined in advance by their character, history and degree of maturity at the given moment.[26]

There were also signs in 1847, however, of the same friction between Kavelin and Belinsky that arose at that time between the critic and his beloved friends, Granovsky and Botkin. Like Granovsky, Kavelin was reluctant to commit all his articles to *Sovremennik*, for which Belinsky was now demanding wholehearted support. Thus in January 1847 Kavelin wrote to Krayevsky, assuring him that he would continue to send work to *Otechestvennyye zapiski*, which he still held in high regard, even though his sympathies and friendships naturally inclined him towards *Sovremennik*.[27] Belinsky, it is true, continued to express his affection for Kavelin, but clearly regarded his attitude as perfidious, and even accused Kavelin, as he had accused Granovsky, of conspiring to ruin *Sovremennik* by assisting its rival.[28] And in November 1847 he expressed his horror at seeing that Krayevsky had advertised in his journal forthcoming articles by Kavelin on Russian history: the advertisement provided fresh evidence of Kavelin's treachery.[29] At the same time Belinsky found Kavelin guilty of offering the same sort of effective intellectual support to their opponents as Granovsky and Botkin. In December 1847, for example, he takes Kavelin to task for being too charitable – some would say fair-minded – in his reply to Samarin's criticisms of his 'Brief Survey of the Juridical Way of Life of Ancient Russia'. Kavelin had committed what in Belinsky's eyes was an indiscretion when he acknowledged at the end of his reply that Samarin was a 'gifted person'; in so doing Kavelin had shown Samarin such respect that the reader might have assumed that Kavelin was finding it difficult to combat his opponent. Kavelin ought instead to have routed Samarin with 'polite irony, a contemptuous gibe'. The Slavophiles were 'scoundrels' and Kavelin had inexcusably let one of them escape alive when he had had him under his heel; if one were attacking a reptile, one had to crush it.[30]

Kavelin's intellectual tolerance, the early signs of which gave rise to these objections on Belinsky's part in 1847, became fully apparent in the mid and late 1850s once debate was freer and political opinions began to be clarified. His circle of acquaintances at this period was exceptionally wide. His 'salon', recalled one of those who frequented it, attracted people of 'all possible shades and colours', some of whom were shortly to occupy, or indeed already did occupy, diametrically opposite positions on the political spectrum.[31] In the first place, he stood at the centre of the St Petersburg liberals, among whom were to be found relatively progressive bureaucrats such as the Milyutin brothers, academics such as the historian Solovyov and the economist Babst and writers such as Turgenev. In the second place, he became acquainted at this period with the Grand Duchess Yelena Pavlovna and even served briefly as tutor in jurisprudence to the son of Alexander II. And, in the third place, he now became quite close to Pogodin, the proponent of 'Official Nationality', with whom he had taken issue on several occasions in the late 1840s. Believing that conditions after the Crimean War required all honourable Russians to forget personal animosities and to join forces in faithful service of the motherland, Kavelin wished now to be reconciled with people with whom he had once been at odds. Friendship with Pogodin therefore blossomed, and at the beginning of 1858 Kavelin was able to write to his erstwhile antagonist, in his characteristically effusive manner: 'I appreciate and love you more than ever, Mikhail Petrovich: take this not as a phrase but as a word coming from the heart.'[32]

However, the clearest sign of Kavelin's toleration – and also, admittedly, of the relative unity which still existed in the intelligentsia in the mid 1850s – was perhaps his conciliatory attitude towards the radical young *raznochintsy*. His heart warmed in the presence of the younger generation, he told Pogodin in April 1856: here there were 'treasures of love, and faith and the springs of living life' (*sic*). If the young did have their oddities and caprices then these might be seen as the product of the abnormal environment in which they had grown up.[33] In a letter of 1857 to Herzen he wrote of the young in a similar spirit. The older generation was leaving the centre of the stage and a 'new tribe' was appearing which certainly possessed incomparably more knowledge – though not necessarily more warmth, faith and hope – than their elders.[34] It is possible that Kavelin found it relatively easy to tolerate the younger generation because his poor literary judgement and lack of interest in aesthetics rendered him indifferent to the provocative judgements issuing in the second half of the 1850s from Chernyshevsky and Dobrolyubov on the subject of imaginative literature – judgements which infuriated Botkin, Annenkov and Druzhinin. Be that as it may, his personal relations with the two leading *raznochintsy* remained good even as the opposing liberal and radical positions, of which Kavelin and Chernyshevsky themselves were the main representatives respectively, were being defined. 'I know him well', Kavelin wrote to Katkov in October 1858 with Chernyshevsky in mind, 'and I can assure you most positively that he doesn't deserve to be called a man without conviction'. It might not always be easy to agree with Chernyshevsky's views, but one could not accuse him of insincerity or dishonesty. He deserved 'complete and deep respect and sympathy'.[35] Antonovich tells us that Kavelin was by no means hostile to *Sovremennik* in the late 1850s and that he even placed a high value on its 'hissing' (that is to say its social criticism).[36] Dobrolyubov gave lessons on Russian language and literature to Kavelin's son until the boy's death of scarlet fever, at the age of fourteen, in February 1861. And it is perhaps worth pointing out that Kavelin was one of the small group of people – most of whom belonged to the radical wing of the intelligentsia – who attended Dobrolyubov's funeral in November 1861.[37]

Chernyshevsky, for his part, had regarded Kavelin with some affection ever since his first encounter with him in 1850, when Chernyshevsky had been a student at St Petersburg University where Kavelin was by then teaching. Kavelin was an 'extremely considerate, nice, obliging person', Chernyshevsky wrote at that time.[38] It is clear from a letter written to his family that Chernyshevsky still counted Kavelin among his 'friends' in 1858, and according to one source he remained close to him even as late as the spring of 1862 (though this continuing intimacy may be partly explained by Chernyshevsky's compassion for Kavelin after the death of the latter's son).[39] In his published essays, meanwhile, Chernyshevsky repeatedly praised Kavelin as a scholar, sometimes lavishly. In any case Kavelin deserved the respect of the younger generation for his contribution to the activity of that Pleiad of men of letters, enlightened and progressive in their day, who had clustered around Belinsky in the 1840s.[40] Dobrolyubov, who met Kavelin for the first time in 1858, also felt close to him. Trying to clear up a personal misunderstanding in 1859 Dobrolyubov asked one of his correspondents to refer for a character reference, as it were, to someone who knew him well, Chernyshevsky or Kavelin, for example: their report, Dobrolyubov felt sure, would not be unfavourable to him.[41] His lessons to Kavelin's son, he is said to have given 'out of friendship';[42] and, like Chernyshevsky, he often commended Kavelin's works in his articles.[43] He also had a special fondness for Kavelin's wife, who seems to have acted as a sort of senior confidante to him; at any rate Dobrolyubov pours out his feelings to her in a surviving letter which he wrote from Paris, where he had found an unaccustomed happiness in the lap of the simple and friendly French family with whom he was boarding.[44]

It is undeniable, however, that in spite of this undoubted personal closeness between Kavelin, on the one hand, and Chernyshevsky and Dobrolyubov, on the other, the attitude of the *raznochintsy* to the older liberal was tinged with a certain irony. 'In general Kavelin goes round being good-natured as before', Chernyshevsky wrote to Dobrolyubov from St Petersburg in September 1860.[45] Apparently Chernyshevsky and his militant young disciples took pleasure in frightening the liberal circles they visited by talking of axes, a favourite symbol at the time for violent revolution.[46] Most importantly, Chernyshevsky evidently associated Kavelin with those liberals whom he had been attacking throughout 1858 in his essays on French history and politics.[47] And when in 1859 he reported to Dobrolyubov on his meeting in London with Herzen – who had criticised the revolutionary posture of the younger generation – he summed the *émigré* up, in his disappointment, as 'Kavelin squared'.[48] Dobrolyubov's attitude was equally ambivalent. He was sceptical in the face of Kavelin's naïve optimism that the enlightened members of the editorial commissions would bring about effective agrarian reform, though he did not question the sincerity of Kavelin's zeal and entered into a friendly alcoholic wager with him on the likely date of publication of the emancipation edict.[49] Again, writing to Chernyshevsky from Messina in June 1861, shortly before his death, Dobrolyubov envisaged what he would do on his return to St Petersburg:

I know that . . . as before I shall order a suit from Charmeur's which will fit me as badly as one from any other tailor, that I'll go to the Italian opera, of which I make no sense, that I'll make fun of Kavelin and Turgenev, whom I sincerely love . . .[50]

For Chernyshevsky and Dobrolyubov, then, social intercourse with Kavelin was beguiling, though politically pointless. For Kavelin, on the other hand, the maintenance of amicable relations with the pragmatic young radicals was not only genuinely stimulating but also an essential strand in the politics of conciliation in which he was currently engaged.

Kavelin's 'Memorandum on the Emancipation of the Peasants in Russia' (1855)

While attempting to play down differences of political opinion in the intelligentsia of the mid 1850s, Kavelin remained faithful to the humanitarian ideals of the generation to which he belonged. (Indeed, it was only by promoting those ideals, he believed, that the intelligentsia could prevent dangerous divisions from opening up in Russian society.) This humanitarianism found expression chiefly in Kavelin's vigorous contribution in the mid 1850s to the discussion of the abolition of serfdom, which in a letter of 1856 to Pogodin he described as the 'question of all questions, the ill of all ills, the misfortune of all our misfortunes'.[51]

Kavelin put forward his proposals for the emancipation of the serfs in a long 'memorandum', written in 1855, which was to remain one of the most important projects drafted on the subject for discussion in the liberal and radical intellectual circles. (Other substantial projects were written by Samarin and two other landowners with Slavophile sympathies, Koshelyov and Prince Cherkassky.) The causes of Russia's poverty, Kavelin argues, are many: the system of government, the absence of a rigorous judicial system, the constraints placed on trade and industry and, most important of all, the institution of serfdom. The baneful consequences of this institution were both economic and moral. Unpaid labour was performed 'lazily and unwillingly' and was at least twice as unproductive as free labour. As a consequence vast resources were wasted, with an annual loss to the nation as a whole, Kavelin calculated, of a sum in the region of a hundred million roubles. Moreover, the survival of serfdom was a major reason for the disadvantageous distribution of the population and therefore of the 'artificial direction' taken by the nation's industry: it caused an overwhelming majority of Russia's landowners to concentrate unquestioningly on the production of grain. From the moral point of view, the possession by one human being of almost unlimited power over another was 'always, without exception, a source of unbridled arbitrariness and oppression, on the one hand, and of servility, lies and deceit, on the other'. Any good intentions on the part of landowners gradually gave way to 'indifference, annoyance, strictness, severity, bitterness and tyranny' in their attitude to their serfs, while slavery bred in the serf himself 'slyness, cunning and malevolence, or at least indifference towards his masters'. The serf-owner became idle and parasitic, delegated responsibility to his manager or bailiff and lived as an absentee landlord amusing himself in the capital or abroad. The serfs too developed a parasitic attitude, reasoning that it was the responsibility of their lord to care for them if bad harvest, cattle disease, fire or some other natural disaster caused serious deprivation. In short, serfdom was an 'inexhaustible source of violence, immorality, ignorance, idleness, parasitism and all the vices which flow therefrom, and even of crimes'.[52]

So long as serfdom existed so too did the threat of another peasant uprising of the sort led by Stenka Razin or Pugachov. There was no rumour, however absurd, no grievance, however trivial, which might not revive the people's age-old desire for emancipation and spark off another elemental revolt. Furthermore, the continued existence of serfdom served as a brake on the development of Russian society as a whole, impeding the introduction of every necessary reform, such as the alteration of the method of military recruitment, the education of the lower classes, the improvement of the civil and criminal legal systems and the reorganisation of the police and the administration. Thus serfdom was the 'Gordian knot' – Kavelin maintained in a characteristically inelegant metaphor – to which all Russia's 'social ulcers' could be reduced. The most well-meaning efforts of sovereigns and reformers would come to nought so long as serfdom survived.[53]

Having briefly dismissed some of the arguments which it was conventional to adduce in favour of the retention of serfdom (that the peasants were unready for freedom; that the landlords had an important police function and that they were the main and irreplaceable suppliers of grain; and that the aristocracy would decline if it lost the right of serf-ownership), Kavelin addressed himself to the question of how serfdom was in practice to be abolished. With his usual desire to appear even-handed he considered the interests of the various parties concerned. The landowners would wish to defend property which they had acquired by legal means. The serfs would require complete personal freedom from the lords and the right to retain the land of which they made use, the hut in which they lived and such property as they had acquired. The state, finally, would wish in its own interest to respect and protect the rights of lords and serfs alike. It was unthinkable, therefore, to contemplate the emancipation of the serfs without providing compensation for their former owners. For, in the first place, emancipation without compensation would set a dangerous example of infringement of property rights; in the second place, it would cast the most numerous class of educated and well-to-do subjects into penury; and, in the third place, the owners of estates on which labour costs exceeded the value of produce would be deprived altogether of income from those estates. And yet at the same time the government would have to do its best to guarantee the personal and material well-being of the peasants once they had been emancipated. In the interests of social calm and order it could not permit the peasants' dependence on the lords to continue; nor could it implement a solution which left the peasants without land because in that event they would either be placed in complete economic dependence on the landowners or would be forced to rove from one region to another in search of work; that is to say, they would become a landless proletariat – a prospect which all sections of Russian society, aware of the Western European experience, regarded with dread.[54]

Taking all these factors into account, Kavelin set down three propositions which he considered it essential for those who would frame the terms of the emancipation to bear in mind. Firstly, the serfs must be freed completely from dependence on their lords. Secondly, they must be freed together with land as well as with all the property already belonging to them. And, thirdly, the serf-owners must receive compensation for the loss of their property. Kavelin then proceeds to discuss the question of the amount of land which the serfs should receive when they are liberated. This amount, he believes, may be determined in various ways. The serfs might be freed with all the land belonging to the estate on which they are settled, or with a varying number of *desyatiny** per soul or household according to the locality, or with that amount of land of which they were currently making use. The first method Kavelin finds 'extremely unsuitable', because it would require the government to pay immense sums to the landowners by way of compensation and because much of the land, being superfluous to the peasants' needs, would pass into the hands of the state and would thereupon begin to yield less income. Most importantly, this transfer of land to the state would entail the almost complete disappearance of private landowning, which Kavelin regarded as a prerequisite for a flourishing rural economy. The second possible method of determining the size of the peasant's plot seemed to Kavelin to be impracticable, since the settling of terms on a local basis would require years of painstaking labour and huge expense and would give rise to abuses and irreconcilable conflicts. The third method is the one which commends itself to Kavelin for it preserved and reaffirmed the principle of private landownership which had been established long ago and to which lord and serf alike had grown accustomed. Nor would its implementation require great expense or cause serious misunderstandings.[55]

Turning next to the problem of the compensation of the lords for the loss they would incur, Kavelin again examines various solutions.

* plural of *desyatina*, a land measure equivalent to 2.7 acres.

The lords might be compensated only for the land they lost, or for both land and serfs; the amount of compensation might be based on prices established by the government or average prices at the time of the reform; and there were various procedures by which the compensation might be paid. Kavelin contends that compensation of the lords only for the land they lost and not for their serfs would be unjust, since the serfs at present constituted the rightful property of the lord and since it was only in a few densely populated provinces that land had great value and serfs comparatively little. He also argues strongly that the whole redemption sum due to the lords would have to be paid over to them at the time of the emancipation, rather than spread over a period. For the economic affairs of the lords would have to be put on a sound footing immediately after the emancipation, and the gentry itself would be unable to find the money from its own resources for the extra-ordinary capital expenditure which would suddenly be required. The lords, then, should be compensated by the simplest and fairest means for the loss of their serfs: the serfs and the land to be allotted to them should be valued as honestly and realistically as possible according to the going rate and the redemption sum paid over in full at the moment the serfs ceased to be the lord's private property.[56]

Besides having obvious practical value as a careful and wide-ranging examination of questions relating to the emancipation of the serfs, Kavelin's memorandum also served as an eloquent expression of the political views of the 'men of the 1840s' as those views began to crystallise in the relatively free atmosphere of the mid 1850s. Both in his main concrete proposals and in various passages which form a sort of subtext to the memorandum, Kavelin reveals a number of distinctive traits of the emergent Russian liberalism. In the first place, Kavelin repeatedly makes it clear that the post-reform economy which he envisages is based partly on free enterprise rather than state ownership, which he associates with inefficiency. He explicitly states, after all, that the state should not engage in any manufacturing activity, but should sell all government-owned industrial establishments to private individuals or companies, be they Russian or foreign. He also makes an early statement in the memorandum about the efficiency of wage labour and the benefits which flow from its use. Work was done more quickly than under the serf-owning system because each had the incentive to earn as much as possible. Wage labour had the additional advantage of causing the rapid circulation of money among the masses. This money, 'passing through thousands of hands', distributed prosperity, which in turn was the 'most reliable and abundant source of state revenue', through direct and indirect taxation. The undesirable consequences of the implementation of *laissez-faire* economic policies in the countryside Kavelin, with his habitual optimism, expected Russia to avoid. At any rate he explicitly deplored the prospect of former serfs falling into 'extreme poverty' and becoming a homeless and landless rural proletariat.[57]

In the second place, Kavelin stoutly defends the interests of the gentry (and we may infer from the statements he makes elsewhere that his attitude towards this class is not dictated purely by a tactical desire to diminish the general opposition of landowners to the emancipation). He is anxious to ensure that his projected reform will jeopardise neither the gentry's social standing nor its economic well-being. Thus in his supplement to the memorandum, when he comes to discuss the role which the gentry might play in local administration after the emancipation, he insists that this, the most educated social stratum, must enjoy considerable influence. It was desirable in all countries that it should do so, but nowhere more than in Russia where the masses remained so ignorant.[58] More importantly he required that the lords be compensated for the loss of their serfs as well as for their land and that that compensation be paid in full at the outset. He also argued in favour of the retention of large-scale private landownership by the gentry, claiming that it had been shown 'by experience' that 'private landed property and the existence of large farms alongside small ones' were 'absolutely essential conditions' for rural prosperity,[59] and he tried to ensure that the lords' landholdings would indeed remain substantial after the emancipation by proposing that the peasants receive only such land as they currently cultivated. In fact so striking is Kavelin's concern to safeguard the interests of the gentry that it has even been suggested, by the Soviet scholar Tsagolov, that a desire to preserve the wealth and status of that class after the emancipation out-weighed any humanitarian considerations in Kavelin's mind and, paradoxical as it may at first sight seem, found expression in his proposal that the serf received land as well as freedom. For an emancipated peasantry endowed with a small amount of land would not drift into the towns but would remain in the countryside and serve as a cheap labour force for the principal landowning class.[60]

Certainly Kavelin's belief in the importance of large-scale land-ownership by the gentry is so strong that he does not approve of the introduction of the unfettered competition which might threaten such an institution and he is not therefore to be associated with those Western liberals whose advocacy of a *laissez-faire* economy tended to assist the enterprise of the bourgeoisie and correspondingly to undermine the pre-eminent position of the landed aristocracy. Nor, of course, does Kavelin's vision of large-scale private landownership have anything in common with the collectivist utopia, based on communal landholding, which had already been outlined by Herzen and which, through the writings of Chernyshevsky and later Populist thinkers, came to fascinate the Russian intelligentsia until the end of the 1880s.

In the third place, Kavelin emphasises in his memorandum, and elsewhere, that social change must be gradual and peaceful, that it must not produce antagonisms among the various social classes. Indeed one cannot escape the conclusion that Kavelin's desire to see the prevailing order so greatly modified was prompted not only by his concern to safeguard the interests of the gentry but also, in large measure, by the fear that attempts to preserve it in its existing form might bring even more far-reaching social change and bloody conflict. A satisfactory solution of the problem of serfdom would spare Russia, Kavelin wrote in a letter at this time, 'from senseless carnage' and would give the country the chance to develop peacefully, 'without leaps and jumps, for five hundred years to come'.[61] And in the memorandum itself he emphasises that in order to fulfil her 'great calling' Russia needed above all 'peaceful progress' which everywhere gave firmer results than development by the 'dubious and terrible means of revolutions'. It is with a view to averting such upheavals that Kavelin endeavours – perhaps with little hope of success or universal approval – to take into account and to reconcile the interests of all parties concerned, landowners, serfs and state, when framing his proposals for emancipation. And towards the end of the memorandum he looks forward to a society as unified, despite its inequalities, as that which Botkin thought he had found in Spain in the 1840s. Gentry and peasant, both owning land, would have common interests. The gentry would cease to fear necessary and useful changes, while the peasantry would see in the gentry a natural and trustworthy defender of their interests. The nation would merge into a 'single whole' in which there would, admittedly, be distinctions but no 'enmity and internal fragmentation'.[62]

In the fourth place, Kavelin expressed in his memorandum a strong faith in the feasibility and effectiveness of a benevolent monarchy. In fact, it was the very existence of a firm and impartial monarchy which he felt would guarantee the social harmony he hoped to witness once serfdom had been abolished. The office of the Russian tsar stood 'immeasurably higher' than all sectional interests and would remain 'immovable and inaccessible' so long as the tsar did not abase it by expressing an 'exclusive and partial preference' for the interests of one class at the expense of all others. Certainly Russia's historical past, Kavelin believed, provided plentiful evidence to show that the tsar was by no means to be identified with the gentry.[63] And in his supplement to the memorandum, Kavelin makes the point even more emphatically. The Russian tsar, he wrote here

is not a nobleman, not a merchant, not a military man, not a peasant; he stands above all estates and at the same time is close to all of them. The force of things, which not infrequently goes against personal inclinations, aspirations and concepts, makes the Russian tsar without fail a mediator, the supreme arbitrator of social interests, a just measure of the claims of all classes and estates.[64]

This confidence in the autocracy was underpinned by the view Kavelin had expressed almost a decade before, in his 'Brief Survey of the Juridical Way of Life of Ancient Russia', that the state was the main agent of progress and the instrument of rational social organisation. In retrospect, one is bound to view such confidence as ingenuous and misplaced; but in a society as backward as the Russian it was perhaps the last resort of men who hoped that far-reaching social change would come about without devastating social conflict.

Kavelin's attitude towards the new tsar, Alexander II, clearly reflected the hope expressed in his memorandum that reform from above might avert revolution from below. Some two months after Alexander's accession Kavelin, according to one acquaintance, 'was literally transported with delight when he spoke about the new sovereign'.[65] In January 1856, as the first projects for the emancipation of the serfs were being discussed, he told Pogodin that one could not look on Alexander 'without sympathy'. The tsar was governed by the best intentions and was conducting himself very well. One should be grateful to him for what was being done, especially when one bore in mind the climate of the time.[66] A few months later he wrote again to Pogodin, saying that he was becoming seriously attached to the new tsar, whose good heart was gradually leading Russia out of its benighted state. Kavelin only prayed that Alexander had strength enough not to be misled by the unscrupulous advisers who surrounded him.[67] Finally, his unequivocal approval of Alexander's efforts found public expression at a banquet of 28 December 1857, which Kavelin travelled specially from St Petersburg to Moscow to attend and at which he lauded the 'great deed' of 20 November (the issuing of the Nazimov rescript in which the nobility of Lithuania were instructed to set up committees to prepare proposals providing for the peasants' acquisition of their homesteads and assuring them of the use of some land after their emancipation). At last the task set by centuries of Russian history had been tackled, Kavelin declared, and he invited the assembled men of letters and dignitaries to raise their glasses to the health of the 'peacemaker' who in both foreign and domestic affairs was bringing the blessings of peace to the Russian land.[68]

It is ironic in view of Kavelin's effusions of goodwill towards the monarchy that his memorandum on the emancipation of the serfs should have eventually incurred royal displeasure. The responsibility for Kavelin's fall from favour lay with Chernyshevsky, who in 1858 published a large part of Kavelin's memorandum in *Sovremennik*. Of the many recent projects concerning the abolition of serfdom, Kavelin's adhered 'most faithfully' to the principles upheld by *Sovremennik*, Chernyshevsky wrote in a preamble to the memorandum; the journal's editors were 'in complete agreement' with the general principles of the memorandum.[69] As a matter of fact, Chernyshevsky was greatly exaggerating the extent of his agreement with Kavelin; he could not, for example, have accepted Kavelin's defence of landowners' property rights, his enthusiasm for elements of a capitalist economy or his confidence in benevolent monarchy. But he was prepared for the purpose of securing a major objective, emancipation, to present an apparently united front in the intelligentsia. However, the stratagem, which was put into effect, it seems, without Kavelin's own full knowledge or complete approval,[70] proved a costly failure. The hostility of the gentry to the liberal as well as the radical sections of the intelligentsia was increased by the implication of the memorandum, or rather

Chernyshevsky's version of it, that emancipation was a foregone conclusion. Panayev, as co-editor of *Sovremennik*, was called to account for the publication of the memorandum by the chief of gendarmes and the journal threatened with closure. The liberal section of the intelligentsia lost some of the goodwill it had built up with Alexander, and Kavelin himself was dismissed from his post as tutor to the tsarevich.[71]

Relations with Herzen and Chicherin, 1855–8

Kavelin's hope that the intelligentsia might be able to work together with the autocracy in the interests of reform and his pleas for caution and moderation found expression not only in his memorandum on the emancipation of the serfs but also in the programme he began to formulate in collaboration with Chicherin for the liberal circles which emerged in Russia immediately after the death of Nicholas.

As soon as the political climate changed in 1855, Kavelin began vigorously to encourage the production and circulation, in manuscript form, of articles examining current problems and containing moderate plans for their solution. So rapid was the output of such articles, however, that it soon became desirable to seek some means of publishing them. Inside Russia, of course, the press remained inhibited by censorship, in spite of the greater freedom which it quickly began to enjoy. In London, where Herzen had recently set up a free Russian press, on the other hand, expressions of moderate opinion could be printed without constraint. Herzen was therefore approached and his help solicited, and early in 1856 the first of nine collections of articles from Russia was published by him under the title *Voices from Russia*.[72] (The political sentiments expressed by the contributors to *Voices from Russia* did not, however, receive Herzen's blessing; indeed, Herzen reminded the reader in his own brief foreword to the first issue that he was only a 'printer' ready to publish anything that might be useful to the common cause.)[73]

The first number of *Voices from Russia* began with a letter, signed by 'a Russian liberal', which had been written by Kavelin and Chicherin and which was considered a programmatic statement for the anthology. Kavelin, who was the author of the first half of this letter, took pains to emphasise at the outset that the programme was of a gradualist nature: secret societies, a political opposition, revolutionary and destructive plans – these phenomena were 'immeasurably distant' from the present 'awakening' in Russia. He even went so far as to say – though nonsensically, as Herzen implied by a question-mark in the text – that nobody inside Russia had suggested the need for a 'secret society, revolution, *the limitation of autocratic power* or anything of the sort'. Kavelin then proceeded to attempt to explain Russia's ills as a product of the gulf that separated tsar and people rather than as the consequence of autocratic policy. In the reign of Nicholas a 'greedy, corrupt and ignorant' bureaucracy had insinuated itself between tsar and people and on the pretext of serving the sovereign and protecting his throne had prevented the voice of Russia from reaching him. The present 'well-intentioned tsar', however, seemed to sense his remoteness from his subjects, even though he was surrounded by unscrupulous advisers who inhibited that free blossoming of thought and letters which would help to dispel traditional misapprehensions about the intentions of both tsar and people. Finally, Kavelin criticised Herzen for his impatience with the autocracy and his rejection of a policy of cautious reform and invited the *émigré* to listen '*sine ira et studio*' to the voice of liberal opinion. Kavelin did not approve of the criticisms which Herzen had made of the autocracy since his emigration (and he claimed that a vast majority within Russia shared his disapproval). At a time when educated Russians were wondering how to improve their laws, eradicate abuses, emancipate the peasants without shaking the whole social organism, introduce freedom of speech and bridle the censorship, Herzen was preaching the destruction of all government, advocating Proudhonist anarchy and devising utopian social plans of no current or practical interest. Kavelin and the Russian liberals on whose behalf he claimed to be speaking, on the other hand, were ready to 'rally round any government that was in any way liberal and support it with all their strength'.[74] Chicherin's contribution to the letter from the 'Russian liberal', incidentally, contained an even stronger condemnation of Herzen for his espousal of socialism, his apparent acceptance of revolution, in which streams of innocent blood would flow, and his ignorance of the ever-present historical 'law of gradualness'.[75]

It is clear from a letter which Kavelin sent to Herzen in August 1857 that he hoped the *émigré* might himself come to adopt the moderate views put forward by the 'Russian liberal' in *Voices from Russia* and even transform *Kolokol* (*The Bell*) into an organ for their expression. It is true that Kavelin's love of Herzen was undiminished (and it would be wrong to see his effusive expressions of that love as cynical ploys intended to make his practical advice more acceptable to Herzen). Nor did Kavelin believe that he and Herzen disagreed about ends and basic principles. On the question of means, however, they did differ. In the present circumstances, Kavelin argued, a foreign organ should be 'moderate' in order that it might serve as a mouthpiece 'for all opinions'. When Old Believers, Poles, Germans, Finns and Jews all asked Herzen to publish their views, then *Kolokol* would fulfil that purpose, but at present it was 'too exclusive'. Kavelin also makes the interesting suggestion that Herzen should contemplate the publication of a paper in French: the government would look with comparative favour on such a paper because it would be inaccessible to the common people, whose unrest the government greatly feared, and the paper would be the more useful as a result.[76] By the beginning of 1858 Kavelin had to concede that *Kolokol* in fact exercised great influence in its present form, but he did again counsel moderation, this time on the grounds that the intentions of Alexander II were unquestionably good. Certainly Herzen should continue to expose 'all the foul deeds, follies and villainies' which he was now renowned for discovering; but he should be very careful when writing about the royal family.[77]

Whatever differences of opinion arose between Kavelin and Herzen in the second half of the 1850s, however, they did have a common intellectual and spiritual past, having both imbibed the humanitarian idealism of the 1840s, and at the end of 1858 an event took place which underlined the strength of this bond. Chicherin sent Herzen a long screed in which he again strongly attacked Herzen's radicalism and reiterated the merits of the moderate approach for which he, Chicherin, was a leading spokesman. (Herzen published the letter under his own title, 'A Bill of Indictment', in *Kolokol*.)[78] Chicherin claimed in his letter that many 'thinking people' in Russia reproached *Kolokol* for 'frivolity'; one read in it 'not the word of reason but the word of passion'. Unbridled impulses might have a certain poetic charm, but in public life rational qualities, such as political sense, tact, and a sense of proportion and timing were more important. It was an historical moment, moreover, when public figures should not be fanning flames or rubbing salt in wounds but calming tempers. Herzen seemed to Chicherin not to value civic virtues and enlightenment or to respect the law but to be ready to see these sources of social stability swept away in a 'fatal struggle' and to encourage people to seize the axe. He had chosen his end and the question as to what means, peaceful or violent, might be used in the attempt to achieve it had only secondary significance for him. As for the emancipation of the serfs, since the tsar had already announced his intention to carry out that reform it seemed foolish to Chicherin to counsel haste: such reforms took time to devise because they were not nearly so simple as the penning of an article for *Kolokol*.[79]

Given Chicherin's youth and Herzen's national and international standing as a sincere and high-principled opponent of the Russian régime, this 'bill of indictment' seemed arrogant and insulting and gave offence even to men such as Kavelin, who as a matter of fact was now in many respects closer to its author than to its recipient. Kavelin immediately sent Herzen a letter of protest against Chicherin's outburst together with a supporting letter signed by Turgenev, Annenkov, Babst and others. This letter of protest – which Herzen out of 'decorum' declined to publish immediately but was persuaded to include in a subsequent number of *Kolokol* – is by virtue of its tone no less typical of the liberalism of the older generation, the 'men of the 1840s', than specific views expressed by Kavelin in the letter from a 'Russian liberal'. Kavelin announced at the outset that he was not going to discuss the fairness or unfairness of the charges made by Chicherin; one could suppose that he actually considered them valid. Rather, it was the 'deed' itself that Kavelin wished to discuss. He upheld the view that 'heart' was essential in thought, that the 'public figure and thinker without heart' was a 'grave'. Thought imbued with warmth, heart and soul was 'fullness, life and freshness' and would for long survive, whereas Chicherin's, being 'soulless', would quickly perish. As for judgement of Herzen, one could perceive his mistakes, but it was necessary also to take into account his 'heartfelt ardour', his 'burning love of good and truth'. He had a vocation to 'stir, awaken, animate and enliven', whilst Chicherin, proud of his cold principles, should take his place beside his 'cousins, the noble representatives of the French Revolution of 1848, who themselves called forth the slaughter and then mercilessly executed the innocent'. Here Kavelin aptly invoked the memory of Belinsky, who might have been moved by Chicherin's letter to deliver one of his thunderous denunciations. Finally, reaching a crescendo of indignation, Kavelin declared that the Russian people had a mission to rebuild society on the principle 'Love thy neighbour as thyself.' Chicherin stood in their path and would have either to step aside or to go with the people, otherwise he would perish ignominiously. Kavelin appeals to the young generation who will be called upon to save the world and bring into being the true Kingdom of Christ. The young should be ready to die like martyrs, like the first Christians, in defence of the equal right of each peasant to the land and of the '*communal principle*' which survived in the Russian countryside, where one could still find peace and breathe freely.[80]

There is admittedly in Kavelin's impassioned letter some evidence of a departure from positions he had seemed previously to occupy. He appears in particular to have moved closer to Herzen in his view of the Russian commune as an institution which might provide a base for future social development. It is worth noting too that his messianic vision of a young intelligentsia sacrificing itself in the countryside anticipates the revolutionary Populism of the early 1870s, which Herzen helped to inspire. But in the main Kavelin's letter reveals a man faithful to the spirit of the 'Westernisers' of the 1840s. Indeed, so reminiscent is it of Belinsky's famous 'letter to Gogol' that it is perhaps not fanciful to suggest that Kavelin, whose quixotism was always ostentatious, believed himself to be taking up the role of moral judge which Belinsky had played with such authority. At any rate Kavelin's insistence on the importance of heart, warmth and enthusiasm in social thought is entirely characteristic of his generation. (These are the very qualities, after all, with which Turgenev had endowed Rudin, his own summary, written in 1855–6, of the character of the 'men of the 1840s'.) Thus those same qualities that had animated the Westernist intelligentsia of the 1840s seemed to unite Kavelin the liberal to his contemporary Herzen the socialist rather than to Chicherin the younger fellow liberal, and thereby still tended in the second half of the 1850s to blur political distinctions in the intelligentsia, although in truth unity was already imperilled by fundamental differences of opinion and could not now be long preserved.

Kavelin's essay of 1859 on the peasant commune

There is one further work of Kavelin's which reveals his search for compromise, his hopes and fears in the second half of the 1850s, namely his important article published in 1859 under the title 'A Brief Look at the Russian Rural Commune'.

Kavelin conceded that the commune in its present form did not efficiently utilise the land at its disposal, and he even predicted that the practice of allotting equal plots of land to each member of the commune would in time have to be abandoned as a result of the growth of the population. Nevertheless communal landholding would still have important features which would ensure the survival of the institution in some form. Firstly, a member of the commune would have no property rights over his plot, only the right to hold and use it; he could not therefore bequeath, sell or otherwise dispose of it. Secondly, the holding of communal land presupposed constant residence in the commune; the landholder could not therefore hold land in various places or lease the land he held. Thirdly, orphans or an eldest son left after the death of a landholder without a plot of their own might have the right to retain their deceased father's plot. These features of communal landholding did not deprive the landholder of incentive to improve the land, as detractors of the institution supposed; the landholder, like the man renting land, would improve his plot even if he could not pass it on to his heirs because he himself might directly benefit from its improvement. Nor would the prohibition of landholding by the same individual in more than one commune and the requirement that he remain on the land act as a brake on economic and civil development provided that two conditions obtained (and these conditions were fundamental to Kavelin's conception of the future of the commune): first, communal landholding should not be the *only* form of landholding in the realm and, second, the individual farmer should not be compelled to choose this form of landholding. So long as private property existed alongside communal property, and so long as the farmer could freely choose whether to take a communal plot, Kavelin contended, the institution of communal landholding would not seem restrictive.[81]

Such land as was in the first instance communal might be gradually turned, Kavelin believed, into land which could be rented for life and under certain circumstances inherited by a man's son after his death. This method of renting property would be quite different, however, from private renting, which sooner or later inevitably turned into 'industrial speculation'. The small farm, held in this way, would not be suitable for the 'wealthy capitalist, or the entrepreneur, or the well-to-do property owner, or the man who, having no abilities or any proclivity to rural pursuits and occupations, provides for himself and feeds his family by urban or some other occupations and pursuits'. It would be utilised instead by the poor peasant, who hoped not to amass large profits but merely to make ends meet, or by the family peasant who was glad to work, or by the enterprising commoner who had lost his capital in unsuccessful speculation, or by the poor orphan or the widow with children to raise. In short, communal landholding, as Kavelin envisaged it, would provide life-long security for the weak and defenceless and for all people who were not endowed with particular talent, energy or ambition.[82]

Kavelin's thinking as it is revealed in this article is strongly coloured, like that of many contemporaries of all shades of political opinion, by fear that unbridled capitalist development might be imminent in Russia (and their knowledge of Western European conditions furnished Russian thinkers with abundant evidence of the misery that such development would in all probability cause). The 'principle of private property', Kavelin admitted, had greatly stimulated the spirit of free enterprise and helped to bring about the industrial achievements of which Western Europe and America were justly proud. But the principle had its adverse effects too. It produced widespread poverty and encouraged the voracious accumulation of material wealth by the few and the concentration of that wealth in fewer hands. Small property holders – as indeed Marx and Engels had recently argued in *The Communist Manifesto* – could not survive in capitalist society and gradually fell into the ranks of the workers. Philanthropy, the 'solemn *culpa mea*' of modern society, would be powerless before that society's 'fateful laws'. The principle of 'social anarchy' would hold sway, serving as an 'inexhaustible source of deep social ulcers'. The growth of personal property, then, like individualism, would cause 'ruin and destruction', eating away the social organism, if it were not modified and counterbalanced by the other 'organising principle of landholding', the communal principle as Kavelin had described it.[83] Thus fear of the emergence of a landless and homeless proletariat and awareness of the threat such a proletariat would pose to social stability compelled Kavelin by 1859 to give more attention to the institution which Herzen had long defended but which Kavelin himself, as recently as August 1857, had said could not serve as Russia's 'anchor of salvation'.[84]

Kavelin's plan for the future development of the commune, however, did not in essence resemble that of radical thinkers such as Herzen, Chernyshevsky and the later Populists. Rather, it represented a characteristic attempt at compromise. For, unlike the socialists, Kavelin was not intending that Russia should altogether circumvent a capitalist phase of economic development; only that the harsher aspects of that phase should be mitigated. The small farm which, he hoped, would develop out of the commune was not to be an embryo of a socialist collective that would eventually embrace all of Russia, but merely the 'only possible refuge' of the less privileged members of Russian society from the unavoidable and in fact desirable capitalism which would be establishing itself at the same time. Indeed, Kavelin's plan was shaped not only by fear of capitalism but also by fear of the political extremism to which capitalism, if unchecked, gave rise. Care should be taken to ensure that the masses were not driven to a point at which they might develop a hatred for social institutions, begin to demand the 'impossible and the unattainable' and enter into conflict with other social groups. The creation of a popular mass with deep roots in the land was the best means of averting such dangers. For wherever the rural masses were firmly settled they were the 'most conservative social element'. And the Russian mass, granted the opportunity Kavelin outlined, would not lose the habit of 'standing on their own feet'; they would not exhibit the idleness and parasitism that came of dependence on charity. The 'future ills', then, against which the commune might serve as a 'secure' bulwark, were not merely the ills of capitalism but also those of socialism.[85]

On one level, of course, Kavelin's article of 1859 may be seen as one contribution to the extensive debate on the commune which continued in the Russian intelligentsia from the 1840s to the 1880s and which at certain periods – notably the late 1850s, late 1860s and early 1880s – assumed very great importance for prospective social reformers and revolutionaries. At the same time the article also provides further illustration of the lengths to which Kavelin, as a leading spokesman of liberal opinion, was prepared to go in order to reconcile conflicting points of view. It must be said, moreover, that his attempt at compromise had in this instance a superficial success. Admittedly Leontyev, one of the editors of *Russkiy vestnik*, to whom Kavelin initially submitted the article, demanded some changes, which were unacceptable to Kavelin, lest it should seem that the author sympathised with the Slavophiles; but even he, Leontyev, was in agreement with Kavelin on the fundamental principles.[86] The radical Dobrolyubov welcomed the article as a 'very serious defence of the commune'.[87] And Samarin, the Slavophile who had been one of Kavelin's main antagonists a decade before, naturally considered it 'excellent' since Kavelin had argued in it for the preservation of an institution the Slavophiles had long regarded as sacred.[88]

Finally, it is worth mentioning in connection with Kavelin's essay of 1859 on the peasant commune one further attempt in which he was engaged at this time to reconcile conflicting opinions as the gap between his own position and that of the radical wing of the intelligentsia widened. At the end of a long letter of August 1859 to Herzen, in which he addresses the *émigré* almost as an idol, he takes up an unfinished philosophical dispute which he had been carrying on, in a friendly tone, with Ogaryov on the subject of materialism. Try as Ogaryov might to reduce everything to mechanical and natural-historical causes, he was still bound, Kavelin contended, to come up against phenomena of another order which had their own distinctive, albeit analogous, laws of development, phenomena which related to and derived from man's 'intellectual and spiritual nature'. These phenomena had a 'physiology' and 'pathology' of their own, different from the 'physiology' and 'pathology' of the natural sciences. That both sets of phenomena, the physical and the moral, did indeed have their laws, and that these laws could be analysed rationally, Kavelin was prepared, then, to accept. Nor did he deny that there was the closest connection between the physical and the moral worlds, that they were in constant interaction with one another.[89] But he fought against the confusion of the two and therefore against a Chernyshevskian reduction of man's moral and intellectual world to the status of a product of physiological and environmental factors. Like Lavrov, who at the same period was arguing that determinism (or 'fatalism', as Lavrov called it) was not for all practical purposes a tenable doctrine, since man had to base his actions on the assumption that he did have moral responsibility for them,[90] so Kavelin too resisted Ogaryov's alluring comprehensive solution to philosophical questions, preferring instead what Zenkovsky terms a 'semi-positivism' which shunned both the abstract idealism of German philosophy and the crude materialism espoused by so many early Russian socialists.[91]

Towards defence of the 'status quo'

However fundamental the differences between Kavelin and Chernyshevsky, between the liberal and socialist positions of the late 1850s and early 1860s might seem in retrospect, they were still partly obscured, until 1862 at least, by Kavelin's lingering association with radical causes. Thus in 1861 Kavelin was supporting Lavrov's candidacy for a chair in St Petersburg University (much to the annoyance of the conservative professor Nikitenko, who scathingly suggested that only in the Sandwich Islands might Lavrov's thought pass for philosophy and who associated Lavrov – incorrectly, as it happened – with the materialism currently being propagated by the radicals).[92] More importantly, Kavelin adopted an indulgent attitude towards the rebellious students involved in the disturbances which affected St Petersburg University in the autumn of 1861 and which resulted in its temporary closure. The illegal student meetings and demonstrations he saw as the 'inevitable consequence' of the retention of the old university charter of 1835, which was plainly inadequate in the new conditions that had arisen after the Crimean War. Under the provisions of this charter, he pointed out, the students were treated like schoolchildren, the official inspector was granted enormous power over them, students and staff were kept at a distance from one another and staff were prevented from participating in the running of the university. Given the 'police character' of the university, it was wrong to see the student meetings as attempts to form embryonic political and revolutionary clubs. In any case, these meetings would instantly lose much of their attraction for the students if the government were to give them its blessing. And in general student protest, which was prompted in the main by noble impulses, would be more effectively treated by the moral influence of academics than by repressive measures on the part of the police.[93]

The committee of professors set up in the summer of 1861 in order to find a means of applying new rules devised by the recently appointed Minister of Education, Putyatin, found itself in an impossible position, Kavelin felt, and all its liberal proposals were rejected by the Ministry. In October 1861 several members of staff in the Law Faculty – to which a large proportion of the students involved in the disturbances belonged – decided not to lecture and Kavelin supported them. On 25 October Kavelin, always prone to make the impulsive gesture, resigned his teaching post and several other professors of liberal persuasion followed his example. He was prominent in the attempt made after the closure of the university to set up a 'free university' in St Petersburg and did indeed contribute to a programme of lectures delivered independently of the official university in January 1862. And in April 1862 he still dissociated himself from attempts to condemn the students involved in the disorders of the previous autumn, refusing to support a reprimand of the students written by Chicherin, Leontyev and Solovyov. He considered himself to have parted with this company; Moscow, where they congregated, was a 'cemetery' and Chicherin was a 'dolt' with whom Kavelin did not wish to be compared.[94]

On the other hand, Kavelin's expressions of support for radical causes began to seem increasingly hollow in 1861–2 as his fear of sweeping change led him in effect to condone government policy at the very time when it was becoming more conservative. He cools, for example, towards the Polish cause, for which he had previously had much sympathy.[95] Not that he had unequivocally advocated independence for the Poles even in the late 1850s; but he had hoped that if the Poles renounced the use of force then Russo-Polish co-operation might be possible and he had helped his friend Ohryzko to obtain permission for the publication of a daily Polish newspaper, *Słowo (The Word)*, in St Petersburg, for the purpose of promoting this ambition.[96] In 1862, however, he appears to defend the *status quo*: 'senseless' and 'revolting' as Russian sovereignty over the Poles might have been in the past (and Kavelin was inclined to think that it was not now so bad as it had previously been), the Poles would not benefit at this juncture from shaking it off.[97]

Kavelin's extreme reluctance to agitate for other fundamental reforms after the emancipation of the serfs finds further and most emphatic expression in his pamphlet, *The Gentry and the Emancipation of the Peasants*, which he wrote in May 1861 and had published in Berlin in 1862.[98] The pamphlet is a paean to the enlightened gentry (to which Kavelin himself belonged), a plea that this group be given a 'happy future and a brilliant role' in the life of the state and, at the same time, a defence of the gentry's right to landed property. Many people, Kavelin wrote, believed that the unequal distribution of possessions was 'arbitrary, artificial, and coincidental' and that this inequality could be ended by the abolition of private property and inheritance. Such socialist demands, however, were quite unreasonable, because they contradicted the 'law of freedom', a law as inexorable as the law of communal life. If the right to own property and the right to bequeath it to one's children were withdrawn, few people would continue to labour.[99] For these rights respected man's freedom, without which he would become an 'animal and human society a flock of sheep'. Inequality, innate personal virtues and talents, and property were to be found at all times and in all places; they were a 'basic law of human societies'. It was not because these inequalities existed, nor because societies had their upper classes that social struggles developed. Those struggles arose when upper classes, not understanding their proper function, evolved into closed hereditary castes hedged around with privileges and began to rule a country in their own interests. The gentry ought rather to be the first among equals, as they were in England. There the aristocracy 'with rare prudence had renounced its privileges and spirit of exclusiveness at an early stage'. It had granted all social estates the same rights which it enjoyed itself and by this means had retained both its standing in the eyes of the English people and its political influence in the state.[100]

The Russian gentry, when the question of the emancipation of the serfs had been raised by Alexander II, had in Kavelin's opinion demeaned itself by making miserly calculations, by invoking its obsolete privileges, by demanding fabulous sums in return for the surrender of these privileges and by attempting to frighten the government with threats of popular rebellion and with demands for a constitution. Nevertheless, in the new conditions which obtained after the emancipation, the Russian gentry might still play a worthy role if it emulated the English aristocracy. It should take note of the English aristocracy's healthy relationship with the lower classes and its recognition of the 'organic unity' of all social elements, for these factors made possible an endless process of peaceful development by gradual reform and removed the threat of rebellion by the lower classes against the upper. The Russian gentry might even have a certain advantage over the English aristocracy; for the survival in Russia of large-scale landed property – the 'kernel, the main interest' around which the Russian gentry would rally – would enable Russia to avert the emergence of a large landless proletariat.

The Russian gentry should therefore apply itself not merely to the management of its economic affairs but also to the task of winning the sympathy of other social classes. Conditions were not yet ripe, however, for the constitution for which there was currently a clamour. For Russia lacked the foundations necessary for representative government. Russian society consisted only of land-owners and peasants and had no middle class; nor was there any tradition of civil or political activity at the local level. As for a constitution which gave the gentry exclusive political rights, that was unthinkable, for such a privilege would be opposed by the government, by the masses and by all the 'enlightened' and 'liberal' elements of Russian society. The best course for the gentry, therefore, was to attempt to 'regenerate itself' through work and education and by parting with the luxury and unearned income it had traditionally enjoyed.[101]

As a piece of political thought, with its lame supposition that 'force of circumstances and things' is a moving force in history,[102] with its glib assumptions about the English aristocracy and its weak pleas for a disinterested gentry in Russia, Kavelin's pamphlet is very poor. Moreover, its proposal that the gentry should remain the 'first estate',[103] its rejection, for whatever reasons, of a constitution as premature and its implicit confidence in the capacity of the autocracy to carry out reform – these features served finally to reveal the gulf that now separated Kavelin from the radical intelligentsia in general and to alienate Herzen in particular. Kavelin replied, in May 1862, to Herzen's first rebuke by pleading that he had written his pamphlet the previous year when the gentry had been 'bawling' for a constitution, by which they meant the annulment of the emancipation edict.[104] But Kavelin's reply did not placate Herzen, who drafted a further passionate rejoinder. Kavelin was the last active representative of Herzen's Moscow period, the second youth which he remembered with such fondness. It was to Kavelin that Herzen had dedicated his essay on Robert Owen, the best thing, he thought, that he had ever written. How, Herzen asked, could such a person produce this 'scraggy, absurd and harmful' pamphlet? Only Kavelin's repudiation of his paean to the aristocracy could now remove the barrier it had placed between them.[105] Kavelin, however, refused to recant and once again tried to defend himself by reiterating arguments familiar from his article of 1859 on the commune, concerning the need to preserve private property as a

basis for 'individuality and freedom', and by raising the spectre of
the French Revolution as an omen of the fate that might befall
Russia if the old order were modified too quickly and funda-
mentally.[106]

Kavelin himself clearly sensed now that liberals and socialists had
reached a parting of the ways. His fear of revolutionary upheaval
made him increasingly intolerant of radicalism. Thus in June 1862
he lamented that 'some illness' seemed to have seized the youth like
an 'epidemic'.[107] In August he again told Herzen that he was
spoiling *Kolokol*: the more openly the journal supported the cause
of social revolution in Russia, the more its former influence would
decline.[108] And at the same time he spoke with equanimity of the
arrests that were beginning to take place in Russia. These arrests
did not surprise him, nor, he confessed to Herzen, did they even
seem 'disgraceful' to him, for Russian society was now in a state of
war. The 'revolutionary party' considered all means of over-
throwing the government acceptable, and the government, for its
part, defended itself with the means at its disposal. The arrest and
exile of the political opponents of the régime should not be seen in
the same light as the repression which had taken place in the time of
the 'rogue Nicholas'; then people had perished 'for an idea, for
convictions, for faith, for words'. Kavelin even taunts Herzen: he
would like to see, he says, how Herzen, if he were in a position of
authority, would deal with parties which plotted against him. As for
Chernyshevsky, who had been arrested in 1862, Kavelin very much
loved him; but he had never come across such a 'trouble-maker',
such a 'tactless and cocky person'. Nor did Kavelin have the
slightest doubt about the truth of the rumours that the fires which
had broken out in St Petersburg in spring 1862 were connected in
some way with the seditious proclamations that had recently
appeared.[109]

Kavelin's proposition that it was legitimate for the government to
arrest persons plotting to overthrow it is in itself not unreasonable.
At any rate it is difficult to agree with the inference drawn from it by
Lenin, on the basis of his reading of the letters in which the
proposition was put forward, that Kavelin was 'one of the most
revolting examples of liberal effrontery'.[110] And yet clearly the
spirit of Kavelin's words, if not their logic, was bound to be
offensive to any who considered the autocratic régime more barbarous than its militant opponents, just as Chicherin's famous letter to

Herzen had seemed offensive to Kavelin himself. The equanimity with which Kavelin viewed Chernyshevsky's arrest underlined yet again the fact that in the final analysis, when difficult choices had to be made, Kavelin preferred to live in a stable society with a buoyant and privileged gentry and to entertain the prospect of indefinite monarchic rule, rather than to risk social turmoil by attacking an unyielding autocracy too vigorously. His acceptance of Chernyshevsky's arrest as a necessary measure and his attempt to distinguish it from the persecution visited on the intelligentsia in the reign of Nicholas indicated that by the middle of 1862 he too, like Botkin and Druzhinin, had irrevocably aligned himself with the 'fathers' with whom he had in any case always had the greater affinity.

Kavelin lived on until May 1885 and, although buffeted by personal misfortunes such as the premature death of his daughter in 1877, at the age of twenty-six, and the death of his wife in 1879, immersed himself as ever in tireless and selfless work. In 1862 he was sent abroad by the new Minister of Education, Golovnin, to study the organisation of higher education in France, Germany, Belgium, Holland and Switzerland,[111] and he remained abroad until 1864. On his return to Russia he took up a position obtained for him by his friend Grot in a fiscal department of the Ministry of the Interior, and from 1877 he lectured in the St Petersburg Academy of Military Law, where his students found him as sociable and as responsive to topical issues as before. But his day was past. His friend Spasovich describes him in the late 1860s, when he was barely fifty, as 'prematurely aged physically'.[112] He no longer enjoyed any great influence in the intelligentsia. And even his intellectual interests indicated his retreat from practical matters: his energies were now concentrated in the fields of psychology and ethics,[113] fields in which the younger generation of the 1860s had built foundations for their radical politics but in which Kavelin sought mainly refuge from a larger battleground now dominated by the forces he most feared.

Conclusion

The Russian liberals whose thought has been examined in this study shared many views and attitudes, although they did not constitute or belong to any political party or even any intellectual circle in the formal sense. They were all humanitarian men who – before the event at any rate – favoured the abolition of serfdom. They all cultivated enlightened values derived from the West, whose civilisation they admired and in which Granovsky, Botkin and Annenkov at least spent long periods. They cherished friendship and personal relationships and refused to look on individuals as mere ciphers in some sociological or political calculation. Like John Stuart Mill, and in opposition to the Slavophiles, they bemoaned the deadening effect of custom, posited in the human personality a need for self-development and individuality, and believed that there was a 'need of persons' – as Mill put it, more eloquently than they – who might not only 'discover new truths, and point out when what were once truths are true no longer' but also 'commence new practices, and set the example of more enlightened conduct, and better taste and sense in human life'.[1] They also demanded that the intellectual bring fairness and toleration to assessments of the society and culture of a given nation, including his own. Where there was contention they endeavoured to understand both points of view, to weigh the evidence more or less dispassionately and to come to rational and sober conclusions. Both Granovsky and Kavelin therefore commend Tacitus' disavowal of indignation and partisanship, and Druzhinin explicitly advocates *bespristrastiye* in literary criticism. They appreciated how important it was that the expression of opinion should be free if the discussion on which impartial conclusions might be based were to flourish. Again, they would have endorsed Mill's belief that the

only way in which a human being can make some approach to knowing the whole of a subject, is by hearing what can be said about it by persons of every variety of opinion, and studying all modes in which it can be looked at by every character of mind.

For them, as for the Victorian Englishman, it was not the 'violent conflict between parts of the truth, but the quiet suppression of half of it' that was the more 'formidable evil'.[2]

Most importantly, the early Russian liberals placed great value on political stability. It is no coincidence that Botkin, Annenkov, Druzhinin and Kavelin (like Chicherin, Katkov, Turgenev and others) all showed an increasing affection, indeed admiration, for England in the late 1850s as the prospects for peaceful change in their own country seemed, in spite of the current preparation of legislation to abolish serfdom, to be threatened by the ascendancy of the socialist wing of the intelligentsia. For England, although it was despised by Russian socialists as the home of the most rapacious and prosperous bourgeoisie, was also the most stable nation in Western Europe from the political point of view. More than any other Western European country England seemed to have avoided destructive social convulsions and instead to have gradually evolved peacefully as a result of the implementation of timely reforms. The readiness of Alexander II to contemplate the abolition of serfdom and the steadfastness with which he held to this purpose heartened the liberals, particularly Annenkov and Kavelin, and seemed to betoken the possibility of adequate reform from above in Russia too. If, however, the government were to prove unwilling to make opportune concessions in the interests of social harmony (as the English aristocracy seemed to Kavelin, for example, to have done), then the existing order, with all its shortcomings, would still be preferable, in the opinion of these Russian thinkers, to the bloodshed and destruction that would come if axes were wielded and to the social uniformity, the tyranny of the majority, that might follow in the wake of revolution. They would perhaps have agreed with Montaigne, to whose humanist tradition they really belonged, that 'there is, in public affairs, no state so bad, provided it has age and continuity on its side, that [it] is not preferable to change and disturbance'.[3] Therefore they could not cross the Rubicon with Herzen and fight for a society which, though far more just than the present one, would lack their own civilised values, they could not wholeheartedly espouse the cause of the peasant who in Herzen's vision would stand by 'with dry eyes' as the 'lunatic asylum' of their civilisation was burned down.[4] They would attempt instead to reconcile antagonistic forces, and their writings do indeed reflect an attraction to what are perceived, however implausibly or misguidedly, as unifying factors and personalities. Thus Granovsky, like Chaadayev, admires Christianity in its Western form, Charlemagne and Alexander the Great. Botkin praises the supposed lack of class-consciousness in the Spanish character and commends the equality before the law which British citizens enjoy. Annenkov delights in what he takes to be the social harmony that stems from Italian indifference to political controversy. Druzhinin exalts the comprehensive artistic vision that reconciles opposites and breathes serenity. And Kavelin, simultaneously on close terms with royalty and *raznochintsy*, tries to defend both peasant interests and communal landholding, on the one hand, and gentry landownership and an economy based on the free circulation of money on the other.

The tendency which Granovsky, Botkin, Annenkov, Druzhinin and Kavelin represented, however, was not destined to flourish in Russia. Occupying the middle ground between an autocratic government which continued to resist change after the brief period of reform in the 1860s and a radical intelligentsia which was able to generate a vigorous revolutionary movement from the early 1870s, Russian liberals remained weak and ineffectual until at least the 1890s. From that decade, it is true, a liberal movement found a following in the developing professional middle classes and began to attract elements of both the Populist and Marxist wings of the radical intelligentsia. And yet even when conditions were more propitious for the growth of liberalism after the famine of 1891–2 and the death of Alexander III in 1894, Russian liberals continued to be easily dispirited and their movement, in the admission of its main Western historian, still lacked 'vitality and resilience'.[5] Only in the early years of the twentieth century did Russian liberals form an organisation and formulate a programme that enabled them to challenge the various brands of Russian socialism as an effective opposition to tsarist autocracy.

In attempting at last to evaluate the contribution of the five subjects of this study to nineteenth-century Russian intellectual life, one must above all offer an explanation for this failure on their part to establish a strong and durable tradition. One reason for such failure, as scholars have frequently pointed out, is undoubtedly the absence of a large and coherent middle class or bourgeoisie in nineteenth-century Russia. One need not go so far as Harold Laski, who describes liberalism in all its manifestations in clearcut Marxist terms as an ideology answering to the needs of the bourgeois world, a 'by-product of the effort of the middle class to win its place in the sun'.[6] Nevertheless the liberal political position – insofar as one can be clearly defined at all, for liberalism has of course taken numerous forms in the various countries and periods in which it has been represented – has generally been closely connected in Western Europe with the bourgeoisie and the growth of capitalism. Liberals have advocated a *laissez-faire* economy, the reduction of state intervention in the affairs of the individual and the assertion of individual rights and freedoms, including property rights, conducive to the development of a new industrial society in which the bourgeoisie could prosper. However, the middle class which in the West profited from the weakening of monarchic power, aristocratic privilege, ecclesiastical authority and what one writer has called the 'crust of custom'[7] was more a potentiality than an established social force in nineteenth-century Russia. It is true that the various elements that comprised the Western European bourgeoisie – a trading or entrepreneurial group, a bureacracy and a professional group, consisting of teachers, doctors, lawyers and others – were all in evidence in Russia (though until the post-reform period the first consisted largely of merchants and the last, owing to the rudimentary level of education and medical provision for the populace and the nature of the legal system had barely begun to develop before the 1860s). But these various groups had no common interests which could bind them together as a class. Those engaged in trade and industry had from Muscovite days pursued their business in a state whose rulers, as Richard Pipes has put it, 'regarded monopoly on productive wealth a natural complement to autocracy'.[8] They depended on the favour of the crown and responded to protective treatment with a servility which found political expression, especially at the beginning of the twentieth century, in staunch monarchism. Among the bureaucracy the standards of a gentry owing allegiance to the crown persisted: the state, in Seton-Watson's words, 'was placed before the individual, military values above civil values' and – as the imaginative writers of the period repeatedly complain – the 'good opinion of the hierarchical superior was preferred to the approval of public opinion'.[9] Finally, to the intelligentsia, which absorbed large sections of the professional groups when they did at last begin to develop in the second half of the century, the ethos of the merchant class and the bureaucracy seemed equally alien and odious, the former being associated with greed and philistinism and the latter with arbitrariness and corruption.

The early Russian liberals we have examined do have some affinity with the Western tradition to which the development of capitalism and the growth of a bourgeoisie had given rise. Granovsky and Kavelin, indeed all the Westernisers, recognise in the individual a need to be free of the dead weight of social custom. Botkin and Annenkov defend the bourgeoisie against the tirades of Herzen, enjoy the comforts of bourgeois civilisation and admire the freedoms and rights of its citizens. Kavelin speaks of the advantages of wage labour. Nevertheless their defence of the Western bourgeoisie, and of the individualism and *laissez-faire* economy which were crucial to Western liberalism, was very equivocal. Botkin, while voicing the wish that Russia might have a bourgeoisie, also claimed that his sympathies lay with the working class, and it is largely by virtue of his ability to dissociate himself from the *mores* of the *kupechestvo* or merchant class, to which he himself belonged by birth and within which he continued to seek his livelihood, that he gained acceptance in the intelligentsia. Granovsky and Kavelin sought to reconcile the quest for individuality with reverence for the enlightened autocrat. Kavelin viewed aspects of bourgeois society with profound distaste, feared the social disorders to which its ills might lead and pleaded for legislation to avert the creation of the landless proletariat on which Western capitalism had thriven. Nor did any of these Russian liberals espouse the ethic of self-interest, the utilitarianism which in Britain had underpinned liberal social and economic theories but which in Russia was turned to advantage by the liberals' own radical opponents. In any case Granovsky, Annenkov, Druzhinin and Kavelin all belonged to the landed gentry and wished to preserve values that might be associated with that class, such as respect for nobility of character and conduct, and a sense of honour, which were embodied in Granovsky's conception of the knight errant, Botkin's conception of the *caballero*, Druzhinin's conception of the English 'gentleman' and even Kavelin's vision of the young *intelligént* sacrificing himself for the Russian peasant. They also envisaged a society in which the gentry's status and wealth would be protected, indeed they considered the preservation of a privileged nobility vital for the health of the nation as a whole. Thus they seem to take up a position between the standpoints of two separate and antagonistic classes, bourgeoisie and gentry, the first of which, insofar as it existed at all in Russia, was fragmented and very different in character from its Western European counterpart, and the second of which, although in a moribund state, for the most part linked its fortunes to an institution, serfdom, which the liberal Westernisers themselves regarded as no longer economically or morally defensible.

A second crucial reason for the liberals' lack of impact was the absence in Russia of any proper political forum for the expression of their views. Politics in nineteenth-century Russia, like so much else, were monopolised by the autocracy, which tolerated neither elective legislature nor political parties. Russian society was therefore of the sort in which political activity should be seen as an avocation rather than a vocation, a speculative pastime rather than a means of livelihood for professional advocates. The liberal gentry failed even during the period of reforms in the early 1860s to persuade the government to grant the constitution which might have guaranteed some outlet for political ambitions. And although such 'senseless dreams', as Nicholas II was to describe constitutional demands, tended to be revived in times of political crisis, for example in 1880 and 1894, they continued to be vehemently opposed by men such as Pobedonostsev, who as mentor to Alexander III and chief Procurator of the Holy Synod wielded great power during the 1880s and who described a constitution as an abhorrent phenomenon to which the Russian soul could never be reconciled, a 'poison to the entire organism, destructive by its inherent deceit'.[10] Given the restrictions placed on political life, the only formal bodies in which liberal aspirations could find expression were the *zemstva*, but these, in spite of the hope nourished by some that they might eventually support a 'parliamentary roof', a representative assembly at the national level, remained in fact only organs of local self-government. In any case their autonomy was increasingly curtailed by central government in the first thirty years after their creation in 1864.[11] They attracted well-intentioned men who did not lack social conscience but whose caution prevented them at least until the last decade of the century from effectively challenging an unyielding government and made them content to busy themselves with what was known as *kulturtregerstvo* or attempts to civilise the backward nation, 'small deeds' of the sort that Annenkov had required of the 'weak type' in the 1850s. Denied any meaningful political role, then, the liberal wing of the intelligentsia occupied itself with agitation for palliative measures. But since liberals were therefore ineffectual as social reformers, their fundamental belief – that political activity must remain within the law – was discredited, and Populist revolutionaries, who for the most part looked on parliamentary democracy only as an insidious means of achieving the political ends of the bourgeoisie, benefited accordingly from their observable impotence. Looking at the relative fortunes and appeal of the gradualist liberal and revolutionary socialist wings of the intelligentsia after 1861, it is impossible to escape the conclusion that the government itself was responsible in large measure for the benumbing of the former and the invigoration of the latter. By doggedly refusing to establish any representative assembly or even to pay any attention to the opinions of the small educated public it lent plausibility to the utterances of its revolutionary opponents, who believed that only popular revolt or terrorism would bring substantial change, and correspondingly damaged the political fortunes of men of more moderate persuasion.

In addition to these social and political explanations for the failure of the early Russian liberals to generate a powerful current in Russian intellectual and political life we should also bear in mind the inherent weaknesses of their thought. For one thing their outlook was flawed by a fundamental inconsistency: it had grown out of the general movement of the 1840s, in Russia and the West, to emancipate individuality, nowhere stifled more than in Russia, from political, social and philosophical oppression, and yet it betrayed a faith in strong government of a sort which Mill, engaged in a similar crusade in the West, had considered legitimate only for societies in a state of barbarousness. Furthermore, the advocates of this early Russian liberalism were poorly equipped to defend their standpoint in a new age of belligerent publicism. They had little taste or aptitude for factional controversy, for they were dilettanti, gentlemen who loved the humanities for their ennobling effect but were loath to seek for a baser utility in them lest in so doing they should sterilise or pollute a source of freshness and invigoration. Besides, the literary heritage they bequeathed was not impressive. Granovsky, inspiring as he undoubtedly was as a lecturer, left only a small body of scholarship, and in that something of the spirit of the original utterance was evidently lost. Botkin wrote little and a great deal of what Annenkov produced was unreadable. Druzhinin, perhaps at his liveliest in sketches of no consequence, often lapses into mediocre narrative in his longer essays, while his shorter pieces are sometimes flaccid and one-dimensional. Kavelin is neither consistent in his ideas nor elegant in his style. Most importantly, none of the five liberals we have examined, with the partial exception of Kavelin, brought to his published work the true originality or distinction which raises Chaadayev and Herzen, for example, above most of their contemporaries or which assures foreign thinkers with whom the Russian liberals have a superficial kinship, such as Mill and Arnold, of a more secure place in their own native tradition. The substance of Druzhinin's aesthetic credo, after all, is to be found in Belinsky's writings of his Hegelian phase, and Kavelin's work on Russian history represented a more popular, less scholarly parallel endeavour to that of Solovyov.

Such weaknesses, however, are not confined to the thought of these liberal thinkers. Inconsistency, ingenuousness, an inelegant or actually opaque style and a tendency to recapitulate or reformulate the ideas of others are all failings to be found also in the writings of some of their most influential radical contemporaries. Belinsky, for instance, was notoriously prone to take up extreme positions which he could not long hold and to allow himself to be intoxicated by ideas received at second hand in simplified form. Likewise Chernyshevsky may be faulted for his unquestioning faith in the applicability of scientific method to the examination of all human problems, his sometimes simplistic reasoning and his frequently banal examples and infantile tone. The inherent weaknesses to which one might draw attention in the thought of the early Russian liberals, therefore, are a necessary but by no means sufficient explanation of the relative lack of impact of these thinkers.

A much more important reason for the difficulty they experienced in establishing their position was the alien quality of some of their most important views and basic attitudes. It was not just that so much in their thought was derived from Western sources (as were also the fundamental tenets of the *Weltanschauung* of the *raznochintsy*); it was also that their views and attitudes did not fall on fertile ground. For one thing the very amorphousness of liberalism, its lack of dogmatism, its repudiation of the revolutionary quality that the Westernisers themselves had found in Hegel's philosophy and that Belinsky had found in socialism, reduced its appeal to an educated class inclined to seek comprehensive intellectual explanations and social panaceas. Liberalism was not an effective competitor after the mid 1850s for the integral outlook of the 'new angel', as Annenkov had called Chernyshevsky, who proclaimed Robert Owen a 'holy old man' and who preached materialism and rational egoism with a missionary zeal as if they were irrefutable creeds. Furthermore, the liberal Westernisers tended to defend groups and notions whose value was not appreciated in Russia at either end of the political spectrum. For example, the bourgeoisie, about whom Botkin and Annenkov spoke with respect, excited equal animosity among both Russian conservatives and radicals. The Slavophiles, like the Prussian aristocrat Haxthausen, were no less dismayed by the prospect of capitalist industrial development, which threatened to destroy the poetic and spiritual side of life, than were Belinsky (before the last months of his life, at any rate) and Herzen by the possibility of the pauperisation of the masses. A similar fear of the development of capitalism and a bourgeoisie in Russia was also to be one of the mainsprings of both *pochvennichestvo* and Populism (which entered its openly revolutionary phase at the very time, the early 1870s, when the Russian intelligentsia was becoming aware, through the first Russian translation of the first volume of *Capital*, of Marx's analysis of the mechanism of capitalist society). Again, the respect shown by Granovsky and Botkin for Western European law was no more shared by the Slavophiles and the *pochvenniki* (who regarded that body of law as formalistic and devoid of a true spirit of justice) than by the radical *raznochintsy*, who tended to view it as a sanctification of the rights of the bourgeoisie and to consider infringements of it as inevitable consequences of social privation. For the former groups of Romantic conservatives it was moral law, not positive law, that should have authority in human affairs, while for the latter, radical group law in its scientific sense – that is to say definition of invariable and necessary causes and effects in the life of the individual and society, as well as in the natural world – took similar precedence over any jurisprudential considerations. Nor was a sense of the importance of the temporal law to become deeply embedded in the consciousness of the intelligentsia even after the attempt to reform the judicial system in the mid 1860s. As late as 1909 Kistyakovsky, in his contribution to the collection of essays entitled *Landmarks*, still insisted that the Russian intelligentsia, in its quest for 'higher and absolute ideals', had 'never respected the law, never seen any value in it'.[12]

Most importantly, the spirit of calm, dispassionate inquiry which the liberal Westernisers sought to promote was regarded with deep suspicion by a large section of the Russian intelligentsia. No sooner had the liberals tried to introduce a learning independent of official doctrine than the nascent intelligentsia to which they themselves belonged perceived the potential utility of such an endeavour as an instrument of change. The nation into which such learning was being introduced, moreover, was so manifestly backward and barbarous when measured against those nations in which this learning had its sources that to humanitarian men it seemed immoral to give the new culture time to put down deep roots in Russian soil before attempting to gather some of the fruits it might yield. Thus in place of an ability to examine contributions to philosophy and culture 'according to their essence, from the point of view of their absolute value', Berdyayev contended in his own contribution to *Landmarks*, one found an 'almost maniacal tendency to assess philosophical doctrines and philosophical truths according to political and utilitarian criteria'. A '*love of truth*' had been paralysed by a '*love of equalising justice, of the social good, of the people's wellbeing*'. The conditions of Russian life had made the flowering of what Berdyayev called an 'objective social philosophy and science' impossible[13] and the hold of liberalism was weakened accordingly. The pleas of liberals in the mid 1850s for a serene and apolitical literature and a dispassionate literary criticism addressing itself to the problem of evaluating artistic merit before all else fell on ears already deafened by Belinsky's impassioned demands – which in the 1840s the liberal Westernisers had themselves applauded and supported in their way – for a literature harnessed to the cause of national salvation as well as to eternal aesthetic ideals. While Druzhinin, aided by Botkin and Annenkov, tried in the manner of Matthew Arnold to remain independent, patiently to seek fresh knowledge and to create an atmosphere in which the 'best ideas might prevail', others were affirming the principle of social utility as the paramount criterion for the judgement of the arts and the various branches of philosophy. The intellectual, a more or less disinterested seeker after truth, was being ousted by the *intelligént*, the ardent champion of doctrines useful in the pursuit of social justice.

It was the misfortune of the liberal Westernisers, moreover, that the utilitarian tendency in Russian culture was greatly strengthened in the second half of the 1850s by that peculiar combination of circumstances that forced thinking men to make unpleasant choices and express firm commitments to one set of values or another. The death of Nicholas I, Russia's defeat in the Crimean War, the decline in the power of the gentry, the emergence of the *raznochintsy*, the growth of peasant unrest and the sudden revival of literature and thought – all these factors served to create what Lenin was to describe as Russia's first 'revolutionary situation' in the late 1850s and early 1860s and brought about a sharp polarisation of opinion. 'Of course, it is safer to go where the wind blows', Nikitenko mused in his diary in October 1861 as ugly student demonstrations disrupted the academic life of St Petersburg University;

but there are now various winds blowing and they are against one another. At such a time as this any honourable man is bound to define his position, to be *something*, not *all things* . . .[14]

Botkin, Annenkov and Druzhinin might still try to stand back, like Turgenev's Nikolay Kirsanov, in order to admire the beauty of nature, to savour their fondest memories of youth and to delight in Pushkin's lyrical celebrations of the spiritual and emotional world dear to every individual. But in so doing they laid themselves open to the charge that they were self-indulgent, that they were averting their gaze from an unpleasant reality and thereby accepting or even condoning it. Radical publicists such as Dobrolyubov had little difficulty in associating such liberals with *oblomovshchina*, the malady of inertia that afflicted a gentry nourished and pampered at the cost of the toiling serf. A liberal, as he was defined in a radical 'dictionary' of the early 60s, was faint-hearted and hypocritical,

a man loving freedom, usually a boyar [who enjoys] freedom to look through a window without doing anything, then to go for a walk, to the theatre, or a ball – that is what is known as a liberal man.[15]

He was specious and charming, but disingenuous. He 'glowed with such sincerity and zeal, and moreover was such a dear and was so nice to everyone', as Saltykov-Shchedrin lampoons him in one of his 'fables', 'that he was forgiven for being politically unsound. He knew how to vindicate truth with a smile, could, when necessary, play the simpleton, and could show off his disinterestedness to advantage'.[16] But he was ineffectual: 'liberalism', one of those 'foreign' and 'useless' words which Bazarov condemns, could not disguise his bankruptcy, both moral and economic, to which the ramshackle estate through which Nikolay Kirsanov drives his son and his guest at the beginning of *Fathers and Children* is a damning testimony. Worst of all in the eyes of so many of his contemporaries was his striving for impartiality, his search for means of reconciling conflicting interests and his ultimate quiescence. For there were institutions so objectionable that any attempt to come to terms with them, or merely to mitigate their harsher aspects rather than altogether to destroy them, might seem a bargain with evil and an implicit profession of allegiance to the established order. The defendants of 'unconditional and independent knowledge' in Russia, 'knowledge as a principle standing far above topical social matters', wrote Berdyayev in his essay in *Landmarks*, were 'still suspected of reactionary sympathies'.[17] Even the symbolist poet Blok was to interpret the attempt to stand 'outside politics' as a retirement into 'aestheticism and individualism', and pointed to Turgenev – a writer on such intimate terms with the liberal Western-isers examined here and so close to them in his views – as a prime example of the 'pure artist' whose attempts to shun political commit-ment had given him the 'anaemic complexion' of a 'flaccid liberal-constitutionalist living the idle life of a lord'. To attempt to live 'outside politics' was 'humanism inside out' and it harmed the humanist's cause, for by concealing a side of reality, by failing to remove a few bricks when it was necessary in the interest of the whole truth to do so, one made it more probable that other coarser and more brutal reformers would destroy the whole edifice.[18] Thus in Russian conditions after the 1850s those who attempted to defend middle ground were characterised not so much as noble advocates of truth and reason but rather as pusillanimous egotists trying to conceal their essential conservatism behind a cloak of rhetoric.

The liberals themselves, it must be added, lent force to the gibes of the socialists and plausibility to their criticisms by refusing to break altogether with the established order. Botkin and Annenkov, in particular, led an epicurean existence financed not so much by their own journalistic labours as by inherited wealth derived from commerce, in Botkin's case, and landowning in Annenkov's. Not only were they disinclined to give up this style of life, they also tended throughout the 1850s to pursue it with an ostentatiousness offensive to the more plebeian members of the intelligentsia who did not have the means to indulge such tastes and were in any case of an ascetic temperament. Most importantly, the liberals compromised themselves by their determination to preserve an aristocracy, social, aesthetic and moral, of the sort to which they themselves belonged, by their defence of strong, even authoritarian government and by their effusive expressions of gratitude and loyalty to Alexander II during the early years of his reign. Their reasons for this monarchism may have been various, and not necessarily purely selfish. Admittedly they had no personal experience of the breakdown of order in society, as had Thomas Hobbes when he wrote his own defence of authoritarian government in seventeenth-century England, for they lived in a period of reasonable domestic stability. They may, however, have been disturbed by the distant memory of the great peasant rebellion led by Pugachov in the 1770s or by what they had read on the subject of the French Revolution, or by their parents' accounts of the Napoleonic period which had followed that revolution and by which Russia, of course, had been so deeply affected. Certainly they were shaken by the disturbances in the West in 1848. Perhaps temperament too was the mother of their conviction, for all had peace-loving natures. Whatever the motives for their defence of the Russian autocracy, though, this monarchism ultimately rendered them ineffectual. For it is arguable that despite the personal initiatives of Alexander II, the institution of autocracy was already too discredited by the beginning of the 1860s to enable the tsar to provide leadership acceptable to the whole nation as it strove to catch up the Western European powers with which it was now in competition. Unable either to escape this fact or to accept it, the liberals I have examined lived out their last years without the influence they had formerly enjoyed and, with the exception of Granovsky, they died too late to end their days with a sense of richness and fulfilment.

There is, finally, one further reason for the failure of the liberal Westernisers to make a lasting impact in Russia, and one for which they themselves can scarcely be blamed. By the time they began to clarify their aesthetic, social and political views in the late 50s, the intellectual and political climate in Europe as a whole was no longer quite so propitious for the promotion of liberalism as it had once been. In France and Britain liberal opponents of a powerful monarchy and landed aristocracy had emphatically asserted themselves during the 1830s and 40s, while in both Germany and Italy liberalism had in the same period benefited from its association with the aspiration towards a unified nation. By the time the Russian intelligentsia came to contemplate the modernisation of their own values and society in the mid 1850s, however, liberals in the West were for the most part either content with their gains or in retreat. In France Louis-Napoleon had reintroduced authoritarian government after his *coup d'état* in 1851; in Germany the liberal successes in the towns had not spread to the countryside; and in Italy Cavour's attempt to introduce an English brand of liberalism was confined to Piedmont and did not flourish on a national scale after the unification of the country in 1861. Thus after 1848, when liberals had had the opportunity to take power over much of the continent, the liberal's former zeal and confidence was gone and his outlook, which in the first half of the century had seemed dynamic and progressive, increasingly became what one historian has described as a 'static rather than a revolutionary force'.[19] The most vigorous force for change in the West was now the socialist movement about which Granovsky, Botkin and Annenkov had all expressed reservations in the 1840s and whose momentum Botkin, Annenkov, Kavelin (and Druzhinin, in his capacity as critic of 'Gogolian' art) had anxiously tried to check in the second half of the 1850s. The utopian vision of Fourier, Cabet and others, and the agitation of Blanqui and Louis Blanc and their supporters had helped to generate the unrest which resulted in the downfall of the July monarchy in 1848. Marx's and Engels' critique of bourgeois society, particularly in its Victorian English form, the anarchist teachings of Bakunin and Proudhon, the agitation of Lassalle and the development of a German socialist movement in the 1860s, the foundation of the First Workingmen's International in 1864 – all these factors attested to the vigour of that new tendency in Western European political thought to which the Russian *raznochintsy* and their Populist successors responded. Thus at that very period when some members of the Russian intelligentsia were beginning to form an outlook in some measure comparable to that of Western liberals, a new stream of thought antithetical to their liberalism flooded into Russia and immediately threatened to engulf them. It need only be added that the traditional dependence of Russian thinkers on inspiration and nourishment from the West made this development in Western thought the more decisive – and the more destructive – for the early Russian liberals.

The fact that the liberal Westernisers had little lasting impact on Russian thought and political life does not entitle us to conclude, however, that their achievement was nearly so insignificant as their rapid eclipse in the 1850s and their subsequent confinement in relative obscurity would seem to indicate. Like Turgenev's Rudin they sowed 'many good seeds in young souls'. For one thing they had all made important individual contributions to Russian culture. Granovsky and Kavelin had helped to lay foundations for Russian historical scholarship. Botkin and Annenkov increased Russian knowledge of Western Europe and Annenkov has left valuable accounts of the life of the intelligentsia to which he belonged. Druzhinin, through his novella *Polinka Saks*, helped to mould the sensibility of a generation earnestly espousing humanitarian causes and, in his literary criticism, put forward the fullest and most lucid defence of the view, to which Turgenev, Goncharov, Fet and the young Tolstoy were greatly attracted, that art should remain uncommitted to any social or political cause. Kavelin also made a significant contribution to the discussion of the emancipation of the serfs, the most momentous and far-reaching reform in nineteenth-century Russia. Even more important than these individual contributions, however, was the part which Granovsky, Botkin, Annenkov, Druzhinin and Kavelin (together, of course, with many others) played collectively in the intellectual life of their time. The gentry culture they partially represented was in its final bloom and could not effectively compete with the more robust plebeian growths nourished by the latest Western influences, but it did even now confer many benefits on a nation just becoming conscious of a role for itself in the modern European world. For a brief period, as Victor Frank has expressed it in a felicitous metaphor, the houses of the gentry, almost the only stone buildings against a background of peasant huts, were a 'cradle of civilisation' in Russia; their

pseudo-classical contours with moulding on the façade, surrounded by neglected parks and overgrown ponds, became for Russia what the cities had been for ancient Greece, the monasteries for medieval Europe, the 'manses' of Presbyterian ministers for Scotland, the *Pfarrhäuser* for Protestant Germany.[20]

They had helped to introduce a humane culture into a backward nation, and it was a culture that, in Isaiah Berlin's words, 'meant more to the Russians, late-comers to Hegel's feast of the spirit, than to the blasé nations of the west'.[21] With their wide-ranging literary, artistic, philosophical and historical interests, their erudition, their good taste, their linguistic prowess and their extensive knowledge of the contemporary West they were able to make accessible to their compatriots – and especially to Belinsky, perhaps the most important figure in the intellectual life of their age – an immense repository of intellectual and spiritual treasures. By fulfilling this task – which they conceived as a noble one and approached with sincerity and humility, if with frequent naïveté – they helped considerably to foster an enlightened intelligentsia in Russia and to refine its taste. They had played a worthy role in that sudden awakening which took place in the mid nineteenth century on the fringe of Europe, where in 1839 the Marquis de Custine had found only tyranny and desolation – an awakening which already in the lifetime of the liberal Westernisers themselves began to find expression in a literature still unsurpassed in depth and humanity.

Key to abbreviations used in the notes

BT   *V. P. Botkin i I. S. Turgenev: neizdannaya perepiska, 1851–1869*, Moscow–Leningrad, 1930.
LN   *Literaturnoye nasledstvo.*
PSS *Polnoye sobraniye sochineniy.*
PVA *P. V. Annenkov i yego druz'ya*, St Petersburg, 1892.
Soch. *Sochineniya.*
SS   *Sobraniye sochineniy.*
TKS *Turgenev i krug 'Sovremennika': neizdannyye materialy, 1847–1861*, Moscow–Leningrad, 1930.
VKO P. V. Annenkov, *Vospominaniya i kriticheskiye ocherki*, 3 vols., St Petersburg, 1877–81.

A few other abbreviations occur in the notes. These are explained when reference is first made to the work which they indicate.

Notes

FOREWORD

1 Alexander Herzen, *My Past and Thoughts: The Memoirs of Alexander Herzen*, trans. by Constance Garnett, revised by Humphrey Higgins, 4 vols., London, 1968, II, p. 529.

2 K. D. Kavelin, *SS*, 4 vols., St Petersburg, 1897–1900, II, cols. 1175–77. There is no reason not to take Kavelin's words at their face value. Kavelin was, after all, recording his conversation for his own private reference, not for publication. In any case dissimulation was alien to him: he was forthright to the point of being ingenuous.

3 See Chapter 1, pp. 33–41, for fuller examination of Chernyshevsky's essays on liberalism.

4 See bibliography for details of all the works cited here.

5 It is, however, a good indication of the continuing lack of Soviet enthusiasm for the work of Granovsky, Botkin, Annenkov, Druzhinin and Kavelin that there is no post-revolutionary collection of the works of any one of them. Annenkov's memoirs have been republished in the Soviet period, but it is perhaps significant that these throw as much light on Belinsky and writers such as Gogol and Turgenev, whose literary reputation is secure, as on Annenkov's liberal contemporaries. There is also a recent Soviet edition of Botkin's *Letters on Spain*.

6 V. A. Kitayev, *Ot frondy k okhranitel'stvu: iz istorii russkoy liberal'noy mysli 50-kh–60-kh godov XIX veka*, Moscow, 1972, (hereafter *Ot frondy k okhranitel'stvu*), p. 3.

7 *Ibid.*, p. 282.

8 Isaiah Berlin, *Russian Thinkers*, London, 1978, p. 303.

9 viz. 'Druzhinin and the "Pushkin School" of Russian Literature' (paper delivered at the Convention of the American Association for the Advancement of Slavic Studies, New Haven, Conn., October 1979, and article under the same title in a *Festschrift* for N. Ye. Andreyev, *Poetry, Prose and Public Opinion of Russia, 1850–1950*, ed. William J. Harrison, and Avril Pyman, Letchworth, 1984, pp. 19–42; 'Vasiliy Petrovich Botkin, (1810–69)' (paper delivered at the Conference of the British Universities' Association of Slavists, Bangor, April 1982, and article under the same title in *Oxford Slavonic Papers*, XVI, 1983, pp. 141–63; 'T. N. Granovsky: the Historian as Liberal Westerniser' (paper delivered at meeting of the Nineteenth-Century Russian Literature

Group of the British Universities' Association of Slavists, Bristol, October 1982).

CHAPTER I

1 Quotations from the first English translation of the work by the Marquis de Custine, *Russia*, London, 1854, pp. 135, 66, 151, 53, 131, 197, 70, 88, 25, 79, 100, 32, 203. The French original, *La Russie en 1839*, was published in Paris in 1843.

2 Michael T. Florinsky, *Russia: A History and an Interpretation*, 2 vols., New York, 1953, II, p. 754.

3 Quoted by Florinsky, p. 755.

4 Custine, p. 169.

5 Quoted by Florinsky, p. 797.

6 *Ibid.*, p. 799.

7 Custine, pp. 69–70, 57.

8 D. S. Mirsky, *A History of Russian Literature*, London, 1949, p. 172.

9 Quoted by Sidney Monas in *The Third Section: Police and Society in Russia under Nicholas I*, Cambridge, Mass., 1961, p. 163.

10 The phrase is used by Dobrolyubov as the title to one of his reviews of the work of the playwright, Ostrovsky (see N. A. Dobrolyubov, *SS*, 9 vols., Moscow–Leningrad, 1961–3, V, pp. 7–139).

11 Quotations from the English translation by Raymond T. McNally in *The Major Works of Peter Chaadaev*, Notre Dame, Ind. and London, 1969, pp. 23–51, see esp. pp. 34, 28, 30–1.

12 Peter K. Christoff, *K. S. Aksakov: A Study in Ideas*, Princeton, N.J., 1982, p. 86.

13 Ivan Kireyevsky, for example, admitted that he was bound to the West by 'many indissoluble sympathies' (see his *PSS*, 2 vols., Moscow, 1911, I, p. 112).

14 *Ibid.*, pp. 109–20.

15 *Ibid.*, p. 119.

16 *Ibid.*, p. 215.

17 Aleksey Khomyakov, *Izbrannyye sochineniya*, ed. N. S. Arsen'yev, New York, 1955, pp. 79–102, esp. pp. 90ff.

18 Kireyevsky, *PSS*, I, pp. 162, 143–4. On the Slavophiles' views on Orthodoxy, see esp. Nicholas V. Riasanovsky, 'Khomiakov on *Sobornost'*' in *Continuity and Change in Russian and Soviet Thought*, ed. Ernest J. Simmons, New York, 1967, pp. 183–196.

19 Khomyakov, *Izbrannyye sochineniya*, pp. 122–4.

20 K. S. Aksakov, *PSS*, 3 vols., Moscow, 1861–80, I, pp. 291–2.

21 See Baron A. von Haxthausen, *The Russian Empire: Its People, Institutions and Resources*, 2 vols., London, 1856, I, pp. 123–35. The German original, *Studien über die innern Zustände, das Volksleben und insbesondere die ländlichen Einrichtungen Russland*, was published in Hanover in 1847.

22 Khomyakov, *Izbrannyye sochineniya*, pp. 80, 84.

23 It is as well to emphasise at the outset that the term 'Westerniser' ('Westernist' and even 'Westerner' are sometimes also used to translate the Russian *zapadnik*) has even greater shortcomings than the term 'Slavophile'. Like the term 'Slavophile', it was first used as a gibe by those who wished to disparage the attitudes it implied. The American historian, Richard Pipes, even goes so far as to say that it is difficult to perceive among the opponents of the Slavophiles 'any unity except that of a negative kind' and suggests that the 'party' designated 'Westerners' is really only a 'ioil for the Slavophiles' invented by historians as lovers of symmetry (see Pipes' book, *Russia under the Old Régime*, London, 1974, p. 268).

24 See Alexander Herzen, *My Past and Thoughts*, II, p. 511. (In the main Russian edition of Herzen's works, *SS*, 30 vols., Moscow, 1954–65, *Byloye i dumy* occupies vols. VIII–XI.)

25 I. S. Turgenev, *Polnoye sobraniye sochineniy i pisem*, 28 vols., Moscow–Leningrad, 1960–8 (hereafter cited as *PSSP* [works] and *PSSP, Pis'ma* [Letters]), XIV, p. 9.

26 Herzen, *My Past and Thoughts*, II, p. 398.

27 Quoted by Frederick Copleston, S.J., *A History of Philosophy*, 8 vols., London, 1961–6, VII, p. 166.

28 The fullest study of Hegel's influence in Russia in Chizhevsky's *Gegel' v Rossii*, Paris, 1939. See also Andrzej Walicki, *The Slavophile Controversy, History of a Conservative Utopia in Nineteenth-Century Russian Thought*, trans. Hilda Andrews-Rusiecka, Oxford, 1975, pp. 287–335.

29 See M. A. Bakunin, *Selected Writings*, ed. Arthur Lehning, London, 1973, p. 58.

30 Ludwig Feuerbach, *The Essence of Christianity*, ed. and abridged by E. Graham Waring and F. W. Strothman, New York, 1957, pp. 30 (Feuerbach's italics), 9–11, 18, 65.

31 P. V. Annenkov, *Literaturnyye vospominaniya*, Moscow, 1960, p. 274.

32 See Herzen, *SS*, III, pp. 7–88, esp. pp. 64ff. and pp. 91–315.

33 Walicki, *The Slavophile Controversy*, p. 375.

34 Custine, p. 174.

35 Turgenev, *PSSP, Pis'ma*, I, pp. 274, 277.

36 Quoted by G. D. H. Cole in *A History of Socialist Thought*, I, London, 1953, p. 42.

37 *Ibid.*, p. 176.

38 Annenkov, *Literaturnyye vospominaniya*, p. 209.

39 *The Communist Manifesto*, Part III, Section 3.

40 Annenkov, *Literaturnyye vospominaniya*, p. 269.

41 *Ibid.*, p. 270.

42 V. G. Belinsky, *PSS*, 13 vols., Moscow, 1953–9, XI, pp. 386–7.

43 *Richard II*, Act III, scene ii.

44 Belinsky, *PSS*, III, pp. 325–56, esp. pp. 330–1, 334, 341.

45 *Ibid.*, pp. 385–419, esp. pp. 392ff.

46 *Ibid.*, IV, pp. 193–270, esp. pp. 235ff., 265.
47 *Ibid.*, pp. 479–547, esp. pp. 520ff.
48 *Ibid.*, VII, pp. 49–50; see also Walicki, *A History of Russian Thought from the Enlightenment to Marxism*, trans. by Hilda Andrews-Rusiecka, Oxford, 1980, p. 124.
49 Belinsky, *PSS*, XI, p. 556.
50 *Ibid.*, XII, pp. 22–3. See Dostoyevsky's novel, *Brat'ya Karamazovy*, Part V, Chapter IV.
51 Belinsky, *PSS*, XII, pp. 70, 66.
52 *Ibid.*, VII, p. 311.
53 *Ibid.*, X, p. 257.
54 *Ibid.*, p. 302.
55 *Ibid.*, p. 311.
56 *Ibid.*, pp. 213, 217.
57 *Ibid.*, p. 311.
58 *Ibid.*, p. 302.
59 See Georg Lukács, *Studies in European Realism*, London, 1972, pp. 97–125, for a Marxist analysis of the school of criticism founded by Belinsky.
60 Belinsky, *PSS*, X, pp. 17–18.
61 *Ibid.*, VII, pp. 435ff.
62 *Ibid.*, X, pp. 17, 302.
63 *Ibid.*, VIII, pp. 472, 479.
64 *Ibid.*, X, pp. 9, 19–20.
65 *Ibid.*, pp. 12–13.
66 *Ibid.*, I, pp. 22–4.
67 *Ibid.*, VII, p. 503.
68 *Ibid.*, X, pp. 292–4.
69 N. A. Nekrasov, *Polnoye sobraniye sochineniy i pisem*, 12 vols., Moscow, 1948–53 (hereafter *PSSP*), IX, p. 142.
70 Belinsky, *PSS*, X, pp. 295–9.
71 *Ibid.*, pp. 300–2.
72 *Ibid.*, p. 212.
73 Annenkov, *Literaturnyye vospominaniya*, p. 192.
74 Belinsky, *PSS*, VII, p. 392.
75 The phrase belongs to D. V. Grigorovich, *Literaturnyye vospominaniya*, Moscow, 1961, p. 103.
76 Herzen, *SS*, V, pp. 15–67; see also p. 317. Quotations are from pp. 317, 34, 35, 37, 63.
77 See esp. *ibid.*, VI, pp. 150–86; VII, pp. 9–132, 271–306; XII, pp. 134–66. Quotations from VI, p. 151, XII, p. 154, VII, p. 288, XII, pp. 144, 152.
78 Annenkov, *Literaturnyye vospominaniya*, p. 533.
79 Quoted by Hugh Seton-Watson, *The Russian Empire, 1801–1917*, Oxford, 1967, p. 277.
80 Florinsky, *Russia: A History and an Interpretation*, II, p. 805.
81 Annenkov, *Literaturnyye vospominaniya*, pp. 535–6.

82 Quoted by Seton-Watson, p. 335.
83 See *Ranniye slavyanofily. A. S. Khomyakov, I. V. Kireyevskiy, K. S. i I. S. Aksakovy*, ed. N. L. Brodsky, Moscow, 1910, pp. 69–96.
84 Kireyevsky, *PSS*, I, pp. 223–64; see esp. pp. 224–5, 228–9, 237, 246–7.
85 Khomyakov, *Izbrannyye sochineniya*, pp. 172–206.
86 Herzen, *My Past and Thoughts*, II, pp. 600–30.
87 Chicherin is an important thinker who has not been sufficiently studied. He falls outside the scope of the present study because, as a younger man than the liberals examined here, he did not make an impact on Russian thought until the 1850s. He did not therefore participate in the discussions of the Westernisers in the 1840s or pass through a youthful phase of idealistic humanitarianism inspired by Belinsky. The spirit of his thought is consequently different from that of Granovsky, Botkin, Annenkov and Kavelin, although its content is not dissimilar (see esp. Chapter 6, Section 5, below). For a recent Soviet view of him see Kitayev, *Ot frondy k okhranitel'stvu, passim*. The best discussion of Chicherin in English is to be found in Leonard Schapiro's book, *Rationalism and Nationalism in Russian Nineteenth-Century Political Thought*, New Haven, Conn., and London, 1967, pp. 89–101.
88 See *TKS*, p. 104. On *Russkiy vestnik* and its platform and the mood of its contributors in the mid 1850s see Kitayev, *Ot frondy k okhranitel'-stvu*, pp. 25–85.
89 B. N. Chicherin, *Opyty po istorii russkogo prava*, Moscow, 1858, p. 369.
90 See V. N. Rozental', 'Obshchestvenno-politicheskaya programma russkogo liberalizma v seredine 50-kh godov XIX v.', *Istoricheskiye zapiski*, LXX, 1961, pp. 220–1.
91 *Ibid.*, pp. 208–9. Rozental' is quoting from an article by Chicherin which appeared in *Russkiy vestnik*, October, 1856, vol. v., book 2.
92 The pioneering studies of Russian liberalism in its infancy are by Rozental' 'Pervoye otkrytoye vystupleniye russkikh liberalov v 1855–1856 gg.', *Istoriya SSSR*, 1958, no. 2, pp. 113–30; 'Obsh-chestvenno-politicheskaya programma russkogo liberalizma v seredine 50-kh godov XIX v.', *Istoricheskiye zapiski*, LXX, 1961, pp. 197–222; 'Narastaniye "krizisa verkhov" v seredine 50-kh godov XIX veka', in the symposium *Revolyutsionnaya situatsiya v Rossii v 1859–1861 gg.*', ed. M. V. Nechkina *et al.*, Moscow, 1962, pp. 40–63; 'Ideynyye tsentry liberal 'nogo dvizheniya v Rossii nakanune revolyutsionnoy situatsii', in another volume of the same symposium, Moscow, 1963, pp. 372–98. Kitayev, in his book *Ot frondy k okhranitel'stvu*, concentrates on the thought of Katkov, Chicherin and Kavelin; and Sh. M. Levin's *Ocherki po istorii russkoy obshchestvennoy mysli: Vtoraya polovina XIX–nachalo XX veka*, Leningrad, 1974, contains a substantial section on liberalism from an unfinished monograph (pp. 348–404).
93 See Rozental', 'Obshchestvenno-politicheskaya programma russkogo liberalizma v seredine 50-kh godov XIX v.', p. 200.
94 *Ibid.*, p. 201.

95 N. G. Chernyshevsky, *PSS*, 15 vols., Moscow, 1939–50, VII, pp. 240, 258.
96 Chernyshevsky's dissertation appears in *PSS*, II, pp. 5–92; see esp. pp. 10ff.
97 See Dostoyevsky's article 'G.-bov i vopros ob iskusstve', *PSS*, 30 vols. planned, Leningrad, 1972–, XVIII, pp. 70–103, esp pp. 76ff.
98 Turgenev, *PSSP, Pis'ma*, II, pp. 287, 290, 293, 294, 296, 297.
99 See Chernyshevsky, *PSS*, III, pp. 5–309.
100 *Ibid.*, VII, pp. 222–95; see esp. pp. 240, 278, 260–61, 264, 266.
101 *Ibid.*, p. 286.
102 *Ibid.*, V, pp. 357–92; see also IV, pp. 303–48, esp. 316–17, 328, 334, 340–1; *ibid.*, pp. 737–61, esp. 744–6, 756, 760; V, pp. 576–626, esp. 615ff.
103 *Ibid.*, V, pp. 5–64, esp. 37, 48.
104 *Ibid.*, pp. 213–91, esp. pp. 214–16.
105 *Ibid.*, pp. 217–18.
106 *Ibid.*, p. 378.
107 *Ibid.*, pp. 292–317, esp. pp. 300, 305.
108 The *Velikoruss* leaflets were reprinted in M. Lemke, *Ocherki osvoboditel'nogo dvizheniya 'shestidesyatykh godov'*, St Petersburg, 1908, pp. 359–68.
109 See N. V. Shelgunov, L. P. Shelgunova, M. L. Mikhaylov, *Vospominaniya*, Moscow, 1967, 2 vols., I, pp. 332–50.
110 The proclamation is reprinted in Lemke, *Politicheskiye protsessy v Rossii 1860–kh gg.*, 2nd ed., Moscow–Petrograd, 1923, pp. 508–18.

CHAPTER 2 (GRANOVSKY)

1 Turgenev, *PSSP*, VI, p. 371.
2 Herzen, *My Past and Thoughts*, II, p. 499.
3 The phrase belongs to Annenkov, being the title of his best known memoirs (*Zamechatel 'noye desyatiletiye*); see his *Literaturnyye vospominaniya*, pp. 135–374.
4 Most of the main Russian works on Granovsky are pre-revolutionary. See esp. A. V. Stankevich, *T. N. Granovskiy i yego perepiska*, 2nd ed., 2 vols., Moscow, 1897 (hereafter Stankevich, I, and Stankevich, II; vol. I is a biography, vol. II contains Granovsky's correspondence, which is an invaluable source of information on his life and thought). See also N. I. Kareyev, *Istoricheskoye mirosozertsaniye Granovskogo*, St Petersburg, 1896; Ch. Vetrinsky [V. Ye. Cheshikhin), *V sorokovykh godakh: Istoriko-literaturnyye ocherki i kharakteristiki*, Moscow, 1899, pp. 62–95; and M. Gershenzon, *Istoriya molodoy Rossii*, Moscow, 1908, pp. 202–43, where the influence of Granovsky's personality, as opposed to his scholarship, is rightly emphasised. In the Soviet period material on Granovsky has been published by, among others, V. P. Buzeskul, 'Vseobshchaya istoriya i yego predstaviteli v Rossii v XIX i

nachale XX veka', part I, in *Trudy komissii po istorii znaniy*, VII, Leningrad, 1929, pp. 47–64; I. Ivashin, 'Rukopis' publichnykh lektsiy T. N. Granovskogo', *Istoricheskiy zhurnal*, 1945, nos. 1–2 (137–8), pp. 81–4; and S. A. Asinovskaya, *Iz istorii peredovykh idey v russkoy mediyevistike (T. N. Granovskiy)*, Moscow, 1955. There is also an exhaustive bibliographical work on Granovsky by S. S. Dmitriyev, ed., *Granovskiy, Timofey Nikolayevich. Bibliografiya, 1828–1967*, Moscow, 1969.

For discussion of Granovsky in English, see Schapiro, *Rationalism and Nationalism in Russian Nineteenth-Century Political Thought*, pp. 73–81; and esp. the long monograph by Priscilla R. Roosevelt, 'Granovskii at the lectern: a conservative liberal's vision of history', *Forschungen zur osteuropäischen Geschichte*, XXIX, Berlin, 1981, pp. 61–192, where attention is focused primarily on Granovsky's university lectures on world history.

5 See Asinovskaya, ed., *Lektsii T. N. Granovskogo po istorii srednevekov'ya*, Moscow, 1961; idem, *Lektsii T. N. Granovskogo po istorii pozdnego srednevekov'ya*, Moscow, 1971. See also P. Milyukov, *Iz istorii russkoy intelligentsii*, 2nd ed., St Petersburg, 1903, pp. 212–65; and 'Neizdannyye universitetskiye kursy Granovskogo', introduced by M. N. Kovalensky, in *Golos minuvshego*, Moscow, 1913, no. 9, pp. 210–33.

6 Belinsky, *PSS*, XI, pp. 456, 494, 377.

7 Herzen, *My Past and Thoughts*, II, pp. 499, 489.

8 I. I. Panayev, *Literaturnyye vospominaniya*, Leningrad, 1950, p. 230.

9 Stankevich, II, p. 68.

10 *Ibid.*, I, p. 67.

11 *Ibid.*, p. 61; Granovsky's italics.

12 *Ibid.*, p. 62.

13 *Ibid.*, II, p. 364.

14 *Ibid.*, pp. 90, 201.

15 *Ibid.*, p. 62.

16 *Ibid.*, p. 355.

17 *Ibid.*, p. 190.

18 *Ibid.*, p. 364. For Belinsky's attitude towards Schiller see his letter of 29th September 1839 to N. V. Stankevich in *PSS*, XI, p. 385.

19 T. N. Granovsky, *Soch.*, 4th ed., 1 vol., Moscow 1900, pp. 288–99, 420–37. All subsequent references to Granovsky's collected works are to this edition.

20 Stankevich, I, p. 267.

21 Granovsky, *Soch.*, p. 96.

22 Stankevich, II, p. 400.

23 *Ibid.*, p. 395.

24 Tacitus, *The Annals of Imperial Rome*, Book I, Chapter I.

25 Stankevich, II, p. 358.

26 Panayev, p. 225.

27 Turgenev, *PSSP*, VI, p. 373.
28 Stankevich, II, p. 98.
29 Herzen, *My Past and Thoughts*, II, p. 510.
30 Granovsky, *Soch.*, p. 308.
31 Annenkov, *Literaturnyye vospominaniya*, p. 214.
32 See Stankevich, I, p. 130.
33 *Ibid.*, II, p. 459.
34 *Ibid.*, pp. 365–6; Granovsky's italics.
35 *Ibid.*, I, p. 127.
36 Annenkov, *Literaturnyye vospominaniya*, p. 213.
37 Herzen, *My Past and Thoughts*, II, pp. 504–5.
38 Stankevich, I, p. 127.
39 *Ibid.*, p. 283.
40 See Milyukov, *Iz istorii russkoy intelligentsii*, pp. 252–3.
41 See Asinovskaya, *Lektsii T. N. Granovskogo po istorii srednevekov'ya*, p. 169.
42 Granovsky, *Soch.*, pp. 203, 206.
43 *Ibid.*, p. 555.
44 *Ibid.*, p. 419.
45 *Ibid.*, p. 414; Stankevich, II, p. 419.
46 Stankevich, II, p. 420.
47 *Ibid.*, pp. 176–7.
48 *Ibid.*, I, p. 138.
49 *Ibid.*
50 *Ibid.*, II, pp. 369–70.
51 Granovsky, *Soch.*, pp. 134–71, esp. 154, 162.
52 *Ibid.*, p. 266.
53 Stankevich, II, pp. 351, 412–13.
54 Granovsky, *Soch.*, p. 562.
55 Asinovskaya, *Lektsii T. N. Granovskogo po istorii srednevekov'ya*, p. 100.
56 Granovsky, *Soch.*, p. 456.
57 *Ibid.*, pp. 273–4.
58 *Ibid.*, pp. 190, 193.
59 *Ibid.*, pp. 180–2, 225.
60 Milyukov, *Iz istorii russkoy intelligentsii*, p. 246; see also Granovsky, *Soch.*, p. 536; Annenkov, *Literaturnyye vospominaniya*, p. 214.
61 Granovsky, *Soch.*, pp. 256–7.
62 Stankevich, II, p. 370.
63 *Ibid.*, p. 448.
64 *Ibid.*, pp. 437, 453.
65 Chaadayev, *op. cit.*, p. 38.
66 See Stankevich, II, p. 439.
67 Granovsky, *Soch.*, pp. 420–37, 540–50.
68 Asinovskaya, *Lektsii T. N. Granovskogo po istorii srednevekov'ya*, p. 174.

69 Granovsky, *Soch.*, p. 268.
70 Annenkov, *Literaturnyye vospominaniya*, p. 270.
71 Stankevich, I, pp. 184–5.
72 *Ibid.*, II, pp. 450–1.
73 Turgenev, *PSSP*, VIII, pp. 171–92.
74 See N. V. Chaykovsky, 'Cherez polstoletiya: Otkrytoye pis'mo k druz'yam', *Golos minuvshego na chuzhoy storone*, 3 (16), 1926, p. 183.
75 Herzen, *My Past and Thoughts*, II, p. 545.
76 N. M. Yazykov, *Polnoye sobraniye stikhotvoreniy*, Moscow–Leningrad, 1964, p. 394.
77 Annenkov, *Literaturnyye vospominaniya*, p. 226.
78 See Granovsky, *Soch.*, pp. 517–35.
79 See e.g., Stankevich, II, p. 457.
80 Herzen, *My Past and Thoughts*, II, p. 499.
81 Annenkov, *Literaturnyye vospominaniya*, p. 291; Stankevich, II, pp. 402, 415, 442.
82 Stankevich, II, pp. 445–6.
83 *LN*, LXII, p. 94.
84 Stankevich, II, p. 363.
85 *LN*, LVI, p. 132.
86 Belinsky, *PSS*, XII, p. 132.
87 *Ibid.*, XI, p. 377; Stankevich, II, p. 363.
88 Belinsky, *PSS*, XII, p. 105. See also *LN*, LVI, p. 80.
89 Stankevich, II, pp. 439–40.
90 See *ibid.*, I, pp. 194–5.
91 Herzen, *My Past and Thoughts*, II, p. 586; Annenkov, *Literaturnyye vospominaniya*, pp. 274–5.
92 Granovsky, *Soch.*, p. 472.
93 The same reluctance on Granovsky's part to abandon notions which warmed human life is apparent in his belief in the hortative potential of historical scholarship and in the existence of pattern in history. In the preamble to his doctoral dissertation, published when his differences with Herzen had come to a head, for example, he declares that historical judgement is pronounced not in order to disturb the peace of the dead but to strengthen the moral sense of the living and to bolster 'their shaky faith in good and truth … In the possibility of such judgement there is something profoundly comforting for man.' It gives the 'weary soul new strength for its quarrel with life' (*Soch.*, p. 174). And in the introduction to the first of a new series of public lectures delivered in 1851 he talks of periods of intellectual and moral weakening when man ceases to believe in the 'legitimate movement of events' and loses sight of the 'divine link, which embraces the whole life of mankind'. But in fact the sense of events does at last become clear even if it is not revealed for thousands of years (*ibid.*, p. 242).
94 Stankevich, II, pp. 448–9.
95 Belinsky, *PSS.* XII, pp. 406, 428.

96 Stankevich, II, p. 424.

97 Granovsky, *Soch.*, p. 447.

98 See Stankevich, I, p. 219. The quatrain is from Goethe's *Zahme Xenien*, V, and appears in *Goethes Werke*, Weimar ed., 1887–1919, section I, vol. 3, p. 325. The last two lines also appear as Paralipomenon 62 of *Faust* (*ibid.*, I, 14, p. 313). A literal translation of the quatrain would be: 'Come! Let us sit down to dine./Who would be moved by such folly!/The world is coming apart like a rotten fish./We shall not embalm it.

99 Stankevich, I, pp. 218–19.

100 *Ibid.*, p. 246.

101 Annenkov, *Literaturnyye vospominaniya*, pp. 273–4.

102 Granovsky, *Soch.*, p. 25.

103 Stankevich, I, pp. 150–1.

104 Granovsky, *Soch.*, pp. 483–4, 439.

105 *Ibid.*, p. 25.

106 *Ibid.*, p. 445.

107 Belinsky, *PSS*, x, p. 368.

108 Granovsky, *Soch.*, p. 241.

109 *Ibid.*, p. 245.

110 Roosevelt, *op. cit.*, p. 63.

111 Granovsky, *Soch.*, pp. 590–1; Stankevich, II, p. 456.

112 See Zven'ya, no. 5, Moscow–Leningrad, 1935, p. 753.

113 See Stankevich, I, pp. 225–6.

114 *Ibid.*, II, p. 425.

115 Herzen, *My Past and Thoughts*, II, p. 500.

116 Turgenev, *PSSP*, VIII, p. 23.

117 Chernyshevsky, *PSS*, IV, pp. 692, 761; Dobrolyubov, *SS*, II, pp. 382, 397. The articles to which Chernyshevsky and Dobrolyubov were reacting were by V. V. Grigor'yev, 'T. N. Granovskiy do yego professorstva v Moskve', *Russkaya beseda*, 1856, book III, pp. 17–46, and book IV, section 5, pp. 1–57.

118 Chernyshevsky, *PSS*, III, pp. 346–68; see esp. p. 349.

119 Dostoyevsky, *Pis'ma*, A. S. Dolinin, ed., Moscow–Leningrad, 1928–59, II, p. 256.

120 *Idem*, *PSS*, 30 vols., Leningrad, 1972–, X, e.g. pp. 7–12, 16, 19–20, 30, 33–4, 61, 64. See also Richard Peace, *Dostoyevsky: An Examination of the Major Novels*, Cambridge, 1971, pp. 143–4, 320–1. (It is true that Dostoyevsky's narrator says that Stepan Verkhovensky should *not* be compared to an 'actor on the stage' – but given the tactlessness of the narrator and Dostoyevsky's own scathingly ironical treatment of Verkhovensky it is quite legitimate to take these words as *confirmation* rather than refutation of the comparison.)

121 Dostoyevsky, *Pis'ma*, II, p. 364. Dostoyevsky is referring to the republican commune established by the Parisian proletariat in March 1871 and to the radical journalist and dramatist who served on the

Committee of Public Safety and the Finance Commission of the Commune.

CHAPTER 3 (BOTKIN)

1 *Letters and Memorials of Jane Welsh Carlyle*, London, 1883, II, pp. 355–6.
2 See V. P. Botkin, *Soch.*, 3 vols., St Petersburg, 1890–3.
3 B. F. Yegorov, 'V. P. Botkin – literator i kritik', *Uchonyye zapiski Tartuskogo gos. univ.*, 139, 1963, pp. 20–81; 167, 1965, pp. 81–122; and 184, 1966, pp. 33–43 (hereafter Yegorov 1, 2 and 3 respectively). These most informative articles are based on archive material as well as published sources; the first contains a useful catalogue of Botkin's travels and is followed by a list of his writings.
4 Isaiah Berlin, *Russian Thinkers*, pp. 25, 134. See also, e.g., E. H. Carr, *Michael Bakunin*, New York, 1961, pp. 70–1. For a nineteenth-century assessment, see Vetrinsky, *V sorokovykh godakh: Istoriko-literaturnyye ocherki i kharakteristiki*, Moscow, 1899, pp. 129–195.
5 Stankevich, II, p. 364.
6 Turgenev, *PSSP, Pis'ma*, IV, p. 381.
7 Annenkov, *Literaturnyye vospominaniya*, p. 331; see also Grigorovich, *Literaturnyye vospominaniya*, Moscow, 1961, p. 119.
8 Herzen, *My Past and Thoughts*, II, p. 491.
9 *Ibid.*, pp. 491–2. I have changed the phrase '"listening" to the fragrance of a turkey . . .' ('*slushaya . . . zapakh indeyki*') in Constance Garnett's translation to 'scenting the aroma of a turkey . . .'
10 The phrase belongs to Turgenev, *PSSP*, XIV, p. 30; Turgenev's italics.
11 Belinsky, *PSS*, XII, p. 81.
12 *Ibid.*, XI, p. 355.
13 *Ibid.*, p. 179.
14 *Ibid.*, p. 190.
15 *Ibid.*, pp. 262, 264.
16 *Ibid.*, pp. 366, 372.
17 A. N. Pypin, *Belinskiy, yego zhizn' i perepiska*, 2nd ed., St Petersburg, 1908, p. 271.
18 See Norman W. Ingham, *E. T. A. Hoffmann's Reception in Russia*, Würzburg, 1974, pp. 199, 205–6; see also pp. 267, 278.
19 *PVA*, p. 578.
20 *Ibid.*, p. 527.
21 Stankevich, II, pp. 378–9.
22 *PVA*, p. 526.
23 Stankevich, II, p. 190.
24 Belinsky, *PSS*, XI, pp. 189–90.
25 Annenkov, *Literaturnyye vospominaniya*, p. 183.
26 e.g. Herzen, *My Past and Thoughts*, II, p. 632.
27 See Yegorov, 1, p. 29.

28 Belinsky, *PSS*, XI, p. 314.
29 See Yegorov, I, p. 28 n.
30 Belinsky, *PSS*, II, pp. 556ff., 754 n.
31 *Ibid.*, XI, p. 351.
32 *Ibid.*, p. 438.
33 *Ibid.*, p. 494.
34 *Ibid.*, p. 556.
35 *Ibid.*, pp. 523–4.
36 *Ibid.*, pp. 552–3, 564.
37 *Ibid.*, XII, pp. 26, 54.
38 *Ibid.*, XI, p. 439.
39 *Ibid.*, p. 456.
40 *Ibid.*, p. 528.
41 Belinsky, *Pis'ma*, ed. Ye. A. Lyatsky, St Petersburg, 1914 (hereafter Lyatsky), II, p. 383.
42 See Yegorov, I, p. 34.
43 Lyatsky, II, p. 401.
44 See Yegorov, I, p. 37.
45 See Lyatsky, II, pp. 416–21.
46 Belinsky, *PSS*, XII, p. 94.
47 Lyatsky, II, p. 425.
48 Belinsky, *PSS*, XII, p. 22.
49 Lyatsky, II, p. 421.
50 Botkin, *Soch.*, II, pp. 257–8. Engels' pamphlet appears in Karl Marx and Frederick Engels, *Collected Works* (Lawrence and Wishart), London, 1975–, II, pp. 189–240.
51 Botkin, *Soch.*, II, pp. 270–1, 275–80, 165, 291.
52 Belinsky, *PSS*, XII, p. 152. See also p. 131.
53 Herzen, *My Past and Thoughts*, II, pp. 630–8. See also Belinsky, *PSS*, XII, pp. 156, 159–60; and *Literaturnaya mysl'*, no. 2, 1923, pp. 183ff.
54 See Carr, *Michael Bakunin*, p. 132.
55 See *LN*, LXII, pp. 786–7.
56 Botkin, *Soch.*, II, pp. 205–6.
57 *PVA*, pp. 538–40, 533, 530.
58 *Ibid.*, p. 530.
59 *Ibid.*, p. 525.
60 *Ibid.*, p. 523.
61 *Ibid.*, pp. 521, 527.
62 Annenkov, *Literaturnyye vospominaniya*, p. 331.
63 See, e.g. Belinsky, *PSS*, XII, pp. 410–11, 453; Chernyshevsky, *PSS*, IV, pp. 222–45; A. V. Druzhinin, *SS*, 8 vols., St Petersburg, 1865–7, VII, pp. 381–414.
64 *PVA*, p. 543.
65 Belinsky, *PSS*, XII, p. 453.
66 Botkin, *Soch.*, I, pp. 138, 153, 117ff., 175, 81–2.
67 Belinsky, *PSS*, X, p. 353; *PVA*, p. 502.

68 Botkin, *Soch.*, I, pp. 42, 59, 43, 35, 130–1, 68.

69 *PVA*, p. 533.

70 Botkin, *Soch.*, I, pp. 59–60, 42, 66, 99–100, 112, 49, 69, 249, 70–1, 75.

71 *PVA*, p. 522.

72 Belinsky, *PSS*, XII, pp. 404–5.

73 *Ibid.*, p. 411.

74 *Ibid.*, p. 340.

75 *Ibid.*, p. 445.

76 See *PVA*, pp. 553–5.

77 Belinsky, *PSS*, XII, pp. 446–52.

78 *LN*, LXII, p. 46.

79 *PVA*, pp. 542, 551–3. No doubt Botkin's reaction to Herzen's *Letters from the Avenue Marigny* accounts to a large extent for Belinsky's unfavourable comments on Botkin in the last months of his life. According to Kavelin, Belinsky said that Botkin had become acquainted with the West 'like a Scythian' (i.e. member of the nomadic tribe that had once roamed the South Russian steppes; the word had also acquired the figurative meaning of an ignorant and backward person), he had been infected by 'European debauchery', but the 'great European ideas' had passed him by. Kavelin himself echoes the view that Botkin returned from the West corrupted by bourgeois civilisation (Kavelin, *SS*, III, col. 1095).

80 A. Ya. Panayeva, *Vospominaniya*, Moscow, 1956, pp. 179–80.

81 Annenkov, *Literaturnyye vospominaniya*, p. 537.

82 See Yegorov, 2, pp. 81–2.

83 Botkin, *Soch.*, II, pp. 335ff.

84 *BT*, p. 14.

85 *Ibid.*, pp. 22, 25.

86 *Ibid.*, pp. 62–3.

87 See Yegorov, 2, p. 91; *Golos minuvshego*, 1916, X, p. 83.

88 *TKS*, pp. 372, 385.

89 *BT*, pp. 61–2; see also p. 69.

90 *TKS*, p. 175; Turgenev, *PSSP, Pis'ma*, II, pp. 272ff.; Grigorovich, pp. 137ff.

91 Druzhinin, *SS*, VII, pp. 30–82. See Chapter 5, pp. 162–6.

92 *Golos minuvshego*, 1916, X, p. 84.

93 *TKS*, pp. 316, 329.

94 *PVA*, p. 571.

95 *Golos minuvshego*, 1916, X, pp. 92–3; *ibid.*, 1922, I, pp. 129–30.

96 *BT*, p. 96.

97 Botkin, *Soch.*, II, p. 3.

98 Thomas Carlyle, *On Heroes, Hero-Worship and the Heroic in History*, Cambridge, 1924, pp. 20–1, 10, 102, 114, 117.

99 *Ibid.*, pp. 1, 30, 12–16.

100 *BT*, p. 110.

101 Botkin, *Soch.*, II, pp. 352–94, esp pp. 352–5, 360–3, 367, 369, 374.

102 *Ibid.*, pp. 325–35.
103 *TKS*, p. 434.
104 Botkin, *Soch.*, I, pp. 284–338, esp. pp. 286, 294, 291, 325, 332, 337–8.
105 *BT*, pp. 176, 237, 222.
106 *Ibid.*, p. 177.
107 *Ibid.*, pp. 176–80; A. Fet, *Moi vospominaniya, 1848–1889*, 2 vols., Moscow, 1890, II, p. 8.
108 Ye. M. Feoktistov, *Vospominaniya. Za kulisami politiki i literatury*, Leningrad, 1929, pp. 30–1.
109 *BT*, p. 221.
110 Turgenev, *PSSP, Pis'ma*, IV, p. 199.
111 Feoktistov, p. 10.
112 *BT*, p. 230.
113 *PVA*, p. 581.

CHAPTER 4 (ANNENKOV)

1 *Zamechatel'noye desyatiletiye*. The work is reprinted in V. P. Doro-feyev's well annotated edition of Annenkov's memoirs, *Literaturnyye vospominaniya*, Moscow, 1960, to which reference has already been made in the preceding chapters. All subsequent references to Annen-kov's literary memoirs are to this edition. There are also a pre-revolutionary edition and an early Soviet edition of the memoirs (both entitled *Literaturnyye vospominaniya* and both including *Zamechatel'-noye desyatiletiye*), published in St Petersburg, 1909, and Leningrad, 1928, respectively. *Zamechatel'noye desyatiletiye* was first published in *Vestnik Yevropy*, 1880, and was reprinted in *VKO*, III, pp. 1–224. The work has been translated into English by Irwin R. Titunik under the title *The Extraordinary Decade: Literary Memoirs*, ed. Arthur P. Mendel, Michigan, 1968.

Annenkov's phrase *'zamechatel'noye desyatiletiye'* is generally trans-lated as 'remarkable decade'. I have translated it as 'marvellous decade' on the grounds that Annenkov would seem to be drawing attention to the intellectual splendour of the period as much as to the fact that it was especially noteworthy. This is in any case the translation preferred by Isaiah Berlin in the original version of his essay on the 'birth of the Russian intelligentsia' (see *Encounter*, IV, no. 6, June 1955, p. 27).

Zamechatel'noye desyatiletiye is an important source for the present study, but I have not discussed the work itself since it was not written until the 1870s, that is to say long after the period with which I am mainly concerned.

2 Lavrov's article on Annenkov, entitled 'Russkiy turist 40-kh godov', was published in *Delo*, 1877, VIII, and is cited by N. Mendel'son in his preface to a collection of Annenkov's letters published in *Trudy Publichnoy biblioteki SSSR imeni Lenina*, no. 111, Moscow, 1934 (see pp. 48–9).

3 Quoted by D. Ryazanov, *Ocherki po istorii marksizma*, Moscow, 1923, p. 396.
4 Turgenev, *PSSP, Pis'ma*, I, p. 274.
5 Stankevich, II, p. 288.
6 Nekrasov, *PSSP*, x, p. 116.
7 I. V. Annenkov, *Istoriya leyb-gvardii Konnogo Polka, 1731–1848*, St Petersburg, 1849.
8 Annenkov, *Literaturnyye vospominaniya*, p. 59.
9 Belinsky, *PSS*, x, pp. 559, 580, 530, 554.
10 On the dates of Annenkov's departure from Russia and his return, see his *Literaturnyye vospominaniya*, pp. 189 and 209 and nn. 52 and 71 on pp. 580 and 585 respectively. The 'Letters from Abroad' (*Pis'ma iz-za granitsy*) are reprinted in *PVA*, pp. 122–247. They are discussed by Pypin in his article 'P. V. Annenkov' in *Vestnik Yevropy*, 1892, book III, pp. 301–43 (see pp. 306–25), and, briefly, by Kuleshov in his work *Literaturnyye svyazi Rossii i Zapadnoy Yevropy v XIX veke (pervaya polovina)*, 2nd ed., Moscow, 1977, pp. 73–6.
11 Annenkov and Katkov soon parted company in Berlin where Katkov was to attend lectures in the university (see Annenkov, *Literaturnyye vospominaniya*, p. 200).
12 See Annenkov's first four letters (*PVA*, pp. 122–40).
13 *Ibid.*, pp. 157–8.
14 *Ibid.*, p. 161. I have not attempted in my translations of Annenkov's writings to remove the woolliness and imprecision of his style.
15 *Ibid.*, pp. 163, 175.
16 Contrast his detailed and generally favourable remarks about Guizot in *The Marvellous Decade*, written in the 1870s (see Annenkov, *Literaturnyye vospominaniya*, pp. 204–8).
17 *PVA*, pp. 197–8, 203, 184–5, 187–9.
18 *Ibid.*, pp. 221–2.
19 *Ibid.*, pp. 235–6.
20 *Ibid.*, pp. 246–7.
21 Belinsky, *PSS*, XI, p. 530.
22 Annenkov, *Literaturnyye vospominaniya*, p. 182.
23 On the date of the meeting, see *ibid.*, p. 608, n. 162.
24 *Ibid.*, pp. 302–3.
25 *Ibid.*, pp. 302–4. The meeting Annenkov describes is no doubt a sitting of the Brussels branch of the network of communist correspondence committees which Marx and Engels had recently set up in order to facilitate the exchange of ideas among German, French and British socialists (see David McClellan, *The Thought of Karl Marx: An Introduction*, London, 1971, p. 30).
26 *PVA*, p. 249. Botkin, having read Annenkov's first 'Parisian Letter', endorsed Annenkov's opinion of Proudhon's book. 'It's not just a question of attacking what is', Botkin wrote to Annenkov, 'but of

discovering why it is, in a word, discovering the laws operating in the industrial world' (*ibid.*, p. 525).

27 [Marx and Engels], *Perepiska K. Marksa i F. Engel'sa s russkimi politicheskimi deyatel'yami*, 2nd ed., Moscow, 1951 (hereafter cited as [Marx and Engels], *Perepiska*), p. 9.

28 *Ibid.*, pp. 10–21; Marx's italics.

29 *Ibid.*, p. 21.

30 *Ibid.*, pp. 21–2.

31 Quoted by George Woodcock in his book, *Anarchism: A History of Libertarian Ideas and Movements*, Harmondsworth, 1970, p. 111, in which there is a most useful chapter on Proudhon (pp. 98–133).

32 [Marx and Engels], *Perepiska*, p. 23. For Annenkov's letters to Marx which are not published in [Marx and Engels], *Perepiska*, see Ryazanov, *Ocherki po istorii marksizma*, pp. 416–19, 423–4. On Annenkov's relations and correspondence with Marx, see also P. N. Sakulin, *Russkaya literatura i sotsializm*, Moscow, 1922, pp. 234–52. The subject is also briefly discussed by D. Zaslavsky in his article, 'K voprosu o politicheskom zaveshchanii Belinskogo', *LN*, LV, pp. 65–6, 68, where Marx's views are presented as inaccessible to the inveterate Russian liberal. Annenkov did meet Marx and Engels again when they came to Paris after the February revolution in 1848, but he had no further contact with them after his return to Russia later that year (see Annenkov, *Literaturnyye vospominaniya*, pp. 304, 306–7).

33 N. V. Gogol', *PSS*, 14 vols., Moscow, 1940–52, XIII, p. 363. Botkin, on the other hand, thought very highly of Annenkov's letters precisely because they were ends in themselves (see *PVA*, pp. 545–7).

34 *PVA*, pp. 277, 249, 255. Considérant was a disciple of Fourier's.

35 *Ibid.*, pp. 278–9.

36 *Ibid.*, pp. 318–19, 316.

37 See Belinsky, *PSS*, XII, pp. 338, 341, 345.

38 On this itinerary, see *LN*, LVI, p. 192, and Belinsky, *PSS*, XII, pp. 386–7.

39 Belinsky, *PSS*, XII, p. 378.

40 *The Marvellous Decade* ends with Annenkov's account of Belinsky's stay in the West (see Chapters XXXIV, XXXV and XXXVI, *Literaturnyye vospominaniya*, pp. 332–74). There is some doubt as to Annenkov's reliability here. He is attempting retrospectively to present a portrait of Belinsky as more moderate in his aesthetic and political beliefs (and therefore closer to the Annenkov of the period in which these memoirs were written) than was in all probability the case.

41 *LN*, LVI, p. 190.

42 Belinsky, *PSS*, XII, p. 402. Belinsky's view seems to foretoken Chernyshevsky's dismissal of liberal advocacy of political freedom (see Chapter 1, pp. 33–41). It is not clear from Belinsky's comments on the constitutional experiment in Germany, however, that he fully understood the position there (although he was correct in believing that Frederick William had no enthusiasm for parliamentary government).

The King did not formally dissolve the Combined Parliament in 1847,
but forced it to elect small standing committees which would conduct the
parliament's annual business and thus effectively deprive the majority of
the parliament's members from exercising the democratic rights they
were supposed now to enjoy.

43 Belinsky, *PSS*, xii, pp. 436–9.
44 *Ibid.*, pp. 446–52 (see also Chapter 3, pp. 94–7).
45 *Ibid.*, pp. 467–8. Belinsky refers to Bakunin in this letter as their 'friend
the believer [*veruyushchiy drug*]'. Bakunin had contrasted himself to
Annenkov in the same terms. 'You are a sceptic, I am a believer', he
wrote to him in December 1847 (*PVA*, p. 622).
46 *PVA*, p. 624.
47 Gogol', *PSS*, xiv, p. 87.
48 Herzen, *SS*, xxiii, pp. 96–7.
49 See *Sovremennik*, vol. iii, 1847, section i, pp. 57–84. The story is
published with the signature ***. It is not reprinted in either *VKO* or
PVA.
50 Belinsky, *PSS*, xii, p. 430.
51 *The Artist* (*Khudozhnik*) was published in *Sovremennik*, 1848, vol. vii,
section i, pp. 5–20, and *She Will Perish* (*Ona pogibnet*) in *ibid.*, 1848,
vol. viii, section i, pp. 105–42.
52 Belinsky, *PSS*, xii, p. 465.
53 See *VKO*, i, pp. 1–160. On these sketches see Yegorov, 'P. V. Annenkov – literator i kritik 1840-kh–1850-kh gg.', *Uchonyye zapiski Tartuskogo gosudarstvennogo universiteta*, no. 209, 1968, pp. 68–70.
Annenkov was also the author of the article 'Zametki o russkoy literature proshlogo goda' (see *VKO*, ii, pp. 23–45) which was written in this
period and published in *Sovremennik* in 1849. The article, a review of the
works published in 1848, was reminiscent of Belinsky's annual surveys of
Russian literature, though it was modest by comparison and presaged
the enfeeblement of the critical tradition Belinsky had established (see
esp. Chapter 5, pp. 131–6, see also Yegorov, *Bor'ba esteticheskikh
idey v Rossii serediny XIX veka*, Leningrad, 1982, pp. 39–53, on the
decline of this genre of criticism during the 'dismal seven years').
54 Gogol', *PSS*, xiii, p. 363.
55 See e.g. *VKO*, i, p. 111.
56 Nekrasov, *PSSP*, xii, pp. 262–3; see also p. 145, and x, p. 154.
57 Turgenev, *PSSP, Pis'ma*, ii, p. 109. A lengthy account of Turgenev's
relations with Annenkov (though mainly with reference to the 1860s and
1870s), is to be found in N. M. Gut'yar, *Ivan Sergeyevich Turgenev*,
Yur'yev, 1907, pp. 347–67.
58 Turgenev, *PSSP, Pis'ma*, ii, pp. 144–5. See also iii, pp. 46–7, for further
remarks by Turgenev on Merck.
59 *Ibid.*, iii, p. 45.
60 *Ibid.*, xi, p. 161; x, p. 209.
61 *Ibid.*, ii, p. 103; see also pp. 116, 121, 159.

62 See L. N. Nazarova, 'K istorii tvorchestva I. S. Turgeneva 50–60-kh godov', in *I. S. Turgenev (1818–1883–1958): Stat'i i materialy*, ed. M. P. Alekseyev, Oryol, 1960, pp. 139–40..See also Yegorov, 'P. V. Annenkov – literator i kritik 1840-kh–1850-kh gg.', pp. 72–3n.

63 Turgenev, *PSSP, Pis'ma*, II, p. 144.

64 See Yu. Oksman, 'Vospominaniya P. A. Katenina o Pushkine', *LN*, XVI–XVIII, 1934, p. 630; Turgenev, *PSSP, Pis'ma*, II, p. 121.

65 Turgenev, *PSSP, Pis'ma*, II, pp. 488, 138, 490, 141. Annenkov and Turgenev have in mind Nekrasov's poems 'Akh, byli shchastlivyye gody!' and 'Stariki' (see Nekrasov, *PSSP*, Moscow, 1948–53, I, pp. 70, 402).

66 *Pis'ma P. V. Annenkova k I. S. Turgenevu*, published in *Trudy Publichnoy biblioteki SSSR imeni Lenina*, no. 111, Moscow, 1934 (hereafter *Pis'ma Annenkova*), p. 60. (Complaints about his various ailments, particularly digestive troubles, abound in Turgenev's letters!)

67 See e.g. *ibid.*, pp. 60, 65, 68; and Turgenev, *PSSP, Pis'ma*, e.g. II, pp. 79, 145, 152, 232, 292, etc. For a fuller account of what the liberals understood by 'poetry', see Chapter 5, Section 5 below.

68 *Pis'ma Annenkova*, pp. 74, 76.

69 *Ibid.*, p. 72.

70 *Ibid.*, pp. 81–2.

71 The edition of Strauss' book with which Annenkov was familiar was the first German edition, *Ulrich von Hutten*, Leipzig, 1858. I have quoted from the elegant English translation done by Mrs G. Sturge from the second German edition (Leipzig, 1871), entitled *Ulrich von Hutten: His Life and Times*, London, 1874, and it is to this translation that reference is made here. (Figures in brackets refer to the corresponding pages in the two parts of the first German edition.) See pp. 31, 13, 70, 197, 253, 34, 257, 68, 88 (i.e. German ed., I, pp. 58, 19, 133; II, 33–4, 125; I, 67; II, 133; I, 128, 170–1).

72 *Ibid.*, pp. 95, 316, 319, 315, 324 (i.e. German ed., I, p. 188; II, 245, 249, 244, 259).

73 *Ibid.*, p. 321 (i.e. German ed., II, pp. 253–4).

74 *Ibid.*, pp. 315–16, 346 (i.e. German ed., II, pp. 245, 300).

75 *VKO*, II, p. 151.

76 Turgenev, *PSSP, Pis'ma*, III, p. 45; Nekrasov, *PSSP*, I, p. 427. Annenkov's literary criticism is discussed by S. A. Vengerov in his entry on Annenkov in his *Kritiko-biograficheskiy slovar' russkikh pisateley i uchonykh*, 6 vols., St Petersburg, 1889–1904, I, pp. 596–612. The fullest Soviet discussion of Annenkov's criticism is to be found in Yegorov's article, 'P. V. Annenkov – literator i kritik 1840-kh–1850-kh gg.' (see esp. pp. 78–83, 92–108). Yegorov's book, *Bor'ba esteticheskikh idey v Rossii serediny XIX veka*, incorporates the same material on pp. 212–58. See also N. Bel'chikov, 'P. V. Annenkov, A. V. Druzhinin, S. S. Dudyshkin', in *Ocherki po istorii russkoy kritiki*, ed. A. Lunacharsky and Val. Polyansky, 2 vols., Moscow–Leningrad, 1929–31, I,

pp. 263–304; N. I. Prutskov, '"Esteticheskaya" kritika (Botkin, Druzhinin, Annenkov)', in *Istoriya russkoy kritiki*, 2 vols., Moscow–Leningrad, 1958, I, pp. 444–69; and Kuleshov, *Istoriya russkoy kritiki XVIII–XIX vekov*, 2nd ed., Moscow, 1978, pp. 223–6.

77 Dobrolyubov's article, 'Kogda zhe pridyot nastoyashchiy den'?', appears in his *SS*, VI, pp. 96–140. See pp. 96–7.

78 Annenkov, *VKO*, II, pp. 5–6, 12, 14–16, 22; Annenkov's italics. The position Annenkov is adopting is defended much more powerfully by Druzhinin (see Chapter 5 below, esp. Sections 4 and 5), though in fact an article of Annenkov's, 'O mysli v proizvedeniyakh izyashchnoy slovesnosti', published in *Sovremennik* in January in 1855, was the earliest statement of the case for 'pure art' at this period (see Yegorov, 'P. V. Annenkov – literator i kritik 1840-kh–1850-kh gg.', p. 80).

79 Annenkov, *VKO*, II, p. 32.

80 *Ibid.*, p. 62.

81 *Ibid.*, pp. 120–1.

82 *Ibid.*, p. 178. Annenkov greatly valued the talent of Pisemsky, whom he knew well and about whom he has left valuable memoirs (see his *Literaturnyye vospominaniya*, pp. 489–526).

83 Chernyshevsky, 'Russkiy chelovek na *rendez-vous*', *PSS*, V, pp. 156–74.

84 Annenkov, *VKO*, II, pp. 153, 157, 163, 165, 167–72.

85 Belinsky, *PSS*, VII, p. 579.

86 *Sochineniya Pushkina s prilozheniyem materialov dlya yego biografii. Izdaniye P. V. Annenkova*, 7 vols., St Petersburg, 1855–7. Documents relating to Annenkov's work on Pushkin are published in *PVA*, pp. 383–485.

87 Turgenev, *PSSP, Pis'ma*, II, p. 261.

88 *PVA*, p. 493.

89 Nekrasov, *PSSP*, IX, pp. 369–70.

90 Chernyshevsky, *PSS*, IV, pp. 719–20. (Chernyshevsky also had in mind Annenkov's works on Stankevich and Gogol'.)

91 See Turgenev, *PSSP, Pis'ma*, II, p. 555.

92 Turgenev, in a jocular epigram contained in a letter to Annenkov in 1857, described his friend as the 'God of misprints' (*ibid.*, III, p. 72). See also the epigram by Nekrasov and Druzhinin (Nekrasov, *PSSP*, I, p. 427); *PVA*, p. 493; and Dobrolyubov, *SS*, IX, p. 286.

93 *N. V. Stankevich. Perepiska yego, i biografiya napisannaya P. V. Annenkovym*, 2 parts, Moscow, 1857. The biography was first published in nos. 2 and 4 of *Russkiy vestnik* for 1857. It is reprinted in *VKO*, III, pp. 268–383.

94 Annenkov, *VKO*, III, p. 304.

95 *Ibid.*, p. 331.

96 *Ibid.*, p. 382. See also B. Eykhenbaum, 'Naslediye Belinskogo i Lev Tolstoy (1857–1858)', *Voprosy literatury*, 1961, no. 6, pp. 139–44; and

S. I. Mashinsky, 'Kruzhok N. V. Stankevicha i yego poety', in his *Poety kruzhka N. V. Stankevicha*, Moscow–Leningrad, 1964, pp. 8–12.

97 Annenkov, *VKO*, III, p. 383.

98 *Pis'ma k A. V. Druzhininu (1850–1863)*, ed. P. S. Popov, *Letopisi Gosudarstvennogo literaturnogo muzeya*, book IX, Moscow, 1948 (hereafter *Pis'ma k Druzhininu*), p. 26.

99 *Ibid.*

100 For comments on Annenkov's memoirs, see e.g. *ibid.*, p. 51; *TKS*, pp. 207, 330, 332; Turgenev, *PSSP, Pis'ma*, III, p. 102; Chernyshevsky, *PSS*, IV, p. 719.

101 Annenkov, *Literaturnyye vospominaniya*, p. 52.

102 *Ibid.*, pp. 54–5.

103 Turgenev, *PSSP, Pis'ma*, III, p. 102. See also *TKS*, p. 207.

104 These memoirs, together with their third and final part, which was first published in 1862, are printed in *VKO*, I, pp. 241–328. They were in all probability drafted some years before their publication, when the events of 1848 were still fresh in Annenkov's mind.

105 *Ibid.*, p. 311.

106 *Ibid.*, pp. 241, 268–9, 294, 318, 307.

107 See *idem, Literaturnyye vospominaniya*, pp. 451–4. A programme for such a society was drafted jointly by Annenkov and Turgenev in 1860 (see Turgenev, *PSSP*, XV, pp. 245–52; see also *ibid.*, pp. 425–7, and *ibid., Pis'ma*, IV, pp. 120–1, 497). No such society was actually formed, however, and after the early months of 1862 the political climate in Russia was hardly conducive to ventures of this sort, as Annenkov himself observed (*Literaturnyye vospominaniya*, p. 454). The government was strongly opposed to such initiatives, which seemed to some even to have revolutionary significance (see e.g. A. V. Nikitenko, *Dnevnik*, 3 vols., Leningrad, 1955–6, II, p. 168).

108 *Pis'ma Annenkova*, p. 75.

109 *Ibid.*, p. 105.

110 *Ibid.*, pp. 117–8.

111 *Ibid.*, p. 118.

112 *Pis'ma k Druzhininu*, p. 29.

113 *Pis'ma Annenkova*, p. 111; Turgenev, *PSSP, Pis'ma*, IV, p. 195.

114 *Pis'ma Annenkova*, p. 115.

115 *PVA*, pp. 370–82. The 'letter' was printed in an appendix to *Russkiy vestnik*, entitled 'Sovremennaya letopis'', in which Katkov also published criticisms of Herzen and Ogaryov.

116 See Herzen, *SS*, XXVII, pp. 500–1, 510, 513. Annenkov also has a very hostile passage on Herzen's socialism in the memoirs he drafted (but did not complete) on the 'dismal seven years' (see *Literaturnyye vospominaniya*, p. 541).

117 See *VKO*, II, pp. 313–22.

CHAPTER 5 (DRUZHININ)

1 See Bel'chikov, 'P. V. Annenkov, A. V. Druzhinin, S. S. Dudyshkin', *op. cit.*, pp. 263–304, esp. p. 267; K. Chukovsky, 'Druzhinin i Lev Tolstoy', in Chukovsky, *SS*, 6 vols., Moscow, 1965–9, V, pp. 55–125; see also *idem*, 'Pushkin i Nekrasov', *SS*, IV, pp. 23ff.

2 See e.g. *LN*, LI–LII, p. 237; *Bol'shaya sovetskaya entsiklopediya*, 2nd ed., XV, p. 242.

3 *Bol'shaya sovetskaya entsiklopediya*, 2nd ed., XV, p. 242.

4 Chukovsky, 'Pushkin i Nekrasov', pp. 23ff.; *idem*, 'Gogol'', *SS*, IV, p. 128.

5 Yegorov, '"Esteticheskaya" kritika bez laka i bez degtya', *Voprosy literatury*, 1965, no. 5, pp. 142–160 (see esp. pp. 143, 148). For further Soviet work on Druzhinin, see Prutskov, '"Esteticheskaya" kritika (Botkin, Druzhinin, Annenkov)', *op. cit.*; Kuleshov, *Istoriya russkoy kritiki XVIII–XIX vekov*, pp. 218–22; and Yegorov, *Bor'ba esteticheskikh idey v Rossii serediny XIX veka*, esp. pp. 49–52, 78–84, 104–5, 120–1. The most exhaustive study of Druzhinin's life and work, however, remains the entry in Vengerov's pre-revolutionary *Kritiko-biograficheskiy slovar' russkikh pisateley i uchonykh*, *op. cit.*, V, pp. 376–433.

6 See e.g. Nekrasov's comments, published in Druzhinin, *SS*, VIII, pp. xv–xvi. *Biblioteka dlya chteniya* is hereafter referred to simply as *Biblioteka*.

7 See e.g. Chernyshevsky, *PSS*, XIV, p. 329; M. P. Alekseyev, ed., *Shekspir i russkaya kul'tura*, Moscow–Leningrad, 1965, e.g. pp. 558, 559, 643, 703. The plays Druzhinin translated were *King Lear*, *Coriolanus*, *Richard III* and *King John*.

8 The 'Obshchestvo dlya posobiya nuzhdayushchimsya literatoram i uchonym' was founded on Druzhinin's initiative in autumn 1859 and survived throughout the remaining years of the tsarist régime. Chernyshevsky, Nekrasov, Ostrovsky, Tolstoy and Turgenev were among its early organisers. On its foundation and early activity, see the commemorative volume, *XXV let:1859–1884. Sbornik, izdannyy komitetom obshchestva dlya posobiya nuzhdayushchimsya literatoram i uchonym*, St Petersburg, 1884, pp. 1–199. On Druzhinin's role in the society's foundation and early activity, see V. P. Gayevsky's article, 'A. V. Druzhinin kak osnovatel' literaturnogo fonda', *ibid.*, pp. 423–34.

9 See Druzhinin, *SS*, IV, pp. 246–362; V, pp. 211–36; *ibid.*, pp. 236–47; and *ibid.*, IV, pp. 363–587 respectively.

10 *Ibid.*, VII, pp. 668–714.

11 See the memoirs of P. I. Veynberg in the collection *F. M. Dostoyevskiy v vospominaniyakh sovremennikov*, ed. V. V. Grigorenko *et al.*, Moscow, 1964, I, p. 330.

12 Nekrasov, *PSSP*, X, p. 308.

13 Ye. Ya. Kolbasin in *TKS*, p. 299.

14 L. N. Tolstoy, *PSS*, 90 vols., Moscow–Leningrad, 1928–58, LX, p. 153.
15 Turgenev, *PSSP, Pis'ma*, III, p. 84.
16 *TKS*, pp. 76–7.
17 Turgenev, *PSSP, Pis'ma*, II, pp. 92, 213.
18 *Ibid.*, p. 137.
19 *Ibid.*, p. 239.
20 *Ibid.*, pp. 296, 284, 289, 291.
21 *Ibid.*, pp. 281–2, 292, 294, 296.
22 *Ibid.*, p. 367. Turgenev uses the English word 'reviewer' in his letter.
23 *Ibid.*, IV, pp. 53–4; *I. S. Turgenev v vospominaniyakh sovremennikov*, 2
    vols., Moscow, 1969, I, pp. 288, 368.
24 *TKS*, p. 299.
25 Tolstoy, *PSS*, LX, pp. 86–7, 93.
26 *TKS*, p. 202. On relations between Tolstoy and Druzhinin see also the
    excellent article by Eykhenbaum, 'Naslediye Belinskogo i Lev Tolstoy
    (1857–1858)', *op. cit.*, pp. 124–48, esp. pp. 124ff.; and A. M.
    Shteyngol'd, 'Ranniye proizvedeniya Tolstogo i literaturno-
    kriticheskaya mysl' 1850–kh godov', in G. Ya. Galagan and N. I. Pruts-
    kov, ed., *L. N. Tolstoy i russkaya literaturno-obshchestvennaya mysl'*,
    Leningrad, 1979, pp. 133–57.
27 Turgenev, *PSSP, Pis'ma*, II, pp. 307–8.
28 Grigorovich, p. 148.
29 A measure customarily interpreted at the period as a sign of liberalism
    on the part of the landowner. See also Pushkin's *Yevgeniy Onegin*,
    Chapter II, stanza 4, and Turgenev's sketch *Burmistr* ('The Bailiff') in
    Zapiski okhotnika (though in neither case is the liberalism sincere).
30 The novella is reprinted in Druzhinin, *SS*, I, pp. 1–66. I have given this
    detailed *résumé* of it not merely for the sake of providing background to
    the discussion which follows but also because the work, as far as I am
    aware, is quite unknown to the English reader. Druzhinin's further
    novellas and stories (all written between 1847 and 1855) and a novel in
    three parts *Obruchonnyye* [1857], occupy the remainder of vol. I and
    vol. II of his *SS*.
31 Belinsky, *PSS*, XII, pp. 444, 467; X, p. 347.
32 Panayeva, pp. 183–4. On the reception of *Polin'ka Saks* in 1847–8,
    see also Annenkov, *VKO*, II, p. 38.
33 See Leonid Grossman, *Dostoevsky: A Biography*, trans. by Mary
    Mackler, London, 1974, p. 235.
34 Dostoyevsky, *PSS*, XIII, p. 10.
35 See N. Gusev, *Lev Nikolayevich Tolstoy: materialy k biografii s 1828 po
    1855 god*, Moscow, 1954, p. 239.
36 Quoted by Patricia Thomson, *George Sand and the Victorians: Her
    Influence and Reputation in Nineteenth-Century England*, London,
    1977, p. 12.
37 Belinsky, *PSS*, VII, pp. 390ff. It is also worth comparing Belinsky's views
    on marriage, as they are expressed here, with those of Granovsky (see

Chapter 2, Section 5 above); Belinsky's attitude is very similar to Granovsky's chivalrous idealism.

38 *Ibid.*, p. 392.

39 See Turgenev, *PSSP*, IV, p. 537.

40 The 'Letters' ('Pis'ma inogorodnego podpischika o russkoy zhurnalistike') occupy vol. VI of Druzhinin's *SS*; see pp. 22, 24.

41 *Ibid.*, pp. 87–8.

42 *Ibid.*, V, pp. 47–86.

43 *Ibid.*, pp. 86–120 and 120–72.

44 These *feuilletons* are printed in *ibid.*, VIII, pp. 3–110. Druzhinin returned to the genre and produced further cycles under the headings 'Zametki peterburgskogo turista' (1855–6; *SS*, VIII, pp. 111–462); 'Zametki i uveselitel'nyye ocherki peterburgskogo turista' (1856–7, 1860; *ibid.*, pp. 463–545); 'Russkiye za granitseyu' (1860; *ibid.*, pp. 546–84); 'Novyye zametki peterburgskogo turista' (1861; *ibid.*, pp. 585–688); and 'Uveselitel'no-filosofskiye ocherki peterburgskogo turista' (1862–3; *ibid.*, pp. 689–750).

45 Nekrasov, *PSSP*, X, pp. 211, 230; IX, pp. 366–7, 291.

46 *TKS*, p. 201.

47 *Ibid.*, pp. 390, 397.

48 Chernyshevsky, *PSS*, III, pp. 708–12; XIV, pp. 326–8.

49 In the first number for 1857.

50 Turgenev, *PSSP*, *Pis'ma*, II, p. 378; III, p. 29.

51 *TKS*, p. 194.

52 Nekrasov, *PSSP*, X, pp. 247, 308.

53 *TKS*, p. 418.

54 Chernyshevsky, *PSS*, XIV, p. 345.

55 *TKS*, p. 207.

56 Druzhinin, *SS*, VII, pp. 30–82. The quotation is from p. 57. It should be noted that a significant contribution to the defence of Pushkin was also made by Katkov, who wrote an unfinished cycle of articles on the poet which were published in the January and February books of *Russkiy vestnik* in 1856.

57 Chernyshevsky, *PSS*, III, pp. 10–11.

58 Druzhinin, *SS*, VII, pp. 189–242.

59 *Ibid.*, IV, pp. 363–587, esp. pp. 364–6. Druzhinin's other major critical articles which may be taken as belonging to the polemic with Chernyshevsky are on Fet's verse (*SS*, VII, pp. 115–30); Tolstoy's *Metel'* and *Dva gusara* (*ibid.*, pp. 168–89) and his *Sevastopol'skiye rasskazy* and Saltykov-Shchedrin's *Gubernskiye ocherki* (*ibid.*, pp. 242–57); Pisemsky's *Ocherki iz krest'yanskogo byta* (*ibid.*, pp. 257–86); Turgenev's prose works (*ibid.*, pp. 286–374); the poetry of A. N. Maykov (*ibid.*, pp. 487–514); Pisemsky's *Tysyacha dush* (*ibid.*, pp. 514–27); Ostrovsky's plays (*ibid.*, pp. 528–67); the Ukrainian folk tales of Marko-Vovchok (*ibid.*, pp. 567–79); and Goncharov's *Oblomov* (*ibid.*, pp. 579–601).

60 Druzhinin, *SS*, VII, pp. 214ff. Druzhinin himself admitted that his use of the term 'didactic' was very loose and broad. He applied it not merely to what he saw as obvious examples of practical or instructive literature, such as Lomonosov's ode on the use of glass or Boileau's *Art poétique*, but also to the 'philosophical dithyrambs' of George Sand and the German poets who had derided Goethe; in short, to all artists who did not strive to create 'pure art' as he had defined it.

61 *Ibid.*

62 *Ibid.*, pp. 215, 221–3, 227–8.

63 *Ibid.*, pp. 232ff.

64 *Ibid.*, pp. 279ff.

65 *Ibid.*, pp. 331–2.

66 *Ibid.*, v, p. 216.

67 *Ibid.*, VII, pp. 575–7.

68 *Ibid.*, p. 273.

69 *Ibid.*, p. 551.

70 *Ibid.*, pp. 59–60.

71 *Pis'ma k Druzhininu*, p. 41.

72 *Ibid.*

73 Druzhinin, *SS*, VII, pp. 59–60.

74 *TKS*, pp. 240–1.

75 Druzhinin, *SS*, VII, p. 32.

76 *Ibid.*, pp. 59–60. The Tat'yana mentioned in this passage is of course the heroine of *Yevgeniy Onegin*, Selifan is Chichikov's coachman in Gogol''s *Myortvyye dushi* and Akakiy Akakiyevich the poor clerk in *Shinel'* by the same author. There are also allusions to the text of the following works by Pushkin: *Yevgeniy Onegin*, Chapter VII (stanzas 1–20), Chapter V (stanza 2) and Chapter IV (stanza 42); 'Besy' (1830); 'Zimniy vecher' (1825); and the cycle of poems written by Pushkin to celebrate the anniversary of the opening of his school at Tsarskoye Selo on 19 October.

77 Belinsky, *PSS*, VII, pp. 576–8.

78 Druzhinin, *SS*, VII, pp. 58–9.

79 *Ibid.*, p. 581.

80 *Ibid.*, p. 186.

81 *Ibid.*, p. 57.

82 *Ibid.*, p. 187; Druzhinin's italics.

83 *Ibid.*, IV, p. 365.

84 *Ibid.*, VII, p. 544.

85 *Ibid.*, IV, pp. 365, 450.

86 *Ibid.*, VII, pp. 514, 517.

87 *Ibid.*, p. 297.

88 *Ibid.*, p. 174.

89 *Ibid.*, p. 514.

90 *Ibid.*, p. 192.

91 *Ibid.*, pp. 193ff., 205–6.

92 *Ibid.*, p. 530; Druzhinin's italics.
93 *Ibid.*, p. 548.
94 *Ibid.*, p. 373.
95 *Ibid.*, pp. 240–2.
96 Turgenev, *PSSP, Pis'ma*, III, pp. 84, 54, 37.
97 Druzhinin, *SS*, VII, pp. 211, 223, 264.
98 Grigorovich, p. 146.
99 *LN*, LXXIII, book II, 1964, p. 115.
100 Herzen, *SS*, XXVI, pp. 68–9.
101 Turgenev, *PSSP, Pis'ma*, III, p. 50, and *PSSP*, XV, p. 46.
102 Druzhinin, *SS*, VII, p. 549; my italics.
103 Nekrasov, *PSSP*, X, p. 308.
104 Druzhinin, *SS*, VII, p. 315.
105 Belinsky, *PSS*, VII, pp. 344ff. Pushkin's poem is entitled 'Chern''. See, e.g., Pushkin's lines, spoken by the poet:

Molchi, bessmyslennyy narod,
Podyonshchik, rab nuzhdy, zabot!
Nesnosen mne tvoy ropot derzkiy.
Ty cherv' zemli, ne syn nebes . . .

(Be silent, foolish people,
Labourer, slave of necessity and [earthly] cares!
I find your impertinent grumbling insufferable.
You are the worm of the earth, not the son of the heavens.)

106 Druzhinin, *SS*, VII, p. 314. Druzhinin himself uses the English expression the '*vile multitude*'.
107 *Ibid.*, pp. 312, 314. N.B. the similarity of Druzhinin's aesthetic credo to that of Belinsky in his Hegelian phase, as expressed in his article on Menzel (see Chapter 1, pp. 15–26).
108 See Druzhinin, *SS*, III, pp. 35–40.
109 *Ibid.*, VII, p. 519.
110 *Coriolanus*, Act II, scene ii; II, i; I, i; III, i.
111 Druzhinin, *SS*, VII, p. 219.
112 Turgenev, *PSSP, Pis'ma*, III, p. 30; *Pis'ma k Druzhininu*, p. 50. It should be added that Druzhinin's admiration of nobility, social as well as moral, combined with his Anglophilism to make him attempt to popularise the English concept of a 'gentleman' in Russia. He frequently drew attention to the nuances of gentility, courtesy, decency, delicacy and detachment conveyed by the English word. (See e.g. *SS*, V, p. 312.) The attempt was in vain, however; the word already had pejorative associations in Russia and these persisted as the intelligentsia learned more of the deep social divisions in Victorian England.
113 Druzhinin, *SS*, V, pp. 247–74, esp. p. 250.
114 Chernyshevsky, *PSS*, XIV, pp. 316–17.
115 *LN*, LXXIII, book II, 1964, p. 121.
116 Tolstoy, *PSS*, LX, p. 325.

117 This apt phrase belongs to Mirsky, *A History of Russian Literature*, p. 219.
118 Druzhinin, *SS*, vII, pp. 115ff.
119 This episode is described by Nikitenko, *Dnevnik*, II, pp. 403–4. Reference to the funeral is also made by Fet, *Moi vospominaniya*, II, pp. 5–6. See also Turgenev, *PSSP*, *Pis'ma*, v, p. 222.

CHAPTER 6 (KAVELIN)

1 *LN*, LXI, pp. 783–4.
2 For biographical material on Kavelin see esp. the introductory articles in volumes I, II and III of his collected works: D. A. Korsakov, 'Zhizn' i deyatel'nost' K. D. Kavelina', in Kavelin, *SS*, I, pp. ix–xxx; V. D. Spasovich, 'Vospominaniya o K. D. Kaveline', *ibid.*, II, pp. vii–xxxi; A. F. Koni, 'Pamyati K. D. Kavelina', *ibid.*, III, pp. vii–xx. (All subsequent references to Kavelin's works are to this edition.) Korsakov, who was Kavelin's nephew, had already published a great deal of biographical material, including correspondence, shortly after Kavelin's death, in *Vestnik Yevropy* (see 1886, book V, pp. 5–30); book VI, pp. 445–91; book VII, pp. 21–38; book VIII, pp. 539–64; book X, pp. 731–58; book XI, pp. 162–94; 1887, book II, pp. 608–45; book IV, pp. 457–88; book V, pp. 5–32; book VIII, pp. 765–76; 1888, book V, pp. 5–51). Soviet scholars have devoted more attention to Kavelin (and to three of his works in particular: his memorandum of 1855 on the emancipation of the serfs, his article of 1859 on the peasant commune and his pamphlet of 1861 on the gentry and the emancipation [see Sections 4, 6 and 7 below]) than they have to the other subjects of this study. See esp. the articles by Rozental', cited in n. 92 to Chapter 1 above, and the monographs (to which further reference will be made below) by N. G. Sladkevich, *Ocherki istorii obshchestvennoy mysli Rossii v kontse 50-kh–nachale 60-kh godov XIX veka*, Leningrad, 1962; Kitayev, *Ot frondy k okhranitel'stvu*, *op. cit.*; Levin, *Ocherki po istorii russkoy obshchestvennoy mysli*, *op. cit.*; and N. A. Tsagolov, *Ocherki russkoy ekonomicheskoy mysli perioda padeniya krepostnogo prava*, Moscow, 1956, pp. 298–346, where Kavelin's economic views are closely examined. Western scholars have paid little attention to Kavelin (but see Daniel Field, 'Kavelin and Russian Liberalism', *Slavic Review*, XXXII, no. 1, 1973, pp. 59–78).
3 Turgenev, *PSSP*, *Pis'ma*, IV, p. 356.
4 Nikitenko, *Dnevnik*, II, p. 114.
5 *Pis'ma k Druzhininu*, p. 386.
6 Belinsky, *PSS*, XII, pp. 432, 461.
7 Kavelin's essay, entitled 'Vzglyad na yuridicheskiy byt drevney Rossii', is reprinted in *SS*, I, cols., 5–66. See cols., 8, 14–15. Kavelin's italics.
8 *Ibid.*, cols., 10–18. Kavelin maintains that the Tartars ruled over the Russians 'from afar' and did not settle among the Russian people; their influence on the Russian way of life was therefore minimal (col. 12).

9 *Ibid.*, cols. 26–45.

10 *Ibid.*, cols. 46–53. The *oprichnina* was the new administrative élite with which Ivan surrounded himself. Belinsky's evaluation of Ivan the Terrible was similarly favourable (see his *PSS*, VII, p. 593; X, p. 195; XII, p. 267).

11 *Ibid.*, cols. 57–63.

12 *LN*, LXIV, p. 244.

13 For Kavelin's views on Solovyov's works see *SS*, I, cols. 253–508. On Kavelin as an historian of the étatist school see also N. Rubinshteyn, *Russkaya istoriografiya*, Moscow, 1941, pp. 293–301.

14 *PVA*, p. 530.

15 Belinsky, *PSS*, XII, pp. 262, 267; *ibid.*, X, p. 354. On the probable influence of Kavelin's historical views on Belinsky see D. L. Tal'nikov, 'Kontseptsiya Kavelina i istoricheskiye vzglyady Belinskogo', *Voprosy istorii*, 1956, no. 9, pp. 130–40.

16 Belinsky, *PSS*, X, pp. 7–50.

17 Yu. F. Samarin, *Soch.*, 12 vols., Moscow, 1877–1911, I, pp. 28–108. Samarin's article is entitled 'O mneniyakh "Sovremennika" istoricheskikh i literaturnykh'.

18 *LN*, LXII, p. 40.

19 Kavelin, *SS*, I, col. 8. Kavelin's italics.

20 *Ibid.*, cols. 17–18. For further discussion of Kavelin's essay, see Walicki, *The Slavophile Controversy*, pp. 404–12, and *idem, A History of Russian Thought*, pp. 148–50.

21 Wilhelm von Humboldt, *The Limits of State Action*, ed. J. W. Burrow, Cambridge, 1969, p. 37.

22 J. S. Mill, *On Liberty and Considerations on Representative Government*, ed. R. B. McCallum, Oxford, 1946, pp. 1–2, 50, 55–6, 8.

23 *Ibid.*, p. 9.

24 Paul R. Sweet, *Wilhelm von Humboldt: A Biography*, 2 vols., Columbus, Ohio, 1978–80, I, p. 112.

25 Kavelin, *SS*, I, cols., 73–4.

26 *Ibid.*, IV, cols. 41–5. The image Kavelin uses here – the conversion of what is consumed into the flesh and blood of the consumer – would appear to be borrowed from Belinsky's 'Brief Survey of Russian Literature for 1846' (see Belinsky, *PSS*, X, p. 9, and Chapter 1, pp. 15–26).

27 *LN*, LVI, p. 186.

28 Belinsky, *PSS*, XII, pp. 361, 406. See also p. 334.

29 *Ibid.*, p. 413.

30 *Ibid.*, pp. 456–7.

31 Spasovich, p. xvii.

32 See N. P. Barsukov, *Zhizn' i trudy M. P. Pogodina*, 22 vols., St Petersburg, 1888–1910, XIV, pp. 201–2, 516.

33 *Ibid.*, p. 216.

34 *Pis'ma K. D. Kavelina i Iv. S. Turgeneva k Al. Iv. Gertsenu*, ed. M. Dragomanov, Geneva, 1892 (hereafter *Pis'ma Kavelina*), p. 4.

35 *Zapiski otdela rukopisey Publichnoy biblioteki im. V. I. Lenina*, Moscow, 1940, no. 6, p. 62.
36 See *N. G. Chernyshevskiy v vospominaniyakh sovremennikov*, 2 vols., Saratov, 1958–9, I, p. 351; L. F. Panteleyev, *Vospominaniya*, Moscow, 1958, pp. 197–8.
37 See *N. G. Chernyshevskiy v vospominaniyakh sovremennikov*, I, p. 185.
38 Chernyshevsky, *PSS*, XIV, p. 205.
39 *Ibid.*, pp. 367, 409; *N. G. Chernyshevskiy v vospominaniyakh sovremennikov*, II, p. 269.
40 e.g. Chernyshevsky, *PSS*, II, p. 666; III, pp. 181, 223; IV, pp. 686, 863.
41 Dobrolyubov, *SS*, IX, p. 353.
42 *N. A. Dobrolyubov v vospominaniyakh sovremennikov*, Leningrad, 1961, pp. 273, 288.
43 e.g. Dobrolyubov, *SS*, III, p. 312; IV, pp. 101, 180.
44 *Ibid.*, IX, pp. 453–5.
45 Chernyshevsky, *PSS*, XIV, p. 409.
46 *N. G. Chernyshevskiy v vospominaniyakh sovremennikov*, II, p. 89. The symbol of axes is used in Zaichnevsky's proclamation 'Young Russia' (see Chapter 1, pp. 41ff. and p. 236, n. 110).
47 See Chapter 1, pp. 33–41.
48 Chernyshevsky, *PSS*, XIV, p. 379. Kavelin is the model for the character of Ryazantsev in Chernyshevsky's novel *Prolog*, written in the late 1860s when Chernyshevsky was in Siberian exile. Like Kavelin, Ryazantsev is a university professor, jurist and landowner who has long been interested in the question of the emancipation of the serfs and has written a substantial work on the subject. His home is a meetingplace for the 'progressives' of the capital. (Volgin himself [i.e. Chernyshevsky] attends Ryazantsev's gatherings on occasion.) Ryazantsev is a 'good-natured fellow' who appears an erudite and authoritative scholar and an ardent supporter of the popular cause. Volgin, however, is sceptical about the effectiveness of Ryazantsev's views and treats them with some condescension. He regards Ryazantsev as bombastic and naive and considers him in effect a mouthpiece for the views of the gentry, whose interests he will support when difficult choices finally have to be made. Chernyshevsky, then, has clearly endowed Ryazantsev with the characteristics he had long associated with Kavelin and the name Ryazantsev confirms the identity of the character's model: Kavelin was brought up in the province of Ryazan'. (Similarly Chernyshevsky, in giving the name Volgin to his leading character, was underlining the character's relation to himself, a native of the Volga town of Saratov.) See Chernyshevsky, *PSS*, XIII, e.g. pp. 31, 138, 193–4, 198–9, 203–4, and A. P. Skaftymov's notes in his edition of Chernyshevsky's *Prolog*, Moscow–Leningrad, 1936, pp. 514–15.
49 Dobrolyubov, *SS*, IX, pp. 459–60.
50 *Ibid.*, p. 473.
51 Barsukov, XIV, p. 213.

52 See Kavelin, *SS*, II, cols. 5–6, 25–31. Kavelin's memorandum, 'Zapiska ob osvobozhdenii krest 'yan v Rossii' (*SS*, II, cols. 5–64) was written in 1855. (On the precise date of its composition see Levin, *Ocherki po istorii russkoy obshchestvennoy mysli, op. cit.*, pp. 380–1.) A supplement to the memorandum, in which Kavelin answers comments and criticisms that had been made about it, was written in 1856 and is printed as the second part of the memorandum in *SS*, II (cols. 64–8). Sections of the memorandum were printed, in a slightly abridged form, in *Golosa iz Rossii*, book III, London, 1857, pp. 114–44, and the bulk of it was published in *Sovremennik* in 1858 (see n. 69 below). There is a large literature on the memorandum. See Sladkevich, *Ocherki istorii obshchestvennoy mysli*, pp. 36–7; Kitayev, *Ot frondy k okhranitel'stvu*, pp. 169ff., and esp. Tsagolov, *Ocherki russkoy ekonomicheskoy mysli*, (to which detailed reference is made in n. 60 below).

In a further statement on the subject, entitled 'Mysli ob unichtozhenii krepostnogo sostoyaniya v Rossii' (*SS*, II, cols. 87–102), Kavelin retreated somewhat from the position he had adopted in his memorandum. This statement was written in response to questions put in 1857 by members of the Secret Committee considering the emancipation of the serfs and reflects Kavelin's pessimism about the possibility of speedy implementation of reform at a time when peasant unrest was growing and violent social upheaval seemed increasingly likely. Kavelin reiterated the main points of his memorandum but now suggested that it would not be possible to put them into effect straightaway and recommended cautious transitional measures: while the unconditional rights of landlords over the person and property of the serfs should be abolished, he suggested for example, the peasants should continue to fulfil certain obligations (*obrok* or *barshchina* [corvée]), albeit in a limited form (see esp. cols. 91–3). On this statement see esp. Levin, *Ocherki po istorii obshchestvennoy mysli*, pp. 383–7.

53 Kavelin, *SS*, II, cols. 32–4.
54 *Ibid.*, cols., 34–6, 40–2.
55 *Ibid.*, cols. 43–4.
56 *Ibid.*, cols. 46–8.
57 *Ibid.*, cols. 14–19.
58 *Ibid.*, cols. 66–7.
59 *Ibid.*, col. 44.
60 Tsagolov, *Ocherki russkoy ekonomicheskoy mysli, op. cit.*, esp. pp. 300–2, 310, 316, 331, 336. Tsagolov's analysis is an example of Soviet methodology both at its most persuasive and its most rigid. Tsagolov portrays Kavelin as a spokesman for a serf-owning order which had outlived its effectiveness and which now inevitably had to face the challenge of a system of bourgeois economic relations. Sensing that these new relations would lead to social antagonisms which would threaten the supremacy of the gentry, Kavelin set himself, in Tsagolov's view, a difficult task: to allow for the free development of the bourgeois

system of relations, but in such a way that the superiority of the gentry would be maintained and the class antagonisms characteristic of bourgeois society avoided (p. 304). Tsagolov does not allow, however, of the possibility that individual thinkers might be anything more than faithful spokesmen, albeit ingenious ones, for the social class to which they belong. He therefore refuses not only to treat the course which Kavelin advocates – and which does not lead to socialism – as having any intrinsic merit or historical feasibility, but even to accept that Kavelin may sincerely have believed that classes other than the gentry would benefit as much from the solution he was commending as from any other (see e.g. Tsagolov's imputation to Kavelin of insincerity [p. 327] and hypocrisy [p. 329] and his implicit endorsement of Lenin's bitter denunciation of Kavelin [p. 346; see also below, pp. 203–8]).

61 Barsukov, xiv, p. 215.
62 Kavelin, *SS*, ii, cols. 54, 71–2.
63 *Ibid.*, col. 36.
64 *Ibid.*, col. 68.
65 Feoktistov, *Vospominaniya*, p. 100.
66 Barsukov, xiv, p. 208.
67 *Ibid.*, pp. 210–11.
68 See Kavelin, *SS*, ii, cols. 1181–3.
69 Chernyshevsky printed the memorandum under the title 'O novykh usloviyakh sel'skogo byta', which appears in his *PSS*, v, pp. 108–36. For Chernyshevsky's preamble see p. 108. Chernyshevsky made some changes in and significant omissions from Kavelin's text. He did not include, for instance, Kavelin's expression of faith in the benevolence and impartiality of the Russian autocracy, his statement of the need for peaceful progress rather than revolutionary upheaval, or his plea for a united society in which the gentry would retain a privileged position (cols. 36, 54, 71–2 in Kavelin, which are omitted from Chernyshevsky pp. 113, 120, 126–7 respectively). For further details on Chernyshevsky's changes and omissions, some of which were calculated to placate the censor but others of which concerned matters of principle, see Levin, *Ocherki po istorii obshchestvennoy mysli*, pp. 391–3.
70 See Kavelin's letter of 1885 to Semevsky (printed in *Russkaya starina*, 1886, xlix, p. 132). The circumstances of the publication of the memorandum, however, are confused. Kavelin's claim that Chernyshevsky published it without his knowledge or approval was made much later in 1885 and is not entirely trustworthy. In a letter of 1858 to Katkov he explained that he had handed the memorandum over to Chernyshevsky as 'literary property' (*Zapiski otdela rukopisey Publichnoy biblioteki im. V. I. Lenina*, p. 62), and presumably therefore he could not have been altogether surprised when Chernyshevsky decided to publish it, though clearly he did not realise that Chernyshevsky would publish it when he did and in the form in which it appeared in *Sovremennik*. Levin argues plausibly that Kavelin would in fact have had time to protest after

the printing of the memorandum but before its publication had he wished to do so, and that he regretted not so much the fact that it appeared in print as that it appeared in *Sovremennik* rather than in Katkov's *Russkiy vestnik* (see *Ocherki po istorii obshchestvennoy mysli*, p. 389).

71 See Nikitenko, *Dnevnik*, II, p. 19; Herzen, *SS*, XIII, pp. 300–5.

72 *Golosa iz Rossii*, I, London, 1856. Book II also appeared in 1856, books III and IV in 1857 and books V and VI in 1858 and 1859 respectively.

73 *Ibid.*, I, pp. 5–7, and Herzen, *SS*, XII, pp. 329–30.

74 *Golosa iz Rossii*, I, pp. 10–20; Kavelin's italics. Tacitus' axiom '*sine ira et studio*' may be taken as a slogan for the subjects of this study in the mid 1850s, for it aptly gave expression to their sober and conciliatory approach to the solution of the nation's problems, both philosophical and practical.

75 *Golosa iz Rossii*, I, pp. 20–36. On authorship of the letter see B. N. Chicherin, *Vospominaniya*, 4 parts, Moscow, 1929–34, I, p. 172.

76 *Pis'ma Kavelina*, pp. 3–7.

77 *LN*, LXII, p. 386.

78 In *Kolokol*, no. 20, 1 December 1858.

79 Chicherin's letter is also published in *Pis'ma Kavelina*, pp. 21–9.

80 *Ibid.*, pp. 32–42; Kavelin's italics. The letter which accompanied this protest is printed in *ibid.*, pp. 30–1. See Turgenev, *PSSP, Pis'ma*, III, p. 268, for the list of those who associated themselves with Kavelin's protest. Herzen's comments on his refusal to publish this protest at the first opportunity are in *Pis'ma Kavelina*, p. 29, and Herzen, *SS*, XIII, p. 416.

81 Kavelin, *SS*, II, cols. 167–75. On this article see also Sladkevich, *Ocherki istorii obshchestvennoy mysli Rossii*, pp. 70–2; and Kitayev, *Ot frondy k okhranitel'stvu*, pp. 193ff., where the article is treated as reflecting the breakdown of the liberal Westernism which Kavelin represented. Kavelin continued to write a great deal on the commune after 1861: see esp. his 'Obshchinnoye vladeniye' (1876), reprinted in *SS*, II, cols. 217–86, and 'Krest'yanskiy vopros' (*ibid.*, cols. 393–598, esp. pp. 455–83). See also Tsagolov, *Ocherki russkoy ekonomicheskoy mysli*, pp. 333–42.

82 Kavelin, *SS*, II, cols. 176–7.

83 *Ibid.*, cols. 177–83.

84 *Pis'ma Kavelina*, p. 4.

85 Kavelin, *SS*, II, cols. 177, 179, 186, 188–9, 194. Kavelin still continued to defend the coexistence of private and communal landholding in a letter of 1862 to Herzen (see *Pis'ma Kavelina*, pp. 58–9).

86 See *Russkaya mysl'*, 1892, no. 3, pp. 10–11. The article was finally published in *Ateney*, 1859, no. 2.

87 Dobrolyubov, *SS*, IV, p. 101.

88 *Russkaya mysl'*, 1892, no. 10, p. 4.

89 See *Pis'ma Kavelina*, pp. 14–15.

90 See e.g. P. L. Lavrov, *Filosofiya i sotsiologiya: Izbrannyye proizvede-niya*, 2 vols., Moscow, 1965, I, pp. 373–5.

91 See V. V. Zenkovsky, *A History of Russian Philosophy*, trans. George L. Kline, 2 vols., London, 1953, I, pp. 345–8.

92 Nikitenko, *Dnevnik*, II, pp. 175, 166. In fact Lavrov's early philosophical works, in which he formulates the ideas that are to underpin his *Historical Letters* of 1869, contain arguments designed to refute the popular materialism and the determinism to which materialism seemed to lead.

93 See Kavelin's 'Zapiska o besporyadkakh v S.-Peterburgskom univer-sitete, osen'yu 1861 goda', *SS*, II, cols. 1191–1206.

94 *Pis'ma Kavelina*, pp. 48–9, 58. Herzen had printed the reprimand of Chicherin *et al.* in *Kolokol*, nos. 126 and 127 (1862). See also Herzen, *SS*, XVI, pp. 80–2, 282, 375–7, 456. Turgenev's attitude to Chicherin was similar in 1862 (see *PSSP*, *Pis'ma*, IV, p. 335). On the atmosphere and events in St Petersburg University in the autumn of 1861, see esp. Nikitenko, *Dnevnik*, II, pp. 206–52; and on Kavelin's career in the university, see esp. Panteleyev, *Vospominaniya*, Moscow, 1958, pp. 196–202.

95 Panteleyev, pp. 170, 174–5.

96 Spasovich, p. xv.

97 *Pis'ma Kavelina*, p. 78.

98 Kavelin's pamphlet 'Dvoryanstvo i osvobozhdeniye krest'yan' is reprinted in *SS*, II, cols. 105–42.

99 This assertion appears to contradict one of the points Kavelin had made in his article of 1859 on the peasant commune in defence of the partial retention of the institution of communal landholding.

100 Kavelin, *SS*, II, cols. 109–15. On the pamphlet see esp. Kitayev, *Ot frondy k okhranitel'stvu*, pp. 125ff and 164, where it is argued that the defence of a landowning gentry in effect marks the end of Kavelin's Westernism, since it presupposes a different historical path for Russia.

101 Kavelin, *SS*, II, cols. 124–9, 133, 138–42.

102 *Ibid.*, col. 139.

103 *Ibid.*, cols. 107, 111.

104 *Pis'ma Kavelina*, p. 50–1.

105 *Ibid.*, pp. 52–3, reprinted in Herzen, *SS*, XXVII, pp. 226–7. Herzen's essay on Robert Owen is printed in *SS*, XI, pp. 205–53, and also appears in the translation of Herzen's *My Past and Thoughts*, III, pp. 1205–51. (It in fact constitutes Part VI, Chapter 10 of *Byloye i dumy*.)

106 *Pis'ma Kavelina*, pp. 56–8.

107 *Russkaya starina*, XCVII, p. 141.

108 *Pis'ma Kavelina*, p. 80.

109 *Ibid.*, p. 82.

110 V. I. Lenin, *PSS*, 5th ed., 55 vols., Moscow, 1958–65, XXI, p. 259. Lenin's judgement is contained in his article 'Pamyati Gertsena'; see also his article 'Goniteli zemstva i Annibaly liberalizma', (*ibid.*, V,

pp. 32–3). The intensity of Lenin's antipathy to Kavelin is no doubt due partly to the fact that he held Chernyshevsky in the highest esteem.
111 His observations on his findings are published in *SS*, III, cols. 5–226.
112 Spasovich, p. xxix.
113 His works in these fields are published in *SS*, III, cols. 365–1074; see esp. *Zadachi etiki – Ucheniye o nravstvennosti pri sovremennykh usloviyakh znaniya*, published in *Vestnik Yevropy* in 1884 and as a separate edition in 1885, and dedicated to the 'young generation' (*SS*, cols. 897–1018). Tsagolov makes the point that whereas in the mid 1850s economic questions had seemed to Kavelin to be of paramount importance, in the 1870s and 1880s, when his vision of a healthy economy based largely on aristocratic landowning was being undermined by the emergence of the kulak as a powerful economic factor in the countryside, he sought the solution to socio-economic problems outside the sphere of economics (see Tsagolov, *Ocherki russkoy ekonomicheskoy mysli*, pp. 344–5).

CONCLUSION

1 Mill, *On Liberty and Considerations on Representative Government*, ed. R. B. McCallum, Oxford, 1946, p. 57.
2 *Ibid.*, pp. 18, 46.
3 Michel de Montaigne, *Essays*, II, xvii. (The quotation is from the trans. by J. M. Cohen, Harmondsworth, 1958, p. 217.)
4 Herzen, *SS*, XVI, p. 13.
5 George Fischer, *Russian Liberalism: From Gentry to Intelligentsia*, Cambridge, Mass., 1958, p. 76.
6 Harold J. Laski, *The Rise of European Liberalism: An Essay in Interpretation*, London, 1962, p. 167.
7 Thomas P. Neill, *The Rise and Decline of Liberalism*, Milwaukee, Wisc., 1953, p. 38.
8 Pipes, *Russia under the Old Régime*, London, 1974, p. 194.
9 Seton-Watson, *The Russian Empire, 1801–1917*, Oxford, 1967, p. 538; see also pp. 28–9.
10 Quoted by Florinsky, *Russia: A History and an Interpretation*, New York, 1953, p. 1089.
11 See Fischer, *Russian Liberalism: From Gentry to Intelligentsia*, pp. 10–13.
12 B. A. Kistyakovsky, 'V zashchitu prava. (Intelligentsiya i pravosoznaniye)', in *Vekhi. Sbornik statey o russkoy intelligentsii*, ed. N. A. Berdyayev *et al.*, 2nd ed., Moscow, 1909, pp. 125–6.
13 N. A. Berdyayev, 'Filosofskaya istina i intelligentskaya pravda', *ibid.*, pp. 7–8, 14; Berdyayev's italics.
14 Nikitenko, *Dnevnik*, II, p. 222; Nikitenko's italics.
15 Quoted by James H. Billington, *The Icon and the Axe: An Interpretive History of Russian Culture*, London, 1966, p. 378.

16 Quoted by Fischer, *Russian Liberalism: From Gentry to Intelligentsia*, p. 1.
17 Berdyayev, 'Filosofskaya istina i intelligentskaya pravda', pp. 3–4.
18 Aleksandr Blok, *SS*, 8 vols., Moscow–Leningrad, 1960–3, VII, pp. 358–9.
19 Fischer, *Russian Liberalism: From Gentry to Intelligentsia*, p. 77.
20 Victor Frank, 'Ottsy i deti', in his *Izbrannyye stat'i*, ed. Leonard Schapiro, London, 1974, p. 175.
21 Isaiah Berlin, *Russian Thinkers*, *op. cit.*, p. 303.

Selected bibliography

The intellectual life of mid nineteenth-century Russia revolved around the so-called 'thick journals' and it was in these that the bulk of the works examined in this study – essays on literary, philosophical, social and political subjects, travel sketches, poetry, drama, short stories and novels – were first published. From the point of view of the present study the most important among these journals during the period c. 1838–61 were *Biblioteka dlya chteniya* (1834–65); *Otechestvennyye zapiski* (1839–67 and 1868–84); *Russkiy vestnik* (1856–1906); and *Sovremennik* (1836–66).

In addition to these journals and the works cited in the bibliography below one has constantly to keep in mind in any study of nineteenth-century Russian thought the major fiction of the period. For an examination of the liberal Westernisers the works of Pushkin, Lermontov, Gogol', Turgenev, Grigorovich, Nekrasov, Ostrovsky, Fet, Goncharov, Pisemsky and Tolstoy are particularly important sources, since they provided a starting-point for discussion of different conceptions of art and different attitudes towards contemporary Russian reality.

Primary sources (works, memoirs, correspondence)

Aksakov, K. S., *Polnoye sobraniye sochineniy*, 3 vols., Moscow, 1861–80.

Annenkov, P. V., *Literaturnyye vospominaniya*, St Petersburg, 1909.

Literaturnnyye vospominaniya, Moscow, 1960.

Pis'ma P. V. Annenkova k I. S. Turgenevu, Trudy Publichnoy biblioteki SSSR imeni Lenina, no. 111, Moscow, 1934, pp. 45–184.

P. V. Annenkov i yego druz'ya. Literaturnyye vospominaniya i perepiska, 1835–1885 godov, St Petersburg, 1892.

(ed.), *Sochineniya Pushkina s prilozheniyem materialov dlya yego biografii*, 7 vols., St Petersburg, 1855–7.

The Extraordinary Decade: Literary Memoirs, trans. by I. R. Titunik, ed. A. P. Mendel, Ann Arbor, Mich. 1968.

Vospominaniya i kriticheskiye ocherki, 3 vols., St Petersburg, 1877–81.

Arnold, Matthew, *Essays in Criticism; First and Second Series*, with intro. by G. K. Chesterton, London, 1924.

Belinksy, V. G., *Pis'ma*, ed. Ye. A. Lyatsky, 3 vols., St Petersburg, 1914.

Polnoye sobraniye sochineniy, 13 vols., Moscow, 1953–9.

Botkin, V. P., *Lettres sur l'Espagne*, trans. and ed. by Alexandre Zviguilsky, Paris, 1969.

Pis'ma ob Ispanii, ed. B. F. Yegorov, A. Zvigil'sky [Alexandre Zvi-guilsky], Leningrad, 1976.
Sochineniya, 3 vols., St Petersburg, 1890–3.
V. P. Botkin i I. S. Turgenev: neizdannaya perepiska, 1851–1869, Moscow–Leningrad, 1930.
Brodsky, N. L., ed., *Ranniye slavyanofily. A. S. Khomyakov, I. V. Kireyevsky, K. S. i I. S. Aksakovy*, Moscow, 1910.
Carlyle, Thomas, *On Heroes, Hero-Worship and the Heroic in History*, Cambridge, 1924.
Chaadayev, P., *The Major Works of Peter Chaadaev*, trans. by Raymond T. McNally, Notre Dame, 1969.
Chernyshevsky, N. G., *Polnoye sobraniye sochineniy*, 15 vols., Moscow, 1939–50.
Chicherin, B. N., *Vospominaniya*, 4 parts, Moscow, 1929–34.
Custine, Astolphe, Marquis de, *La Russie en 1839*, 4 vols., Paris, 1843.
Russia, trans. and abridged from the French, London, 1854.
Dobrolyubov, N. A., *Sobraniye sochineniy*, 9 vols., Moscow–Leningrad, 1961–4.
Dostoyevsky, F. M., *Polnoye sobraniye sochineniy*, 30 vols. planned, Leningrad, 1972–.
Druzhinin, A. V., *Sobraniye sochineniy*, 8 vols., St Petersburg, 1865–7.
Feoktistov, Ye. M., *Vospominaniya. Za kulisami politiki i literatury*, Leningrad, 1929.
Fet, A. I., *Moi vospominaniya, 1848–1889*, 2 vols., Moscow, 1890.
Feuerbach, Ludwig, *The Essence of Christianity*, ed. and abridged by E. Graham Waring and F. W. Strothman, New York, 1957.
Gogol', N. V., *Polnoye sobraniye sochineniy*, 14 vols., Moscow, 1940–52.
Golosa iz Rossii, 9 books, London, 1856–60. (Facsimile ed. in 3 parts, with commentaries and index in 4th part, Moscow, 1974–5.)
Granovsky, T. N., *Lektsii T. N. Granovskogo po istorii pozdnego sred-nevekov'ya*, ed. S. A. Asinovskaya, Moscow, 1971.
Lektsii T. N. Granovskogo po istorii srednevekov'ya, ed. S. A. Asinovskaya, Moscow, 1961.
'Neizdannyye universitetskiye kursy Granovskogo', ed. M. N. Kovalensky, *Golos minuvshego*, Moscow, 1913, no. 9, pp. 210–33.
Sochineniya, 4th ed., 1 vol., Moscow, 1900.
Grigorovich, D. V., *Literaturnyye vospominaniya*, Moscow, 1961.
Haxthausen, Baron A. von, *The Russian Empire: Its People, Institutions and Resources*, 2 vols., London, 1856.
Herzen, (A. I. Gertsen), *My Past and Thoughts: The Memoirs of Alexander Herzen*, trans. by Constance Garnett, revised by Humphrey Higgins, 4 vols., London, 1968.
Sobraniye sochineniy, 30 vols., Moscow, 1954–65.
Humboldt, Wilhelm von, *The Limits of State Action*, ed. J. W. Burrow, Cambridge, 1969.

Kavelin, K. D., 'Iz pisem K. D. Kavelina k K. K. Grotu', *Russkaya starina*, xcvii, 1899, pp. 135–57.

'Pis'ma K. D. Kavelina k M. N. Katkovu o Chernyshevskom (iz arkhiva M. N. Katkova)', *Zapiski otdela rukopisey, Vsesoyuznaya biblioteka imeni V. I. Lenina*, no. vi, Moscow, 1940, pp. 59–63.

Pis'ma K. Dm. Kavelina i Iv. S. Turgeneva k. Al. Iv. Gertsenu, ed. M. Dragomanov, Geneva, 1892.

Sobraniye sochineniy, 4 vols., St Petersburg, 1897–1900.

Khomaykov, A. S., *Izbrannyye sochineniya*, ed. N. S. Arsen'yev, 1 vol., New York, 1955.

Kireyevsky, I. V., *Polnoye sobraniye sochineniy*, 2 vols., Moscow, 1911.

Koni, A. F., 'Pamyati K. D. Kavelina', in Kavelin, *Sobraniye sochineniy*, iii, pp. vii–xx.

Korsakov, D. A., 'Konstantin Dmitriyevich Kavelin', *Russkaya starina*, liii, 1887, pp. 433–50.

'Konstantin Dmitriyevich Kavelin. Materialy dlya biografii, iz semeynoy perepiski i vospominaniy', *Vestnik Yevropy*, 1886, book V, pp. 5–30; book VI, pp. 445–91; book VII, pp. 21–38; book VIII, pp. 539–64; book X, pp. 731–58; book XI, pp. 162–94; 1887, book II, pp. 608–45; book IV, pp. 457–88; book V, pp. 5–32; book VIII, pp. 765–76; 1888, book V, pp. 5–51.

'Zhizn' i deyatel'nost' K. D. Kavelina', in Kavelin, *Sobraniye sochineniy*, 1, pp. ix–xxx.

Koshelyov, Alexander I., *Zapiski, 1806–1883*, Berlin 1884 (republished with introduction by Nicholas Riasanovsky, Newtonville, Mass., 1976).

Lenin, V. I., *Polnoye sobraniye sochineniy*, 5th ed., 55 vols., Moscow, 1958–65.

Literaturnoye nasledstvo, xlix–l, Moscow, 1946 (on Nekrasov).

li–lii, Moscow, 1949 (on Nekrasov).

lv, Moscow, 1948 (on Belinsky).

lvi, Moscow, 1950 (on Belinsky).

lvii, Moscow, 1951 (on Belinsky).

lxi, Moscow, 1953 (on Herzen and Ogaryov).

lxii, Moscow, 1955 (on Herzen and Ogaryov).

lxiii, Moscow, 1956 (on Herzen and Ogaryov).

lxiv, Moscow, 1958 (on Herzen).

lxvii, Moscow, 1959 (on the 'revolutionary democrats').

lxxiii (2 books), Moscow, 1964 (on Turgenev).

lxxvi, Moscow, 1967 (on Turgenev).

Marx, K., and Engels, F., *Perepiska K. Marksa i F. Engel'sa s russkimi politicheskimi deyatel'yami*, 2nd ed., Moscow, 1951.

Mill, J.S., *On Liberty and Considerations on Representative Government*, ed. R. B. McCallum, Oxford, 1946.

Nekrasov, N. A., *Polnoye sobraniye sochineniy i pisem*, 12 vols., Moscow, 1948–53.

Nelidov, F. F., ed., *Zapadniki 40-kh godov: N. V. Stankevich, V. G. Belinskiy, A. I. Gertsen, T. N. Granovskiy i dr.*, Moscow, 1910.

Nikitenko, A. V., *Dnevnik*, 3 vols., Leningrad, 1955–6.

Oksman, Yu. G., ed., *N. G. Chernyshevskiy v vospominaniyakh sovremennikov*, 2 vols., Saratov, 1958–9.

Panayev, I. I., *Literaturnyye vospominaniya*, Leningrad, 1950.

Panayeva, A. Ya. (afterwards Golovachova), *Vospominaniya*, Moscow, 1956.

Panteleyev, L. F. *Vospominaniya*, Moscow, 1958.

Popov, P.S., ed., *Pis'ma k A. V. Druzhininu (1850–1863), Letospisi Gosudarstvennogo literaturnogo muzeya*, book IX, Moscow, 1948.

Putintsev, V. A., ed., *Gertsen v vospominaniyakh sovremennikov*, Moscow, 1956.

Samarin, Yu. F., *Sochineniya*, 12 vols., Moscow, 1877–1911.

Shtakenshneyder, Ye. A., *Dnevnik i zapiski (1854–1886)*, Moscow–Leningrad, 1934.

Spasovich, V. D., 'Vospominaniya o K. D. Kaveline', in Kavelin, *Sobraniye sochineniy*, II, pp. vii–xxxi.

Stankevich, A.V., *T. N. Granovskiy i yego perepiska*, 2nd ed., 2 vols., Moscow, 1897.

Strauss, David Friedrich, *Ulrich von Hutten*, 2 parts, Leipzig, 1858.
 Ulrich von Hutten: His Life and times, trans. from the 2nd German ed. by Mrs G. Sturge, London, 1874.

Tolstoy, L. N., *Polnoye sobraniye sochineniy*, 90 vols., Moscow, 1928–58.

Tuchkova-Ogaryova, N. A., *Vospominaniya*, Moscow, 1959.

Turgenev, I. S., *Polnoye sobraniye sochineniy i pisem*, 28 vols., Moscow–Leningrad, 1960–8.
 Turgenev i krug 'Sovremennika': neizdannyye materialy, 1847–1861, Moscow–Leningrad, 1930.

XXV let 1859–1884. Sbornik izdannyy komitetom obshchestva dlya posobiya nuzhdayushchimsya literatoram i uchonym, St Petersburg, 1884.

Zhdanov, V. V. *et al.*, ed., *N. A. Dobrolyubov v vospominaniyakh sovremennikov*, Leningrad, 1961.

Secondary sources

Acton, Edward, *Alexander Herzen and the Role of the Intellectual Revolutionary*, Cambridge, 1979.

Alekseyev, M. P., ' "Pis'ma ob Ispanii" V. P. Botkina i russkaya poeziya', in his book *Ocherki istorii ispano-russkikh literaturnykh otnosheniy XVI–XIX vv.*, Leningrad, 1964, pp. 171–206.
 (ed.), *Shekspir i russkaya kul'tura*, Moscow–Leningrad, 1965.

Asinovskaya, S. A., *Iz istorii peredovykh idey v russkoy mediyevistike (T. N. Granovskiy)*, Moscow, 1955.

Barghoorn, Frederick C., 'Russian Radicals and the West European Revolutions of 1848', *Review of Politics*, XI, 1949, no. 3, pp. 338–54.

Barsukov, N. P., *Zhizn' i trudy M. P. Pogodina*, 22 books, St Petersburg, 1888–1910.

Bel'chikov, N., 'P. V. Annenkov, A. V. Druzhinin, S. S. Dudyshkin', *Ocherki po istorii russkoy kritiki*, ed. A. Lunacharsky and Val. Polyansky, 2 vols., Moscow–Leningrad, 1929–31, I, pp. 263–304.

Berdyayev, Nicolas, *The Russian Idea*, trans. by R. M. French, London, 1947.

et al., *Vekhi. Sbornik statey o russkoy intelligentsii*, 2nd ed., Moscow, 1909.

Berlin, Isaiah, *Fathers and Children*, the Romanes Lecture, Oxford, 1972.
Karl Marx: His life and environment, 3rd ed., Oxford, 1970.
Russian Thinkers, London, 1978.

Bowman, Herbert E., *Vissarion Belinski, 1811–1848: A Study in the Origins of Social Criticism in Russia*, Cambridge, Mass., 1954.

Brown, Edward J., *Stankevich and his Moscow Circle, 1830–1840*, Stanford, Calif., 1966.

Buzeskul, V. P., 'Vseobshchaya istoriya i yego predstaviteli v Rossii v XIX i nachale XX veka', part I, *Trudy komissii po istorii znaniy*, VII, Leningrad, 1929.

Carr, E. H., *Michael Bakunin*, New York, 1961.
The Romantic Exiles. A Nineteenth-Century Portrait Gallery, London, 1968.

Chizhevsky, D. I., *Gegel' v Rossii*, Paris, 1939.

Christian, R. F., *Tolstoy: A Critical Introduction*, Cambridge, 1969.

Christoff, Peter K., *K. S. Aksakov: A Study in Ideas*, Princeton, N.J., 1982.

Chukovsky, Korney, 'Druzhinin i Lev Tolstoy', in his *Sobraniye sochineniy*, 6 vols., Moscow, 1965–9, V, pp. 55–125.

Cole, G. D. H., *A History of Socialist Thought*, vols. I and II, London, 1953–4.

Copleston, Frederick, S. J., *A History of Philosophy*, 8 vols., London, 1961–6, VII, part I.

Dement'yev, A. G., *Ocherki po istorii russkoy zhurnalistiki 1840–1850 gg.*, Moscow–Leningrad, 1951.

Dmitriyev, S. S., ed., *Granovskiy, Timofey Nikolayevich. Bibliografiya, 1828–1967*, Moscow, 1969.

Dorofeyev, V., 'P. V. Annenkov i yego vospominaniya', in Annenkov, *Literaturnyye vospominaniya*, Moscow, 1960, pp. 5–43.

Dowler, Wayne, *Dostoevsky, Grigor'ev and Native Soil Conservatism*, Toronto, 1982.

Druzhinin, N. M., 'Moskva v gody krymskoy voyny', *Istoriya Moskvy*, III, Moscow, 1954, pp. 728–83.

Emmons, Terence, *The Russian Landed Gentry and the Peasant Emancipation of 1861*, Cambridge, 1968.

Eykhenbaum, B., 'Naslediye Belinskogo i Lev Tolstoy (1857–1858)', *Voprosy literatury*, 1961, no. 6, pp. 124–48.

Field, Daniel, 'Kavelin and Russian Liberalism', *Slavic Review*, xxxii, 1973, no. 1, pp. 59–78.

The End of Serfdom: Nobility and Bureaucracy in Russia, 1855–1861, Cambridge, Mass., 1976.

Fischer, George, *Russian Liberalism: From Gentry to Intelligentsia*, Cambridge, Mass., 1958.

Florinsky, Michael T., *Russia: A History and an Interpretation*, 2 vols., New York, 1953.

Freeborn, Richard, *Turgenev: The Novelist's Novelist*, Oxford, 1963.

Galagan, G. Ya. and Prutskov, N. I., ed., *L. N. Tolstoy i russkaya literaturno-obshchestvennaya mysl'*, Leningrad, 1979.

Gershenzon, M., *Istoriya molodoy Rossii*, Moscow, 1908.

Gleason, Abbot, *European and Muscovite: Ivan Kireevsky and the origins of Slavophilism*, Cambridge, Mass., 1972.

Gooch, G. P., *History and Historians in the Nineteenth Century*, 2nd ed., London, 1952.

Granjard, Henri, *Ivan Tourguénev et les courants politiques et sociaux de son temps*, Paris, 1954.

Gratieux, A., *A. S. Khomiakov et le mouvement Slavophile*, 2 vols., Paris, 1939.

Gut'yar, N. M., *Ivan Sergeyevich Turgenev*, Yur'yev, 1907.

Illeritsky, V. Ye., 'O gosudarstvennoy shkole v russkoy istoriografii', *Voprosy istorii*, 1959, no. 5, pp. 141–59.

Ivanov, Iv., *Istoriya russkoy kritiki*, St Petersburg, 1898–1900, parts III and IV.

Ivanov-Razumnik, *Istoriya russkoy obshchestvennoy mysli*, 2nd ed., 2 vols., St Petersburg, 1908.

Ivashin, I., 'Rukopis' publichnykh lektsiy T. N. Granovskogo', *Istoricheskiy zhurnal*, 1945, nos. 1–2 (137–8), pp. 81–4.

Kaplan, Frederick I., 'Russian Fourierism of the 1840's: a Contrast to Herzen's Westernism', *American Slavic and East European Review*, xvii, 1958, no. 2, pp. 161–72.

Karatayev, N. K., *Russkaya ekonomicheskaya mysl' v period krizisa feodal'nogo khozyaystva (40–60-ye gody XIX veka)*, Moscow, 1957.

Kareyev, N., *Istoricheskoye mirosozertsaniye T. N. Granovskogo*, 3rd ed., St Petersburg, 1905.

Karpovich, M. M., 'Chernyshevskii between Socialism and Liberalism' *Cahiers du monde russe et soviétique*, 1960, no. 1, pp. 571–83.

Katz, Martin, *Michael N. Katkov: A Political Biography, 1818–1887*, The Hague, 1966.

'Timofey N. Granovskii: An Historiographical Interpretation', *Canadian Slavonic Papers*, xv, no. 4, pp. 488–98.

Kitayev, V. A., *Ot frondy k okhranitel'stvu: iz istorii russkoy liberal'noy mysli 50–60-kh godov XIX veka*, Moscow, 1972.

Koshovenko, A. Ye., 'K voprosu o londonskoy vstreche N. G. Chernyshevskogo s A. I. Gertsenom v 1859 g. i formule "Kavelin v kvadrate" ', in *Revolyutsionnaya situatsiya v Rossii v 1859–1861 gg.*, ed. M. V. Nechkina *et al.*, Moscow, 1960, pp. 271–82.

Kos'minsky, Ye. A., 'Zhizn' i deyatel'nost' T. N. Granovskogo', *Vestnik Moskovskogo universiteta*, 1956, no. 4, pp. 119–28.

Kovalyova, I. N., 'Slavyanofily i zapadniki v period krymskoy voyny (1853–1856 gg.)' *Istoricheskiye zapiski*, LXXX, 1967, pp. 181–206.

Koyré, Alexandre, *Etudes sur l'histoire de la pensée philosophique en Russie*, Paris, 1950.

Kuleshov, V. I., *Istoriya russkoy kritiki XVIII–XIX vekov*, 2nd ed., Moscow, 1978.

Literaturnyye svyazi Rossii i Zapadnoy Yevropy v XIX veke (pervaya polovina), 2nd ed., Moscow, 1977.

Natural'naya shkola v russkoy literature XIX veka, Moscow, 1965.

'Otechestvennyye zapiski' i literatura 40-kh godov XIX veka, Moscow, 1958.

Lampert, Evgeny, *Sons against Fathers: Studies in Russian Radicalism and Revolution*, Oxford, 1965.

Studies in Rebellion, London, 1957.

Laski, Harold J., *The Rise of European Liberalism: An Essay in Interpretation*, London, 1962.

Lavretsky, A., *Belinskiy, Chernyshevskiy, Dobrolyubov v bor'be za realizm*, Moscow, 1941.

Lemke, M., *Nikolayevskiye zhandarmy i literatura, 1826–1855 gg.*, St Petersburg, 1909.

Ocherki po istorii russkoy tsenzury i zhurnalistiki XIX stoletiya, St Petersburg, 1904.

Leontovich, V. V., *Istoriya liberalizma v Rossii, 1762–1914*, Paris, 1980 (a Russian trans. from the German original, *Geschichte des Liberalismus in Russland*, Frankfurt-am-Main, 1957).

Levin, Sh. M., *Ocherki po istorii russkoy obshchestvennoy mysli: Vtoraya polovina XIX–nachalo XX veka*, Leningrad, 1974.

Lincoln, W. Bruce, *Nicholas I; Emperor and Autocrat of All the Russias*, London, 1978.

Nikolai Miliutin: An Enlightened Russian Bureaucrat, Newtonville, Mass., 1977.

'Russia's "enlightened" bureaucrats and the problem of state reform, 1848–1856', *Cahiers du monde russe et soviétique*, 1971, XII, no. 4, pp. 410–21.

'The Circle of the Grand Duchess Yelena Pavlovna, 1847–1861', *The Slavonic and East European Review*, 1970, XLVIII, no. 112, pp. 373–87.

'The Genesis of an "Enlightened" Bureaucracy in Russia, 1825–1856', *Jahrbücher für Geschichte Osteuropas*, 1972, XX, pp. 321–30.

Malia, Martin E., *Alexander Herzen and the Birth of Russian Socialism, 1812–1855*, Cambridge, Mass., 1961.

'Schiller and the Early Russian Left', *Russian Thought and Politics*, ed.

Hugh McLean, Martin E. Malia, George Fischer, Cambridge, Mass., 1957, pp. 169–200.

Masaryk, Thomas Garrigue, *The Spirit of Russia: Studies in History, Literature and Philosophy*, trans. by Eden and Cedar Paul, 2 vols., London, 1919.

Mathewson, Rufus W., *The Positive Hero in Russian Literature*, New York, 1958.

McClellan, David, *The Thought of Karl Marx: An Introduction*, London, 1971.

Milyukov, P., *Iz istorii russkoy intelligentsii*, 2nd ed., St Petersburg, 1903.

Mirsky, D. S., *A History of Russian Literature*, London, 1949.

Monas, Sidney, *The Third Section. Police and Society in Russia under Nicholas I*, Cambridge, Mass., 1961.

Myakotin, V. A., 'Publitsisticheskaya deyatel'nost' K. D. Kavelina', *Russkoye bogatstvo*, 1902, no. 9, pp. 70–97, second pagination.

Nahirny, Vladimir C., 'The Russian Intelligentsia: from Men of Ideas to Men of Convictions', *Comparative Studies in Society and History*, 1961–2, IV, pp. 403–35.

Neill, Thomas P., *The Rise and Decline of Liberalism*, Milwaukee, Wisc., 1953.

Nol'de, Baron B. E., *Yuriy Samarin i yego vremya*, 2nd ed., Paris, 1978.

Pereira, N. G. O. *The Thought and Teachings of N. G. Černyševskij*, The Hague, 1975.

Pipes, Richard, *Russia under the Old Régime*, London, 1974.

Prutskov, N. I., '"Esteticheskaya" kritika (Botkin, Druzhinin, Annenkov)', *Istoriya russkoy kritiki*, Moscow–Leningrad, 1958, I, pp. 444–69.

Pypin, A. N., *Belinskiy, yego zhizn' i perepiska*, 2nd ed., St Petersburg, 1908.

'P. V. Annenkov', *Vestnik Yevropy*, 1892, book III, pp. 301–43.

Racheotes, Nicholas S., 'T. N. Granovskii: on the Meaning of History', *Studies in Soviet Thought*, 1978, XVIII, pp. 197–221.

Reeve, Helen S., 'Utopian Socialism in Russian Literature: 1840's–1860's', *American Slavic and East European Review*, 1959, XVIII, no. 3, pp. 374–93.

Riasanovsky, Nicholas V., *A Parting of Ways: Government and the Educated Public in Russia, 1801–1855*, Oxford, 1976.

Nicholas I and Official Nationality in Russia, 1825–1855, Berkeley and Los Angeles, 1959.

Russia and the West in the Teaching of the Slavophiles, Cambridge, Mass., 1952.

Roosevelt, Priscilla R., 'Granovskii at the Lectern: a Conservative Liberal's Vision of History', *Forschungen zur osteuropäischen Geschichte*, Berlin, 1981, XXIX, pp. 61–192.

Rozental', V. N., 'Ideynyye tsentry liberal'nogo dvizheniya v Rossii nakanune revolyutsionnoy situatsii', in *Revolyutsionnaya situatsiya v Rossii*

v 1859–1861 gg., ed. M. V. Nechkina *et al.*, Moscow, 1963, pp. 372–98.
'Narastaniye "krizisa verkhov" v seredine 50-kh godov XIX veka', in *Revolyutsionnaya situatsiya v Rossii v 1859–1861 gg.*, ed. M. V. Nechkina *et al.*, Moscow, 1962, pp. 40–63.
'Obshchestvenno-politicheskaya programma russkogo liberalizma v seredine 50-kh godov XIX v.', *Istoricheskiye zapiski*, 1961, LXX, pp. 197–222,
'Pervoye otkrytoye vystupleniye russkikh liberalov v 1855–1856 gg.', *Istoriya SSSR*, 1958, no. 2, pp. 113–30.
Rubinshteyn, N., *Russkaya istoriografiya*, Moscow, 1941.
Ryazanov, D., *Karl Marks i russkiye lyudi sorokovykh godov*, 2nd ed., Moscow, 1919.
Ocherki po istorii marksizma, Moscow, 1923.
Sakulin, P. N., *Russkaya literatura i sotsializm*, 1st part, Moscow, 1922.
Schapiro, Leonard, *Rationalism and Nationalism in Russian Nineteenth-Century Political Thought*, New Haven, Conn., 1967.
'The Pre-Revolutionary Intelligentsia and the Legal Order', in *The Russian Intelligentsia*, ed. Richard Pipes, New York, 1961, pp. 19–31.
Turgenev: His Life and Times, Oxford, 1978.
Seton-Watson, Hugh, *The Russian Empire, 1801–1917*, Oxford, 1967.
Sladkevich, N. G., *Ocherki istorii obshchestvennoy mysli Rossii v kontse 50-kh–nachale 60-kh godov XIX veka*, Leningrad, 1962.
Squire, P. S., *The Third Department: The Establishment and Practices of the Political Police in the Russia of Nicholas I*, Cambridge, 1968.
Tal'nikov, D. L., 'Kontseptsiya Kavelina i istoricheskiye vzglyady Belinskogo', *Voprosy istorii*, 1956, no. 9, pp. 130–40.
Terras, Victor, *Belinskij and Russian Literary Criticism: The Heritage of Organic Aesthetics*, Madison, Wisc., 1974.
Tsagolov, N. A., *Ocherki russkoy ekonomicheskoy mysli perioda padeniya krepostnogo prava*, Moscow, 1956.
Utechin, S. V., *Russian Political Thought. A Concise History*, London, 1964.
Vengerov, S. A., *Kritiko-biograficheskiy slovar' russkikh pisateley i uchonykh*, 6 vols., St Petersburg, 1889–1904.
Venturi, Franco, *Roots of Revolution: A History of the Populist and Socialist Movements in Nineteenth-Century Russia*, trans. by F. Haskell, London, 1960.
Vetrinsky, Ch., [V. Ye. Cheshikhin], *T. N. Granovskiy i yego vremya*, 2nd ed., St Petersburg, 1905.
V sorokovykh godakh: istoriko-literaturnyye ocherki i kharakteristiki, Moscow, 1899.
Walicki, Andrzej, *A History of Russian Thought from the Enlightenment to Marxism*, trans. by Hilda Andrews-Rusiecka, Oxford, 1980.
'Hegel, Feuerbach and the Russian philosophical left, 1836–1848', *Annali dell'Istituto Giangiacomo Feltrinelli*, 1963, VI, pp. 105–36.
The Slavophile Controversy: History of a Conservative Utopia in Nine-

teenth-Century Russian Thought, trans. by Hilda Andrews-Rusiecka, Oxford, 1975.

Wellek, René, *A History of Modern Criticism, 1750–1950*, 5 vols. planned, London, 1966– , vols. III and IV.

'Social and Aesthetic Values in Russian Nineteenth-Century Literary Criticism (Belinskii, Chernyshevskii, Dobroliubov, Pisarev)', in *Continuity and Change in Russian and Soviet Thought*, ed. Ernest J. Simmons, Cambridge, Mass., 1955, pp. 381–97.

Willey, Basil, *Nineteenth Century Studies: Coleridge to Matthew Arnold*, London, 1949.

Woehrlin, William F., *Chernyshevskii: The Man and the Journalist*, Cambridge, Mass., 1971.

Woodcock, George, *Anarchism: A History of Libertarian Ideas and Movements*, Harmondsworth, 1970.

Yegorov, B. F., *Bor'ba esteticheskikh idey v Rossii serediny XIX veka*, Leningrad, 1982.

'"Esteticheskaya" kritika bez laka i bez degtya', *Voprosy literatury*, 1965, no. 5, pp. 142–60.

'P. V. Annenkov – literator i kritik 1840-kh–1850-kh gg.', *Uchonyye zapiski Tartuskogo gosudarstvennogo universiteta*, no. 209, 1968, pp. 51–108.

'V. P. Botkin – literator i kritik', *Uchonyye zapiski Tartuskogo gosudarstvennogo universiteta*, nos. 139, 1963, pp. 20–81; 167, 1965, pp. 81–122; 184, 1966, pp. 33–43.

Yevgen'yev-Maksimov, V., *'Sovremennik' pri Chernyshevskom i Dobrolyubove*, Leningrad, 1936.

Zamotin, I. I., *Sorokovyye i shestidesyatyye gody: ocherki po istorii russkoy literatury XIX stoletiya*, 2nd ed., Petrograd, 1915.

Zapadov, A. V., ed., *Istoriya russkoy zhurnalistiki XVIII–XIX vekov*, 2nd ed., Moscow, 1966.

Zenkovsky, V. V., *A History of Russian Philosophy*, trans. by George L. Kline, 2 vols., London, 1953.

Zviguilsky, Alexandre, 'Les "Lettres sur l'Espagne" de V.-P. Botkine', in his French ed. of Vassili Botkine, *Lettres sur l'Espagne*, Paris, 1969, pp. 13–54.

Index

Hegel, Georg Wilhelm Friedrich 10–12, 15, 18–19, 48–50, 71, 85–8, 116, 182, 221, 228; Hegelian aesthetics 10, 12, 34, 86, 170–1; Hegelian dictum 'the real is rational' 12, 15, 86, 170; Hegelianism 10–11, 13, 15, 18–19, 49, 85–7; Young Hegelians 12, 88, 161
Heine, Heinrich, 106, 160
Herder, Johann 5
Herwegh, Georg 106, 160, 163
Herzen (A. I. Gertsen) xi–xii, xvi, 9–10, 13, 17, 23, 26–7, 29, 32, 38, 42, 44–7, 52–4, 56–7, 61, 65–6, 73, 75–6, 80, 82–3, 104, 107–8, 114–15, 121, 123–4, 142, 155, 169–70, 176, 182, 188, 190, 196, 205–7, 213, 215, 218, 221–2; relations with Granovsky 68–71; relations with Kavelin 199–203, 211–12; 'Buddhism in Science' 13; 'Dilettantism in Science' 13; *Letters from the Avenue Marigny* 26–7, 70, 95–6, 110, 119; *My Past and Thoughts* 31, 89
Hobbes, Thomas 226
Hoffmann, Ernst 110; *Kreisleriana* 85; *The Serapion Brothers* 85
Homer 160
Hugo, Victor-Marie 17
Humboldt, Wilhelm von 184–5
Hutten, Ulrich von 129–31, 140

individual, rights of xiii, 10, 118, 184–5, 217; struggle against oppression 13, 18, 153, 184–5, 218; crushed by state 16, 18, 62, 185–6; role of individual in history 71–4, 134–6; great historical individual 12, 73–4, 101–2, 185; individualism 7–8, 183–4, 205, 218, 225; individuality (or personality) 18, 178–86, 214, 218
Italy, Annenkov's travels in and views on 110–12, 139–40, 216
Ivan the Terrible (Ivan IV) 180–2, 185

Jacobins 19, 67
Johnson, Samuel 156

Katenin, P. A. 127
Katkov, M. N. xiv, 31–3, 50, 86, 104, 110, 136, 142, 188, 215
Kavelin, K. D. xi–xvi, 9, 26, 31, 46, 74, 76, 107, 126, 136, 148, 173, 175–213 *passim*, 214–16, 218, 221, 227–8; 'A

Brief Look at the Russian Rural Commune' 204–7; 'A Brief Survey of the Juridical Way of Life of Ancient Russia', 177–87, 197; *The Gentry and the Emancipation of the Peasants* 209–11; *Memorandum on the Emancipation of the Peasants in Russia* 190–7; 'Reply to *Moskvityanin*' 186
Ketcher, N. Kh. 31–2, 52
Khomyakov, A. S. 5, 7, 57, 65, 90; 'Epistle to the Serbs' 31; 'The Opinions of Foreigners about Russia' 6–7
Kireyevsky, I. V. 5–6, 57, 62, 66, 68, 90; 'In Reply to A. S. Khomyakov' 5–6; 'On the Need for and Possibility of New Principles for Philosophy' 30–1, 'Review of the Contemporary Condition of Literature' 7
Kireyevsky, P. V. 5, 65–6, 68
Kistyakovsky, B. A. 222
Kitayev, V. A. xiv
knighthood 6, 62–3, 218
Kolokol (The Bell) 200–2, 212
Korsh, A. F. 31
Korsh, F. F. (Kavelina) 176, 189, 213
Korsh, Ye. F. 31
Koshelyov, A. I. 191
Krayevsky, A. A. 94, 186–7
Krylov, N. I. 53, 64, 175
Kryukov D. L. 52, 175
Kudryavtsev, P. N. 31, 56
Kulchik (A. Ya. Kulchitsky) 83
kulturtregerstvo 219

laissez-faire economic policy 41, 195–6, 217–18
Lamartine, Alphonse de 124
Laski, Harold 216
Lassalle, Ferdinand 227
Lavrov, P. L. 73, 106, 207–8
law 4, 7–8, 10, 58–60, 90, 103, 222
Lawrence, G. A.: *Guy Livingstone* 172
Lazhechnikov, I. I. 56
Lenin, (V. I. Ulyanov) xiv, 212, 224
Leontovich, V. V. xv
Leontyev, P. M. 206–7, 209
Lermontov, M. Yu. 3, 17–18, 88, 108; *A Hero of Our Time* 4, 17, 152
Leroux, Pierre 14, 89, 106, 119
Liszt, Franz 101
Lobachevsky, N. I. 34